GOOD
BOOTY

ALSO BY ANN POWERS

★ ★ ★

Weird Like Us: My Bohemian America

Tori Amos: Piece by Piece

GOOD BOOTY

LOVE AND SEX, BLACK & WHITE, BODY AND SOUL IN AMERICAN MUSIC

ANN POWERS

DEY ST.

An Imprint of WILLIAM MORROW

Portions of this book in different forms have appeared on The Record blog at NPR Music and in the great, now-defunct journal *Black Clock*.

HarperCollins books may be purchased for educational, business, or sales promotional use. For information please e-mail the Special Markets Department at SPsales@harpercollins.com.

FIRST EDITION

Designed by Suet Yee Chong

Photography credits: chapters 2 and 7: © The New York Public Library; chapter 3: from the collection of Kip Lornell; chapter 4: © *Sepia* magazine; chapter 5: © Jim Marshall Photography LLC; chapter 7: © Getty Images

Library of Congress Cataloging-in-Publication Data has been applied for.

ISBN 978-0-06-246369-2

17 18 19 20 21   LSC   10 9 8 7 6 5 4 3 2 1

CONTENTS

PREFACE

I think I was around nine years old when I realized music is sexy.
From the first time I heard the songs that moved me to distraction in childhood, by the Beatles and the Jackson 5, I loved them
because they affected my whole body, making me think hard and
respond deeply and jump like a jelly bean. Music gave me a way
to engage with those "funny feelings" my friend Lisa said rose up
in her when she looked at a picture of Keith Richards slouching
around in the Rolling Stones, feelings my mother wouldn't mention and the boys in the schoolyard snickered about but wouldn't
own. The girls in my life were the ones who wanted to name those
feelings, and we did it by dancing to the beat of the Bee Gees and
Queen and Blondie, and once we all hit college, Prince. We became
sexual by playing records, sweating in the crowd at rock shows,
making out with boys in bands or other fans or each other while
music played loud in cars and basements and through the walls of
the bathrooms at the Odd Fellows Hall.

When I started writing about music for a living, I felt driven
not to merely acknowledge its erotic pull, but to really understand
it. This took time, a lot of listening, more sweating in clubs, more

dancing. I eventually realized that in order to grasp how the sounds I loved related to the sex I was having—that everyone was having—I'd need to learn more about how music factored into the history of the places where it originated. Rock and jazz and soul and hip-hop are American inventions, born of and nurtured by people mixing and mingling, claiming themselves and reaching for others. I knew that; I could see the connections forming all around me in the music world. Digging into record crates and spending time with my nose buried in books helped me understand the context for these developments.

My own movement back and forth from the archive to the audience has continually shaped my understanding. I've learned more than I can easily express from the examples of women, queer folk, and people of color who've refused to remain on the margins, both as musicians and as writers filling in the gaps in the standard histories of the American experience. I gained my rebel attitude from punk, my joy from disco, my openness from singer-songwriters, my seriousness from soul. I went to thousands of shows. What I remember most from them is the physicality of it all: the heat of the Metallica mosh pit and the tenderness of tears shared at a Tori Amos sing-along; the way someone I'd never met before grabbed my hand while Kirk Franklin led his gospel choir toward an anointing. The growing literature of popular music scholarship and criticism helped me understand the lost histories and inner drives that lie behind these experiences. I came to understand that American popular music, our nation's first original art form, is made of our best impulses toward freedom, community, and self-realization, and our worst legacies of racial oppression and sexual hypocrisy. I decided I wanted to write a book about American music and American sex, one that would really be about American dreaming, violence, pleasure, hunger, lies, and love.

This book is my offering: a collection of scenes from behind the veil of propriety about a subject we don't discuss openly anywhere near as much as we should. It's grounded in testimonies about the way music ripped down that veil, or made it into a costume its makers could drop to reveal themselves. This is not the standard history of guitar heroes and superstars, though some do appear here. It belongs equally to the dancers in the crowd, the groupies backstage, the couples huddled in the corner as a greasy band lays down the blues.

My account doesn't contain everything I wish it could. Another volume would give Latin music much more of its due, and reach across the ocean to England more often, and go into inner space on the electronic waves of techno and rave. A whole volume could be written on the rap life of Nicki Minaj, someone who makes only a brief appearance here. That's one thing about popular music: despite the canonizing efforts of certain thinkers and industry types, at its heart it's anti-hierarchical and inexhaustible, always renewing itself and skewing its own history in the process. As I explored its many avenues, I found that certain ones connected to illuminate the story I wanted to tell, of how the people of a nation founded on both liberty and oppression found a way to abide together by dancing and singing together, and, eventually, by listening to strangers who did those things in different ways. The story of how music shows us our beauty and our ugliness. The pride it can conjure. The longing it shapes and that sometimes undoes it, as such longing undoes and remakes us.

INTRODUCTION

American music originates in the bodies of its people, in the pull of a moan from the throat and a spine-loosening roll of the hips. From the beginning, it scandalized those who didn't understand it, or maybe felt its impact all too well. Do you think the birth of rock and roll happened in 1956? Try 1819, when John F. Watson, a Methodist layman, noticed that throughout Philadelphia, worshipers were not sticking to the script of the hymnals they held in their hands.

Watson saw and heard the behavior that so worried him not only in churches, but also in camp meetings held outdoors, where pretty much anyone could wander in. He described what he witnessed in a religious tract with the finger-wagging title *Methodist Error, or Friendly Christian Advice to Those Methodists Who Indulge in Extravagant Religious Emotions and Bodily Exercises*: "We have, too, a growing evil, in the practices of singing in our places of public and society worship, *merry* airs, adapted from old *songs*, to hymns of our composing; often miserable as poetry, and senseless as matter, and most frequently composed and first sung by the illiterate *blacks* of the society."[1] These combinations of holy and profane texts, and

of African and European musical sources, stimulated excessive behavior (folks would just keep going all night long) and spiritual
vanity in participants, Watson thought. "In the meantime, one
and another of musical feelings, and consonant animal spirits, has
been heard stepping the merry strains with all the precision of an
avowed *dancer*." In other words, the subjects of Watson's concern
weren't just singing. They were shaking it, baby, shaking it.

The religious practice he observed—a form that eventually
became crystallized within the ring shout, a fluid series of movements blended with call-and-response singing that Africans had
carried over through the horrific Middle Passage and into their
enslavement—had parallels outside the church, in dances from
around the world performed in the streets of new cities and at rural fairs and holiday celebrations. It also echoed the rituals of the
natives that early Americans encountered. But what were the "animal spirits" he mentioned? The phrase sounds racist to contemporary ears, invoking ideas of the primitive often attached to both
African Americans and native people. In Watson's time, it signified
something else: an ancient philosophical concept that also shows
up in Descartes and many post-Enlightenment religious writings,
rooted in the word *anima,* a name for the soul. Perhaps it's more
useful now to call them animating spirits, the ineffable mobilizing
forces that make people feel alive.

These spirits, the philosophers thought, were elements within
the human bloodstream that conveyed the stirrings of the soul
throughout the body. They enabled and regulated the passions.
Music was often invoked as a similar catalyst. Later, Freud's concept of the libido would refocus thinking about the animal spirits
on the sex drive, while the economist John Maynard Keynes would
connect the phrase to the vitality behind capitalism. Combine all
these different ways of trying to grasp what animates both the
spiritual and the emotional—what inner surge awakens people to
themselves and makes them reach out to others—and you might

also hit upon a new way of thinking about the erotic, one that goes beyond simple assumptions about sexual arousal.

What Watson encountered was an erotic exchange that's at the heart of American popular music. This method of sharing and communicating the most personal, difficult to articulate, and indeed intimate aspects of the human experience has been taken up by every kind of American as a conduit for both joy and pain. Through it, communities formed and sustained themselves. From the beginning, music's ability to open people to each other also made it an avenue for exploitation, and a kind of theater where Americans acted out the ways they violated and oppressed one another and dreamed up ways they might heal those wounds. But the erotic as a force in music is rarely discussed in these more complicated terms. Instead, it's the subject that makes people squirm—misunderstood, feared, underestimated, and oversimplified for more than two centuries. Call it sex to keep it simple, and often this vital spirit is reduced to a litany of crude gestures and lewd jokes, or, even in our age of so-called liberation, held up as a threat. Waxing poetic, however, can lead to resurrecting old stereotypes that equate sexiness with a kind of raw instinctiveness, ideas rooted in the racism and sexism that assume that certain people have superpowers in the dark and are menaces to society everywhere else.

The real reason American popular music is all about sex is that we, as a nation, most truly and openly acknowledge sexuality's power through music. This music, infinite in its variety, is rooted in the experiences of people who made a new nation within a dynamic of unprecedented mobility, horrific exploitation and oppression, constant mixing, and the ongoing renegotiation of limits. From colonial times onward, the sounds that inspired dancing and loud sing-alongs in the streets, in ballrooms, in bars, and in people's homes exuded erotic energy and often directly discussed the problems and possibilities of sex and love that people were facing in their times. This was always rhythmic music, too, grounded in those drumbeats carried from Africa within enslaved people's bodies, because their instruments had been taken from them. They stomped and slapped out its meanings in ways that were arousing and miraculous. Popular music's very form, its ebb and flow of excitement so closely resembling the libido, drew people to it as a way to speak what, according to propriety, couldn't be spoken.

And always, this music was a mix, and about mixing. It arose from those streets and semi-private places as a product of Afro-Caribbean, European, Latin American, and native cultures colliding and mingling. America's erotic drive emerged inseparable from the fact of its troubled multiculturalism, rooted in both oppression and the hope for freedom. American music came into being as a bastard child refusing that damning label, shaking off the guilt of perceived illegitimacy. True erotic expression is a kind of truth-telling, bringing out into the open the most joyful and painful aspects of living in a particular body at a particular place and time. It's also a vehicle for what Dr. Martin Luther King Jr. called "some-bodiness . . . the sense of selfhood and dignity that nothing in all the world can take away."[2] Music, which runs through the body, has been able to encompass this profound and necessary aspect of human experience. And it gave us a way to bring it out in the open and share it.

It's impossible to talk about American bodies without acknowledging the legacy of gross inequality that begins in the enslavement of Africans. That's another quality American eroticism shares with American music. It is very difficult to speak of race and sex together in language that's not corrupted by centuries of violent oppression; terms like *miscegenation*, conveying legacies of forced unions across color lines, instantly evoke dangerous prejudices. Yet because the struggle to be human together while acknowledging a legacy of wrongdoing—the struggle to absorb the stain of slavery without erasing it, and to fully acknowledge the countless acts of violence that are elemental to our hybrid national character—is central to what it means to be American, it's no surprise that American eroticism is as much a means to reflect upon these differences, written in the body, as it is a route to the pleasures that can sometimes seem to erase them. This is why Dr. King's "somebodiness" matters so much: eroticism is the full experience of being human, every inch of flesh and spirit, nothing denied.

In the twenty-first century, mainstream popular music often feels very disconnected from this ideal. It has become the product of a global industry, branded and rebranded through the images of stars who can seem interchangeable and are certainly objectified. How does somebodiness survive within a body that doesn't even seem real, due to plastic surgery, vocal Auto-Tuning, and a performer's seeming adherence to a porn script? In 1998 a former Mouseketeer, Britney Spears, donned a schoolgirl fetish costume in a music-video high school hallway and sang an ode to sadomasochism; "Hit me, baby, one more time," Spears cooed. In 2004, Janet Jackson, a superstar known for balancing raciness with a wholesome demeanor, lost half of her bustier during the halftime show at the Super Bowl; actually, it was torn off by the overeager teen idol Justin Timberlake in what became known as "Nipplegate." American families munching chips and dip in their dens were exposed to the horrors of a finely crafted metallic sunburst jewel decorating Jackson's pierced nipple. The fallout was considerable: morally outraged lawmakers soon enacted new restrictions governing the broadcast of explicit material, and Jackson's own career arc took a deep downward turn. Yet predictions of a chilling effect on sexual explicitness in the music world proved inaccurate.

As the age of social media dawned, more people than ever were sampling "blue" material in wide-open cyberspace. Song lyrics grew franker than ever—one mid-decade hit, "Wait (The Whisper Song)" by the Ying Yang Twins, turned on the phrase "Wait 'til you see my dick"—and this ever more explicit language was matched by visuals that often seemed indistinguishable from pornography.

In the 2000s, the videos that promoted pop hits became more like sex tapes, those hybrid products of reality television's connections to the Triple-XXX industry, especially in Los Angeles, where heavy metal stars dated sex workers, and their bedroom performances, leaked on the Internet, became yet another marker of the rock and roll lifestyle.

Simulated sex became a predictable climax during arena shows when stars would pull audience members onstage and dry hump them to the roar of the crowd. Topics once limited to innuendo, from sadomasochism to multiple-partner encounters to vibrator play, were frankly discussed in Top 10 hits. Former teen idols like Justin Bieber hurried to prove themselves as adult pop stars with thorough descriptions of what they enjoyed during the act: "From the door to the wall, coffee table, girl, get ready . . . From the stove to the countertop, dining room table, are you ready?" Bieber sang in 2013's "PYD"—short for the distinctly unromantic "Put You Down."

The elevated feelings brought on by contemplating the nineteenth-century ring shout do not come easily when the mind turns to the outbreak of explicit behavior that's overtaken mainstream pop in the past few years. The movements and sounds that scandalized John F. Watson two hundred years ago now strike most people as affirmative and beautiful; the ring shout is considered foundational within American music and dance, the kind of thing that's taught on educational television. This is what happens to the erotic in music as its expressions fade into history. The lessons it offers are forgotten, and new scenarios arise stimulating the same old debates and anxieties, always perceived as far more shocking than anything that's come before.

The connection between the scandals of 1819 and those surrounding stars like Spears today are actually quite clear once you consider popular music's long tail. A resonant example is the transformation of the former schoolchildren's sweetheart Miley Cyrus, which culminated in her shocking appearance at the MTV Video Music Awards in 2013. During that summer, one of America's nicest girls became its naughtiest. Her blossoming, as it were, as booty-popping, tongue-wagging, nudity-flaunting provocateur was the logical end of the cycle that Spears had begun anew a decade earlier. Like the older gamine, Cyrus was raised on a Disney lot, nabbing the lead role in the series *Hannah Montana* at fourteen. Her father, Billy Ray Cyrus, had been a one-hit wonder in the 1990s, cashing in on a country music line-dance craze that was the G-rated equivalent of burlesque. He raised his daughter to be a performer, and she was never not commodified and objectified, never not, in some way, working what God gave her.

How do you grow up when you're an object of other people's desires? Reaching sexual maturity at a time when pop's culture of pleasure and sensual awareness had never been more frankly explicit, Cyrus did the sensible thing. She performed awakening, the same way she'd performed awkward adolescence for years on prime time. Cyrus devoted herself to twerking—performing a street dance that had long been popular among African Americans in cities like New Orleans. The dance's rapid-fire hip movements lead to an earthquake of jiggle in the buttocks. The slender, tomboyish Cyrus performed her tricky undulations on awards shows and the late-night talk circuit; in the video for her hit "We Can't Stop," she showed herself learning how to make her butt wag harder from a couple of more prodigiously endowed African American friends. The public was shocked, for about six months. Debates raged over whether Cyrus was being racist, sexist, or simply crass with her faux-primitive dance.

In fact, Cyrus had chased a rhythm from the ring shout to the present day, one that connects the weekend recreation of slaves in New Orleans's Congo Square with the faux-exotic Middle Eastern "hootchie kootch" performed by Algerian immigrants at the Chicago World's Fair of 1893; turn-of-the-twentieth-century vernacular dances like the Funky Butt and the Snake Hips with Elvis's famous pelvis; and the heightened theatrics of African American gospel quartets who dazzled worshipers in the 1950s with the self-styled sanctified perversity of Prince and Madonna in the 1980s. Nothing, it seems, is ever really new in the way the inner surge manifests in music. The specifics change in each period, with different kinds of music better capturing the spark of the moment, and different communities—urban immigrants, African Americans of the Great Migration, teenagers in the South, hippies in the West—pushing the conversation forward. This book explores many of the key stories that illuminate how this American conversation about sexuality and the erotic has developed. These scenes show how eroticism, at the deeper level of physical and soulful joy enriching people's understandings of themselves and connections with one other, has given American popular music its central force of meaning. These same stories show how music takes on forbidden topics, opens them up, and makes them irresistible.

Yearning and satisfaction in the body and the psyche are universal experiences, but they come clothed in different guises, depending on the time. Some fundamentals, like that pelvic shake that Cyrus mastered, can be traced from the beginning. Other expressions now seem quaint. What connects the sublime spiritualized need expressed in the 1932 gospel love song "Take My Hand, Precious Lord" to Donna Summer's moaning epiphanies in the disco classic "I Feel Love" is a feeling that can be recognized only if we understand that as morality shifts, music does, too, helping people navigate those boundaries. In nineteenth-century New Orleans, for example, the risky thrills that women and men felt dancing the quadrille at the dozens of balls that took place every week allowed them to imagine intimate connections with new neighbors who were nothing like themselves. Love stories of Creole life, often written by white men about (or stolen from) women of color, were surprisingly frank in describing the perilous closeness between masters and those subject to them, and suggested ways to negotiate the kinds of intimacies that might topple an entire societal structure. Close encounters between slaves dancing in Congo Square and white observers established an element of voyeurism that runs through popular music culture from the days of minstrelsy onward, while also creating the framework for rock and roll spectacle, a performance ritual that, a century later, would lend carnal power to many a white man "channeling" black legacies.

When America was a young country just beginning to grasp the means of creating its own culture, newcomers from disparate homelands made hybrids from the seeds of very different heritages. Central to this process was the absorption of African fundamentals into the very core of American cultural expression, through the appropriations the white owner class made both unthinkingly and in fear and unspoken desire; and through the remarkable perseverance of those enslaved people who, against all odds, became American, and continued to bless the culture with inimitable creativity, virtuosity, and depth. The historian Eric Lott famously called this grounding process "love and theft"; that term aptly illustrates the way the animating spirits in American music are simultaneously earnest and unscrupulous, lofty and corrupt. In every era, expressing the erotic through music has required Americans to confront the ways in which this culture is grounded in exploitation and violation as well as democratic openness and liberty. Americans have continually transformed themselves, but not everyone has the opportunity to do so in the same ways. The sex scenes of American music reveal the most intimate cruelties we have wrought upon each other, alongside the pleasures and kindnesses.

As the country's first full century gave way to its second, new scenarios expanded people's notions of what they could become. The first decades of the 1900s saw women asserting themselves in new ways; the next few made possible the Great Migration that allowed African Americans to begin to take control of their own social realities. Youths emerged as a cultural force in mid-century and redefined both leisure and the life cycle. By the 1980s, communities demanding acknowledgment and civil rights for myriad gender and sexual identities were challenging long-held assumptions and inspiring a new generation toward openness. In each of these phases, music moved people to dare, to keep pushing the edge, even as it helped them negotiate the limits they sometimes chose or still had to endure.

All of this happened in spaces that were social and commercial, where money was exchanged and people sought not just status and fame, but real physical satisfaction. In the original, explicit version of what would become his breakthrough hit "Tutti Frutti"—a song that defines the spirit of rock and roll as succinctly as did anything by Elvis or the Beatles—the unstoppably libidinal superstar Little Richard called his music's (and life's) governing force "good booty." Within those two words are all the glories and contradictions raised—aroused—by American eroticism as expressed through popular music. There's the unapologetic crudeness, an openness that refuses to veil sex in niceties. There is an acknowledgment that this is also a realm of commerce and plunder, of booty earned and stolen. There is, of course, that reference to the ass, the centrifuge in a dancer's body, which can be both an exploited fetish object and a partner's cherished private pleasure. And there is the assurance that, fundamentally, the desire for the erotic is good, something that can make a person whole, make them shout and sing.

Music has created the spaces where Americans can publicly share deep experiences of selfhood and connection. Through the drum and the guitar and the electronic thrum, people feel their own physical drives and longings for emotional connection. Rhythm is quite literally the reason. It's the musical element that guarantees what scientists call "entrainment"—the merging of two ongoing processes, like a heartbeat and a drumbeat. Scientists also call this "coupling": forgetting where one ends and the other begins. The musical experience of entrainment unites a listener with what is being played, the performers playing it, and everyone around her enjoying it, too; it encourages identification and produces sympathy. Entrainment is the reason people dance and what makes them feel a song speaks for them.

Musical rhythms thrive in places where people gather freely—cabarets and dive bars, arenas that rock and festival fields that bloom with a thousand naked flowers. The performance studies scholar Joseph Roach describes such environments as "behavioral vortices": hot spots occupied by hot bodies where concentrated cultural meanings surface. A vortex is a storm that grabs you, but is also made stronger by the motion you contribute. In such a whorl, overlooked or deliberately unacknowledged realities can come to light. Seemingly improper feelings can flourish. What emerges within the vortex would otherwise have remained in the shadows: not only pleasure and physical pride, but anxiety, fear, repulsion. The everyday experience of American eroticism arises from buried prejudices and violent impulses as well as tender ones. In specific places and times, including within the space of a musical recording or live performance, all that hunger and rage, yearning and hope, become visible and audible. The storm throws open a closet and empties out its contents.[3]

To talk about what's revealed within the sexiest moments of American music (and they may not be the most obviously lascivious or titillating ones) is to recast its history in terms that are more inclusive, and less dominated by old ideas of artistic genius or great works, than what's been offered in the past. The conversation calls for celebrating the unsung—the domestic servant, the tango dance instructor, the church mother, the street corner singer, the groupie, the local DJ, the kid making a YouTube video—next to the legendary. This is what acknowledging the erotic does: it expands definitions and switches up hierarchies. This retelling of American popular music doesn't always focus on the big stories. It has gaps.

It is necessarily incomplete, and open. Other music lovers will have different perspectives on what turned them on and turned them around. Taking the turn-on seriously is the point: every moment's pleasure illuminates whole worlds of need, conflict, and possibility, and in its own way, sets the stage for the next.

The vortex abounds with complexities. Music allows people—players, dancers, observers—to ride the storm that arises when desire encounters the roadblocks of prejudice, moral judgment, or cruel circumstance. American eroticism wants to be easy, but for most of history, American life has been hard. Our music grinds pleasure from hardship. It creates whirlwinds but also provides a means to manage them. Music is not chaos, and even though the sounds that became rock and roll have often been discussed or even dismissed as too wild to have sophisticated meanings, in fact the skilled player or dancer has always known exactly which note or step comes next. Sexual experience is most pleasurable when it involves finesse, great attention to detail, and the best kind of surprise. The same is true of the erotic power of American music: cultivating joy, acknowledging vulnerability, it comes in multiple, unexpected ways.

1

THE TABOO BABY

THE BAMBOULA

NEW ORLEANS, 1800–1900

Popular music gives shape, in time, to desire; and desire always crosses boundaries. In the United States, one line underlies all the rest: the artificial one separating the citizens who came to be called "white" from all the other people who inhabited the soil and shaped the nation. Music is so much more than the clearly delineated racial dialogue that several early-twentieth-century jazz musicians slyly called "black notes on white paper," but it is that, too—a means for understanding the racial limits power imposes and the ways that, in lust, love, or careless leisure, people challenge, deny, reinforce, and momentarily obscure those limits. And so any discussion of America's erotic musical life must confront the complexities of American race relations. It's impossible to talk about it otherwise.

A close encounter with someone dangerously different was one of the most explosive possibilities of life in a young America. The fear of racial "mixing"—a more useful and musical term than the overused and stigmatized "miscegenation"—is as old as our colonial past, tied to an ideal of whiteness that was never pure and always embattled. Laws against intermarriage were adopted in Virginia and Maryland as early as 1691. Yet the mobility that kept America expanding continually challenged these hierarchies. In nascent culture capitals, immigrant cities like New York, frontier towns like St. Louis and San Francisco, and most of all in the cosmopolitan Southern center of New Orleans, daily life required the forward thinking to venture beyond their own kind—to exploit others and to learn from them. Able bodies worked together in the bustling streets of these entrepreneurial towns despite language barriers and wildly different points of origin, because the work had to be done; hierarchies of oppression temporarily unraveled in the processes of building and selling, though they were quickly reimposed. At leisure, men took pleasure from women as various as themselves, exploiting them, but sometimes also forging long intimacies. Many of these women danced in the saloons where they met their men: they danced Spanish *cachuchas,* Moorish *alahambras,* Greek *romaikas.* Music granted mobility, however provisional, to those marked as nonwhite—not just for these dancers but for leaders of all-black bands like James Hemmenway and Francis Johnson, who in the early nineteenth century forged a "Negro" sound that blended German military elements with Latin touches and an underlying African current.[1] Music was often the language people employed to talk across lines of prejudice. On one level this tolerance and the leeway it afforded was all a delusion. Yet a vocabulary of freedom, not directly verbalized but written in the beats and tones between those black notes on white paper, began to form. It took well over a century for that feeling to gain the name rock and roll.

Here's one story that says a lot about its time. Thomas C. Nicholls, a decorous military school student of seventeen, had spent all his years within fifty miles of Washington, DC, when, in 1805, his diplomat father summoned his family to join him at a new outpost: the recently acquired American port of New Orleans. Nicholls the younger left his studies at Maryland's Charlotte Hall and joined his siblings and mother on an unpleasant journey aboard the ship *Comet*. Finally, they landed in the city on the southern banks of the Mississippi, which struck Nicholls as "revolting"—the buildings were ramshackle and windowless, the streets muddy, the tavern where he and his brother had to stay had no glass in the windows. But Nicholls found one aspect of his new home beautiful: its female residents, who lived to dance.

One night Nicholls relaxed at the home of a wealthy new friend, watching the women of the house prepare to attend a grand ball at one of the fifteen ballrooms that served this city of around ten thousand people. (The population would double within just a few years.) The women, attended by silent slaves, donned elaborate finery and then stood for inspection in front of their menfolk. The scene, as described by our young Northerner, evokes more brutal ones of slave and livestock auctions. But when they left the house, these human ornaments broke their bonds and became regular people out for fun. Nicholls wrote of this startling development in his memoir forty years later:

> Everything prepared, the order was given to march; when, to my horror and astonishment, the young ladies doffed their shoes and stockings, which were carefully tied up in silk handkerchiefs, and took up the line of march, barefooted, for

the ballroom. After paddling through mud and mire, lighted
by lanterns carried by Negro slaves, we reached the scene of
action without accident. The young ladies halted before the
door and shook one foot after another in a pool of water close
by. After repeating this process some half a dozen times, the
feet were freed of the accumulated mud and were in a proper
state to be wiped dry by the slaves, who had carried towels
for the purpose. Then silk stockings and satin slippers were
put on again, cloaks were thrown aside, tucked-up trains were
let down, and the ladies entered the ballroom, dry-shod and
lovely in the candle-light.[2]

The slaves were not permitted to join in the moment of disorder that put their mistresses in the mood to dance.

This remembrance is a pioneer story glorifying vigor at civilization's edge. Had Nicholls been waxing poetic about discoveries he'd
had a few states to the West, the ladies might have climbed into
a covered wagon assisted by "noble savages." Instead, his details
reflected a different kind of American exoticism, whose elements
were muggy heat, the romance languages of France and Spain, and
the skin—from warm brown to earthy rust to coffee-with-milk to
peachy—of a populace that called itself Creole and, according to
Nicholls, was nearly as diverse as America would ever get.

The people themselves differed in complection [sic], costume,
manners and language, from anything we had ever seen. The
eternal jabbering of French in the street was a sealed book to
us. Drums beat occasionally at the corners of the streets, suspended for a moment to allow the worthy little drummer to
inform the public that on such and such a night there would
be a Grand Ball at the Salle de Conde, or make announce-
ments of a ball of another sort, for colored ladies and white
gentlemen. Such were our visions of New Orleans in 1805.

At this time, New Orleans, which leaders had recently bought, was barely part of the new nation. Yet it already had many of the characteristics of a twenty-first-century megalopolis. The years of French and Spanish rule that preceded the Louisiana Purchase in 1803 established its polyglot nature, as did the city's role as a hub of the slave trade, which connected it to the Caribbean and to Africa. In the streets, African-born residents of this active port carried heritage on their heads, in woven baskets containing the ingredients for gumbo z'herbes, an Americanized version of the diaspora stew callaloo. History rolled off their tongues in newly forming dialects. Free blacks mingled with Irish and Italian immigrants, mixed-blood Creoles, and slave artisans, who ran small shops for the profit of their owners.

Scenes like the ones Nicholls recalled, which became commonplace among travel writers as the century unfolded, created the image of New Orleans as the kitchen garden of American hedonism. To be intrepid here was to seek pleasure as much as material prospects, and this desire to be sensually fulfilled was often attributed to the mixed-up blood of the city's residents. Not only did African people, slave and free, move more freely in New Orleans than they did in many other cities; deep connections to the Latin and French communities differentiated even the so-called whites of the town.

"Those called the Whites are principally brunettes with deep black eyes; dark hair, and good teeth," wrote Thomas Ashe, an Irish travel writer primarily known for spinning tall tales of the American West, in 1806. "Their persons are eminently lovely, and their movements indescribably graceful, far superior to any thing I ever witnessed in Europe. It would seem that a hot climate 'calls to life each latent grace' . . . In the dance these fascinating endowments are peculiarly displayed."[3]

Such descriptions of languid, vaguely Mediterranean Louisiana belles fed into the widespread belief that the South was a place where morals ran as loose as the temperatures ran hot. Abolitionist rhetoric furthered the linkage of plantation life and debauchery. Historian Ronald G. Walters calls this "the Erotic South." "Plantations, like a moralist's equivalent for the settings of pornographic novels, were simply places where the repressed could come out of hiding. Abolitionists saw both what was actually there—erotic encounters did occur—and what associations of power with sex prepared them to see."[4]

The mix is the fundamental form of all American popular arts. Born of Saturday night dance battles in rural barns or urban squares, and of songs shared among family members or working-men in saloons, the music and movement that uniquely belonged to this country were a conglomeration from the beginning. The mingling and mutual appreciation forbidden by law among individuals was constantly enacted symbolically, especially in music and dance. And often, what singers said and how dancers shook and shimmied brought into the open the erotic charge of such encounters. The story of how American music and American sex shaped each other doesn't only begin in New Orleans, but the city's erotic excitement, racial anxiety, and openness to mixing arose early and was noticed. The effect, which theorist Tavia Nyong'o has dubbed "the amalgamation waltz," still feeds American pop. It's what made Miley Cyrus's hips go up and down.[5]

Scholars have struggled to come up with a powerful term to describe American hybridity that doesn't also reinforce stereotypes. Eric Lott's famous formulation of minstrelsy, the foundational form through which white Americans appropriated African American culture as "love and theft," remains the most widely invoked—Bob Dylan even used the phrase as an album title in 2001.[6] But the necessary uncovering of minstrelsy as the source of so much twentieth-century popular culture has led us to overstress the most theatrical appropriations of identity, instead of harder-to-track histories of more common and close-quartered musical encounters. Before the 1830s, when the white itinerant comedian Thomas Rice became widely known for his "Jim Crow" routine, whites and blacks were learning each other's dance steps in ballrooms and plantation parlors and commenting on each other's daily lives in domestic songs. Dance-based or informally voiced expressions of cultural mixing were more widespread than theatrical ones and included all members of American society, including children and women who were not professional entertainers. Music played in the streets and at home could trip into anyone's life. It could feel like a gift, or a violation.

A music-inspired brawl that the New Orleans *Times-Picayune* reported in 1850 was emblematic of the whole period:

> Elizabeth Hyser, a young lady with a red skirt, gipsy hat and blooming countenance, yesterday appeared before Recorder Genois, and made a terrible complaint against Andrea Lobeste, whom she charges with having assaulted her with a dangerous weapon on the levee. It appears that she was discoursing eloquent music on her tamberine, as an accompaniment to an ear-piercing organ, when Mr. Lobeste expressed his disapprobation of the entertainment by cutting up her tamberine with a knife. This grave matter will be inquired into.[7]

Although Hyser's name is German, the way she's described makes her a racial amalgam. Her "gipsy" hat hints at the Latin tinge that has always been essential in American music, and her tambourine was originally a North African instrument. Accounts of New Orleans in the first half of the eighteenth century abound with scenes like this one. And they're almost always set to a lively beat.

The fact of race mixing was amplified through the fear of it—and the excitement it stimulated. Abolitionist declamations that THE SOUTHERN STATES ARE ONE GREAT SODOM formed a hysterical counterpoint to appreciations of the free and easy Southern life published in magazines and travelers' diaries.[8] The true extent of sexual intimacy among people of different races and ethnicities during this period is very difficult to determine. What was real in this polyglot place, and what spun out quickly into myth? How did these mixing, melding, clashing bodies move?

As many chroniclers like Nicholls noted, New Orleans was dance-mad. The fifteen ballrooms he found upon arriving offered entertainment every night of the week, and their number doubled in the next decade. There were balls for the white and Creole upper crust, for free people of color, and even for slaves; there were children's balls and smaller soirees in people's homes. People danced every afternoon on the levee and sometimes out in the Tivoli Gardens amusement park at Bayou St. John.[9]

In the ballrooms, British reels and French quadrilles preserved and expanded the customs of disparate homelands and brokered evenings of peace within a newly multicultural community. Nationalist tensions sometimes burst through the genteel façade, as in the great "quadrille wars" of 1803, when conflicts over whose national dances were performed led to duels and, one memorable night, to the ladies of the party fleeing into the night after someone shouted, "If the women have a drop of French blood in their veins, they will not dance!"[10] Mostly, though, music became the medium through which dancers absorbed the city's myriad subcultures—even ones that law and propriety might have kept them from openly embracing.

African musicians, slave and free, played in bands, just as they did at parties on plantations. The architect Benjamin Latrobe witnessed one such music maker at a ball he attended in 1819, a "tall, ill-dressed black, in the music gallery, who played the tambourin standing up, & in a forced & vile voice called the figures as they changed." The fiddle was also a pacifying force used by slavers to create an illusion that, in their galleries, those people being torn from their families and put into chattel were actually as merry as the tunes one of them played. So music was both a tool of oppression and the weapon that could momentarily defeat it. In Solomon Northup's slave narrative, recently brought to light again by director Steve McQueen's 2013 film version *12 Years a Slave,* the fiddle he calls "notorious" allowed him to travel well beyond the borders of his master's plantation, but also caused him agony when his keeper forced him to use it as others were whipped until they danced.[11]

Slaves did dance in happier circumstances, too, on holidays and other fleeting occasions, sometimes alongside free folk. What effect did European music that incorporated African and Latin elements have on the dancers who willingly and joyfully moved to it? The rhythms of the diaspora are hard to trace within the straight lines of sheet music, which is our primary evidence of this period's sound. But accounts suggest that what jazz historian Marshall Stearns called "rum in a teacup"—"the addition of Congo hip movements to the dances of the court of Versailles"—gave many local dances the added kick that travelers to New Orleans celebrated. The choreography of European dance was still performed, but in a new way—with hips swinging, shoulders delicately shaking, and feet moving more quickly.[12]

This is probably how the women who'd removed their shoes to get to the dance Thomas Nicholls attended gallivanted across the ballroom floor. In dance, the imaginary merges with the real; movements motivated by rhythm stimulate desires that otherwise would remain unspoken and lend them a proper but necessarily flexible shape. The theorist Joseph Roach has written about New Orleans as a particularly verdant seedbed for "the kinesthetic imagination"—the metaphorical place where history is written into bodies and kept alive through movements and rituals that are passed down. The erotic vocabulary that developed within the music and dances in its ballrooms formed a kinesthetic conversation about civic life beyond their ornate doors.[13]

THE QUADROON GIRL

The quadrille—a dance in which four couples traded partners and returned to each other in jaunty polyamory—became inseparable in New Orleans from the feminine character whose name shares its root: the quadroon. By the end of the nineteenth century, the myth of *plaçage*, a system through which mixed-race mothers contracted out their daughters as high-class concubines to sporting men, was accepted as fact and formed the center of virtually every account of social dancing in New Orleans. Dozens of writers described it in fiction and journalism. By 1911, the definition of *plaçage* was fixed. Rixford J. Lincoln, the Poet Laureate of the Louisiana Historical Society, summed it up in "The Quadroon Ballroom":

> *The quadroon girl made white men dance and sigh.*
> *The half-white woman was a creature strange,*
> *A petted, fawning thing, of love and sin.*

The poem depicts the chaos that those Latinized quadrille rhythms caused:

> *There Folly led the dance in madness wild,*
> *When rivals, 'neath the oaks would often meet,*
> *In duel there, to place their lives at stake,*
> *Because they found a quadroon girl so sweet.*

It ends with a moral twist: the ballroom of Lincoln's poetic fantasia has become an asylum dedicated to the care of the orphan descendants of these sinful girls, maintained by nuns.[14]

In Lincoln's portrait, even the most upstanding gentleman, pushed beyond reason and morality by the undulations of young ladies lost in the flow of quadrille, could not be expected to resist a sinful union. In such tales, the idea of music as product and tool of miscegenation most obviously becomes attached to the popular styles that eventually became rock and roll. But what really happened on St. Philip Street on Wednesdays? Not always what so many people feared and were drawn toward. Recent scholarship suggests that the infamous quadroon dances were much like every other dance, connecting would-be lovers who might have found each other anyway. Historians Alecia P. Long, Sharony Green, and Emily Clark have uncovered the wide variety of relations women of color joined in during this period, on a spectrum from coerced sex to complicated "mistress" relationships to common-law marriage (known then as concubinage, regardless of partners' race or gender) to matrimony itself. Kenneth Aslakson, tracing the birth of the *plaçage* myth within travelers' accounts, notes that while the tales we know best "shed only dim light on the nature of white male–colored female relationships in antebellum New Orleans or the quadroon balls . . . these accounts reveal a great deal about the Anglo-American preoccupation with miscegenation."[15]

Why did the quadroon balls come to overshadow all the other ongoing kinds of social dancing in pre-jazz New Orleans, distorting our understanding of music and dance in this era? The abolitionist view of "the erotic South" contributed; so did the armchair tourist's desire for an exotic thrill. Paramount within historic accounts of *plaçage* is the idea that music itself is so seductive that it not only facilitates illicit behavior, but also creates it. The entertainment at quadroon balls was widely considered superior to that available at parties given by white ladies. The promise of close contact with "dusky" beauties definitely added to the enticement, but the dancing was thought to be better, too.

This is where music reenters the frame and determines the story's shape. Within the dance itself, and the subtly elastic form of the music inspiring it, an interracial sound and body language evolved. We can understand this by looking at another dance popular in the South during the same period. According to the dance historian Jurretta Jordan Heckscher, slaves in the Greater Chesapeake area were drawn to the Virginia jig, "a dance type that set a succession of male-female couples in physically demanding encounters within a circle of participant onlookers." This move toward couple dancing—which Africans traditionally considered vulgar—provided a way to act out "perhaps the greatest change in social ideals that marked the transition from Africa to America: the passage from a polygynous to a monogamous paradigm of marriage."[16] Through dancing, Heckscher convincingly argues, slaves absorbed and transformed the unfamiliar customs their masters imposed upon them. The horrors of displacement and bondage dominated slaves' daily lives. Yet the example of the Virginia jig shows how within this dehumanizing process, people preserved Dr. King's sense of "somebodiness"—of dignity and the ability to adapt without vanishing completely. The Virginia jig revealed the subtle movements of Africans becoming African American, with the sorrow that entails, but also the unquenchable fire.

Dancers in early America, slave and free, absorbed the influence of people who could not otherwise be fully acknowledged by following their steps. The African presence in a community altered that community; in dance, whites found the patterns of movement that made slaves' experience concrete and sensual, cultivating a feeling of connection in the flesh. Slaves, in their own changing dances, expressed both defiance and resilience. Dance became a temporary antidote to the spiritually intolerable acts of oppression slavery required. It also became a way of acknowledging that in the close quarters of hybrid America, blending of all kinds was inevitable.

This was a confined kind of openness: it only truly flourished within the symbolically free sphere of leisure realms like the ballroom and the dance hall. And when its effects became too strongly felt, white Americans turned away from it. "From at least the mideighteenth century to the first decade or so of the nineteenth, then, the slaveholding elite habitually danced in ways that they themselves acknowledged had been invented by those they enslaved," Heckscher writes. "And then, gradually but unmistakably, they entirely ceased to do so. One looks in vain after the 1820s for any aspect of wealthy whites' dance that they were willing to attribute to the black aesthetic."

THE POWER OF THE MASK

One other factor made the ballrooms of the early nineteenth century a safer space for explosive symbolic liaisons, including the damning desires those in the white slave-owning class might want to conceal. Masking was common at these events, as were elaborate costumes that turned their wearers into very different people, for an evening, at least. One group described in an 1850 newspaper report ran the gamut:

> A great many prominent New Orleanians attended this ball, and there were Creoles present, as well as American society. George Eustis came as a judge, and his sister Mathilde as a nun, which shocked some of the Catholics present. Mrs. John Slidell was dressed as a "marquise," and the Deslonde girls, one of whom later married General Beauregard, came as French peasants. Colonel and Mrs. John Winthrop were attired as "a gentleman and lady of the nineteenth century." A young man named De Wolf, who was a visitor from Rhode Island, was costumed as "an Arab Sheik," and he seems to have been the sensation of the evening.[17]

Today the brightly colored, feathered headpieces that fill Bour-
bon Street shop windows signal Mardi Gras to most people. That
annual festival blending French Catholic and Afro-Latin influences
has been a part of Southern folk life since the eighteenth century.
Mardi Gras, now a Crescent City staple, concentrates a once much
more diffuse experience of topsy-turvy self-transformation. In the
ballroom era, dancers found liberation in masks nearly every night.

George Washington Cable's quintessential novel of antebellum
New Orleans, *The Grandissimes,* begins with a masked ball in the
theater on St. Philip Street in 1803. The star-crossed lovers Honoré
de Grandissime and Aurora Nancanou first meet in the personae of
a dragoon and a monk, their odd finery enhancing a level of close
engagement that would otherwise not be possible. The strict and
sober bachelor and the young widow spar and entice each other
while sharing a cotillion. The scene unfolds in fairy-tale fashion,
but with a strong sexual pull. "The dance goes on; hearts are beating, wit is flashing, eyes encounter eyes with the leveled lances of
their beams, merriment and joy and sudden bright surprises thrill
the breast."[18] The music has its own costuming effect. It turns the
air into a character, a genie that pushes unlikely lovers toward
each other. Cable's flowery prose suits his romantic tale, written
seven decades after the period it reimagines. Yet his portrayal of
the ball as a free zone where attachments could suddenly establish
themselves—attachments problematic enough to fill a long novel—
accurately represents the role dancing played in social life.

In 1834 a law was established regulating the use of masks during dances. "Ladies who may wish to go out of the ballroom, to
unmask themselves, as well as such as will remain under mask,
will apply for a countermask to the doorkeeper, so as to be identified by the manager, whose duty shall be to recognize masks."[19]
The unstable identities created by masking could not be allowed
to extend into the street, and a witness had to be established to
make sure the costuming remained consistent. The role-playing

a masked event allowed threatened order enough that authorities had to contain it.

Masking was also a part of slave culture. Holidays like Jonkonnu, the winter festival, saw slaves donning costumes, often animal in form, and dancing through the streets. Such customs contributed to the precarious sense of balance in a society fundamentally grounded in inequality. Like dancing, masking was a safety valve that temporarily allowed slaves to experience themselves as different, if not wholly empowered. The threat of genuine resistance always existed in such moments, however, and as the century wore on, events like Jonkonnu were more strongly regulated to prevent rebellion and escape.

New Orleans ballroom culture, too, leaked beyond its own borders. By the late nineteenth century, the quadrille had left polite society and was inspiring a new group of insurgent dancers. In his history of interracial music in New Orleans, Charles Hersch quotes the early jazz bassist Pops Foster and Jelly Roll Morton, who describe the quadrille as a low-down, blatantly sexual dance favored by "the rough gang" who hung out in the uptown clubs where jazz really began. With masks off but fluid identities fully activated, the working people of New Orleans finally turned the courtly turns of a European form into something fleshy and hot and fully American. But that's a story often told. Before music got there, it took a detour behind less visible closed doors.

CREOLE LULLABIES OF
LUST AND LONGING

After a night out, when a Louisiana belle returned to her candlelit bedroom, her slave maid would sometimes sing and talk her to sleep. One antebellum evening brought to life by the novelist and magazine writer Kate Chopin began this way: with the older, "black as the night" Manna Loulou whispering an old song as she turned to her mistress and shared the tragic story of "La Belle Zoraïde."

In Chopin's depiction, Zoraïde was a house slave who was like (but not really like) a sister to her mistress, a delicate girl "whose fingers had never done rougher work than sewing a fine muslin seam." Her mistress doted on her but still controlled her fate. She planned to wed Zoraïde to another slave, the mixed-race manservant of a local doctor. But one day, Zoraïde saw the ebony-skinned field hand Mézor dancing in New Orleans's Congo Square and was smitten. They met and loved; she became pregnant. Her mistress, horrified, arranged for Mézor to be sold and took away Zoraïde's baby, too, telling her it had died during childbirth. Zoraïde eventually went mad, holding on to a bundle of rags as if it were her lost "piti," even when her conscience-stricken mistress tried to return the actual child. She became "Zoraïde le folle, whom no one ever wanted to marry," and lived to be old in that sorry state.

Chopin, a white Missourian who married a Creole cotton trader, meant this chilling story to be a morality tale, though one full of gray areas arrayed on the prism of skin and longing in a mixed-race land.[20] But the frame—the song of Manna Loulou, and her sharing of the story—is what is most interesting. Why would Chopin imagine a scenario like this, in which a slave elicits her owner's sympathy for another slave, cruelly treated?

The author herself came from a Confederate family. Her stories romanticized plantation life, and tacitly, slavery, even as they exposed the realities endured by the black, brown, and white women often forgotten within those grand mansions. (A century later, her famous novel *The Awakening* would become a staple of early women's studies classes.) Chopin sought to acknowledge the voices of those formed within and by these illicit unions; she attached romantic scenarios to the racial boundary crossings that the steps of the quadrille and other dances made palpable. She found her way into doing that, the opening scene of "La Belle Zoraïde" suggests, through the Creole songs that floated through the air in the hallways of her own Southern relations, and which she likely heard when she herself lived in Louisiana as a young wife.

The Creole song tradition is mostly lost now, its revelations re-routed into Acadian folkways or submerged within the torch ballad lineage that later emerged in Harlem and Paris cabarets. Like the rhythm-shifted quadrille, these ballads originated as part of the Afro-Caribbean diaspora, developing within the multicultural milieu of a new nation shaped by empire. Their melodies filled the spaces between official realms of work and leisure. They flourished in the home, forming a dialogue between slaves and the mistresses and children they served. Sometimes white men, expressing their own color line–violating attractions through the voices of others, appropriated the form. Creole songs also filled the streets, where vendors adapted them to advertise delicacies that, like the tunes they sang, located the sweet spot where African and European tastes merged.

Popular before the age of recording and only occasionally adapted by either classical composers or folklorists, Creole songs, like the mixed language in which they were rendered, are not commonly known today. Only a few performers have dedicated themselves to their preservation. Camille Nickerson, known as the Louisiana Lady, performed them in her touring show beginning in the 1930s, when she served as president of the National Association of Negro Musicians. The Jewish immigrant singer Adelaide van Wey (née Silversteen) recorded some florid versions of them in the 1950s. Today, author and performer Sybil Kein maintains the tradition in connection with the Creole Heritage Center in the Northwest Louisiana enclave of Natchitoches. Some Creole songs also figure within the white, French-born Cajun dance repertoire still thriving in bayou Louisiana, though time and adaptation to different communities have shifted their meanings. Creole identity enjoyed a pop moment in 2016, when Beyoncé claimed it in songs and images from her "visual album" *Lemonade*. Still, it remains mostly obscured within today's mainstream narratives, a complex and vital part of American history reduced to the flavor packet in a box of dirty rice.

"Creole" itself is a highly contested term. Asked to explain how it might apply to people, someone with a little knowledge might focus on the French language or on a general Mediterranean bent that allows for some Spanish to slip in. The lingering presence of the Caribbean might also surface. "Creolization" has become a common synonym for hybridity in general, a soaking up of influence the way rice soaks up red. The conflicts and power struggles inherent in that process are often overlooked in favor of simply enjoying a distinct taste. Even the crucial role of Creoles of color as pioneers of jazz and country music, and inventors of the giddy hybrid known as zydeco, is often reduced to a happy nod toward the indulgences of Mardi Gras.

Before jazz and country had those names, however, a different kind of Creole song made a mark on the American imagination. Its form was feminine, even when its practitioners were male, and the dialogue it represented was distinctly interracial. These songs of domestic life and romance fleshed out a private sphere in which erotic exchange was both a defining element and a threat. These little ditties contained much more than mere pleasantries: they were born of the closest mingling imaginable, bringing the facts and fantasies of miscegenation out of the public spaces where it became visible, and back into the bedrooms and kitchens where the American family was evolving.

Nothing is more intimate than the primal scene where these songs were enjoyed, like the one where Chopin's old nanny serenaded her charge. The most frequently cited account of Creole songs is an 1886 article by none other than that master of the fictional dance, George Washington Cable. "How many tens of thousands of black or tawny nurse 'mammies,' with heads wrapped in stiffly starched Madras kerchief turbans, and holding *'lil maitre* or *'lil maitresse* to their bosoms, have made the infants' lullabies these gently sad strains of disappointed love or regretted youth, will never be known," wrote the *Grandissimes* author. Cable was not a Creole himself—his father was a Virginia slaveholder and his mother a New England Puritan. Yet, born and raised in Louisiana, he developed a lifelong fascination with the perils and possibilities of race mixing. On an 1885 speaking tour with Mark Twain, Cable performed a selection of Creole songs, accompanying himself on guitar.[21] Contemporary reports indicate that his "simple, quaint and dignified" performances were gentler than a minstrel's mugging, though equally loved by paying white audiences.

Cable's starched-collar evocations carried forward something very complex. Within the fraught negotiations of still-forming America in the early 1800s, the imagined or distantly observed Creole became one of America's first exotic, not-quite-white characters. A shifting racial category that encompassed people of mixed African blood as well as those with French and Spanish ancestry became linked to a tawny aristocracy demonized as decadent and cruel. The term "Creole" also often included the slaves of that elite who had spent time in the Caribbean, another region where cultures blended as much as they clashed. Antebellum Anglo-Americans presumed a certain unhealthy intimacy between Creoles and their slaves. Accounts of their lives together veered from rhapsodically sensual to sadistic. (One particularly sick variation on the standard cautions about Creole-slave mixing is the tale of the murderous psychopath Madame LaLaurie, retold in the twenty-first-century television show *American Horror Story*—a nightmare with a sexual undercurrent, since LaLaurie's alleged medical experiments on male slaves included genital mutilation.) The melody and romance of Creole songs made palatable these suspect desires.

Like the mixed-race women whose lives became subsumed within the myth of the quadroon, Creoles in the white imagination of antebellum Louisiana became avatars of romantic anxiety

and allure, and their unclear (to outsiders) lineage pushed fantasies of miscegenation to the forefront. The Creole gentlewoman's
life cycle as it was commonly depicted was marked by the touch
of her servants: the mammy who cuddled her; the girlish companion who brushed her hair; the coachman who took her hand and
helped her to the street. Bound together within the daily dance of
domestic life, Creole mistresses (masters are rarely mentioned in
these accounts) and their slaves supposedly spent hours in musical
dialogue.

Creole songs were rarely singled out as a phenomenon in antebellum times, but they became a conduit for Southern nostalgia
after the Civil War ended. A 1925 *New Orleans Item-Tribune* article
featuring songs collected by Ruth Harrison, a socialite and "tireless
worker" at preserving folk tradition, added musical annotation to
this century-old image. It describes a typical afternoon in which a
"dusky" ladies' maid advises her mistress on a new love affair with
"her wiles and manoeuvers, her love potions and subtle magic"—
and with "gay little couplets and quatrains fraught with meaning."
The slave, a figure similar to Kate Chopin's Manna Loulou, sings:

> *Mam'zel Ce-Ce, look in the glass,*
> *Why are you blushing that way?*
> *I don't know what you'll answer him,*
> *But my heart knows you won't say nay!*

She encourages her mistress, already wanton in her tendencies,
to acquiesce to the demands of an ardent suitor. The mistress responds with a "blush to the roots of her hair," turning a darker
color as if to physically reflect her affinity for the African American
advising her.[22]

Like the scene of the mammy with her beloved charges that
Cable painted forty years earlier, this description of how Creole
songs originated turns a relationship based on unpaid labor into

a loving union. Yet the songs themselves were rarely just "gay little couplets"—even the snippet shared by Harrison hints at encounters that go much further than a kiss on the hand. Just as the music and dances in New Orleans ballrooms were musical hybrids that embodied unacceptable erotic unions, these songs constructed a Creole voice that sweetly advertised the temptations—and the dangers—of racial mixing. The songs made audible hushed conversations about illicit liaisons and rivalries; on a deeper level, they communicated the powerful displacement haunting bodies and souls—black, white, and brown—whose longing was for lost homelands and for outlaw loves.

It's important that these songs originated in the home, and were allegedly shared by free and slave women. Even when composed by men, they were a feminine art form intended to uncover the private concerns of the heart. To uncover the Creole song tradition is to find a communal diary of desire; of that yearning's displacement, which broke many hearts and bodies; and of the dangerous negotiations through which women, especially, survived a system that deemed some less than human and subjugated all to the whims of their various patriarchs.

THE FUGITIVE COCOTTE
AND THE CANDIO

The Creole song came to America through the Caribbean. The first one likely written down, called "Lisette Quitté la Plaine," is also the earliest known text in Creole. The writing credit for this song goes to the Haitian landowner and magistrate Duvivier de la Mahautière—a white man. But the lyrics paint a picture of a paramour whose heartbreak is keeping him from an obviously African dance:

My steps, far from Lisette
Stay away from the Calinda;

And my sash fitted with bells
Languishes on my bamboula.

The Calinda is the dance that later fed the central nervous systems of the Afro-American diaspora during Sunday afternoon slave gatherings in New Orleans's Congo Square. The bamboula is the drum used in that dance. "Lisette Quitté la Plaine" wrings pathos from the plight of two slaves whose happiness has been stanched by a forced separation.[23]

That a white overlord-turned-songwriter projected his own emotions into this character reveals how colonial whites, like today's upper-middle-class kids mimicking inner-city rappers, problematically deployed the black Creole culture that surrounded them. As often happens in Creole songs, in "Lisette Quitté la Plaine" romantic love's metaphorical bondage gains extra intensity when linked to literal bondage. The dubious value in this is that it allowed whites to imagine themselves in their own kind of bondage, their desires confined the way they themselves confined the very bodies of others.[24] Chains of iron cut in ways that chains around the emblematic heart do not. Could real, live black Creoles journeying from the Caribbean to the Gulf Coast within the African diaspora have enjoyed any mobility at all? Yes, some: the caricature of the African-born entertainer in the new world was of someone who used music as a freeing tool.

They're in La Mahautière's song: the wandering lover Lisette is a typical female *cocotte,* or flirtatious ingénue, while the narrator is a *candio,* a dancing dandy. In colonial Sainte-Domingue, cocottes were women of mixed race who provided the women of a plantation house with the diversions of song and dance, while candios were men who participated in *voudou* ceremonies and enjoyed a modicum of liberty in both Northern and Southern American cities at the turn of the eighteenth century. Solomon Northup in *Twelve Years a Slave* had some characteristics of the candio. In her book on the slave trade in Haiti, Deborah Jenson calls the candio "the slave who was a little master," a trickster whose hybrid nature allowed him to resist categorical confinement "as much as the female troubadour, black or mulatto, slave or freedwoman, singing to the mistress with whom she might have been in sexual competition."[25]

At least once, a song arose that tried to make light of slaves' provisional empowerment. "Z'amours Marianne" barely made it to the twenty-first century. It was rarely recorded: once by the late-twentieth-century balladeer John DuBois, a few times as an art song with a classical arrangement, and once, in 1929, at an Okeh Records session in Atlanta, Georgia, that was one of the first to lay down the voices of Cajun musicians in a studio. Sybil Kein seems to be the only person performing it today, as part of her lifelong project to preserve Creole culture. It seems likely that the open tone of sexual insurrection in "Z'amours Marianne" made it less than a favorite in the plantation-dominated South. But it's a fascinating document.

Two voices speak through it: a master's and his conquest's. She has the upper hand. "If your love is strong, sir," she sings three times, "You must have money in your pocket!" He replies with a ribald lament implying impotence. "All my canes are burnt, Marianne! My harvest has gone to flames!" And with that, she rejects him.

"If your canes are burnt, sir, your love has gone to flames!" It's impossible to not see the big house burning as she stakes her ground. Kein's research suggests that slaves in New Orleans danced to "Z'amours Marianne" at the end of their free evenings in Congo Square.[26] That's remarkable if true—did slaves really make fun of their owners so openly? But if this is yet another white-authored song, then it's even weirder: a case of sexual humiliation assigned to the master by himself.

"Z'amours Marianne" is included in the 1921 songbook *Bayou*

Ballads, compiled by the composer Kurt Schindler and the folklorist Mina Monroe, who grew up on a plantation in St. Charles Parish.[27] Monroe, like Cable in his author-tour performances, painted a picturesque image of contented black workers whose bodies overflowed with musical feeling. She offered her songs as proof of the harmony of antebellum interracial life. Yet "Z'amours Marianne" is only the most extreme of her twelve selections, most of which paint scenes fraught with tension, struggles over freedom and self-possession that shaped the emerging American character. Violence simmers within these songs. One weapon often wielded is skin color. The female narrator of one "taunt" song expresses rage that the man she loves has fooled her into thinking he was white, while in another, "Michie Preval," a white magistrate throws a dance open to African Americans, and it ends in chaos after the slaves steal their masters' clothes.[28]

Only one character stands outside of this foment: the independent "Suzanne, Suzanne, jolie femme," who chooses to reject the tasty morsels that mingling with white men would guarantee her in favor of the gumbo of her own people. Yet the very idea of such stability within one's own community can't be maintained for long, for every other song in the collection reminds us that the "bed of quality" Suzanne rejects may be one where she is soon physically forced to lie.

Real human beings lived these roles, but they also became characters in song and story, embodying the way African cultural practices permeated America through dancing and music. The cocotte and the candio enjoyed only provisional freedom—or performed freedom as a living fiction, to appease the anger of the whites who dominated them but also lived as their closest intimates. Yet their determination to move, even in bondage, did more than just keep these characters alive. It made them foundational within the psyche of an African American community striving to possess themselves as erotic beings and free people.

CREOLE AFTERLIVES

One song still sung in the twenty-first century is "Michieu Banjo," which celebrates a kind of Creole Yankee Doodle. This is a song for dancing. Pete Seeger brought the song into the American folk revival, but earlier, Camille Nickerson, a Howard University professor and composer–song collector who toured the United States in Creole costume as the Louisiana Lady, brought it to concert halls.[29] With its sprightly tune and fond description of a finely dressed entertainer, "Michieu Banjo" opened up the space where men of color could express pride and sexual prowess even while enduring the Middle Passage and Deep South. Its jauntiness recalls the boast made by Solomon Northup in *Twelve Years a Slave*: that when he strolled the Louisiana backroads with his fiddle, "I was considered the Ole Bull of Bayou Boeuf."[30]

This is the figure, again, of the candio, as sexually charismatic as he is flamboyant. One observer described the candio in a religious rite in nineteenth-century French Guiana: "impassive and majestic, draped in a long robe of crimson calico [. . .] A young girl stands by the Candio, shading him from the ardent sunshine with an umbrella. Another young girl leads him by the left hand, holding a handkerchief in her other hand. Women follow, singing [. . .] An elderly woman steps out of the crowd and goes to congratulate the Candio. He removes his head covering, places it on her head, and invites her to dance. The crowd goes wild . . ."[31] Fancy clothes, female camp followers, the ability to entice the crowd: the candio set a template for male rock and soul stardom. In antebellum times, the candio strutted through song and story, feared and admired by whites and blacks alike for his glamour and his way with women. He had a wild side, often misinterpreted by observers. But he was also an elegant figure whose arch self-possession translated into the early-twentieth-century jazz style of Sidney Bechet, which then became the flash of urban bluesmen like Guitar Slim and the outrageousness of rock and funk stars like Little Richard, James Brown, and Jimi Hendrix. Today, rappers such as Andre 3000 and Kanye West are candio types. The musicians who inhabit this character have always specialized in sounds that cross generic borders and disregard traditionalism. In their moves, we can see the playful subversiveness of Michieu Banjo, who moved through antebellum city streets under the power of his own charm and musical dexterity.

The cocotte survived, too. In the early twentieth century, the international superstar Josephine Baker brought her back to life in the ballads she sang in Paris and Harlem. "J'ai Deux Amours," her 1930 signature song, cast her as a classic *femme doudou*—a colonial woman of color who becomes the mistress of a white man, often a military officer. Baker sang from a heart divided between her homeland and Paris—an internationalist statement that also stands as a metaphor for loving both white and black men. Baker's performances led listeners back to the Caribbean, to the Creole songs that later migrated to Louisiana. To have two loves is to suffer heartbreak, but also to find a way to step outside by going inside: inside the shadowy home, inside the treacherous heart.[32] And so the secrets of the Creole domestic scene, delicately unfolded in songs that barely survived emancipation and the liberation movements of the Caribbean, formed the signature of a twentieth-century performer whose banana dresses and comically subversive African-flavored dancing would enrapture the Western world.

Baker wasn't the only one to heed this lost tradition's siren call. Duke Ellington, jazz's great musical historian, heard it, too, and focusing on its undercover qualities, used it to show how sequestered sexual dialogue could survive not just through playful lyrics but in musical tone and tinge. Ellington recorded his "Creole Love Call" in 1927. The wordless song borrows from a classic New Orleans tune, King Oliver's "Camp Meeting Blues," which had Oliver and his protégé, Louis Armstrong, mooning at each other through their cornets. Ellington's composition is best known for its vocal, by the vaudeville performer Adelaide Hall. It was the first 100 percent nonverbal scat vocal in jazz. Josephine Baker herself recorded a similar vocal line a few months before, during just one verse in the song "Then I'll Be Happy"; doing so, she became an invisible joint in the Creole connection between Oliver and Ellington.[33]

Adelaide Hall's description of how her part in "Creole Love Call" originated involves an exchange as thrilling as the moment when two dancers at a quadrille coyly lower their masks. On tour with Ellington in 1927, she persuaded her husband to linger in the wings as the band played its closing set. "Duke was playing these beautiful tunes," she told an interviewer in 1981. "When it came to this 'Creole Love Call' melody, that's all it was, just the melody. He was playing, and I started humming a countermelody. Duke was catching that melody that I was singing. He came over with his baton right to the edge where I was standing, and he said, 'Well, that's just what I've been looking for. For goodness sakes, sing it again.'"[34]

Hall's woozily suggestive vocal on "Creole Love Call" opened a door for jazz singers to improvise beyond lyrics. It also carried forward the truth that these Creole songs of erotic disruption first made clear: that music offers disclosures that language cannot accommodate. The Creole love song flourished in murmurs, only to survive in scat singing, a vocal practice that helped listeners realize just how much of America's erotic history would reveal itself when transported through rhythm and a wooing tune.

CLOSE ENCOUNTERS IN PLACE CONGO

Creative expression only becomes performance when others outside the circle are observing. The thrill of music, especially in a live setting, arises when the circle feels permeable—artists' sounds, words, and gestures invite others into a space defined by play. In America, performances of American popular song were grounded in the now-taboo minstrel tradition: both the energy and the moral failing of our pop traditions originate in a white man rubbing cork on his face and turning black culture into a grotesque. But that damned and powerful practice had its own inspiration, arising from the places where slaves came together publicly, always under the watch of whites, and experienced provisional freedom to inhabit the culture that was their own. In such rare environments, white onlookers witnessed African-based dance and music and sometimes literally touched those creating it, entering the circle, making it a show. Unlike the male, comically distorted preserve of minstrelsy, these gatherings made room for women and for welcoming music's sensual effects. The most famous was, unsurprisingly, in New Orleans. It became known as Congo Square.

There is a portrait of a handsome dancer in one of the rings that formed on Sunday afternoons in Congo Square. It's the one that very likely inspired Kate Chopin's depiction of La Belle Zoraïde's lover Mézor; in fact, this drawing determined how countless armchair travelers and amateur anthropologists thought about the African, newly American people whose drums and steady-rolling bodies were so important in defining American popular music. In the drawing, from 1886, the man the accompanying text describes as a "black Hercules" has already chosen his companion. They hold hands across their rotating torsos. She demurely turns away, but his chest, naked, is fully displayed and muscular, his other arm thrown back. He sticks out his hip, about to thrust. Half-encircling them is a dense crowd of singers and drummers, mouths open like the dancers' own. All the energy in the scene flows toward the couple about to move together. It is a wedding scene with music as officiant.

This illustration is one of nine that Edward Windsor Kemble, widely known for his "coon" cartoons of Southern blacks, fashioned to accompany an article entitled "The Dance in Place Congo." The author was George W. Cable—the same influential writer whose guitar renditions of Creole songs brought mixed-blood love to the parlors of the North and whose accounts of quadrille dancing bewitched flat-footed readers across the nation. The article and drawings were presented within the pages of *Century* magazine as a close account of the goings-on in this urban park before the Civil War. Its grounds, on the northeast edge of the French Quarter, were the central gathering place for the city's slaves, one day a week, for most of the nineteenth century.[35]

Kemble's portrait of this coupling during a brief respite from enforced servitude has dignity. It is different enough from the popping eyes and watermelon grin of the baby that adorned his 1898 book *A Coon Alphabet* that its shared lineage with the racist caricatures of the minstrel tradition is often overlooked.[36] Yet this admiring view of African grace and virility is, like those images, a fantasia communicating both desire and anxiety. Cable's written descriptions reinforce Kemble's image. His prose practically drools at the muscled, fallen demigod in the ring, deep brown skin gleaming beneath his rags, who takes an initially hesitant young woman by the hand and leads her into a bout of epic dirty dancing.

The account was almost certainly mostly fabrication, one of many similar articles magazine editors commissioned in the wake of the Civil War, in part because they made the defeated and now-needy South seem more attractive to Northerners. Allegedly based on the author's conversations with former slaves, it was more likely cobbled together from various travelers' reports and highly embellished by Cable's own flights of fancy. It wasn't the first white man's frothing narrative of slaves' Sunday dancing at Congo Square; one exists from 1822 and Cable's fellow nonfiction fabulist Lafcadio Hearn noted the lasciviousness of its female rump shakers in a letter in 1885. Yet because it overflows with detail—and puts romantic sexual conquest at the heart of Congo Square's activity—Cable's article became the source to which most people turned when trying to understand the very beginnings of African American (and there-

fore, American) music. No first-person accounts from antebellum
Congo Square dancers have survived. This central birthing place of
American musical performance only comes to us through layers of
glamorous misrepresentation.[37]

Congo Square is the strange Eden of the American musical
consciousness. Its mythos formed after the antebellum South collapsed, as the music born there was traveling along migration's
upside-down tributaries toward the North and the West. A real
place still visited today by tourists who are inevitably disappointed
at its scruffy blankness, it survives as an imaginary planting
ground for key ideas about what makes American music unique.
For the Southern writers who first painted a national portrait
of New Orleans, this open field where slaves could be themselves
(though always watched) became a touchstone for the region's fundamentally conflicted and exotic character.

One way for contemporary music lovers to think of Congo
Square is as the nineteenth-century Storyville. That red-light district, established in 1897, was a place dedicated to genuinely illicit
goings-on. Congo Square was more like a farmers' market. But
both were established to control activity that took place all over
the city—the sex trade in Storyville, slaves' moments of provisional
freedom in the Square—and history has turned both into far more
magical places than they actually were. Both revolved around performance and voyeurism: the ladies of Storyville displayed themselves while ragtime pianists played, while Congo Square's dancers
courted abandon under the eyes of white spectators. And both
have been named as birthplaces for the mixed-race child known as
American music.

Originally covering six or more acres, Congo Square was an
open field on the outskirts of town that became more parklike
over time. As with any city park, it gained and lost features as the
needs of its visitors changed. The research of arts educator Freddi
Williams Evans reveals that Congo Square hosted myriad activi-

ties, including raquette, a lacrosse-like game African Americans appropriated from their Choctaw neighbors; the occasional circus; military activities; and more brutal events, possibly including slave auctions. In its early years, the cannon that signaled curfew for slaves was kept there; later it was home to its own ballroom, the Globe. When the Civil War ended, it played host to an emancipation celebration. By the end of the century it had been renamed Beauregard Square after a dead Civil War general, and blacks were sometimes arrested for walking through it.[38]

Most important, Congo Square was a site of commerce. In his 1819 travelogue, Benjamin Henry Latrobe cited "the useful recreation of going to Market" as equally important for the well-being of slaves as were dancing and playing sports.[39] Using what little money their masters allowed them for the purpose of establishing a business (Article 23 of the Code Noir detailed this practice of providing a "peculium"), "market women" and their customers would purchase or sell ginger beer and cakes, items of clothing, and other small items.[40] This limited chance to participate in capitalism not only bettered the sellers' bare-minimum standards of living; it fed the atmosphere of openness that distinguished Congo Square from other places where slaves gathered, either on plantations or in the sequestered spaces of religious ritual. At the same time, because the homespun products they exchanged reflected their own customs, these women in their colorful *tignon* headdresses shouting out the price of their *calas* rice cakes embodied the qualities whites found alluringly exotic.

Selling, and the small pleasures that the marketplace permitted, fed a distinctly secular mood in Congo Square. Contemporary visitors seek the remnants of ritual there, but despite the clear connections between the dances it hosted and those derived from African diaspora religion, Congo Square was not sacred space. Later depictions have gained a mystical aura by associating the dances performed there with spiritual practices like *voudou*. But those activities were banned by law, and required more secrecy than Congo Square had to offer. Instead, the open, fluid environment of the square made it the perfect setting for blurring lines; what's likely true is that the dances and songs were reflective of African spiritual beliefs without overtly expressing them. Misinterpreting songs and dances as either strange religion or pure debauchery, early chroniclers of Congo Square helped establish the idea that popular music could intermingle the sacred and the profane.

So the origin myths arose and multiplied. By the late twentieth century, the romance of the square—its sexual thrum—was accepted as fact by sensationalists and serious scholars alike. Yet it was all based in fiction: not merely the scattered misperceptions of the well-heeled men who gazed upon people they perceived as savage, but a specific story that originated in legend and was then popularized by Cable, that well-meaning voyeur.

THEY WERE FREE INSIDE THEMSELVES

For Congo Square to become an Eden, it needed an Adam and Eve. Cable gave it that in his writing—not only in the famous *Century* magazine article, but also in his novel *The Grandissimes,* which portrays erotic desire and fulfillment as the central motivator in the antebellum world's complicated realignments of race and class.

Cable fought on the Confederate side in the Civil War, but his mind became troubled after his service. Struggling to reconcile his love of white Southerners with the cruelties he witnessed, he tried to locate vulnerability within the sin of slavery. A key part of this project for Cable was describing how slaves felt, and especially how they loved. He first tried in a short story, "Bibi," which bemoaned the cruel fate of an African king turned slave whose personal rebellion turned bloody. "Bibi" proved too florid for New York publishers, but after Cable found some success with tamer writing about the picturesque South, he made the story of Bibi, recast within the legend of Bras-Coupé, the core of his debut novel, *The Grandissimes*.

The tale of the insurrectionist Bras-Coupé was based on a real incident involving a slave named Squier who fled his owner, fought with police, and was eventually killed, his corpse displayed in the Place d'Armes (now called Jackson Square), the site of most slave executions. Before and after his death, New Orleans authorities helped fashion Squier into Bras-Coupé, a one-armed folk demon designed to maintain order through fear. By the time the story became the centerpiece of *The Grandissimes*—thrice told in the course of the narrative—Cable had given the devil back his arm and made him both a lover and a dancer.

Cable's writing proved inspirational to many. Kate Chopin's short story mirrored Cable's heaving prose: "His body, bare to the waist, was like a column of ebony and it glistened like oil," she wrote in "La Belle Zoraïde," bringing Kemble's illustration to romance-novel life. Less tragic but equally overwrought was composer Henry F. Gilbert's Cable-inspired "ballet-pantomime," which premiered in 1918 at the Metropolitan Opera in New York. A *New York Times* reviewer applauded the spectacle and its star, Rosina Galli, who "achieved an astonishing transformation to the kinky-haired, black-faced vixen of *The Place Congo*."[41] Cable's influence also weighs heavily on the pulp travel writer Herbert Asbury, whose much-reprinted 1936 book *The French Quarter* retells the story of Bras-Coupé, who could "leap higher and shout louder than any of the other slaves who stamped and cavorted in the dance."[42]

Historian Bryan Wagner has followed the trail of Bras-Coupé from its starting point in true stories of the insurrectionist slave named Squier to the present day.[43] He notes that Asbury's book has been a key source for the many jazz historians who trace the American music back to Congo Square. Writers from Rudi Blesh and Marshall Stearns to Frederic Ramsey Jr. and Charles Edward Smith all reference Cable through Asbury, though none mention Bras-Coupé directly. Duke Ellington, in his 1956 musical allegory

"A Drum Is a Woman," did the same more poetically, trying to reclaim the story as African-born; but he, too, got lost in the allure of violence and black macho.

These mistranslations changed the very meaning of Congo Square and became the foundation of a great erotic disconnect: this is the process that, in the nineteenth century, added a lascivious tinge to the idea that would later be articulated as "the blues and country had a baby named rock and roll." Casting African Americans as mute originators and white observers as translators ensured that white appropriations of African American music would always carry a tantalizing tinge of violation. Sexing up the story, Cable and those who followed him submerged the potentially revolutionary power of the dances performed in Congo Square. This cover-up pushed every other meaning—community, soul fulfillment, insurrection, that potent "somebodiness"—under the surface of the music that became African American. But those meanings survived in secret streams. Eroticized performance became a cover and a conduit for self-determination. The voyeurs perceived lust and release; the dancers felt liberation. Knowing they were being watched, the dancers of Congo Square spoke to each other through steps and sounds that they knew would be misread.

One African American artist inspired by Cable did find a way to return the political urgency—and the malice of racism—to the story of the Congo Square candio. The Creole jazz pioneer Sidney Bechet began his autobiography, *Treat It Gentle,* by reaching back to the story of his grandfather Omar—whose life story he reimagines through the legend of Bras-Coupé. Bechet's Bras-Coupé/Omar discovers a young woman dancing in the square, woos and beds her, is accused by her master of rape, flees, returns, and is killed. This rebel motivated by love has a voice and the ability to grasp how erotic desire fits within the larger longing for full selfhood. "He was feeling the Love and the Power working in him," Bechet writes, "and he was feeling strong."

Fashioning a tale of two real true lovers from the unmoored exhibition of eroticism that had become the central meaning of Congo
Square, Bechet frankly states that, for enslaved people barred from
choosing their own life partners, sexual autonomy was key. The
ability to dance in the square had to open up into the possibility
of real lovemaking, of mutual possession. "They had that to give,"
writes Bechet of Omar and the girl Marie's sexual union, "and they
were free inside themselves." Infusing the insight and real longings
of people of color into the story of Congo Square powerfully altered it. But Bechet went further, pointing an accusing finger at
the white observers there. In Omar's story, the master is not simply
angered by the candio's disrespect; he is inflamed with desire for
Marie. What stimulates his lust is the strength and power of the
couple's dance, and his perverse later actions—accusing Omar first
of raping Marie, and then allowing this accusation to mutate into
one of Omar raping his own white daughter—are all dictated by
the hunger that identifies itself when he is captivated by a dance he
would not, and really cannot, join.

To this day, many believers in musical mythologies place the
birth of a distinctly American sound and style within Congo
Square. If it served as the birthplace of anything, however, as the
nineteenth century slid toward the twentieth, it was of mixed messages and misheard phrases, of cultural preservation achieved only
after a rape and a fight. The questions its legends raise about where
"public" ends and "private" begins, and about how the longings
of observers—the audience—shape the meanings of both popular
music and eroticism, remain crucial to this day. New Orleans has
continued to produce and inspire artists who have put eroticism
up front in their work while scrambling its transmitters, making
the listener's own dirty mind complicit in the process.

Little Richard's "Tutti Frutti," recorded in 1955 in the famous
J&M studio just down the street from the then-dormant Congo
Square, was fully pornographic until Richard and a Creole woman

named Dorothy LaBostrie changed its sex-manual verses into code. "If it don't fit, don't force it," the original said, offering advice the way the old Creole songs did, but going further, as the twentieth century did. "You can grease it, make it easy." That sentiment somehow remains implicit in Richard's indelible nonsense whoop: *"a-wop-bop-a-loo-bop-a-wop-bam-boom!"* Feeling its deeper meaning, conveyed through the ululations of a singer who can seemingly shake his own ass with the force of his vocal cords, causes the listener to recognize herself as an observer who reads sex into even the clean versions.

Fast-forward a half century, nearly to the present day. Bounce, a style of music and dance that takes the quadrille's rum-teacup hip roll to its logical extreme in the motions that Miley Cyrus will come to know as twerking, is starting to sweep the nation. One of twerking's anthems is a song called "Wop" by the Florida rapper J. Dash—a song connected to "Tutti Frutti" at its central spoke, the word lifted from the beginning of that delightfully nasty nonsense phrase. "Wiggle wiggle wiggle wiggle wiggle wiggle WOP!" shouts J. Dash.

America complies. Viral videos of women and men twerking—including Cyrus—flood the Internet. The impulse to dance that mixed up America in the first place has reached its logical conclusion. Or so it seems—but this is a harkening back as well, to the many variations on those first, centuries-old attempts to say through the body what remains off-limits, unless music loosens the rules.

In 2016, the African American Queen of Pop, Beyoncé Knowles, released the song "Formation," an anthem aiming to inspire a new generation of civil rights activists whose first stirrings could be seen after Hurricane Katrina devastated many parts of New Orleans—and Congo Square—eleven years earlier. The video, directed by Melina Matsoukas, builds a dream collage of the Crescent City through images exposing its African American cultural understructure. Beyoncé poses as a quadroon in a corset and a bounce dancer in booty shorts; she declares herself the inheritor of a Creole culture that is steeped in blackness. The voice of bounce's emblematic figure, the six-foot-three Big Freedia, booms: "I came to slay, bitch!" "Formation" makes clear that in this century, no white observer can adequately speak for those dancers in the square, who had voices, too.

Many greeted Beyoncé's reclamation as long overdue, but few noted how long: at least two centuries had passed since those unnamed slaves Thomas Nicholls observed had helped their mistresses in and out of their shoes, so that the white ladies could learn routines increasingly redolent of Africa, perhaps while their servants snuck away to try out some French steps of their own. In that long span, countless dances had been danced, many identities blended and forced apart. The taboo baby had grown up and become a matriarch.

2

THAT DA DA STRAIN
SHIMMYING, SHAKING, SEXOLOGY

NEW YORK, 1900–1929

Two years before Sidney Bechet was born into the jazz cradle of New Orleans, Walter H. Ford sat down more than a thousand miles away to write a sketch that would appeal to theatergoers all across America. Ford was a mainstay of the New York popular music scene, a lyricist who would go on to write many successful songs. In 1895, though, he was just an aspiring vaudevillian about to hit the road with his partner, Frankie Francis. We know little about the relationship between Ford and Francis—in 1898, he dedicated the heartsick "Don't Ask Me to Forget" to her—but the little play Ford wrote, which the pair performed everywhere from San Francisco to Trenton, reveals something about what he thought a good lover should do. Entitled "The Tryst," it sparkled with the light of a new dawn of sexual expressiveness.

"The Tryst" takes the form of a travesty, one of the major set pieces in turn-of-the-century vaudeville. Travesties made quick fun of more highfalutin art forms like opera and Shakespearean drama. In their little parody set in the mountains of Andalusia, Ford and Francis played two couples: the young Dolores, in love with a Spanish outlaw, Manuel Cortez; and her spinster aunt and chaperone, Miss Fitt, who foils the chances of a silly suitor, J. Cornwallis Cobb. The latter pair get the skit rolling with broad jokes about each other's unattractiveness:

MISS FITT: Are you sick?

COBB: Sick! Madam, I was singing.

MISS FITT: I wondered what had made that milk turn sour.

And later:

COBB: What's your name?

MISS FITT: Fitt. F-I-Double T-Fitt.

COBB: Married or single?

MISS FITT: Single!

COBB: Oh, I see you're a "mis-fit." [*Miss Fitt enters through door.*] Well, I see you look the part.[1]

Singing and dancing are central activities in "The Tryst." Dolores and Manuel do both naturally, as part of their sexy courtship. Mr. Cobb and Miss Fitt, in contrast, threaten harm with their

attempts. Cobb's warbling of the sentimental ballad "After the
Ball" horrifies Miss Fitt; her thunking balletic leaps, according to
Cobb, make her look like a wooden horse on a merry-go-round.
The younger couple's love ends dramatically when Manuel, hit by
a bullet, dies in Dolores's arms, but it *is* love, sensual and fully realized. Cobb and Fitt, the cuckold and the virgin, bumble offstage
unsatisfied.

Ford and Francis appeared on programs alongside Arabian ac-
robats and Irish character comedians, bird imitators and bicycle
tricksters, and spectacular ladies such as Adele Purvis Onri, who
dazzled with "illuminated rolling globe and rainbow dances."[2]
This was entertainment at the turn of the twentieth century—a
sensational hodgepodge designed to titillate, if not outright shock,
the paying public. Minstrelsy was still popular, both reinforcing
racism and, when performed by African Americans, occasionally
subverting it. But sex—and sexual facility in particular—was rival-
ing race and other identity differences as entertainment's central
subject.

The key connection Ford and Francis made between connubial
and musical success would come to dominate popular culture in
the early years of the next century. As the Victorian age ended, old
hierarchies gave way to a new openness about the body, sex, and in
particular, marital relationships. The Victorian "domino theory of
sex," as the sociologist Steven Seidman calls it, encouraged repression by warning that unleashed desire would become insatiable.[3]
In the 1900s, dancing replaced dominoes: the idea arose that sexual desire could be managed through the skillful mastery of steps,
in sensitive partnerships that resembled the duets heard on the
vaudeville stage or the highly expressive couple dances that moved
from birthplaces like New Orleans into every café, rooftop club,
and cabaret in cities growing up from coast to coast.

Contemporary historians have refuted the image of Victorians
as utterly buttoned down; they enacted their own version of bawd-

iness behind closed doors. But sexuality in America really opened up at the turn of the twentieth century. Before 1900, premarital sex as a concept was almost completely linked to men frequenting prostitutes; in contrast, 40 percent of women born after 1900 reported having sex before marriage. Birth control became a social cause in the 1910s as both the basis of family planning and an unsanctioned aid for the young independent women flooding into cities looking for work and new ways of living. Not long before this, sexology emerged as a scientific discipline, supporting a paradigm shift in the definition of marriage: instead of an arrangement that made families possible, matrimony became the central intimate partnership in couples' lives, expected to serve all emotional and physical needs. Intimacy and satisfaction weren't new to people in the first decades of the twentieth century, but these pursuits *felt* new.

For all of this seemingly sudden frankness and freedom about sex, people still did not act out their lusts in public—except within the symbolic realms of music and dance. There, as Irving Berlin succinctly stated in his 1911 hit, everybody was doin' it. From 1900 through the Jazz Age in the 1920s, a syncopated, hip-shaking revolution took place. Dance floors groaned under the weight of hugging partners doing the Charleston, the tango, and other "nasty" routines. Songwriters pursued the meaty topics of fleshly hunger and abandon. Women artists in particular acted out the changes happening in society, and the blues, which came into vogue as early as 1921, stated the terms of women's desire in language that would make today's hip-hop-savvy pop stars blush.

Fundamental to all these developments was the idea that music and dance could pull out what propriety and morality fought to repress, and that in doing so, it would remake the very bodies of Americans. From this point on, popular music became the orgone box that would help people locate, free, and recharge their sexual fire.

I WANT TO SHIMMIE

The 1890s was a time of sexual crisis, with divorce rates on the rise and women rapidly becoming more independent and forthright about their needs. Courtship and marriage needed a remodel to keep women happy and allow men to retain domestic authority. This mandate made for what sociologist Steven Seidman calls a new "culture of eroticism": a variety of new customs and practices celebrating skill and finesse in the love act.

The nation's literal loosening of the hips began about a decade before the century turned. In 1893, the Chicago World's Fair offered an attraction that allowed thousands of Americans to see a dance technique—allegedly new to America—demonstrated by bespangled Arabic women in the Midway's Algerian Village. The twenty-three-year-old theater producer Sol Bloom imported the dancers after seeing them at a similar fair in Paris.[4] Bloom realized he had a gold mine the minute he saw the women in Paris, immigrants like his own Jewish family, shaking and swerving in their coin necklaces and harem pants. He even wrote a song, "The Streets of Cairo," that would forever be associated with the belly roll.

All the girls in France
Do the hootchie-kootchie dance
And the way they shake
It could really kill a snake
When the snake is dead
They will tie it 'round their head . . .

Bloom's Algerian Village dancers became a living channel reintroducing and exoticizing customs that had actually come to America as part of the slave journey. Paradoxically, this made these dances feel more accessible to nonblack Americans. Parisian "can-can" girls were already popular in 1893, but their leggy high kicks seemed almost coy next to the pelvic thrusts and rolls of the dancers who in fairgoers' minds merged into one performer: the fun and racy harem girl "Little Egypt." Transferred to an imagined Araby, the dances that had frightened white observers of African Americans became both mystical and anthropological. As this "hootchie-kootchie" mutated to eventually become the shimmy-shake—the basis of most popular dances in the 1920s—it would wear many disguises: a Hawaiian grass skirt, an Egyptian queen's robe, a Ziegfeld girl's sequined leotard. Absorbed and incorporated into dance crazes like the Charleston, the shimmy-shake and the ragged, often florid music that inspired it would always serve the same purpose: to make eroticism accessible to even the most fumble-footed dance-floor (or bedroom) novice.

The hootchie-kootch, after all, was an orgasm: the first publicly displayed enactment of sexual excitement and satisfaction in mainstream America. Here's a description of the Algerian Village dancers from the journalist Marian Shaw, who traveled to the Fair in 1893: "A girl dressed in a soft, clinging transparent skirt sways. She trembles with violent emotion, the orchestra plays with furious fervor, she undulates and quivers in what might be called an ecstasy of delirious delight."[5]

Bloom's Algerian Village dancers inspired a craze that took over midways and urban dens where men gathered. Several performers—some Middle Eastern, some not—took the name Little Egypt and made it a vehicle for infamy. Ashea Wabe, born Catherine Devine in Montreal, scandalized Manhattan when a police raid stopped her performance at a high-society dinner in 1896. An early Phonoscope film captured Fatima Djemille, a Coney Island boardwalk dancer, shaking her gold coin–covered costume that same year. "Little Lillian, toe danseuse," a child of about ten, did the hootchie-kootch in full costume in a 1903 film, while "Princess Rajah" capped her recorded 1904 routine by balancing a chair between her teeth. The Syrian-born Fahreda Mazhar, who danced at the Chicago fair at another concession, the Streets of Cairo, held on to the role most tenaciously, performing for years and even filing a copyright-violation suit against Metro-Goldwyn-Mayer for featuring a Little Egypt character in the 1936 film *The Great Ziegfeld*.[6]

These early "belly dancers" are often credited as the mothers of the striptease. That clothes-shedding bump and grind factors heavily into the history of red-light eroticism in America, but until the late twentieth century, such behavior remained mostly hidden within the shuttered world of adult entertainment in saloons and brothels. The hootchie-kootch was different and mattered more, because it could go anywhere—anyone could do it. And by the early 1900s, it *was* everywhere, an instant signifier of a new era in sexual expressiveness for men and women both. "I've got the River Jordan in my hips, and all the women is rarin' to be baptized!" declared the vaudeville star Dewey "Pigmeat" Markham from stages all over the country in the early 1920s. He was right about women's desires, but wrong to think this particular flood needed to be unleashed by a man.

In the 1910s and 1920s, hip- and shoulder-rolling dances and the music that inspired them—not Middle Eastern music, but the rollicking stuff coming out of African American social clubs and Storyville pleasure palaces—would become a means for millions of average Americans to get in touch with their own wild sides. Once people started looking, they found versions everywhere. The shimmy—the name that took over from hootchie-kootch in the 1920s, describing a motion that connected the shoulders to the hips—was never simply a dance. It was a moving manifesto about dance's very purpose and about sexuality's place in public life. The shimmy requires artfulness and discipline, but not rigidity; it's grounded in the flesh and the firm ground beneath the dancer's feet. Unlike dances inspired by ballet or the European court, the shimmy doesn't reach for some ethereal ideal. Moving the torso from neck to tailbone, the dancer directly engages with the physical seat of sexuality—just as a marriage manual might instruct him or her to do in the bedroom, but in public. Learning new dances became a way to show you were open to learning new ways to love.

The music for these dances would quickly settle into genres— Tin Pan Alley, blues, and jazz—but early on, the style that carried forward its spirit was ragtime. In ragtime, the intermingling of African and European elements that surreptitiously fed the ante- bellum quadrille was right out in the open. The bandleader and composer James Reese Europe, a star of the style who died tragi- cally young, once called it "a fun name given to Negro rhythm by our Caucasian brother musicians many years ago." This possibly self-protective remark downplayed the major leap represented by the fact that whites would name a Negro source at all.[7] Though it's remembered through the signature compositions of Europe, Scott Joplin, and Jelly Roll Morton, ragtime was more a revolu- tionary rearrangement of elements than a set of songs. To "rag" a song was to syncopate: to superimpose an irregular rhythm atop a more straightforward one. Ragtime chronicler Terry Waldo has noted that the term has two meanings—to "rag time" was to rip up a song's meter, but "ragging" was also slang for teasing, and, Waldo writes, "the music does just that—it teases the listener. It's full of surprises—unexpected rhythmic shifts and harmonies." Ragtime made the beat music's most essential and exciting element, opened up space for improvisation, and used the pentatonic melodies and harmonies that are at the heart of the blues.[8]

Free play and precision met in ragtime, making it the ideal mu- sical engine for listeners' sensual explorations through dance. This was a technique to be personally explored, not unlike those recom- mended by the new scientists in the field of sexology, whose exper- tise Americans were suddenly seeking. We now think of ragtime primarily as the music in whorehouses—the Storyville establish- ments where Louis Armstrong and Jelly Roll Morton learned their trade—but ragtime was everywhere, including in the home. By the late 1910s the educational entrepreneur Axel Christensen had fifty ragtime schools around the country, advertised in his newsletter, the *Ragtime Review*. Magazines also ran monthly instructions on mastering the style. These lessons put a musical frame around the same lessons people were trying to learn in romance: how to activate one's inner rhythms and respond to another's rhythm, too.[9]

OH, THE FUNNY FEELING

The turn of the twentieth century remodeled courtship and marriage, as new customs like the Niagara Falls honeymoon celebrated mastery of the love act and manuals advocated foreplay and the most pleasurable sex positions.[10] Works like Kate Chopin's novel *The Awakening* and James Herne's drama *Margaret Fleming* depicted tragedy befalling sexually unfulfilled heroines or treacherous men. Extramarital lust became a public preoccupation, whether condemned in "fallen woman" melodramas or giggled about in songs like "Ma Says I Can't Go for a Ride."

It was the perfect time for a loosening of the hips.

"The men and women of races spread all over the world have shown a marvelous skill and patience in imparting rhythm and music to the most unlikely, the most rebellious regions of the body, all wrought by desire into potent and dazzling images," wrote the English sexologist Havelock Ellis in "The Philosophy of Dancing," published in *Atlantic Monthly* in 1914. Ellis, in an Orientalist mode, extolled Africa, Polynesia, and ancient Rome as the sites where "dancing is dancing of the body, with vibratory or rotatory movements of breasts or flanks." Giving a highbrow spin to the scandalous movements of Little Egypt, Ellis encouraged middle-class readers to try a little libertine shake.[11] Other magazines illustrated the sexologist's point with spread after spread of articles on dances of the tropics, the Gypsies, the Far East, and the ancient world.

The hootchie-kootch, absorbed into the shimmy and crossed over to a general public, motivated the turn toward erotic frankness. "Oh, the funny feeling, through my system stealing! What is that? What am I at?" went the lyrics to one popular parody of Bloom's "Streets of Cairo."[12] That funny feeling was frustration dissolving and desire being worked free, the way muscles could be, through movement inspired by fascinating rhythms. In search of pleasure, Americans explored a dazzling array of new steps. Between 1912 and 1914 alone, at least one hundred dance crazes came and went. Virtually every one of these new styles involved some kind of shimmy shaking. Ragtime entered the home through the piano, and the dances that people attempted in their own parlors began to change. At the same time the advent of mass media—film, recordings, and the celebrity-oriented magazines and newspaper columns that promoted these new diversions—made stars of people whose physical skills amazed, challenging novice dancers in the audience.

Every great vocalist of the era was a dancer, too, and usually a dancer first. Recalling his initial meeting with the great blues pioneer Bessie Smith in Atlanta, Georgia, the songwriter Perry Bradford recalled that he didn't even know she could sing: "She was doing an act at the time with a partner named Buzzin' Burton, and they were featuring a dance called Buzzin' Around," he told his fellow musician Noble Sissle in a 1957 interview. "Oh, she was a dancer at first!" Sissle exclaimed. "Yes, a whopping good flat foot dancer," replied Bradford, linking Smith to the anchoring stance that best allows a performer to shimmy and shake.[13] Aspiring stars knew that the right moves could win over a crowd more surely than a great voice might. "I seldom depended on my voice to win social recognition," wrote the theatrical blues queen Ethel Waters of her first teenage performance in a Philadelphia nightclub. "I had developed into a really agile shimmy-shaker. I sure knew how to roll and quiver, and my hips would become whirling dervishes. It was these completely mobile hips, not my voice, that won me friends and admiration."[14]

The shimmy also found its way into high society, through opera. Richard Strauss's *Salome*, inspired by the Oscar Wilde play, caused a sensation when it debuted in 1905. Its unfettered portrayal of the hootchie-kootch dancer who would have John the Baptist's head played one night only at New York's Metropolitan Opera in 1907, then was banned by the opera's board of directors for its "repulsive grewsomeness [*sic*]." The production's star, the ballerina Bianca Froelich, immediately took her Dance of the Seven Veils to the nearby Lincoln Square Variety Theater, where it became a smash. Broadway's greatest producer, Florenz Ziegfeld Jr., had a version of it in his show by the end of the year. Salome remained a favorite role for African American and white theatrical divas alike, including the pioneering Ada Overton Walker, who performed the role with an elegance that made her a critics' favorite as well as a sensation. Just as with Little Egypt, an exotic Orientalist veil—seven of them, in Salome's case—allowed some to turn the shimmy into an intellectual pursuit.[15]

Hitting the culture on so many different levels, the shimmy was more than a fad: it was a means to self-actualization. The external boundaries that nineteenth-century ballroom dance sometimes broke down became internalized as women, especially, sought to get in touch with themselves on the deepest possible level. Through dance, and the bawdy songs and ragged music that nearly always accompanied it, Americans goaded each other into putting old ways aside in favor of what felt good.

"I don't want no 'Hesitation,' all I crave is syncopation," sang Bee Palmer in the 1918 song "I Want to Shimmie," by the interracial songwriting team of Shelton Brooks and Grant Clarke.[16] The song, just one of many hits with the dance's name in the title, enacted what many young white women were dreaming about. An ingénue goes out one weekend, and, by taking a chance on a dance new to her, discovers a route to unanticipated levels of bliss. Clarke's pun-

ning lyrics made light of an outdated version of the waltz, called
the "Hesitation" because of its built-in pauses. But everybody got
the double entendre. The song's story of an adventuress looking for
more than what an uptight ballroom date could offer pointed to
women's growing outspokenness, especially in matters of love. The
freshest stars of the new epoch expressed themselves this way. They
were loud, limber, and ready to party.[17]

Bee Palmer, who grew up in a Swedish family in Chicago,
was the shimmy dancer whose image most easily appealed to the
society wives and embryonic flappers who frequented Florenz
Ziegfeld's spectacular Broadway shows. Palmer—a Ziegfeld girl
herself—radiated health and good nature in her often comical routines. An accomplished pianist and songwriter as well as a dancer,
Palmer was what we now often think of as a Jazz Age heroine: a cute
sort-of tomboy whose can-do spirit helped her flourish in male-
dominated environments. She extolled the shimmy as a boon to
good health. "This constant practice from childhood limbered my
shoulders, developed my chest, kept my body lithe," she told a reporter in 1919. "I have seldom been ill. Every muscle in my body is
in perfect condition. I can stand a tremendous amount of exercise,
of work, without feeling the least fatigue."[18]

Many Jazz Age women took up Palmer's health regimen. Magazines regularly published articles with titles like "Dancing—the
Fountain of Youth" and even "Dancing Is Best Exercise Recom-
mended by Football Coaches."[19] Irene Castle, whose elegant routines with her husband Vernon persuaded a whole generation of
housewives to try steps they initially found shocking, advised her
fans that grace and vigor learned through dancing made women
more attractive. "The woman who dances does not need other
beauty aids," she remarked in a dance manual she and Vernon cowrote. "Beauty will seek her . . . for when a woman is dancing, she is
happily unconscious, and therefore easily carrying out all the exercises taught by beauty experts."[20]

For all its beneficial qualities, the frankness of the shimmy still disturbed many people. Some performers played upon this anxiety. Palmer's rival Gilda Gray, who grew up in a Polish family in Milwaukee, also claimed to have naturally invented the shimmy as a child. Yet the more vampish Gray saw it as the opposite of wholesome. In a magazine memoir published in 1928, Gray described the first night she did the dance, in a saloon where she was a teenage waitress:

> A lean disreputable-looking young man with a cigarette continuously dangling from his lips ran his fingers over the dusty ivory keys . . . Sometimes the patrons were treated to a special concert. On certain gala occasions the lone piano gained company . . . a trombone and a violin. Then the so-called musicians attempted to strum a Negro spiritual. On one of those evenings a girl stepped to the centre of the floor. A girl with yellow hair and blue eyes that tried to laugh upon a cynical world. A girl whose face was thin and white. A girl who stood out there in the limelight; stood singing for her bread and keep. She sang one song. She sang another. The makeshift band played on. There was a primitive strain in their music that night. The girl's shoulders quivered. Somehow the beat of the blues got into her blood. The sensuous tunes caused her shoulders to vibrate. The mad pulsating rhythm crept under her skin, and shivers ran down her spinal column. Great throbbing shivers. Afterwards they told her that she shook like an aspic jelly, but the girl was crying, and tried not to hear . . . for she had been fired! Fired for doing the shimmy![21]

While Palmer stuck to adorable flowered dresses and spangled Ziegfeld costumes, Gray often assumed foreign garb: Egyptian, Himalayan (one remarkable photograph shows her with an Asian drummer in "A Tibetan Monastery"), sometimes a strange amalgam of ancient Greek and African. Her interpretation of the shimmy stressed its cathartic qualities, and connected Gray to other celebrity explorers of femininity's dark side, like the film star Theda Bara and the dancer Alice Eis, whose hypnotic routines with her partner Bert French bore titles like "The Vampire Dance" and "The Dance of the Temptress." That last one featured Eis, only partially dressed and awash in billowing soapy "sea foam," enticing French before pulling him under the suds.[22]

Palmer made the shimmy sweet. Gray reveled in its dangerousness. But even though Palmer sometimes worked with African American musicians, neither shimmy queen talked much about the real source of the dance that made them famous. It was the daring Mae West who unhesitatingly connected it to the thrill and threat of interracial mingling. "We went to the Elite No. 1, and the colored couples on the dance floor were doing the 'Shimmy-shawobble,'" she wrote in her autobiography. "Big black men with razor-slashed faces, fancy high yellows and beginner browns—in the smoke of gin-scented tobacco to the music of 'Can House Blues.' They got up from the tables, got out to the dance floor, and stood in one spot, with hardly any movement of the feet, and just shook their shoulders, torsos, breasts and pelvises. We thought it was funny and were terribly amused by it. But there was a naked, aching sensual agony about it, too."[23]

Mae West didn't pretend the shimmy had sprung from nowhere the way Palmer and Gray did. Yet the scene she painted made the Elite No. 1 seem as foreign to white audiences as the Algerian Village or Congo Square—a primitive, permissive netherworld separate from the happy homes of the bourgeoisie. White slumming—entering predominantly black spaces in search of otherness—remained part of the process of "participatory minstrelsy," as the dance scholar Danielle Robinson has called it. Thinking of black, brown, and Middle Eastern people as more salacious than they ever could be, West and her fans took on their moves and also what they thought were their personalities. "Do like the voodoos do, list'ning to a voodoo melody," Irving Berlin's 1927 song "Shaking the Blues Away," a hit for Ruth Etting, explained. "They shake their bodies to and fro, with every shake, a lucky break."[24]

African American artists used the shimmy as strategically as possible. Ethel Waters writes of her dancing as a way of reminding fans of her recordings that her voice emanated from a powerfully female body. "I really dressed in beautiful gowns for that act of ours," she wrote of her Southern tour in the early 1920s. "For my closing number I sang 'Shake That Thing' and did a dance for the encore. That was a big surprise to my public, which because of my records, thought of me only as a singer."[25] And Waters's dancing was definitely provocative. Mistreatment in an Alabama hospital after a 1918 car accident had left her with a lingering leg injury, so she developed a modified, more sizzling approach to the bump and grind that turned out to be even more provocative than her original approach. It became her trademark.[26]

One of the hits Waters promoted on the road was "That Da Da Strain," a peppy companion piece to the more gut-wrenching blues music that was beginning to gain popularity. "It will shake you, it will make you really go insane" goes the song's chorus; the force bringing delirium is the see-sawing ragtime melody itself. Lyricists of the time paid tribute to the music that enabled dancing to get dirtier. "That Da Da Strain," like the myriad songs about ragtime written by Irving Berlin and other Tin Pan Alley composers, paid tribute to the music that made shimmy shaking possible by carbonating familiar song forms with irresistible rhythm.

Exoticism continued to mask or at least confuse the lineage of the shimmy-shake, though several African American artists made it a trademark. In 1923, Ethel Ridley performed the variation known as the Black Bottom for the first time in a Harlem theater. Alberta Hunter, who tried to copyright the dance, brought it to white audiences in 1925. A white dancer, Ann Pennington, then brought it to

Ziegfeld rival George White's *Scandals* show in 1926; like Gray and
Palmer, she claimed to have invented it.[27] Pennington sometimes
did the shimmy in Hawaiian garb, taking advantage of a concur-
rent craze for all things tropical. Gray also often performed in grass
skirts and claimed to have been crowned a princess of the Philip-
pines when she visited those islands to film the romance *Aloma of
the South Seas* (actually made in Puerto Rico and Long Island).

Yet even as middle-class white women used the shimmy to become more sexually expressive in private and in public, it continued
the thread within African American dance that began in Congo
Square and continues wherever anyone drops it like it's hot. One
dancer of the Jazz Age took it as far as the most salacious exhibitionists do today. Earl "Snake Hips" Tucker, the Baltimore-bred "eccentric dancer" who came to Harlem in the mid-1920s and wowed
the likes of Duke Ellington with his extreme gyrations, wielded his
sexuality as if it were a weapon against propriety, against being as-
similated into someone else's idea of a good time.

Two film clips survive of Tucker doing his astounding routine.
One is of Ellington's "Symphony in Black: A Rhapsody of Negro
Life." Shown mostly in shadow, Tucker dances in an imagined Harlem cabaret. He's much more visible in the 1930 short subject *Crazy
House,* playing one of the inmates in a comical asylum. He's dressed
all in satin, as he was in his nightclub routine, though a shiny belt
replaces the sash that often dangled down to accentuate his pelvis.
For two full minutes, Tucker twists and sways, making slow, sinuous movements that point directly to the spot just over the edge of
good taste, where Elvis Presley would take his own white Southern
hips in the 1950s.

Unlike the women who popularized the shimmy, Tucker seems
to have had little interest in rehabilitating the dance, either through
anthropological association with a distant land or by extolling it
as a healthy way to limber up. Few accounts of Tucker's life survive,
but it seems that he was not one to make nice. Marshall Stearns,

later a pioneering jazz and dance historian, was scandalized as a college undergrad when he escorted "an even less worldly Vassar sophomore" to see Ellington at the Cotton Club in the late 1920s and Tucker opened the midnight floor show. "Tucker performed with deadly and what might have been called artistic seriousness, but that did not lessen the impact," Stearns wrote, declaring Tucker's routing "a public endorsement of depravity."[28] His date, however, had cheered the routine.

Women, in fact, loved Tucker, perhaps for the very menace Stearns considered corrupting. "He used to say, 'I am the Snake, the lowest thing on earth,'" noted his fellow dancer James Berry in a French magazine interview published in 1978. "He did not tell it to the public but to all the people backstage—mostly to the girls." In florid and possibly exaggerated terms, Berry recalled Tucker's temper, and his "very nasty mouth. Mostly about sex. He used to go round and beat on the door with his penis. On the girls' door. They'd open the door and there he was, holding it in his hand."[29]

Making the genital focal point of the shimmy obscenely explicit, Tucker was, in his way, more honest than most. This reincarnation of the dandified *candio*, known for bedding multiple women at a time, could never become an American sweetheart like Bee Palmer or even the racier Mae West and Gilda Gray. Tucker paid for his priapic ways, dying of syphilis before turning forty. Yet his insistent sexuality connects the shimmy to later eras, when the veils of humor or exoticism that softened its impact would fall away and the River Jordan in dancers' hips would be fully released.

APACHE DANCES AND MASOCHISM BLUES

In the steamy late summer of 1925, Charlie Chaplin took Louise Brooks on a date to the Lido. The thirty-six-year-old Hollywood player had come to New York for the August premiere of his movie

The Gold Rush, and hung around to begin an affair with the eighteen-year-old Ziegfeld girl, though he'd left a wife and new baby back in California. Chaplin liked to check out Manhattan's fancy new nightclubs, and this evening he and Brooks did the town with his assistant and one of her girlfriends. "Swirling in chiffons of pink and blue, Peggy and I danced the tango with them at the Montmartre where the head waiters bowed reverently before Charlie and the haughty patrons pretended that they were not thrilled at the sight of him," Brooks wrote much later.[30] The group also watched the exhibition dances staged to incite and inspire amateurs.

They'd come to the Lido, a very exclusive spot that demanded a five-dollar cover, to see Brooks's friend Barbara Bennett debut with a new partner, the infamous Latin Lover Maurice Mouvet. The Chaplin party, seated at a front table, gazed with interest at the violence that ensued. "Barbara muffed a step and giggled," Brooks wrote in her remembrance. "Glaring with rage, Maurice did not kick her then because he was reserving his punishment for their final Apache number at the end of which he sent Barbara skidding on her face to the very edge of the dance floor."

Six years later, Chaplin was still thinking about that disturbing dance. He mined its mixed messages in the famous nightclub scene in *City Lights,* his comical critique of urban life, released in 1931.[31] The film shows his Little Tramp character trying to break up a couple's apache routine, which he misinterprets as a dangerous fight. Chaplin found comedy in the unease that complemented the era's bubbly sexual optimism.

The apache dance (pronounced A-POSH, not like the Native American tribal name) allegedly came from the back alleys of Montmarte in Paris, where the New York–born but Europe-raised Mouvet saw it performed by a street tough and his companion while drinking in a sleazy bar. To a piano waltz, a probable pimp strode toward his woman and grabbed her. "She did not seem willing to dance, but with simple persuasion he raised one of his hands and gave her a smart smack across the mouth," Mouvet recounted in his 1915 autobiography-cum–instruction booklet, *Maurice's Art of Dancing.* "It was a novel way to begin a dance, and I held my breath. She did not seem to resent it. Thoroughly cowed, she submitted to be taken into the middle of the floor, and the peculiarly vicious and savage dance commenced." After several moves that resembled a fistfight, and one spectacular lift that left the woman dangling upside down over the man's shoulder, the apache dance ended with the man spinning the woman around, held by her neck, and then roughly discarding her to return to his poker game.

Mouvet and his drinking buddy, the Parisian actor Max Dearly, were flabbergasted. The commercial instincts of the two young entertainers quickly switched on, however, and they asked the tough to teach them the dance, which he did for the price of another round. Soon both Dearly and Mouvet were dancing a modified apache with their partners in Paris cafés. Mouvet then brought it to New York, where it became a sensation. "It is the dance of realism, of primitive passion," wrote Mouvet. "As a picture of life in the raw, it has beauty and artistic strength.[32]

Mouvet's account of its discovery may be bunk. Joseph C. Smith performed an apache dance in the Broadway show *The Queen of the Moulin Rouge* in 1908, and offered an almost identical origin story to a reporter in a 1912 article. His telling stressed the woman's passivity and the extreme brutality of the dance. After witnessing a man break a glass over his lover's head—"I thought she was dead," Smith said—he observed the dance: "He only cavorted; she really danced, danced with an expressiveness that I had never seen before. Not a word did she speak, but her every movement, all her grace and life, implored him to be merciful to her, to take her back and fold her in his arms."[33]

Here, in movement, was the very same impudently masochistic desire expressed in a new kind of music emerging around the same time that ragtime did—the blues. By 1920, when Mamie Smith had the first hit in the genre with "Crazy Blues," one preoccupation stood out among its many subjects: troubled love. Blues favorites like Smith's song, Ma Rainey's "Sweet Rough Man," and Bessie Smith's "Tain't Nobody's Business If I Do" took on touchy subjects with an unapologetic clarity, transmuting the spirit of tough dancing into song.

Like the blues, the apache gave women power through its physicality but also portrayed their victimization. Some women dancers would refuse to perform the apache; others would add steps in which the woman fights back. While it definitely did glamourize men's abuse of women, the apache also appealed to female observers because it so graphically depicted the frightening loss of control that might result from more expressive sexuality. The apache was like a hidden chapter in the living marriage manual of social dancing; dwelling on the extremes of violence and abuse, it also gave form to more common fears about jealousy, sexual craving, and emotional dependence.

From its inception onward, the apache remained strictly an exhibition routine, never embraced by nonprofessional dancers. Its key moves—especially that strangulating lift—were just too difficult to be executed by amateurs, and a crowded dance floor wouldn't accommodate the throws that sent female apache dancers across the room. Yet we still see traces of this dance everywhere. Dozens of films, from the musical comedy classic *Singin' in the Rain* to director Baz Luhrmann's postmodern *Moulin Rouge!*, rely on versions of it to heighten the drama. Its greatest presence remains in the ballroom. Those dangerous lifts and dazzling throws that win competitions like *Dancing with the Stars*? They're apache in origin.

Partner dancing is now a specialty only some amateurs pursue, but in the first half of the twentieth century it was arguably *the* central American leisure activity. It told stories, the way songs did— the most evocative dances were love songs without words. Jazz Age Americans eager to become more sexually sophisticated learned how to ride the current of their own desires by watching savants like Mouvet and his partners and, after a few champagne cocktails, tentatively trying out their own dramatic routines. They longed to discover how to integrate publicly expressed passion into their daily lives and relationships. Sure, you could shimmy like your sister Kate, as the song said, but could you do it out in the open, with your wife, or husband, or the cutie who'd just caught your eye? These questions both inspired and vexed nightlife explorers as they took to the wide-open interior spaces proliferating across the country and reveled in what Mouvet called "the shining-floored life."

Dance instructors of the Jazz Age took it upon themselves to help the descendants of the Puritans relax and enjoy themselves on the dance floor, if not in the more secluded spaces to which such choreographed flirtations often led. These entrepreneurial artistes cashed in on a surge of interest in partner dancing that began around 1912, when urban cabarets and hotels began installing floors polished with oil sealer and equipped with springs beneath for extra floatiness. "Suddenly in the midst of this money-getting machine-made age," one journalist wrote, "we throw all our caution to the wind; we give up some of our business hours, and we do not only dance in the evening, but in the afternoon and the morning."[34] It was as if every city in the nation suddenly wanted to be New Orleans—as if the purpose of urban life were not commerce, but leisure, and everyone, poor or rich, needed to learn how to have visible fun.

THE COMPLEXITIES OF COUPLING

The dance mania served a serious purpose, providing couples a way to explore each other in a safe, shared zone, as they pantomimed desire, conquest, happiness, and even sometimes sorrow and violence to the sound of a hoppin' band. Coupledom was already a major theme in vaudeville and other traveling entertainments, as well as on Broadway. Mixed double acts—a man and woman working together, as opposed to two Laurel and Hardy–style men—became common in the first years of the twentieth century, with a focus on the ups and downs of matrimony. The most famous of these teams in black vaudeville, Butterbeans and Susie (aka Jodie Edwards and Susie Hawthorne), actually wed onstage in Philadelphia in 1917. Bickering, ribald jokes, and heavy innuendo were the specialties of such acts, foreshadowing the subject matter of the classic blues. Their songs sometimes included the sounds of sex, masked by jaunty melodies.[35]

Dance also created opportunities for displays of sexualized vigor. Individual performers employed the shimmy-shake; stock routines like the famous carnival show-closer "Eph and Dinah" did something similar for couples. In that skit, an elderly plantation couple is celebrating a wedding anniversary, and everyone at their party dances to the syncopated sounds of a string band, except the honored guests themselves. After some goading, Uncle Eph creakily gets up—and eventually proves himself stellar at getting down. Dinah, pulled to the dance floor, starts out hobbling but ends up executing a powerful hootchie-kootch. Soon they're doing a slow grind, to the amused shock of their youngers. Dance brings Eph and Dinah back to life; it's Viagra in motion, resurrecting desires and abilities that by all known logic should be dead.

The boom in urban entertainment gave residents of America's biggest cities ample places to witness and experience the revitalizing power of dance. Most theaters featured a dance contest, open to the public, on Friday nights, enticing participants with the promise of a prize, possible romance, and even a new career—since many vaudeville stars got their start winning such battles.[36] In the more intimate spaces of the cabaret and the rooftop garden, this mingling of the professional and the amateur took a different form. The historian Lewis Erenberg called this world of leisure "a realm of public privacy."[37] Relatively diverse crowds—sometimes even racially mixed ones—could mingle in a fairly exclusive environment. Professional dancers and singers would often hide in plain sight, sitting at a table along with the evening's other guests, until the time came for them to stand up and perform, within touching distance of the crowd.

The most famous of the dancers were Vernon and Irene Castle, the lithe young pair who became the official embodiment of America's dance craze. Though the Castles vehemently rejected "crude" dance elements like the shimmy-shake, their easy way of being in tune with each other still produced an erotic buzz. The Castles symbolized the sexual compatibility of complementary equals and that made them the envy of many middle-class couples. An early Castles film clip shows the duo waltzing through their act; it cuts to an older husband and wife watching. The husband quickly grows excited, grinning and nudging his wife. At first, she resists, but under the Castles' spell she soon softens, throwing googly-eyed glances at her spouse.[38]

The Castles sold themselves as purveyors of clean choreography, which they associated with whiteness. Though Vernon loved ragtime and sought out African American musical collaborators, and Irene took at least one lesson from Ethel Waters's companion (and likely lover) Ethel Williams, the pair claimed to have never performed black dances in their "primitive" state—Irene denounced the shimmy, for example, calling it "very, very crude."[39] Their dance floor chemistry was more cool than hot, their choreography communicating an ideal of intimacy grounded in propriety and mutual respect.

Yet partner dancing, like the blues, could also dwell on the downside of eroticism. The apache, with its seedy pimp-and-whore narrative, is just one example. The most popular "dangerous" dance of the time was the tango, which felt risky because of the clutching grasp it demanded and the narrative of frank passion it embodied. The tango was promoted in New York in the early 1910s by Mouvet, who, in a story that echoed his apache brag, claimed to have learned it from a group of Argentinian youths he befriended while living in Paris. In New York, he opened a studio where he and his wife, Florence Walton, taught all comers who could afford the twenty-five-dollar fee.[40] The tango brought to prominence the Latin elements that ran through all the music of the Afro-Caribbean diaspora. It was foreign-flavored, yet as a hidden but ever-present part of the nation's heritage, it instantly made sense in an American context. The Latin Lover, a character developed by Mouvet and later perfected by the Italian-born Rudolph Valentino, romanticized a familiar presence in every urbanite's life: the immigrant, changing the face of a nation that had never been ethnically stable in the first place.

OF MISERY AND MEN

The advent of recordings coincided with a general shift toward more openly sexual subject matter in virtually all styles of music. By 1920, the top songs included the harem-themed "Dardanella" and sexy dance tunes like Art Hickman's teasing, squeezing "Hold Me." Also at this time, the growing assertiveness of the African American creative class was complemented by the rise of immigrant performers who, burdened with similar stereotypes casting them as primitively passionate, sometimes found in them a way to be more freely emotional. The transition to something closer to naturalness affected all performers. One compelling case is that of Fanny Brice, the Jewish comedienne whose song "My Man" became the massively popular musical equivalent to the apache dance.

Brice, born in 1891, was a child of New York's Jewish merchant class; her parents owned a chain of saloons in New Jersey. As a teenager, she dropped out of school to pursue work as a chorus girl in Florenz Ziegfeld's staged extravaganzas, finding her niche performing comic numbers based on Yiddish stereotypes. She danced.

in the style of Little Egypt and attempted the apache (for the latter, Eddie Cantor played her paramour), but she did so for laughs. Her first big splash came when she did a silly Dance of the Seven Veils to the tune of Irving Berlin's song "Sadie Salome (Go Home)."

Brice longed to transcend comedy, or at least step outside of it for one memorable number. "People like to feel miserable," she said in a *New Yorker* interview in 1929. "You make them laugh, they will forget you, but if you make them cry, they will never forget you."[41] But she couldn't find the right material until 1919, when Ziegfeld, her mentor, suggested a song he'd discovered on a recording by the French musical hall queen Mistinguett, who, as it happened, was Max Dearly's partner when he brought the apache dance to the cabaret of Paris.

The song was "My Man," a mesmerizing chanson with a circular melody and a modal undercurrent. Its original lyric came straight out of the apache legend. The wronged woman who sings it is a prostitute, left alone by her pimp, whom she viscerally misses: "I'm going crazy, because he's under my skin." Brice transformed it into what she called "every woman's song," though she held on to its frisson of violence. She often performed it in what one critic identified as "the apachian black and red, leaning against a lamppost, with great pathos," as "a portrayal of the abused companion of some slum brute singing of her love."[42]

The English lyrics Ziegfeld commissioned from the playwright Channing Pollock soften up that criminal scenario just enough so that the average wife unhappy with the state of her own less-than-ideal marriage could identify with it. The "My Man" we know is a prototypical tale of miscommunication and dependency: "Oh my man, I love him so, he'll never know . . . all my life is just despair, but I don't care . . . what's the difference if I say I'll go away, when I know I'll come back on my knees someday." This was also the story of Brice herself in 1921, when she first performed it. The element of confession cemented the song's place in the history of women speaking their sexual realities in song, alongside the best work of blueswomen like Bessie Smith and Ma Rainey, who were Brice's historical peers.

Brice's man was Jules "Nicky" Arnstein, and though he wasn't a street tough, he was definitely a gangster. She met the handsome racketeer in 1912, when she was twenty-one and he was thirty-three. He quickly abandoned the wife he had in Baltimore and set up house with Brice in New York; six years later they married, and she bore him a daughter and a son. Initially entranced by what she perceived as Arnstein's high-class grace—the press painted Arnstein as a peacock, who didn't like to be interrogated because "it had a way of disturbing the set of his collar and the groom of his hair"— Brice spent much of their marriage trying to keep him out of prison.

She invested heavily in legal battles that ultimately failed, and he did time for criminal acts including bank fraud and wiretapping. Though they divorced in 1927 and Brice went on to marry (and divorce) the songwriter and producer Billy Rose, Arnstein remained the legendary love of her life. Omar Sharif transformed him into a real matinee idol in *Funny Girl*, the 1968 film starring Barbra Streisand, and Arnstein still hovers in the background, a bad boy, every time another singer, from Barbra Streisand to Lea Michele, approaches "My Man."[43]

It's the actual performance, not the costume or even the context, that marks "My Man" as a benchmark in both Brice's career and in the history of the erotic lament. "My Man" created a space in Brice's otherwise frantic routine, allowing her to subdue the freneticism of her shtick and truly connect. Singing slowly, often lapsing into plain speech, Brice acted as both confessor and confidante, offering up a sorrow her fans perceived as real and asking them to feel it as a way of better understanding their own burdens.

"My Man" earned Brice respect as an artist who could truly reveal herself instead of simply relying on jokes and sugary sentimentality. "Hear her, with her castles of romance tumbling about her ears, bravely sing 'My Man,'" read an advertisement for Brice's Victor recording of the song. "[It is] the kind of heart song you want to hear again and again."[44] This copywriter's spiel indicates what was changing in popular song as the 1920s began. The record, a relatively new medium that was also responsible for the rise of the blues, demanded a shift in priorities. No longer did artists have to dance to point to their embodied realities. The disembodied nature of the record allowed for a kind of intimacy that demanded stillness as the listener absorbed a song's emotional impact in relative privacy. Dance would still play a central role in popular music for decades to come, but now it had a competitor: the natural-sounding voice, whispering sweet nothings that meant everything in a listener's ear.

As part of this transition, "My Man" is truly a blues song, admired for its honest depiction of emotions so intense they erase propriety. It also resembles the single biggest hit of the 1910s—a song that would never be called a blues. "You Made Me Love You" is remembered as perhaps the last high point (if you can call it that) of blackface minstrelsy, performed by Al Jolson, whose legacy will forever be tainted by its burnt-cork mark. To modern ears, it doesn't match the pathos of "My Man"—it's an embarrassing relic of a less aware time. Brice herself made Jolson's song into a joke in her routines, showing her undies to the crowd as she winked and grinned.

Yet as Jolson played it, the famous desperate, funny, slightly scary hook of "You Made Me Love You"—"gimme gimme gimme gimme what I cry for"—does tap into the anxieties of the time about love and loss of control. He'd fall to one knee when he sang it during a Winter Garden theater run in 1913. The gesture, first necessitated by an injury, read as human, as did his outstretched arms. Once again, a lyric about the failure to keep sexual feeling in its proper place fascinated listeners and made the singer who conveyed it something more than just another clever mugger.

It's telling that both "My Man" and "You Made Me Love You" later became signature songs for artists associated with bringing older musical styles into the modern age. In 1937, an adolescent Judy Garland sweetly murmured Jolson's plea to a photograph of her heartthrob, Clark Gable; her understated rendition signaled her own move from the broad theatrical tradition toward the more intimate palette of the movie star. The same year, Billie Holiday would record "My Man" as a jazzy blues, applying her intelligence and cool to its overheated lyric and taking the classic blues into the jazz age. Just as the key moves of the era's favorite partner dances would be used in love rituals for decades to come, these songs served as vehicles for popular music to progress, and along with it, for America's expressions of erotic longing and fulfillment to become more subtly shaded and refined.

A NEW, BLUE WOMAN

Young lovers, especially female ones, needed role models in uncovering what they'd been raised to tastefully repress. That's what the era's "It" girls provided, from Irene Castle in her husband's arms to shimmy dancers like Bee Palmer and the heroines, like Louise Brooks and Clara Bow, who sparkled on the silver screen. One "It" girl had a jump on this new way of being. At the very beginning of the 1920s, she set an example that would influence artists across the lines of race, class, and performance style. Yet she has been largely forgotten. Her name was Florence Mills.

"Dresden China and she turns into a stick of dynamite"—that's what Noble Sissle, one of her mentors, called Mills. She exploded one night in the summer of 1921, on the stage of Cort's 63rd Street Theatre in Manhattan. Mills, a woman the size of a girl, stood there for a moment on what an admirer had called "her canary legs." A thousand people gazed into her wide brown eyes. She had been performing for most of her twenty-five years, but this was her chance to leave behind the trials of the vaudeville road and the degradation of playing a pickaninny—a cartoon kid—in minstrel shows, and become a part of the progressive African American theater scene that was then storming New York. Sissle's partner, Eubie Blake, had given her this part in his new musical *Shuffle Along,* though he'd been slightly skeptical about whether such a slender, boyish young lady could replace the bawdy Gertrude Saunders, who'd been a sensation on the road. Now she had to do it: to use her little voice to warm up the show's most lascivious number, "I'm Craving for That Kind of Love," until it cracked her open, along with everyone around her.[45]

She was so slender. The broad bodily movements of a buxom barmaid type just didn't make sense for her. Mills just walked. She strolled ever so slowly out of the spotlight, letting it stalk her, as she sang Noble Sissle's funny lyric about wanting "a modern Romeo—I do not want a phoneo." As the song implored the lover to get closer, Mills inched toward those watching her. "Kiss me"—another step. "Whisper"—two more. "Honey, when there's no one near . . ." The front-row Johnnies could almost touch her now. By this time the crowd was going crazy, each member reaching toward Mills, in dreams at least, through a suddenly shattered fourth wall. A star was born by the time Mills sang the song's final line. This was a new kind of dream girl with a bubbling energy expressive of women's raging struggle to balance self-possession and lingering propriety with the temptation, or perhaps the imperative, to let go.

Florence Mills arrived at this juncture fully prepared to embody the era's transformative possibilities. Her story is one of mobility: she ascended from the working class, defied the strictures that afflicted many African American performers, and startled the world with her new, androgynous, and innately assertive way of being female. Her place in history has been compromised because she never made any records or appeared on film. But even more than her friend Irene Castle or her admirers Ethel Waters and Josephine Baker, Mills expressed the sense of possibility women felt in this age of unanticipated freedoms and risks.

Born in 1896 in Washington, DC, Mills had played the boyish, hardly human characters called "pickaninnies" in traveling tent shows as a child. Before that, her mother took in laundry for local sporting women, and Florence, a preschooler, would sing Irish ballads for the prostitutes, who rewarded her with coins as they waited for their clean clothes. Her construction worker father had a friend who owned a nearby theater, and that's how Florence went from workroom serenades to a real stage. She was a showbiz kid from then on. By her teens, she was in an ersatz sister act and had met her future husband, Ulysses "Slow Kid" Thompson, a dancer with the group the Tennessee Ten.[46]

She was twenty-five when she nabbed the part in *Shuffle Along*. Soon, Mills was New York's biggest African American female star. Irving Berlin sent her a telegram lauding her as "the greatest of all colored performers" when she first traveled to Europe in 1923. Irene Castle envied her enough to emulate her in a gesture of spectacular bad taste, wearing blackface to a London party both attended that same year. (Mills accepted this cruel flattery without comment.) Charlie Chaplin took in her show at New York's Plantation Room, a theater built just for her, the first constructed for a female headliner. Back in Europe, the Prince of Wales attended her star vehicle, *Blackbirds of 1926*, more than a dozen times in one season. She was equally beloved by African Americans and became a spokesperson for racial equality, turning her signature love song, "I'm a Little Blackbird Looking for a Bluebird," into a call for African Americans to be treated with respect and empathy.[47]

Florence Mills was an electric figure at the beginning of the Jazz Age because she turned the broad strokes of contemporary theater into something more intimate and relatable. She was a modern woman, acting like one. "Her slender body is all rhythm; her artistry is instinctive; her power of improvisation—she never sings two verses alike, and frequently interpolates embellishments that would make many a prima donna green with envy—belongs to genius, and that she has in her very eyelids," wrote the British critic Herbert Hughes upon seeing Mills in the New York production of *Shuffle Along* in 1922.[48] In his book *Black Manhattan,* James Weldon Johnson extolled her naturalness as magical. "One might best string out a list of words such as: pixy, elf, radiant, exotic, Peter Pan, wood-nymph, wistful, piquant, magnetism, witchery, madness, flame; and then despairingly exclaim: 'Oh, you know what I mean.' She could be whimsical, she could be almost grotesque; but she had the good taste that never allowed her to be coarse."[49] In photographs, she looks more like a modern pop star—angular and quick-limbed and instinctively chic—than a voluptuous vaudeville-born big mama. Gilbert Seldes wrote in *The 7 Lively Arts,* "She remains an original, with little or nothing to give beyond her presence, her instinctive grace, and her baffling, seductive voice." What could be more modern than a woman who could enrapture crowds just by being herself?[50]

Mills clowned and mugged with all the vigor of her vaudeville training, but her irresistible naturalness allowed her to express overt sexual longing in a way that made audiences identify with her. "May I pay you this compliment," wrote one fan, Lena Trent Gordony. "Even in the number where the music is given to the wildest abandon of jazz rhythm you maintain a refined interpretation that lends a world of color beautiful to all you do . . . And last night you made me feel an intense throb of great pride, Robert Hichens would call it the call of the blood, I do know that I found a great contentment in the knowledge that you and I were akin."[51]

Gordony's pride is that of an African American delighted by Mills's gift for turning the broad strokes passed down through the minstrel line into something relatable and, by her judgment, respectable; but it is also that of a woman who felt her own complicated yearnings mirrored by Mills. "Here we have the key to her magic control of an audience," wrote the African American critic Theophilus Lewis of Mills in 1927, "her ability to express the vulgar and commonplace in terms of delicacy and beauty."[52] If Bessie Smith became what the jazz critic Will Friedwald identifies as "the first fully three-dimensional recording artist" when she claimed the title of Empress of the Blues in 1923, Florence Mills brought the same complete way of being to musical theater two years before that. She was the agent of the modern spirit of unmasked feeling, moving into a space that felt immediate and unplanned.[53]

Mills rode her success in *Shuffle Along* to heights never before achieved by an African American woman in theater, but her triumph was short-lived. Refusing to take a break in her concert schedule to rest, she contracted severe pelvic tuberculosis and died after surgery on November 1, 1927. She was thirty-one years old. Her one reported visit to a recording studio, in 1924, had been a failure; those test pressings are lost. Too busy touring to try again or take advantage of Hollywood's interest, she left no permanent legacy.[54] But 150,000 thronged the Harlem streets where her funeral procession took place. An account in the *Baltimore Sun* revealed the breadth of the mourners, and that, just as she had as a child in her mother's laundry room, she left the world singing across the color line: "The theater and business [*sic*] began to mix in the swelling crowd. An actress would file by between a grocer, able for the first time to leave his store, and a plasterer, with the overalls of his trade across his arm. A white girl came in. She was the Irish nurse to whom Miss Mills sang 'Where the River Shannon Flows' just two hours before she died Tuesday morning."[55]

Today we can only wonder about the particularities of Florence Mills's talent, which made her such a meteorite during the six years she held the theater world in her small hand. One way to understand her is as the harbinger of authenticity in pop, specifically serving as a bridge between vaudeville and the blues. The moment of her rise was the one in which authenticity began to grow in currency as a new artistic ideal, and in music, this quality was tied to the realm of the erotic. Still the least comfortably shared aspect of most people's lives, sexual feeling as expressed in song or dance often takes on the nature of a secret being revealed.[56] In the words of songwriters like Noble Sissle and the voices of singers like Mills, the personal began to assert itself as the most real aspect of anyone's life. In the tiny nightclubs and hotel ballrooms where couples like the Castles danced right past revelers' tables, people felt changed by the way a song hit them—as long as that song seemed natural and therefore true. It was up to the performer to invent a body language that felt more trustworthy than the broad gestures of earlier times.

GOLD-NECK WOMEN

As the 1920s fizzed on, the most sophisticated performers in show business, using the revolutionary new technology of the recording studio to reroute the pathways of American popular music, were the queens of the classic blues: the great innovators in the regional, mostly segregated culture of roadhouses and tent shows, where Florence Mills had begun her journey to bigger and more glamorous stages. Mamie Smith was the first to gain national recognition, beginning the craze with her recording of Perry Bradford's "Crazy Blues" in 1920. Bessie Smith became the most legendary. Her mentor, Ma Rainey, most effectively carried the stage savvy of vaudeville into the blues form. There were many others, from the bawdy Lucille Bogan to the enterprising Victoria Spivey and the elegant Lucille Hegamin, a friend of Mills who occasionally covered the songs Florence made famous. These women turned what the blues was then—a hybrid song form combining Southern folk traditions with vaudeville flourishes and the instrumentation of small-ensemble jazz—into the cornerstone of what would later become rock and roll.

Recording is what made the blues more significant than any
other early-twentieth-century popular music style besides jazz. Bessie Smith and Mamie Smith, Ma Rainey, and the other stars of the
burgeoning "race records" business provided the soundtrack for the
Great Migration that brought African Americans out of the South
and across America, changing the nation's culture and character on
a fundamental level. With lyrics focusing on everyday burdens and
pleasures—sexual encounters chief among them—the blues did away
with the clever tricks of theatrical singing as well as the technical
fussiness of the classical approach. Blueswomen used lung power,
bent notes, and conversational phrasing to make the repetitive verses
of the form sound like language ripped from real life. Increasingly,
the recorded blues became an illicit portal connecting white fans
to the voices who had originally described those new sensations.
Embodied, disembodied, and re-embodied, shared and borrowed
and stolen and reclaimed so many times that it became a common tongue—constantly contested, with room for infinite minute
variations—the blues permeated the 1920s. Classic blues stars like
Bessie Smith and Ma Rainey served as erotic ambassadors.

But the blues queens did not merely exist in a separate sphere
ruled by the patterns their voices cut into shellac. Bessie Smith,
remember, was a "whopping good flat foot dancer," and Ma Rainey
was as known for her flamboyant personal style and "gold neck"
covered in coin jewelry as she was for her songs. As one contemporary writer has noted, "Historically speaking, recording the blues
made Black women socially visible, and physically invisible, for the
first time . . . Song became a smooth, black, grooved body." The facts
of women's flesh, which comes in all sizes and shades of brown,
peach, and tan, are sometimes lost as we fetishize the distance and
mystery that recordings can create.[57] Scholars working today, like
Daphne Brooks, Paige McGinley, and Jayna Brown, have begun to
correct this isolated view, noting that while blues recordings certainly were a mass phenomenon that cemented the genre's primary

place in popular music history, the women who made them also danced, did comedy routines, flamboyantly narrated their performances, and interacted with their fans in all of their fleshly glory. Some began their careers as chorus girls in traveling revues, dancing more than singing, or led troupes that had as many clowns as guitarists. And though the women we most strongly associate with the classic blues were certainly marketed as owning the form—the phrase "queen of the blues" was thrown around on countless record labels and music sheets—it's clear that no limiting notions of authenticity kept performers within a strict genre definition. Like ragtime, the classic blues was more an approach than a set of songs.

Ethel Waters, who began singing blues at the Harlem dive Edmond's Cellar around 1919, recalled in her autobiography that the pianist Lou Henley convinced her to add Tin Pan Alley songs like Fanny Brice's other signature, "Rose of Washington Square," to her repertoire. "To my surprise, I found out that I could characterize and act out these songs just as I did my blues," Waters wrote.[58] By broadening her repertoire but sticking with a blues approach, Waters both distinguished herself and maintained the deep spirit of truth telling that audiences demanded. This slim, tall, androgynous shimmy dancer came up with her own style, one that borrowed from the era's biggest sellers without imitating them. Waters felt confident enough in her take on the blues that, in some shows, her first line would be to answer the orchestra leader's question "Are you Ethel Waters?" with the sassy "I ain't Bessie Smith!"

This catholic definition of the blues represents how it infused American culture during the Jazz Age. An index of American popular songs for the decade of the 1920s compiled by the jazz producer Nat Shapiro noted more than two hundred tunes with "blues" in the title, including ones by every major Tin Pan Alley composer.[59] That number would top five thousand by 1942. In its early years, the essence of the blues remained unbottled, a bootlegger's brew. Its dynamic nature as a symbolic site of the most adventurous outpourings of emotion made it something more than simply a song form. The blues did away with the distancing elements of the stage and brought uncorked emotion into the grasp of the avid listener.

By this definition, Florence Mills was a blueswoman, too, though she's not remembered as one. She brought to life that new sense of music as a personal, provocative force. Bessie Smith herself recorded a song with the same title as one of Mills's signature numbers—the double entendre-laced streetwalker's confession "I've Got What It Takes, But It Breaks My Heart to Give It Away"— though the two lyrics differ somewhat. Both songs tell the same story, a kind of narration of the apache dance: the singer claims her right to the money she's earned by selling her body, singing in defiance of the shiftless boyfriend who harasses her. The version Mills performed in her 1923 *Plantation Revue* was so hot that one critic declared it "the most suggestive song ever heard on a Broadway stage." Did the future Empress of the Blues stand in the back of that Broadway theater absorbing Mills's delivery? It could have happened—Smith was in Manhattan that year, making her first recordings for Columbia.

The blues took shape through such hidden exchanges—women comparing techniques, as they did in every aspect of their lives, and taking words or ideas shaped by men and correcting them to better reflect their own experiences. Female singers and their male accompanists performed a sonic tango. Similarly, theatrical songwriters and improvising actresses sparred and followed each other, holding on tight as they came up with new steps. In midsized theaters and tiny after-hours clubs, listeners joined in, too, shouting back at the stars they loved. Hot trotters crowded close to the bandstand. They'd left their dog-eared sexology books by the bed stand and were trying to bring the ideas zinging through their heads to blood-rushing life.

3

LET IT
BREATHE ON ME
SPIRITUAL EROTICS

CHICAGO, BIRMINGHAM, MEMPHIS,
1929–1958

Even as more and more dancers and fans of "hot" music moved through the 1920s charging themselves up, America's musical-erotic revolution still mostly lacked a key element: the kind of depth that could turn profanity profound. The musical erotic needed a reckoning with spirituality, the other fundamental human activity through which Americans came to understand themselves. As Audre Lorde would later write in her clarifying 1978 essay "Uses of the Erotic: The Erotic as Power"—a central text of second-wave feminism—eroticism is, in essence, both sensual and sacred, self-fulfilling and interpersonal. Spirit plays a central role in meaningful desire, though it need not be named "god." One word Lorde connects to the spiritual erotic is *joy*—the rush that comes forth, unnamable, from within. The shimmy dancers of the Jazz Age had few feminist theorists to make these connections explicit, but they felt them. The spiritual erotic also makes room for sadness that challenges people to grow: the vein that ran from slaves' laments to the "sorrow all on your mind" of Bessie Smith.

Secular performers faced a challenge when trying to convey the seriousness of this inmost power source. They were entertainers. How could they keep fun intact while conveying the release of what Lorde calls "the kernel within myself" that "heightens and strengthens all my experience?"[1] Popular music's lewd gestures and double entendres—however sensual and emotionally rich—were still, at core, outwardly focused. How could performers infuse their down and dirty ways with the expansiveness of the sacred?

The music that answered this question came from within Christianity, but only after believers who had dared to encounter the profane found a way to balance and honor both key elements. Gospel music's songwriters and performers wanted their music to touch people where they lived—in their hearts and guts, and, though they might not admit it, their genitals—but to also reveal that "something within." In the 1930s, holy people and their highly interactive congregants ushered in the Golden Age of Gospel, which extended into the 1950s, when its central elements were secularized within the prime erotic musical movements of our time: rock, funk, and soul.

SATURDAY NIGHT AND SUNDAY MORNING

In the predawn light of this historical moment, Ma Rainey, a tent-show lifer at forty-four, was still on the road. She befriended Thomas Fulbright, a young white actor from Arkansas playing in a touring production of *Charley's Aunt*, when both were traveling the oil towns of East Texas. Fulbright recalled gaining entrance to one of Rainey's "Midnight Rambles"—a raunchy show designed, as Rainey told Fulbright, to "make the old men young and the young men have ideas they shouldn't have in the first place."

Fulbright stood in the back, a delicate theatrical flower retreating from the crowd of drunken oil-field workers spoiling for a fight. "Now one would think these rough looking men would enjoy the risqué performance and scant costumes of the chorus girls, but not this bunch," he later wrote. "They wanted a special song from Ma and kept yelling for it.

"It was a production number with the entire company on stage," Fulbright explained. "The music was that old number 'It's Tight Like That' and each member of the company would sing a chorus and then dance a fast-time step or two. Of course, Ma was the last to sing her part and the words of the chorus she did went like this: 'See that spider crawling up the wall; He's going up there to get his ashes hauled; Oh, It's tight like that.' Then she danced. Now take my word for it, Ma could dance. She would pull her skirt up and step to. The crowd went wild."[2]

While Ma Rainey was lifting her skirts above her worn, intrepid knees, the man who'd given her "It's Tight Like That"—her former bandleader and the song's cowriter, a Georgia-born African American composer named Thomas A. Dorsey—sat home in Chicago, in the midst of a spiritual crisis. It wasn't his first. The son of a failed preacher, Dorsey discovered musical gifts playing his mother's portable organ at home, then found another world as a footloose twelve-year-old in downtown Atlanta, where his family had moved to escape the sharecropping life. He first saw Rainey there, along with Bessie Smith and her partner Wayne "Buzzin'" Burton, who could tap dance so fast he became known as "the boy with the insane feet."[3] Soon young Dorsey was selling popcorn behind a theater's concession counter and wandering into nearby bordellos to tickle the ivories on their parlor pianos. He acquired the less-than-flattering name "Barrel House Tom," which he took with him to Chicago in 1916.[4] There he played ragtime for couples dancing the slow drag at the women-owned funhouses called "buffet flats" because of the smorgasbord of sexual indulgence offered. Dorsey was popular in the flats, because as a Southern-bred musician, he knew how to simmer down a rhythm and burn the blues. But he never left behind his father's church. Torn, he found a special balance in the metaphorical hour when Saturday drifted into Sunday.

At twenty-two, after a nervous breakdown brought on by the kind of performance schedule that killed Florence Mills, Dorsey was persuaded to leave the blues world for a moment and attend the 1921 National Baptist Convention. The fussily dressed proper ladies who thronged the hall put him off, but he stayed to hear a singing preacher named Nix, who'd been hired to promote a new songbook called *Gospel Pearls*. (There's dispute whether this was A. W. Nix, whose fiery sermons full of pop-culture references later made him a recording star, or his brother W. M. Nix.)[5] Nix blew the wavering bluesman into another stratosphere. Dorsey would describe the encounter as a glimpse of "divine rapture" that made him reconsider his low-down ways.[6] But Dorsey also saw in Nix exactly what the blues offered. "I heard a man sing [the popular hymn] 'I Do, Don't You?'" he recounted in an interview fifty years later. "Named Nix: Great, big, healthy stout fellow, handsome fellow. I said, 'That's what I'd like to do.' It looked like he was havin' such a good time with it, and when they passed the collection plate, they took up hundreds of dollars, I said, 'That's where I oughta be!'"[7]

Dorsey realized the power in Nix's blend of appetite and grace, but couldn't find the money in it, so he continued working in the blues world, which was exploding after the recording success of Bessie Smith. In 1924, his old Atlanta pal Rainey came calling, asking Dorsey to become her pianist on the road and hiring his young wife Nettie as her wardrobe mistress. Something kept pulling at Dorsey, though: Sunday morning coming down. In 1926 he found himself getting dizzy after leaving a Chicago club show. It was the onset of a second breakdown that left him incapacitated for two years. Another religious conversion revitalized him, but he kept getting tempted by secular pleasures, like Adam in the garden. He was invited to play with a band called the Whispering Syncopators; he became a go-to guy as cowriter of songs that would sell at the buffet flats.

One of those serpentine seductions led Dorsey to cowrite Rainey's "It's Tight Like That." "One night a young man came to my home," Dorsey told his biographer, Michael Harris. "He had some words written down and wanted me to write the music and arrange a melody to his words. My wife cleared the dishes from the supper table and I looked over the words; the title of the song was 'It's Tight Like That.' I looked it over carefully and told him I did not do that kind of music anymore. I was now giving all of [my] time to gospel songs. But he prevailed with me to make a melody. After a long period of persuasion and much discussion, he said, 'But there is big money in it if it clicks.' I looked around at our poor furnishings and our limited wearing apparel. 'Come on, once more won't matter,' he said quietly with a smile."[8]

Dorsey and that young man, Hudson Whitaker, also known as Tampa Red, enjoyed irresistible success with "It's Tight Like That." They would go on to write and record more than sixty dirty blues songs, with titles like "Pat That Bread," "Billie the Grinder," and "Somebody's Been Using That Thing." Dorsey called himself "Georgia Tom" when he was plying this trade. These songs don't sound like they were conjured by a crossroads devil; they're lighthearted, even silly, with a ragtime flavor and lyrics that turn on puns and tall-tale imagery. It's hard to imagine that Dorsey didn't have a laugh writing them, and he definitely enjoyed the money they made. But on some deep level, they represented failure. Dorsey still hadn't figured out how to manipulate the good feeling of his songs so that it served spiritual striving instead of the sweet lowdown.

When he'd heard the Reverend Nix in 1921, Dorsey had been struck by how personal the preacher's interpretation of the sacred felt. As Harris points out, Nix's emphasis on the "I," on intimacy with Jesus, felt a lot like what Ma Rainey offered her audience.[9] Dorsey tried that in his own work: his first true gospel blues, inspired by the sudden death of a neighbor close to his own age, was an ode to Christ as a best buddy called "If You See My Savior, Tell Him That You Saw Me." But many old-line preachers resisted Dorsey's hymns, judging them too infused with the night spirit that Christian morality sought to suppress.

Things were changing: the book that Nix was selling the day Dorsey heard him sing had opened a door. *Gospel Pearls* featured the stately Protestant hymns that urban African American congregations (mostly Baptists) knew well, but in a new style that made room for the wilder expressions heard in Holiness and Pentecostal churches. *Gospel Pearls* was the first church-distributed hymnal to label itself "gospel," signaling a new hybrid style that was still somewhat subdued, but that allowed room for some improvisation between the melodic lines.[10] But Dorsey wanted to take things further, to feed the fire of God within songs that also had the shimmying feel of the secular.

He knew how this might work, because he'd seen it in the streets. The 1920s abounded with "jack leg preachers," self-ordained messengers who played on street corners. Some made recordings, and we can hear how these early hybridizers combined blues, jazz, and religious forms in idiosyncratic but very influential ways. The blind pianist Arizona Dranes infused her hymnody with an unstoppable ragtime rhythm, becoming renowned in Pentecostal churches and recording for Okeh Records in Chicago. Reverend J. C. Burnett, whose sermons sound a lot like the bluesy 1960s testimonials of the Staple Singers, was a major star of the shellac-disc era. Slide guitar- ist Blind Willie Johnson wrote eerily emotional songs like "John the Revelator," which later became favorites of countercultural rockers. Stars like Bessie Smith and Son House recorded songs with overtly spiritual themes, if not a purely spiritual feel. "Moan, You Moaners," which Smith recorded with Alabama quartet the Dunham Jubilee Singers in 1930, contains a line that describes the centrifugal force that secular artists sought in the church: "Reli- gion turns you inside out."[11]

But in the houses of the officially religious, the blues was still a source of trouble. In 1930, around the same time Fulbright saw Rainey wowing crowds with the song that had put Dorsey on the other side of Eden's garden wall, the backsliding songwriter re- ceived what had to feel like a bitter chastisement. The Reverend A. W. Nix recorded a sermon entitled "It Was Tight Like That." Nix alters the meaning of the song's title to describe the desperation of followers newly suffering in the Depression, throwing wrath to- ward the weak who give in to financial concerns. "The prodigal son had plenty money, but he lost it all when it was tight like that!" Nix shouts. Would Dorsey ever be able to reconcile his love of God and his need for material comfort? Could he find a form rich enough to contain the paradox of a Sunday morning that glowed with the power of Saturday night? Would this music allow for the eroticism of spiritual hunger, of the soul reaching out to God through the body, with arms and singing mouth wide open?

The answer came in 1932, when Dorsey wrote the song that ushered in the Golden Age of Gospel. But it came at a terrible price. Until that year, there was an emotional gap between the blues that Dorsey effortlessly wrote and the gospels he labored to perfect. The blues allowed Dorsey to be frank about life in the flesh. His gospel

compositions, though more personal than many, still floated toward the heavens. The singers in storefront churches and on city
streets were pouring urgency into gospel music, but the songs, even
Dorsey's, avoided the gut. Dorsey was still working with Tampa
Red, making cash from dirty ditties. He poured his investments
into the sanctified side. Partnerships with the singing preacher
Theodore Frye and the foot-patting singer Sallie Martin, a stern
and shrewd businesswoman who oversaw his publishing efforts,
had revved up his career within Chicago's church community. After making a decent-sized splash at the 1930 National Baptist Convention, he became a traveling song salesman with connections
throughout the Midwest. He'd also found his church home, first at
Ebenezer Baptist Church, where he played piano with Frye's choir,
and then at Pilgrim Baptist Church, where he organized the chorus
himself.

Nettie Dorsey was nearly due to deliver the couple's first child
when Thomas decided to jump over to St. Louis to promote his
songs among the local choirs. In a postcard depicting the New Hotel Jefferson and dated August 24, 1932, Dorsey wrote: "Dear Nettie, old dear, I'm having a pretty good time and success. I'll be home
about the last of the week. Take care of yourself, bee [*sic*] sweet."[12]
Two days later, Nettie died in childbirth. Dorsey rushed home in
horror and grief and was able to hold his son before the infant perished the next morning. Dorsey, already prone to depression, fell
into a tailspin. "I became so lonely I did not feel that I could go on
alone," he later told Harris.[13]

Yet bereft as he was, Dorsey wasn't alone. His church community sent him a steady stream of condolence letters, which survive
as the material evidence of what must have been countless visits to
the Dorsey home, covered supper dishes, and Sunday prayers sent
out to envelop the young sacred songwriter in healing love. And
Dorsey also still had his muse, the blues, though it was dragging
him into dark places.

On one of those letters from a congregant, Dorsey scrawled the lyrics of a song, "I Am Thinking of a City," which would be recorded in 1937 by Alabama's Ravizee Family Singers. The song is a dream of escape through death. "I am thinking of a city in a beautiful land where there's joy and pleasure untold," the draft begins. That place offers peace and "riches I'll share"—not the afflictions of the earth or the fickleness of friends who leave. "Some of joy, some of sorrow, all together have gone," the songwriter waxes grimly. He may be next on the program to go, he concludes; "maybe today, maybe tomorrow, I don't know." But he's ready for the Lord to get him out of this uncertain earthly realm. "I Am Thinking of a City" is a nihilistic daydream couched in the language of transcendence. In that way, it's like many old hymns and spirituals, focusing on a land somewhere else—beyond Jordan, beyond Southern clay farmlands or dirty Northern slums, beyond the everyday realities of physical life. This was a crucial survival tool. But it lacked earthiness, literal earthiness, the acknowledgment that we don't live "over there," even when we want to.[14]

Dorsey's church community, especially the women, exemplified that earthiness. The condolence letters they sent after Nettie's death implored him to surrender his grief while in Jesus's arms. These letters did point "beyond the shining shore where better years begin," as one reads. But they also advised Dorsey to take emotional action right away. "The Great Ruler of the Universe doeth all things for the best, and we therefore commend you to Him," reads another letter. "Lean thou upon Him for He will strengthen you for the ordeal—Remember the words—'O Lord, I'm in Your Care.' Nothing can be more consoling."[15] *Lean on Him. Resign yourself to his will. Bow your head and admit you're vulnerable.* The gentle admonishments in these letters foreshadowed what Dorsey would eventually do, writing the song that became his signature and the founding text of the Golden Age of Gospel. One church sister, Mrs. V. Underwood of the Morning Star Baptist Church, went so far as to write a poem. It begins, *A precious one from you have gone / a voice you love is still*, turns on the poignant image of Nettie's empty chair in the Dorsey home, and concludes with yet another call to give in: *Her soul is safe in heaven. So we'll bow our head in humble submission to our Creator.*

Precious Nettie would never return. Therefore, Dorsey's church sisters told him, he needed to turn to his Precious Lord. That's exactly what Dorsey did in the midst of this avalanche of condolence. The composer would tell the story many times of how he took a walk with Theodore Frye and happened into the community room of a beauty school in his neighborhood (a women's space, it's worth noticing), where he found a piano. From memory, he began to play an old hymn, "Must Jesus Bear the Cross Alone," a nineteenth-century update of the eighteenth-century favorite "Amazing Grace." Tweaking the melody a bit to focus on the slow climb of its first few phrases, Dorsey started coming up with new words. He found himself speaking directly to that God the letters told him to seek out, pleading, "Blessed Lord, take my hand!" According to Dorsey, Frye suggested a crucial change—though it's one the songwriter might have already noticed in Underwood's note. Not "blessed," Frye allegedly said. "Precious." The same word Mrs. Underwood used in her poem.

In a song lyric, as in a whispered seduction, one word can make all the difference. "Take My Hand, Precious Lord" would go on to be recorded by virtually every major gospel star and countless secular ones, celebrated as the gospel text that made room for all of the moaning Mahalia Jacksons and crooning Sam Cookes to follow. Within its legend, that one word means everything. Just as he'd heard Reverend Nix make hymns more human by talking about Jesus in the intimate terms of the first person, Dorsey used the possessive, glittering "precious" to step away from transcendence and to live, in pain and the desire to stop that pain, in the here and now. Instead of dreaming beyond the body, "Precious Lord" requires a singer to stay within her body, utterly aware of its demands, calling to God as a bereft blueswoman calls to a straying lover. Spirituals and hymns are meant to soothe need, promising experiences beyond it. "Precious Lord" comes alive within need, showing it as, in fact, desire: yearning for a union so deep it might dissolve you.

In the quickly codifying realm of popular music, the sacred and the profane were at least categorically divided during Dorsey's time. Blues touched the spirit, but in dwelling on the flesh it drew a limit around itself; it couldn't transcend. Sacred music lifted the body, but also questioned the worth of the physical and focused on the hope for a life beyond it. "Take My Hand, Precious Lord" showed how a song could become a passageway reconciling these separate arenas, which, in the experiences of most people, were not so distant anyway.

"Take My Hand, Precious Lord" stands at a crossroads more crucial than any that hosted a devil out to take a bluesman's soul. This song, so seemingly simple, created a space where the beauty and poeticism of desire was revealed, and where the physicality of spiritual longing could be manifest. For Dorsey, it was yet another new beginning. He would achieve legendary status as the "Father of Gospel" on the strength of "Precious Lord" and the songs he wrote in its mold after 1932. But for all of popular music, the song became a landmark hidden in plain sight.

MAGICAL MOTHERS

"Precious Lord" gave modern gospel a template. Singers made it come alive. Dorsey and his fellow hymn writers needed these envoys, mostly women, to carry the music forward within churches and throughout the secular world. Some of their names are familiar: Mahalia Jackson, Rosetta Tharpe, Clara Ward, Marion Williams. Others, like Inez Andrews and Roberta Martin, mostly gained renown within the walls of the sanctuaries where they stomped and squalled, inventing new ways to articulate need and shower listeners with love. Still others, like Clara Hudman (the Georgia Peach) and Queen C. Anderson, are nearly forgotten. But their voices, ripe with that improvisatory ripple that would come to be called melisma and the rich tone of what Williams called "the moan that keeps homes together," gave popular music a new kind of mobility. Their singing overrode the mind-body split that kept the sacred from the profane. Basically, these women invented rock and roll performance.

A description of the performance style of one of Thomas A. Dorsey's early musical companions, Willie Mae Ford Smith, captures the feeling of these electric church mothers. "Mother Smith was dramatic and . . . Holy Ghost–filled . . . When she said she felt like flying away, in your mind's eye, you could visualize this," the gospel radio personality Zella Jackson Price said years after Smith's early heyday. "Folks is just shoutin' everywhere, hats flyin' and car-ryin' on, just somethin' terrible. She'd come in and just wreck all them buildings. That was Mother Smith, and she loved it." Smith was known for flapping her arms while singing, sweating out her sorrow and prancing her joy.[16] Her loud wildness resembled Ma Rainey's, but her earthiness served the Lord.

One thing Willie Mae was not, however, was conventionally sexy. A big-boned woman, known in her later years for outsized eyeglasses, she was a mother figure from the beginning. She em-bodied a gospel ideal that balanced sexuality with other feminine attributes, like humor and huggable warmth. Mothers are sexual beings, of course; but in popular culture they're rarely eroticized bait. Gospel mothers exhibited the fervor of desire while not al-ways worrying whether they fit others' standards of being desirable. Gospel mothers never portrayed themselves as virgins; that luxury of perceived purity didn't present itself within communities where women married young and often multiple times. But they explored what it might feel like to be touched by the Divine, in physical performances that expressed (and often realized) erotic excitement as it flowed from within the body outward, not for show, but in the highest, deepest realization of love.

The vision of black worshipers collapsed upon church floors can quickly become another stereotype, like the ones Florence Mills grappled with playing in musicals about plantations and the jungle. The black church moved into modernity with the rest of American history, adjusting its forms of worship to suit changing times. As romance and sexuality became more openly discussed in the first three decades of the twentieth century, gospel mothers forged a link between everyday interpersonal intimacy and spiritual union. In gospel music of the golden era, the God connection isn't some scary, eyes-rolling-back loss of control; it's intensely satisfying and pleasurable, like sex.

One lesser-known singer working in the spirit-queen tradition described this thrill in no uncertain terms when interviewed in the 1990s. "I *knew* that it was the Lord. 'Cause I've *never felt nothing* like it! *The joy! The fulfillment! The explosion! The everything*—was there! And I had longed for that," she said. Her interviewer, the ethnomusicologist Glenn Hinson, mapped this euphoria in his own description of the gospel singing style: "Start low; rise high; return to low. The worshipful act—be it prayer or preaching, welcome or song—seems to mirror the whole in which it is embedded. Both act and service follow the same trajectory. Turn up the fire; let it sizzle; then turn it down. But never turn it down all the way. Never fully return to the last point of rest. Instead, keep raising the bottom, ever boosting the ambient energy, ever bringing the sustaining lows closer to the fiery peaks."[17]

This approach to singing mirrors the female orgasm. It's what Dorsey needed his hot holy mamas to embody. Women took the holy impulse inward and dwelled upon it as it ebbed and flowed. Their sense of eroticism's pleasure and need as multiple and elusive, needing to be stroked and stoked, translated into a new, shockingly immediate and current framework for sanctified joy. In rock and soul, the secular outgrowths of gospel music, intense privileging of sensual realities became the dynamo that broke down both musical forms and any remaining sense of propriety within performance. This orgasmic authenticity turns what the music historian Craig Werner has called "the gospel impulse"—a striving for connectedness among people seeing themselves "in relation to rather than on their own"—into something erotic.[18] In that moment, when gospel made the erotic divine, popular music's room was wrecked and made ready for the nonsectarian ecstatic innovations of rock and soul.

The women's world of gospel was not a separate sphere; it could complement or overcome male domination as necessary. It was a family realm—sisters often sang together—and its maternal feeling was expansive and erotically charged. Women made waves in a gospel music industry that by the mid-twentieth century was as vital as the one about to host rock and roll's coming-out party.[19] The gospel scene was centered in Chicago, with outposts in Memphis, Harlem, Philadelphia, and Los Angeles. Some artists, like Roberta Martin and Gertrude Ward, became group leaders who flourished as businesswomen as well as musical innovators. The Roberta Martin Singers launched the careers of legends Alex Bradford and James Cleveland in the first major ensemble to include both men and women. Ward's family group, centered on her dynamic youngest daughter Clara and, later, the incomparable soprano Marion Williams, dressed up gospel in sequins and beehives, showing how glitz could serve God.

The most important practitioner of gospel glamour is someone who, later in her life, became such an American institution that we forget how fierce and funky she was when she emerged as the genre's biggest crossover star. Born in New Orleans, raised a Baptist but with a rollicking Holiness congregation right next door, Mahalia Jackson was to gospel what Bessie Smith, the idol of her youth, was to blues. Her 1947 recording of Memphis minister W. Herbert Brewster's "Move On Up a Little Higher" was gospel's breakthrough hit, selling more than two million slices of 78 RPM shellac. Jackson claimed Smith's blues title for herself, calling herself the "Empress of Gospel" after Dorsey, who partnered with her early on in her career, dubbed her that at a 1940 service at the Morning Star Baptist Church.[20]

The bold seventeen-year-old started her Chicago career by standing up in her aunt's proper Baptist church and singing an impromptu Holiness-style solo. She found a marketable balance between the Southern Holiness style of whooping and groaning and the more ordered Northern Baptist approach. Approaching fervor with refinement, Jackson employed just enough theatrical distance within her performances to make gospel translatable to listeners beyond the faithful. She did have rivals as gospel's Golden Age wore on: an accurate retelling of the roots of rock and soul would name Inez Andrews as the originator of the heavy metal wail; Clara Ward as the first glam rocker, in wild wigs and David Bowie–worthy satin and tat; and Marion Williams as the flirtatious force behind the squalling vocal climaxes that Little Richard employed. Richard openly acknowledged that debt.[21]

A revisionist history would also include the men who worked alongside and learned from these women, in what was, in spirit and often in hidden fact, a sexually adventurous world. Many were queer, as Anthony Heilbut has elucidated in his groundbreaking essay "The Children and Their Secret Closet." Sexuality became even more fluid in gospel performance because it wasn't an open focal point. As virile as the women could be, gospel's male soloists embraced femininity. Singers like Brother Joe May—"The Thunderbolt of the Midwest"—and the flamboyant Alex Bradford would run through church aisles, their rotund bodies glistening. As Heilbut puts it, they were in dialogue with the spirit queens, "answering one kind of musical androgyny with another."[22]

All expressed gospel's most important concept when it comes to popular music's erotics: whatever arouses people gains meaning not through outwardly conceived theatrical gestures but by being found and freed from within. In the world of gospel, performance is not merely an act. It is an action, an excavation of that kernel within that Audre Lorde named the erotic: that sex organ known as the soul.

THE TIME BOMB

One gospel mother embodied the fundamental shift from pop showing and telling to rock and soul *being* with unrivaled force and subtlety. Dorothy Love Coates never really crossed over to the mainstream the way Mahalia Jackson did. She didn't experiment with jazz or blues; her offstage personality wasn't flamboyant like that of Rosetta Tharpe (who played to huge crowds and helped popularize the electric guitar) or Clara Ward. Nor is she viewed as a direct link between gospel and pop as readily as is Sam Cooke. Yet Coates directly influenced Cooke, and in her sanctified style, we can see the visceral intensity that figures including James Brown, Janis Joplin, and Bruce Springsteen turned into the very essence of future music.

Born in Birmingham, Alabama, in 1928, Coates became known in the 1960s as an active player in the civil rights movement; her home church was the Sixteenth Street Baptist, where Martin Luther King Jr. centered his Southern activism and where four little girls were murdered in a racist bombing in 1963. Perhaps because of her political nature, or because of the undiagnosed depression that troubled her as it had Dorsey, Coates never moved from the Deep South, though she journeyed with her group, the Gospel Harmonettes, all along the gospel highway. Her most talked-about performances were never captured on film or video.

In her day, though, anyone in gospel understood that Coates commanded the music's spiritualized eroticism. "If you have ever

heard Dorothy Love Coates sing, right away you can tell she is looking for this connection on the inside which matches words that she
is singing," the gospel artist and historian Horace Clarence Boyer
told the filmmaker Dwight Cammeron, whose 2000 documentary
about Coates is a definitive account of the singer's impact.[23] "She
is delivering an experience, she is sharing this experience with you.
And when she begins to sing, all of a sudden she makes that connection, and she is in the sanctified church, she is in the spirit, she
is under the wings of God, and her eyes will pop wide open, and her
body begins to show what she is singing, she becomes a preacher
who is under the Holy Spirit. And when it hits her, it hits you, too."

In her 1950s heyday, Coates and the other four original Harmonettes all drove in one car to California to record for Art Rupe's
Specialty Records. Their Specialty sides were nearly instant hits;
one, "Get Away Jordan," became a centerpiece of the group's shows.
When the Harmonettes played in front of nearly seven thousand
people at the Shrine Auditorium in 1955, on a bill that reads like
a 1950s gospel pantheon—the Soul Stirrers with Sam Cooke, the
Caravans with James Cleveland and Albertina Walker, Brother Joe
May, the beloved quartet the Pilgrim Travelers—"Get Away Jordan"
was the climax of the show. "Get Away Jordan" was originally a
spiritual, heavy with weariness, describing the river of death that
finishes a hard life. Coates's version, included in the live recording
of that 1955 show, places the afterlife's heavenly tomorrow right
smack in gospel's physical now. As the group's road pianist Herbert "Pee Wee" Pickard sets a frantic rhythm, Coates begins with a
sermonette. She's already put the river, the afterlife fantasy, behind
her. She's describing the moment of death. But then she's scold-
ing death—"Get *away*, Jordan, now!"—and putting her arms around
her Savior for a dance. The recording is only audio, so we can't see
Coates doing her famous "quickening"—running and falling to her
knees, calling for a chair, in a routine that James Brown would later
modify in his own cape-shedding finales.

Born three decades later than Willie Mae Ford Smith, Coates didn't have to invent the gospel impulse. She liked secular music as a child, when her name was Dorothy McGriff. She started playing piano in church at age ten and never left after that. Anthony Heilbut has written that Coates didn't need to study the blues because her own life provided enough sadness—her minister father left the family when she was in grade school, and her own firstborn daughter, whom she delivered at age sixteen, suffered from cerebral palsy. Married twice—both times to gospel singers, first Willie Love of the Fairfield Four and then Carl Coates of the Sensational Nightingales—she was no angel. But she loved to demonstrate what heaven on earth felt like.

Even in youth, Coates was a musical tinkerer, an iconoclast disassembling and reassembling sacred texts. "I had a habit of changing the melody sometimes," she told Cammeron. "I would take the song and change the melody that was involved. And once the melody was changed to a little more up-tempo sort of thing, the old people would just knock themselves out over the same song." She'd change the lyrics, too—in one case, she said, a song that included Jesus's words, "Be lifted up to earth, I'll draw all men unto me," became in her hands, "I wonder who will help me lift Jesus." This is the same shove into the present moment Dorsey delivered in "Precious Lord." Coates made what was dry and boring immediate and interactive.

Her passion scared people. Art Rupe worried that she might have a heart attack during the Harmonettes' Specialty recording sessions. "Dorothy's first personal appearances around the country left most gospel audiences in a state of shock!" her sister, Lillian Caffey, wrote in a self-published tribute from the early 1970s. "Her audiences and other artists are still left in awe when this slow-walking, slow-talking, very innocent-looking female explodes like a well-set time bomb."[24]

In the same years when Ray Charles and Etta James were explicitly engaging the gospel impulse in their secular hits, Coates's ability to be both rough and masterful made her music a particularly strong bridge to rock and soul. She herself stuck with gospel all her life, long after the original Harmonettes had left her to form families and get respectable jobs, and she'd reformed the group, and then that one fell apart, too. Coates rarely performed in her later years—her voice, some said, was all shouted out, and because she stayed in Birmingham, she became isolated from her old gospel-highway friends. However, she did have a strange Hollywood moment in the 1990s. Her voice was resurrected as some kind of archetype of suffering in films including *The Long Walk Home* and *Beloved;* she even appeared in those two, leading choruses of grieving or defiant women.

Coates must have enjoyed being acknowledged, but her influence remains hugely underestimated. The spiritualized eroticism she perfected would be similarly engaged by early soul artists like Brown, Charles, and Wilson Pickett, who borrowed directly from her work, and in the voice of Darlene Love, the ubiquitous girl group–era singer whose stage name was a tribute to Coates. And to this day, Coates's shout of "Get Away Jordan"—her embrace of earthy eternal life—can be heard every time a regular person discovers how to be a rock star, quickening under a spark both libidinal and divine.

COCKS IN THE HENHOUSE

Gospel gave rock and soul many musical innovations, but its deepest contribution was the conviction that the soul's erotic fulfillment is a matter of life and death. The same could be said of the blues; but in gospel, there's more movement and more hope. There's also a greater commitment to camaraderie. The mothers and queens who demonstrated longing and satisfaction through their performances found a counterpart in the vocal quartets who showed how yearning and devotion could become even stronger when shared.

These mostly male groups established a way for men to be together erotically that was both inherently queer in its passionate fluidity and reassuringly recognizable to heterosexual men and women not ready to live within a sexually fluid space.

To say it more plainly, gospel quartets were like rock bands. They ran on the shared, sensual, blessed charisma of men who might have otherwise never let loose in the same way. Their antics nearly resembled what the Beatles did ten years later in movies like *Help!* That's the thing about the gospel quartets—they were sex symbols. In their intimacy and competitiveness, their blend of skill and force and bravado, these "cocks in the henhouse," as the Sam Cooke biographer Daniel Wolff once described them, were presenting the world with the prototype of rock-band charisma.[25]

Quartets proliferated throughout the Golden Age of Gospel. Some, like the Golden Gate Quartet and the Soul Stirrers, became nationally famous; others remained beloved in their region, playing the church and revival circuit down home. The tale of the Famous Blue Jay Singers is grounded in a love story, platonic but intense, connecting an older singer with his protégé. In 1926, Silas Steele, a thirteen-year-old country kid who'd recently moved with his family to Birmingham's Jefferson County, met the mentor who would soon turn him into the area's first bona fide gospel star. Clarence Dennis "Tooter" Parnell sang bass in Woodward's Big Four, a group that like many in the area had been formed as a show team playing for visitors to a local factory, in this case the Woodward Ironworks. He recognized that young Steele's big lungs could save the boy from such hard labor and formed the Famous Blue Jays around him.[26]

The fond bond shared by Parnell, Steele, and the other Blue Jays was grounded in machismo. From the beginning, they liked to battle. Sacred song contests took place in the Birmingham area as early as 1929; groups would gather and try to blow each other away with harmonic genius, rhythmic oomph, and showmanship.

Facing off against equally ambitious quartets such as the Kings of Harmony and the Birmingham Jubilee Singers, Steele and his mates learned how to cajole a roomful of believers. Steele shouted in a baritone that grew mightier with every passing year, and could hit a grit-tinged falsetto at opportune moments. Small and thin, he'd strut the stage. And at the right moment, he'd stage-dive right into the arms of the women seated up front.

"They Sing with Their Heads, Hearts, Hands and Feet!" reads a 1934 handbill for the Blue Jays that shows the group looking like Hollywood crooners in tuxedoes, white flowers in their boutonnieres. "Hear Them. They Will Make You Laugh and Cry."[27] Steele, particularly, was known for his emotional power—a quality that can only be called soulfulness, though he perfected his style decades before anyone called music "soul." First with the Famous Blue Jays, and later as the lead voice in the regionally dominant Spirit of Memphis Quartet during that Tennessee group's peak years, Steele was an exemplary quartet king. The Blue Jays recorded for Paramount Records and became one of the first gospel groups to conduct "barnstorming" tours throughout the South. Steele himself never gained great fame, partly because his career ended in 1953, when he left Memphis for California, never to sing again. But within the steamily devotional exchanges Steele shared with his musical companions, he embodied the gospel flourishes that would later help define the dares taken by early rockers and soul men.

The popular conception of gospel's relationship to rock and soul relies on the notion that a few key figures—Ray Charles and Sam Cooke, especially—melded the sacred and secular in a new way at mid-century. But the rock-band-style quartet long predates the emergence of these important players. For example, the group that launched Cooke, the Soul Stirrers, dominated the circuit at the same time Steele was making his mark in the Southeast in the decade before Cooke joined in 1950. Rebert H. Harris, the Stirrers' leading man before Cooke, employed many of the same new ideas Steele explored, including a wide vocal range that slipped into a manly falsetto; a willingness to move onstage and connect with listeners; and a way of connecting spiritual devotion with detailed stories that evoked the daily toils and triumphs of quartet singing's ardent fans.

Devotion to a very personal God fed the heat quartets released. With titles like "I Want Jesus to Walk Around My Bedside," "Let It Breathe on Me," "Here Am I, Send Me," and "Be with Me Jesus," the songs quartets favored allowed men to express an intensity of emotional connection that didn't have many other outlets. Songs about beloved mothers were also common—a safe side step from actual love songs. In a parallel pop realm, white crooners like Bing Crosby wallowed in tenderness. But the mix of masculine strength and open, sweet passion that quartet singing had was distinctive. Women (and, though they might not say so, men) could not resist.

Southern gospel quartets became rugged, skilled working units partly because of the dirt from which they sprang. Dirt, or coal, or steel: in the South, groups often either were put together by factory or mine managers to entertain visiting bigwigs and help workers blow off steam, or came together to help alleviate the dehumanizing drudgery of industrial work. They had to be loud and flashy to rise above the toxic dust. The men who would train these groups, like the pioneering entrepreneur R. C. Foster, urged them to sing "with big voices where you could feel it with your hand!"[28] A city like Birmingham, in its own paradoxical way, was part of the Great Migration that was, as the journalist Isabel Wilkerson wrote in her Pulitzer Prize–winning account of that period, "the first big step the nation's servant class took without asking."[29] Founded in 1871, Birmingham drew in sharecroppers and their families hoping for a better chance at happiness than that slavery-by-another-name offered. In the segregated shantytowns where Jefferson County workers were made to live, they fought to thrive in what sometimes seemed like a much worse "better life."

Gospel quartets grew out of this striving, modeling not just dignity but lionlike pride.[30] Posturing and precision mattered in equal parts as the singers' joined voices shaped elaborate musical patterns only to have one voice break through, nearing ecstatic release. Busting out synchronized moves in their Sunday suits, camouflaging their virility in the language of holy inspiration, these anointed ones were the ultimate alpha males of their popular music era. Swagger, sweat, and rhythm distinguished gospel quartets from glee club–like jubilee groups such as the Golden Gate Quartet. Jubilee groups were jazzy and popular but wouldn't offer much to rock and roll. There just wasn't much craziness there—or much sex.

Men like Silas Steele had sex. "Oh man, popular—is that the word for it?" Spirit of Memphis tenor Robert Reed laughed when asked by the historian Doug Seroff if Steele had pull in Memphis at the group's height.[31] Steele looks fine in publicity photographs from the period, as do all the Spirits. One shot circa 1951 shows the group—eight men strong at this point—in suits that practically shine, with big bow ties and hairstyles that codify the trends of the moment. Steele and the two singers with whom he often exchanged leads, Willmer "Little Ax" Broadnax and Jethroe "Jet" Bledsoe, are lined up in the middle like happy linebackers. Little Ax's hand rests on Steele's arm, his signet ring glittering.

As he did with Parnell in the Blue Jays, Silas had a special understanding with Little Ax, as did many baritone leads and their tenor counterparts during the quartet kings' heyday. Their voices merged with a fluidity that, like the energy exchanged within a rock band, began to feel sexual as it redirected outward, inspiring the audience into greater paroxysms of self-abandonment. Generating a thrill with each other, quartet singers hit upon a pulse that was at once homoerotic and mutually enhancing. Throw Jesus into the mix, the ultimate spiritual lover, and things could get out of control.

Steele and his Blue Jays mentor Tooter Parnell had a dramatic way to show how mutual incitement lay at the heart of quartet gospel. "Parnell, the guy actually that he loved in there so dearly . . . he used to lift Steele up," Reed said. "You know, playing with him on the stand." At a song's high point, Steele would jump right into Parnell's outstretched arms, "like a little baby," John Evans of Detroit's Flying Clouds told Seroff. "Parnell would hold him and the people would go wild."[32]

The geometry of desire within these moves and harmony sounds can be both conventionally masculine—"hard," as the most aggressive quartet singing is called—and unapologetically feelingful. The greatest quartet kings put their own twists on the formula. Claude Jeter of the Swan Silvertones was priest of the falsetto; he caressed and massaged notes with his higher register in ways that would inspire Al Green, soul groups like the Temptations, and later, Prince. Ira Tucker of the Dixie Hummingbirds added a lonesome burr to his delivery that he attributed to the influence of country music. Rebert Harris was the model of power in elegance, a big man who always moved and sang with consummate control. Archie Brownlee of Mississippi's Five Blind Boys was the opposite—a transcendent shouter whose groans and wails foreshadowed the manic sounds of garage rock.

If the preacher directed excitement, and the gospel queen let it fill her up, the gospel quartet demonstrated how to become expert at it, to direct and wield its power. Quartet singers were very self-aware about how women responded to their work, not only because that interest afforded those who wanted it some less-than-pious liaisons, but because that feminine response was what ultimately gave the groups power. Bill Johnson of the Golden Gates came up with the nickname that applied to the church ladies who'd lift up their skirts when they fell out at quartet concerts: Sister Flute. It's a crude, funny name, evoking both the high, climaxing moan that would come from their throats, and an image both phallic and open: insert yourself here. The quartet kings had tricks to please Sister Flute. Jumping into the crowd was one. The Five Blind Boys of Alabama would take one another's hands and leap off a theater stage at once. The smashed guitars and flung microphones of later rock bands were nothing compared to the personal endangerment quartet members risked.[33]

The musical innovations of the quartets also figure later within the geometry of rock's desiring expressiveness. Though the quartets weren't structured around bass and drums, they did introduce the persistent rhythm that rock would further develop, through the bass singer's "pumping" technique. You can hear this early on in Bessie Smith's gospel attempt, "Moan, You Moaners," in which she's backed by a quartet that rocks Smith with a steady roll. The central structural difference quartet singing bequeathed to rock was "the drive," a bold enactment of the journey toward climax. In it, the lead singer breaks free of his fellows, improvising—reaching, teasing, trying out whatever increases the heat in the room. The backing singers focus on a single percussive phrase. They are stroking the song. Together, as Hinson explains, quartet members and their audience "transform the drive into a vehicle of sensuous inducement."[34]

The images of quartet kings running around the aisles of an auditorium are very rock and roll. They're mostly forgotten now, in part because of Sam Cooke. His style was so different—his main analogue was Jeter, who was also calm, intellectual, a subtle seducer. It's worth remembering, though, that other singers who'd pioneer soul and inspire rockers, including Wilson Pickett, O. V. Wright, and Joe Hinton, who replaced Steele in the Spirits when he left for California, showed more allegiance to the "hard" style. Its celebration of roughness and unapologetic masculinity infiltrated rhythm and blues and found a home within the rock bands of the next era.

The hard and the soft both thrived within gospel quartets. Some women found a way to modify the quartet formula. Like the rocker chicks of later eras, they presented themselves as ready and able to play with the boys, in suits, hair done up in pompadours. And they had swagger. The Songbirds of the South, female counterparts of the Spirit of Memphis, had a female "bass" named Elizabeth Darling, who pumped with the skill of a man and even recorded the blues "Bald Headed Daddy" under another name, Lydia Larson and the River Rovers—though some of her Songbird sisters, even the ones who sang anonymously on the session, considered that a disgrace.[35] By contrast, softness with intensity existed within the Spirit of Memphis Quartet, in the person of Steele's favorite counterpart, Willmer "Little Ax" Broadnax. Not as much of a showman as Steele, Broadnax had the more astounding voice. He could hit notes in his natural tenor that other men could only attain in falsetto. His tenor rang out like no other deployed by a quartet king.

That's because Little Ax was a different kind of king. After living as a man into his seventies, Broadnax was killed during a violent fight with a younger girlfriend in 1992. An autopsy revealed that he was assigned female at birth. No one knows why the girl probably named Armatha became Willmer—a census taken when he was thirteen shows he was already identified as male by then—or why he chose a gospel path so heavily populated by alpha males. But Broadnax's secret almost makes sense within the world of the quartet kings, where a man could be himself—or herself—at least and perhaps only within the space of a song.[36]

HOW MEMPHIS MADE GOSPEL ROCK

In Memphis after World War II, gospel's alluring personalities were central to civic life, especially as it connected to the exploding local music scene. Factories springing up along the Mississippi River offered opportunities to rural migrants. At the same time, those new

Memphians, along with returning soldiers, flooded the job and housing markets. Memphis was alive, unstable, and tense.[37] Serving this place abuzz with change was a rapidly expanding medium: radio. Two stations made a particular impact on gospel as it fed the nascent spirit of rock and roll. WDIA was the country's first station programmed by and for African Americans. At WHBQ, maverick DJ Dewey Phillips introduced white listeners—many of them restless, curious teenagers—to the "housewrecking" forces of rhythm, blues, and gospel.

The strides these stations made were motivated by entrepreneurship more than by anti-segregationist or musical goodwill. The former country and pop station WDIA was about to go under when its white owners took a chance on journalist Nat D. Williams, whose *Tan Town Jamboree* hit the airwaves in 1948. A year later, the Reverend Dwight "Gatemouth" Moore, a bluesman whose religious conversion proved to be a great business opportunity, got his own show. Moore brought the blues's mischievousness into the pulpit, pulling stunts like offering to walk on the water (the water proved too "troubled" on the day he chose, and he turned away a disappointed crowd) and running a newspaper contest to name his newborn child. He also survived a stint in jail for stealing a Cadillac. Moore called the gospel concerts he put together "Spiritual Midnight Rambles"—a direct connection to the blues world where Thomas A. Dorsey had left Ma Rainey when he'd made his final conversion in 1932. His successor, Theo Wade, gave Silas Steele and the Spirits their own daily radio show.[38]

WDIA also presented concerts that put gospel acts on the bill with the rising stars of rhythm and blues. One, from 1956, saw the Spirit of Memphis and other gospel artists sharing the bill with Ray Charles, who'd made his breakthrough adapting gospel sounds to blues lyrics in "I Got a Woman" the year before.[39] The gospel portion of the concert was billed as "A Pilgrimage to the Holy Land";

Charles, B.B. King, and doo-wop groups the Moonglows and the Magnificents appeared during the evening's second half, as part of a skit comically reimagining the birth of "Rock'n Roll" within a cartoonish Native American tribe led by "Chief Moohah" and "Chief Rockin' Horse."

One of the other gospel ensembles performing that evening had ties to a more dignified presence on the Memphis gospel radio scene. The Brewsteraires were one of the groups organized by the Reverend W. Herbert Brewster, the composer, community activist, and pastor of East Trigg Avenue Baptist Church. Brewster had written "Move On Up a Little Higher," the song that gave Mahalia Jackson her groove.[40] If Moore and Wade were clowning holy hustlers who reveled in spiritual stunts, Brewster was a self-made dignitary, born into a sharecropper family but versed in several languages, the law, and the works of Shakespeare (all of which he tapped into for his stirring, musical sermons). He found a true star in his protégée Queen C. Anderson, a majestically voiced contralto whose emotional readings of Brewster's hymns were a highlight of his services. "When she sang, she would put everything in her singing. And to tell the truth, you couldn't sit under Queen C. Anderson without shedding tears when she was in the arena singing," Nathaniel Peck of the Brewsteraires once recalled. Anderson was the powerhouse who first presented "Move On Up a Little Higher," which Mahalia Jackson borrowed after Anderson performed it in Chicago. She died relatively young and never reached the fame she deserved. But Brewster made sure Anderson was a star in her hometown; he'd put her, the Brewsteraires, and his other group, the Pattersonaires, on a flatbed truck for mini-tours in front of the town's grocery and furniture stores.[41]

This knack for musical promotion connected Brewster to a valuable friend: Dewey Phillips, a former GI who'd become a DJ on WHBQ the same year WDIA went African American. Phillips was white, but he loved rhythm and blues, and he challenged segrega-tion on the air by playing those "race" records on his three-hour nighttime slot. He also loved gospel. Through Phillips, Brewster established himself as a presence on WHBQ, and the white kids listening soon started showing up at East Trigg. In a destabilizing spin on the norm, they'd sit in the back. "The integrated Sunday night assemblies were unprecedented events in the racially strati-fied city of Memphis before the civil rights era," wrote Phillips's biographer Louis Cantor.[42] These services were something else, too: a hook-up scene.

"It was a groovy 'in' thing to go out to East Trigg Baptist," Phil-lips's office assistant, Bob Lewis, told Cantor. "That used to be date night. A lot of young whites would come with their dates."[43] That was a good idea, especially for poor boys who otherwise might not have been able to take their girls to hear a full band, with saxo-phone, accompany a roster of touring stars that included the Soul Stirrers, Clara Ward, and even the great Mahalia. One of those boys was Elvis Presley, who was courting a fellow high school student named Dixie Locke. Gospel was Presley's favorite music in the early 1950s, and he was definitely interested in making the scene.

Nathaniel Peck recalled that Presley even once came up onto the altar and sang—"he did a number once out there, on a program . . . *one* time."[44] This might seem impossibly bold, especially because in most Elvis biographies, the king-in-waiting's connection to East Trigg is often discussed as illicit: the word *sneak* is nearly always employed to describe Elvis going the mile down the road from his home church, the First Assembly of God, to Brewster's joint. But Peck remembers several white singers who'd sometimes join in the chorus there, and Phillips openly advertised the service as meant for a mixed crowd. Presley may not have had his parents' blessing, but on some level, he was just trying to fit in with the popular kids he admired.

RACE CROSSERS, PRAISE SINGERS

As gospel developed and interacted with secular pop, another strain of spirit-raising music was doing the same thing on the other side of the color line. Southern gospel, as it became known, was connected to the rising field of country music, which developed simultaneously in the 1920s; but it was equally influenced by the sounds of African American musicians, especially quartets. By the 1950s, Southern gospel was a realm distinct from African American gospel; its practitioners, however, did not always observe the rules of the Jim Crow South. One white quartet that regularly crossed the color line at East Trigg was the Songfellows—the very group that Elvis Presley tried and failed to join a few years later.[45] The dimpled and dashing Cecil Blackwood led the group, a junior contingent of a very influential unit called the Blackwood Brothers.

The Blackwoods were the crossover kings of Southern gospel, offering what artists like Pat Boone and, in his calmer moments, Elvis himself would soon provide to rhythm and blues: a respectable alternative to wilder sounds that retained as much juice as pop propriety would permit. Formed in Mississippi in 1934, the Blackwood Brothers did itinerant-musician time in California and the Midwest before reaching Memphis in 1950. Membership evolved as the ensemble, like most gospel quartets, became a brand as much as a band. When Elvis would have discovered them, the lineup included manly baritone R. W. Blackwood and "artistic" bass Bill Lyles, along with teen-idol types James Blackwood and Bill Shaw. Teenage girls—including a young future country music star named Tammy Wynette—particularly liked Shaw, going nuts when he deployed his delicate falsetto in a long vocal tease on his featured number, "Over the Moon."[46] By 1952, when the group's single "Rock-a My Soul" hit the *Billboard* spiritual charts alongside the Spirit of Memphis Quartet's "Atomic Telephone," the Blackwood Brothers were a fully operational music machine.[47] Their

Dixie Lily Flour–sponsored radio show broadcast twice daily on Memphis country station WMPS, which like WDIA had a signal that reached across three states. They had a downtown Memphis record store operated by brother Doyle and a full staff to manage public appearances, merchandising, and tours.

The Blackwoods could be part of the South's white-run "official" culture in ways that even the most entrepreneurial, assimilationist African American gospel artists could not. By 1954, they'd been declared Honorary Tennessee Colonels by Governor Frank Clement and had enjoyed an official Blackwood Brothers Quartet Day in Memphis. Their national fame surged, too; first, the group signed with Presley's eventual home label, RCA-Victor Records, and then it won the televised *Arthur Godfrey's Talent Scouts* show, the *American Idol* of its time. When Elvis saw Cecil and his older brother James in the pews in East Trigg, they must have seemed like princes.

One reason the Blackwoods appealed to kids like Elvis and Dixie was that musically, the group retained an edge—in part by copying black quartets' moves. They crooned dreamily on some hymns, but "Have You Talked to the Man Upstairs"—the one that won on Godfrey's show—was a jazzy number also recorded by the hardest of the hard gospel groups, Archie Brownlee and the Five Blind Boys of Mississippi. Though James Blackwood insisted late in life that black and white Southern gospel were two streams that rarely met, the music says otherwise. It's hard to believe that the Blackwoods didn't hear voices like Silas Steele's growing up, especially considering eldest brother Roy lived in Gadsden, where the white Southern gospel tradition was centered but also just an hour from Birmingham. The musically curious Blackwoods must have checked out a few sides by the Famous Blue Jay Singers and other Jefferson County favorites.[48]

They certainly copped some of the choreography of those leaping, driving, God-serving seducers. In concert, the Blackwoods would often end up in a jumble of lanky limbs, one almost horizontal to the microphone, another on his knees, in a good-natured frenzy. Yet they always retained an air of elegance. As Christian family men, the Blackwood Brothers never pushed the limits of propriety, onstage or off. However, they were selling sex appeal in a package both mothers and daughters could appreciate. The "family albums" they'd sell on the road, Christian versions of fan magazines, featured pictures of the guys with their wives and children showing off the markers of wealth and modernity: ranch homes, shiny sports cars, golf clubs, pianist Jackie Marshall in an apron making biscuits.[49]

If their Christian orientation meant they couldn't quite be Hollywood-style heartthrobs, the Blackwood Brothers found another way to be modern and the opposite of prim. They embraced the newest in transportation technology. The quartet's core members had worked in a San Diego airplane factory during World War II, and R. W. Blackwood decided he wanted to learn to pilot a plane. The group became the Flying Blackwood Brothers in the early 1950s after acquiring both a Cessna 195 and a ten-passenger Beechcraft.[50]

Music critic James M. Curtis has suggested that the Blackwoods were something like the Beatles in their British Invasion moment—clean but representative of the future, with an element of risk built in—and that Elvis Presley's other favorite gospel quartet was the pre-rock equivalent to the Rolling Stones.[51] That group was the Statesmen, led by the boogie-woogie piano man Hovie Lister, known for throwing off his jacket and letting his curly hair fall in his face—moves that Jerry Lee Lewis would invoke when both he and Elvis made it to Sun Records. While the Blackwoods might have kept their interest in African American gospel hidden under their prep school–graduate suits, the Statesmen let it all hang out. They openly covered songs by African American artists—one of their greatest hits is a stomping version of Dorothy Love Coates's "Get Away Jordan"—and had a stage act that sometimes veered dangerously close to minstrelsy, with Statesmen members adopting broad accents and eye-popping facial expressions.

Elvis Presley was a particular admirer of the quartet's lead singer, Jake Hess, and of Statesmen bass Jim "Big Chief" Wetherington, whose pencil-thin moustache made him look like a tango pirate, and who had a habit of wiggling his leg when he sang. If Elvis saw in the Blackwoods a way to be classy and still hip, in the Statesmen he discovered both wildness and humor—a distancing effect that would become central to his own sex appeal. When Elvis shook his hips, especially early on, he'd always raise an eyebrow; it was like a burlesque move, studied, gaining power from his ability to pull back. The sizzle comes as much from the mastery of his self-suppression as it does from the revelation of his lasciviousness.

That's what happened in the music of the Statesmen and the Blackwood Brothers: a channeling not just of African American musical influences but of the quickening eroticism of golden-era gospel, of the quartets' drive, and the spirit queens' sass and self-liberation, and the emotionalism of "Precious Lord." Presley saw in Southern gospel exactly the kind of subversiveness that he could bear as a nice boy who loved his mama but who also needed to be modern and sexually open.

The Blackwood Brothers paid a huge price for their modern ways. Just two weeks after their national breakthrough on the Godfrey show, in the summer of 1954, they were playing a peach festival in Clanton, Alabama, when R. W. Blackwood and his navigator, Bill Lyles, decided to take the group's plane up for a late afternoon spin. The plane crashed, leaving behind the burned bodies of Blackwood, Lyles, and the teenage son of the festival organizer. Five thousand people attended the funeral in Memphis, including African American fans, who sat in the balcony, their presence unusual enough that it was reported in the local newspapers. The Statesmen performed two songs—one, requested by R.W.'s widow, was the country-flavored hymn "Known Only to Him"; the other,

Lyles's favorite, "Does Jesus Care?," had been recorded by quartets including the Soul Stirrers and the Pilgrim Travelers. Even in death, the Blackwood Brothers were pushing the envelope between black and white, between the church and the concert stage.

Presley came to the funeral, of course, with Dixie, a horrible kind of date. Was his belief in gospel music's ability to overcome grief formed that day? A few years later, he turned to it in the darkest moment of his young life, when his mother Gladys unexpectedly died while he was in basic training for the army. The Statesmen and the reconstituted Blackwood Brothers both sang at the funeral. Elvis kept scribbling names of hymns on a piece of paper and passing it to James Blackwood—"Precious Lord" was just the beginning of what turned out to be more than a dozen songs he had them sing.[52]

By then, Presley had recorded some gospel songs himself, though he employed a different gospel quartet, the calm and collected Nashville group the Jordanaires, for sessions partly meant to combat the young rocker's reputation as a troublemaker. "To a great many people, Elvis Presley has been a surprise," the liner notes read on his first religious release, an EP whose lead track was the Dorsey gospel blues "Peace in the Valley." "They have been surprised at his style of singing, at his disarming frankness, and most of all at his rapid success. To them this album will also be a surprise. But to any of the fortunate folks who have known Elvis, whether as a schoolboy, movie usher, delivery man or performer, 'Peace in the Valley' will be no surprise."[53]

The only surprise to the many fans who had heard Elvis's secular sound foreshadowed in both golden-era and Southern gospel might have been how tamely he interpreted the songs others had burned to the ground. In real gospel, the contradictions that often spun out of control in Presley's newborn hits were resolved in a kind of joy that could embrace paradox. Elvis's genuine piety kept him from giving the complex kind of gospel music performance that his idols like the Blackwoods and the Statesmen—and, more so, their role models, the African American quartets—allowed themselves.

But listen to another early Elvis song, the Jerry Leiber and Mike Stoller ballad "Love Me," and you can hear how the singer's time with gospel quartets paid off in a way that led directly to rock and roll. The song itself is a genre buster, written as a country music parody and first recorded by the R&B duo Willy and Ruth. Presley's version signals itself as gospel derived through the Jordanaires' gently pumping backing vocals. Ably supported, he dives down and leaps back in sensual slow motion, letting the song's life force, desire, breathe on him.

"I-I-I would be-e-g and steal . . . Ju-u-ust to feel . . . Yo-u-ur heart . . . BEATING close to mine . . . " Presley is in a state of rapture, his longing its own satisfaction. He paces himself the way a good quartet member would, shaking rhythms out of the song's smooth verses that dissemble the message. He's falling apart but uplifted by the music. He is turning lust divine.

"Gospel music raises the alluring possibility that the outcast might find a single language through which both the desires of the heart and the habits of the soul can merge and find expression," writes Douglas Harrison in his landmark book on Southern gospel and queer identities.[54] Every contradiction Elvis would tap into—"rightness-wrongness, saved-lost, saint-sinner, white-black, straight-gay"—was in gospel at its most erotically charged. Faith was the element that resolved gospel's disturbances. Downplay it, and you have a clearer picture of the human condition that deeply informed early rock and roll: the feeling of being, as Elvis so eloquently put it, all shook up.

4

TEEN DREAMS AND GROWN-UP URGES

THE AMERICAN HEARTLAND, 1950–1960

In the mid-twentieth century, while gospel was schooling Elvis and many other young musical initiates about eroticism's deepest elements, secular music continued to expand America's vocabulary of sex. Jazz mutated in myriad ways, sometimes favoring the New Orleans street sounds that first gave it an identity at the end of the last epoch, sometimes going more Latin via Cuba, the Southwest, and immigrant New York, sometimes blending with the blues. Big-band swing kept people dancing as the fresh athletic steps of the Lindy hop and the jitterbug eclipsed the tango and the shimmy. Virtuoso soloists like Charlie Christian on guitar and Lester Young on saxophone showed how their instruments could share intimacies the same way human voices do. As for those voices—a major new tool, the ribbon microphone, gave singers like Bing Crosby and Billie Holiday a luxury Florence Mills never had. It was sensitive enough to pick up whispers and murmurs, and when the recordings that made use of it hit listeners' ears via the radio, the experience was shockingly intimate. Defending Crosby's slippery vocal technique in a 1932 *Los Angeles Times* article, the critic Isabel Morse Jones paraphrased a female fan's gush: "When Bing sings, it seems as if he is singing just for me. There isn't anyone else in the room." The crooner's move into the lover's position had men "green-eyed" with envy, worried they'd never live up to the exquisitely gentle seductive pressure such a voice revealed was possible.[1]

Intimacy met explicitness in rhythm and blues, a catchall category that emerged in the 1940s to describe the music being sold via "race records" mostly to African American listeners. Stars of this scene, like Joe Turner and Wynonie Harris, projected an intense machismo in aggressive songs staking out sexual territory. "Battle of the Blues," a two-part 1947 Turner and Harris duet, is emblematic of the form: the two men good-naturedly shout at each other about whose woman can last longer in a love session, who can "party" harder, and how "a chick" can't be trusted, no matter how game she is in the bedroom. Women performers gave as good as they got: kiss-offs like Dinah Washington's "Baby Get Lost" and proto-rockers like Ruth Brown's "Mama, He Treats Your Daughter Mean" showed women to be armed with wit and soul and ready to cast light on male inadequacy and even brutality.[2]

If pop produced subtle romantics, and rhythm and blues created strong erotic warriors, the genre that would become country music excelled at describing the intimate sexual politics of the kitchen and the barroom. White rural and Southern regional artists connected with both blues and immigrant folk traditions to offer plainspoken accounts of love's consequences, like the Carter Family's "Single Girl, Married Girl," which reminded women that romance often led to burdensome young motherhood. Jimmie Rodgers, country's first big personality, took listeners into illicit spaces, including the roadhouses known by the 1930s as honky-tonks, which formed a kind of scattered Storyville for male workers and their female night-companions throughout small-town America. "The wild side of life"—adultery, alcoholic excess, the loneliness of the wanderer—and how it impacted the family became a primary musical theme of country music, intertwining the genre thematically with the blues.[3]

America's erotic life had been complicated in the first half of the twentieth century by cataclysmic events. The Great Depression of the 1930s halted the climb of the middle class and led working people and the poor into nearly unimaginable levels of privation. The African American Great Migration that laid the ground for gospel music affected every level of secular urban life, too, including the leisure realms where the language of romance kept developing. After the Depression, World War II stole away millions of American men and changed women's standing at home. After the war ended, a new wave of peace and prosperity allowed Americans time and space to absorb these changes. Unsurprisingly, though, the mood beneath the economic boom of the 1950s was anxious—especially about sex, and about the young generation emerging, the first to proudly wear the title of "teenagers." Into this confusing world came a new sound that was paradoxically wild and redolent of repression. The kids and their observers—their parents and other adults who just didn't understand—called it rock and roll.

THE POMPATUS OF LOVE

Rock and roll was a big bang that came from a thousand small crashes. Chaos crept into virtually every corner of popular music: in gospel, as we've seen, but also in wild Western swing and scary hillbilly stomps; in the breakneck harmonies of the Boswell Sisters and other vocal groups; in the raw jump blues of Ike Turner's "Rocket 88"; in Big Jay McNeely's saxophone exorcisms, which made white and black kids scream in equal measure. And the list goes on. "What came first, the rock & roll chicken or the rock & roll egg?" mused the songwriter and critic Steve Leggett in a review of *The First Rock and Roll Record,* an eighty-two-track compilation of songs that have all been put forward, at one time or another, as the phenomenon's starting point. "No matter. The chicken crossed the road, and that's when rock & roll really started."[4]

One way to tell the story of how rock and roll started is to follow a chick who crossed the road. This specific woman, who would have likely been fine with that hipster's slang term for a female in the know about nightlife and new sounds, was named Nyla Van Rees, and in 1953 she was dating a DJ named Dick "Huggy Boy" Hugg. Nyla was a beauty whose attentiveness in Hugg's DJ booth caused one music journalist to remark, "The way Miss Rees was taking everything in looks like 'Huggy Boy' is trying to make a female deejay out of her."[5] She knew what she liked in music. That's what got her back across the road, and got the Crows' song "Gee" on Los Angeles radio, spreading a new sound that tipped America into the rock and roll revolution.

"Gee," a tune written by the New York group's baritone Bill Davis in less than ten minutes, is a frantic number that adds steroids to its message about the pleasures of hugging and squeezing and kissing with some aggressive *doot-doot-doot*s. The extra syllables push lead singer Sonny Norton's pleading into overdrive. This kind of music had no name until some revivalists named it "doo-wop" a decade after it had reached its early peak. Its playful carnality was breaking out all over American neighborhoods via gangs of young showboating singers who gathered to compete, impress girls, and maybe claim some fame. Huggy Boy was a popular jock who liked these new vocal groups. He worked out of the storefront of Dolphin's record store on Central Avenue, the heart of mid-century African American Los Angeles. The first white DJ to broadcast from the black-owned shop, Hugg cultivated a fan base that crossed racial lines—he was particularly popular with the city's young Mexican American crowd—and his endorsements turned songs into national hits.

That's what happened with "Gee," even though he'd tossed the song in his dud pile. "The 'Gee' story was quite an accident," Hugg told the radio host and music historian Steve Propes in a 1985 interview. "When 'Gee' came out, 1953, I was dating a girl, I was on the night shift. She liked that song, she found it in the box-o-bombs and she said, 'Honey, will you play this record?' She liked the record, we didn't particularly play it a lot . . . it was going to be lost. We had an argument in the studio. She left. I found the record, played 'Gee.' I kept playing it over and over again. By the time she got to North Hollywood, she called the studio. 'Gee, Huggy, you've been playing the same record for ten or twelve minutes. You're going to get fired!' I said, 'I don't care. I'm not going to stop playing this record until you come back here.' She said, 'I don't want you to be fired.' So, I took the record off. I went into the next record. Two days later, when I went into the distributor, they said, 'Huggy, we got a smash hit.'"[6]

"Gee" is a funny song, like most early rock and roll records. It's full of joy, but also nervousness, as if expressing emotions its makers know aren't decorous but just can't hide anymore. The first bursts of rock and roll sound like this: the return of the repressed. But it's simplistic to call what rock and roll communicated liberation. It's just as much a witness to confinement and confusion.

This is especially true of how the music took on sexuality as subject and substance. Rock and roll contained all the ugly and problematic things about sex as well as its pleasures, demonstrating how yearning and sensual release could reduce a person to gibberish. The music's much-touted craziness—many adults heard it as nonsense—changed America's view of sex because it acknowledged desire's ungainliness as well as its fun. In fact, it showed how those things were interrelated. It did so at a moment when sex, as embodied by teenagers, was being viewed as both a menace and a force that would remake the world in a new era.

What function does nonsense serve in the development of healthy sexuality? Concepts set forth by the British pediatrician and psychoanalyst D. W. Winnicott frame childhood sexuality's relationship to play: play is an open-ended sense of absorption—in music making, for example—while sexual desire focuses that absorption on a need and pushes the desiring person toward its end. "Sex, to put it as crudely . . . as possible, is what threatens play, what constantly threatens to put a stop to it," writes modern-day Winnicottian Adam Phillips in his essay "Talking Nonsense, and Knowing When to Stop." Phillips suggests that incoherence creates the transition between childlike play and adult sexual feeling. "One kind of chaos occurs when absorption, or preoccupation, begins turning into appetite and the hope of satisfaction. The nononsense self cannot make that move. Wanting comes out of an incredible muddle."[7]

Considering the nonsense sound of doo-wop within this psychoanalytic framework, the music becomes newly coherent. Or rather, it forcefully asserts its incoherence as a means for doo-wop's creators and fans to remain in that state of play preceding full adult sexuality. Teenagers in the 1950s certainly wanted to experiment with adult behavior, and to learn how to satisfy their freshly born lust. But going too fast also undid them. Doo-wop and other musical styles driven by nonsense offered a way to remain in this disassembled state while still moving through the world with power and confidence.

Nonsense echoed through the streets where young America roamed in the mid-1950s, from New York to Philadelphia, Memphis to New Orleans, Lubbock to Los Angeles. Groups like the Crows tipped away from the "plain talk" of R&B and toward the revelatory babble of an emerging generation. This music was made not by men fronting bluesy bands, but by kids singing on the street and in the bathrooms of their high schools. They were the children of the Great Migration, awash in hormones and hope and a stubborn insistence on liberty, pushing against the bonds of Jim Crow. Doo-wop appealed within African American communities, but via the radio its reach extended: at a time when national attention turned to atrocities like the killing of fourteen-year-old Emmett Till, falsely accused of flirting with a white woman, this was the sound of young black men being amorous, openly and innocently. In a way, it was a form of protest. If conventional language had no room for these voices, they'd make up their own.

The same spaces that might be used for a sexual encounter—with a sneaked-in girl, or between boys—became conduits for expressing what went beyond words. "The boys' bathroom . . . furnished the best echo chamber for singing slow songs with 'wooo' in the background," one singer of the era, Johnny Keyes of the Magnificents, wrote in his 1991 memoir.[8] "All of that tile and porcelain were tailor-made for singing." A teenage Etta James agreed: when the R&B powerhouse auditioned for her future manager Johnny Otis with her vocal group, the Creolettes, she insisted they decamp to a nearby ladies' room. Almost entirely male and originally African American (later, Italian American kids, also suspect on the era's city streets, would adopt the form), doo-wop belonged to what the scholar Jeffrey Melnick calls "good-bad" boys, borrowing that term from the girl group song "Leader of the Pack" by the Shangri-Las: boys who crossed boundaries, especially linguistic ones, for

fun and with no harm intended. These singers reimagined the empowering force of eroticism as not a battle but a game.[9]

Though many certainly had a fame-seeking sparkle in their
eyes, 1950s vocal harmonizers clung to the spirit of play within
their performances, which usually began informally and involved
all sorts of subtexts: competition, swaggering, flirting. Al Frazier of
the Los Angeles group the Lamplighters once reminisced about the
small crowd of geniuses that would gather at the home of Gaynel
and Alex Hodge, both stars of the scene, in Watts. "We used to sit
around the living room and harmonize. Back then I wanted to be a
part of the music, a part of the fun at parties. It wasn't about being
a star." On a given afternoon, Gaynel and Jesse Belvin might compete for the attention of Zola Taylor of the Platters (then at nearby
Jordan Junior High), while Etta James, fresh from a singing lesson
with local gospel luminary James Earle Hines, tried out a new song
with Hollywood Flames singer Bobby Day and his friend Richard
Berry, who'd later go on to write the classic nonsense rocker "Louie,
Louie." The creative process of these young experimenters couldn't
be confined within the boundaries of conventional songs. They
were trying on whatever move worked in the moment.

Gatherings like this, giving birth to groups that mutated with
the speed of a chemistry-class experiment, made doo-wop explode
as a nationwide regional phenomenon. Around fifteen thousand
vocal groups recorded singles during the 1950s, though many never
went beyond that session. The structure of these groups clearly
borrowed from gospel quartets as well as from secular vocal ensembles like the Ink Spots and the Mills Brothers; yet the new wave
was different, partly because its members were so young. Imagine a
whole field of Silas Steeles, most of them under age eighteen. "Dic-
tion isn't always clear, but side is strong and could stir," *Billboard*'s
reviewer wrote of "On Your Radio," the debut single by twelve-year-
old Richard Lanham and the Tempo-Tones, in 1957.[10]

The immortal phrase announcing "On Your Radio"—a bass voice singing "doo doot doo doot dat doo doot doo deet whoop whoop"—was fundamental doo-wop talk. "Gee" combined it with the titular exclamation and a fistful of "oh-ho-whoa"s. "Sh-Boom" by the Chords, which broke around the same time as "Gee," propelled an attempted seduction forward with repeated sputters of its silly title and threw in a "ya da da" or two at the climax. Every doo-wop song relied on nonsense syllables for both percussion and harmonic heft, and by the mid-1950s many were dominated by them, with titles like "Ding Dong," "Chim-Bam-Bah," "Ding a Ling," "Shtiggy Boom," "Vadunt-Un-Va-Da," "Zoom Boom Zing," and so on toward infinity. Most songs weren't entirely nonsense; instead, the absurdity formed a sort of internal dialogue with the words of romance or frustration being expressed. The voices behind these songs seemed to always be dipping back into baby talk to make their points.

After all, they were practically babies. Lanham was one of many singers who were under the age of consent. From hitmaker Frankie Lymon, who started at thirteen, to "old" men like sixteen-year-old Gaynel Hodge, who cowrote the immortal "Earth Angel" and got his start hanging around Huggy Boy and the other DJs at the Dolphin's record shop, these boys possessed unstable voices that reflected their unstable identities, employing the high notes of pubescence to make their leaps and runs thrilling to young ears. Though they may have aimed for the precision of their older role models, they inevitably communicated a different kind of bravado—one grounded in inexperience and hormonal flux. And they pushed it. The doo-wop sound was somehow inappropriate, even to the singers themselves. After Lymon's Harlem-based Teen-agers became international sensations with the 1956 single "Why Do Fools Fall in Love?" he wrote an article entitled "I'm Too Young for Girls" for the African American women's magazine *Tan*. "Sing-

ing about love, romance and all that kissing stuff gives the girls the
wrong idea," he wrote, though he added that he did have a sweetheart of his own, who simply wasn't into "that mushy stuff."[11]

Lymon probably "wrote" this article (if he penned it at all) at
his publicist's behest, to tone down his image. In 1954, rhythm and
blues DJs had begun organizing to discourage artists working in
the new style from recording suggestive songs. They were particularly ruffled by ones like "Such a Night" by the Drifters, which
clearly used nonsense as double entendre. "This suggestivity [*sic*]
vanished from the doo-wop genre with the dawning of the classical period in 1955," doo-wop experts Anthony Gribin and Matthew
Schiff assert in their exhaustive history of the form.[12] But did it,
really? Did Frankie Lymon really mean to not be sexy when he hit
those flirty blue notes on the verses of his breakthrough single? Or
did someone so young simply experience sexuality differently?

This was a relevant question in the 1950s, when fears about a
shortage of men after World War II fed a trend toward early marriage. Girls often began dating at twelve. Parents sanctioned this
by organizing middle-school dances and other "adult" activities
for their children.[13] At the same time, as Lymon's declarations indicate, young teens were not supposed to fully explore the feelings
such encounters inevitably stimulated. This began a pattern that
continues today in American teen social circles still affected by
conservative forces like abstinence-only sex education programs. It
forced teenagers to struggle regularly with partial arousal, to seek
spaces where they could honor their urges in semiprivate (since
they were denied real independence), and to find ways to express
not simply enjoyment, but anxiety.

Mirroring the indeterminate state of adolescence itself, doo-
wop music was both a fugitive form originating in the spaces where
young people headed to find momentary privacy and a conduit
toward respectability, the dream of full manhood. (Female and
mixed-gender doo-wop groups existed, but were few; the feminine

moment would come at the start of the 1960s, with the rise of girl groups.) Historians like Brian Ward have noted the connection between young vocal groups in the early 1950s and gangs. "Both were essentially transient, adolescent affiliations: who else had the time to practice the harmonies or fight in the rumbles?" Ward writes. "Both were inherently unstable aggregations: members regularly came and went, their departure often related to the assumption of adult responsibilities, like marriage, parenthood, the draft, or a job."[14]

The music vocal groups made allowed their young stars to imagine adulthood, but also to show how their identities and emotions didn't fit into the simulacrum of it that society was foisting upon them. Similar to the tic-ridden performances of James Dean in *Rebel Without a Cause* and Vic Morrow in *Blackboard Jungle,* these heartthrobs seemed to leak excess from their very pores. In doo-wop, this created a tension with harmony's inherent elegance. Nonsense was the safety valve that also somehow further fed its energy.

Before the 1950s, ungrammatical syllables had meant many things in popular music. Often, they served as obvious double entendres: that "da da strain" which for Ethel Waters signified sexual excitement had many antecedents, from comical numbers like Spike Jones's version of "Cocktails for Two" to ribald R&B like Dave Bartholomew's "My Ding-a-Ling." The gospel quartets had shown how such ways of masking sexual talk could become sub-lime—a way of invoking an erotic drive that went beyond simple tactile stimulation. At its most emotional, in songs like the Orioles' "It's Too Soon to Know," the Diablos' "The Wind," or "The Letter," the divinely incomprehensible metaphysical poem by sixteen-year-old Vernon Green and his Medallions (which gave us the phrase "the pompatus of love," whatever that means), doo-wop touched upon this sublimity, infusing romance with a sense of wonder and recasting R&B's grown-up leer as a winning smile.

Less promisingly, lyrical absurdism also often signified racial difference. African American performers had to contend with the vigorous ghost of minstrelsy surfacing in "jungle" songs like the primate romance "Aba Daba Honeymoon," written in 1914 but a hit in 1950, when it was featured in the Debbie Reynolds movie *Two Weeks with Love*. These invocations of an Africa where brown beings babbled were complicated by the occasional presence of actual African music. Early doo-wop groups found themselves on the singles charts alongside "Skokiaan," an often-recorded Rhodesian big-band dance number that became a US smash in 1954, and "Wimoweh," the Weavers' folksy 1952 version of South African Solomon Linda's improvised 1939 Zulu refrain. In 1961, a white vocal ensemble with the ironic name the Tokens turned Linda's lovely melody into the perennial family favorite "The Lion Sleeps Tonight."

Beyond clear cases where nonsense substituted for language deemed inappropriate (because it was sexual) or impenetrable (because it was African) lay the realm of nonverbal vocal improvising. As we know from the encounter between Adelaide Hall and Duke Ellington in 1927's "Creole Love Call," this musical practice was always erotic, too. When singers became instruments, the way Ella Fitzgerald did on her career-launching version of the nursery rhyme "A-Tisket, A-Tasket" in 1938, they tested the limits of the body in ways that were openly sensual. Often these acts would also invoke the language of children, allowing listeners to feel a connection to the polymorphous pleasure that preceded the sexual policing they began to encounter as adolescents.

In late 1958, the *New York Times* reporter Gertrude Samuels ventured out to a show at the Paramount Theatre organized by the founding rock and roll DJ Alan "Moondog" Freed that included performances by the vocal groups Frankie Lymon and the Teenagers and the Chantels, alongside solo stars like Jerry Lee Lewis. She asked Roseann Chasen, "a black-haired, starry-eyed beauty of 15," what drew her to rock and roll. "It's just instinct, that's all," Chasen told her. "I come to hear it because I can sing and scream here. Because it's not like at home where your parents are watching TV and you can't."[15] Not like at home, where your parents are watching *you*. Today we think rock and roll emancipated teenagers in the 1950s, and it did—but only provisionally, and in ways that left their problems and fears intact. Rock and roll created a metaphorical free space in which teenagers could scream their inner chaos as well as their emerging desires.

LOTTA SHAKIN' GOIN' ON

As kids singing together carved out temporary free spaces in hallways and on street corners, their goal was to enter a realm where those magic moments of incoherent clarity could be made to last forever: the recording studio. Certain special studios became particularly fertile seedbeds for revelatory teen gibberish. The most famous, then and now, is in Memphis, Tennessee, the same city where so many gospel quartets found their way to deeper truths in harmony. It was a shabby little place called Sun, run by a thirtysomething businessman who'd been robbed of his own teenage freedom when his father died during the Great Depression and he had to go to work to support his family. His name was Sam Phillips, and he became the guru of a whole lotta shakin' goin' on.

Phillips was good at letting kids mess around while making music. He'd started the Memphis Recording Service as a way of making money from the dreams of amateurs, and though his ambition led him to seek out musicians whose singles he could push for a profit, Phillips never let go of that preference for the raw over the cooked. Initially he worked with fairly seasoned African American bluesmen, but he took Sun to another commercial level by turning his attention to barely legal country upstarts trying to avoid lives spent driving trucks or farming. They were interested in becoming regional stars who could play dances throughout the small-town

South and find fans via the cheap new records being pressed on vinyl—45 RPM singles. Phillips helped these flashy itinerant workers stay in touch with the parts of themselves that didn't take so well to upward mobility. When the guitarist Carl Perkins, more meticulous than most, once fumed that a session had been "a big original mistake," Phillips replied "that's what Sun Records is."[16]

Sam Phillips has been memorialized as a Great Man of 1950s rock and roll. He was great, it's true, at staying out of the way of the wave of noise moving through his studio. Sam would get himself in the mood to mess up so that his charges would know he was in solidarity with them. "He was just sitting up there having just as good a time as we were," recalled Billy Lee Riley, a wild man known for the song "Flying Saucers Rock 'n' Roll," in a 1999 interview. "And probably just as drunk as we were—or drunker."[17] A nonmusician, Phillips had help from technology—specifically, recording equipment that guaranteed the weirdest warble and loosest guitar line would be salvageable. Phillips realized his own sense of play by inventing studio tricks like slapback echo, in which two takes of a song could be combined to add yet another layer of fruitful incoherence, pushing the voice and the instruments apart just so, making something that might have seemed totally aggressive at the moment its makers laid it down more tentative—decentered, like a thought process unfolding. When he found his perfect improviser in a gospel-loving, vocal groups–obsessed kid named Elvis Presley, Phillips was ready to get him real, real gone and get every bit of the process down on tape.

If rock and roll was a virus, Elvis was its irresistible Typhoid Mary. That's a fact that no amount of revisionism valuing other players in the genre's birth can overcome. Even before he became a national phenomenon, Elvis was a regional one, touring throughout the South and leaving local versions of himself everywhere in his wake. These callow pretenders played in makeshift clubs set up in community halls, their acts merging the legacies of snake oil salesmen, freak show contortionists, and gospel tent revivalists. Girls flocked to see them. The rockabilly historian Craig Morrison describes these scenes: "There might be Christmas lights strung across the back of the stage, tables and chairs around the perimeter of the room, food available for purchase, and maybe booze ... Since the sound system is rudimentary and there are no stage monitors on the more rocking tunes, the singer sings louder and closer to the microphone to hear himself, sending the audience a distorted vocal sound. The small guitar amp is also distorting. The drummer has a snare, a big bass drum, a ride cymbal and a high hat and sits low, sitting stiff armed." These bands seemed like they had been shot out of a cannon. Often, they only had fifteen minutes to play. It was a competition reminiscent of the all-night gospel battles Elvis witnessed as a high schooler, but with leering replacing sanctified shouts.[18]

Pretty soon, the sound these giddy country boys made had a name: rockabilly. Its creators shared a certain personality—what Phillips's associate, the producer Jack Clement, called "overt." Jerry Lee Lewis hurled his blond curls over his forehead and then would comb them back like some kind of snaggletooth tiger. Ronnie Self would start his shows by running from the back of the stage, grabbing the microphone, and flopping down almost into the audience. Janis Martin, one of a handful of female rockabilly stars, shook her hips like a burlesque dancer. At a time when teenagers were being policed for any sign of going out of control, these rockers did it every night, showing their fans how to survive and even profit from behaving exactly as they weren't supposed to.

Of utmost importance was the way rockabillies confused categories of race, gender, and sexuality, interrupting the "natural" progression young people were expected to make from impulsive childhood to orderly adulthood. And no one confused categories more gracefully than Elvis. Phillips once described the chaos that ensued at the singer's first show after recording for Sun. "It was just a joint," the producer said of the Memphis hall where Presley played. "Here is a bunch of hard-drinking people, and here is a kid up there on the stage, and he ain't playing country, and he ain't necessarily playing rhythm and blues, and he didn't look conventional like they did. He looks a little greasy, as they called it then. And the reaction was just *incredible*."[19]

Elvis was certainly slippery—deep voiced but childlike in his exuberance, he had a sound that messed with received ideas about maturity and stomped all over the racial divisions that ruled both public space and the music charts at that time. He crossed into America's mainstream from a margin, the white Southern side, the same way the doo-wop groups did from its segregated black urban centers. He also blurred gender lines, his soft features perfectly suited to an exaggerated emotionalism that did not diminish his boyish swagger. He sings a threat in "Baby, Let's Play House," his greatest early single: "I'd rather see you dead, little girl, than to be with another man." But he hiccups in the middle of the phrase, like he's breaking into a giggle, or like he's too distracted by Bill Black's cantering bass line to hold thoughts of doing damage in his mind. The violence surfaces and dips away, submerged again. To his teenage listeners—both boys and girls—hearing it in 1955, this must've felt like their own rarely acknowledged experiences of inner volatility.

Using the language of semiotics in his study of modernism and popular song, *Sweet Air*, Edward P. Comentale writes that the young Elvis was "first and foremost an affective/gestural phenomenon." A caption writer for an Elvis photo spread in the first volume of the *Teenage Rock 'n Roll Review* (a short-lived publication founded in 1956) saw the same thing in the star, comparing him to the comical dancer who'd played the Scarecrow in *The Wizard of Oz*. "Possessing one of the most mobile faces of any singer today, Elvis's facial movements clearly indicate the seriousness and sincerity he puts into each and every word he sings," she wrote. "Just as Ray Bolger dances with everything he's got—his eyes, nose, ears, and feet—so Elvis sings with everything he's got, too. That is what makes them greater than other singers or dancers."[20]

Elvis was a genius of feeling and moving, including the way he moved his voice. He found a perfect balance between immediacy and distance. When he jerked his soft body around, he almost lost control—but only ever almost, pulling back that hip thrust or knee wobble just as he did his voice on his earliest hit singles. His actions mirrored the constant and multidirectional internal agitation of the teenage psyche, governed by mysterious drives and emotions that, though they were increasingly named by psychologists, were still not acceptable to air in public. And with that graceful snicker that was half deferential and half permanently subversive, he showed teenagers how to manage the whirl.

Elvis did have artistic role models, and he also had peers who might have matched his level of significance had fate and American prejudices gone a different way. His predecessors included the male torch singer Johnnie Ray, who became a phenomenon in 1952 for, in the words of his supposed friend and fellow vocalist Patti Page, "selling hysteria." The bisexual and floridly effeminate Ray cried publicly during his performances, and partial deafness caused him to exaggerate his responses to the music around him, flailing about in ways that caused a similar response in his fans. Clyde McPhatter, who began his career in the vocal groups the Dominoes and the Drifters, reached the same heights of flamboyance in his recordings that Ray did in performance. Part gospelizing, part operatic, and part a vaudevillian drop to the knee, McPhatter's tragicomic emoting on songs like "The Bells"—a mourner's blues transformed into delirium by the singer's yelps, screams, and cries—was the first major step away from the orderly rambunctiousness of rhythm and blues and toward the rich apparent madness of rock and roll.

Elvis's two greatest contemporaries were Little Richard and Buddy Holly, each standing at either end of the spectrum upon which nonsense flourished. The Memphis King claimed the middle ground between his rivals' two extremes: the strategic outrageousness of Richard Wayne Penniman, the original Black Weirdo, bursting every seam apparently for the hell of it, but really as a way of sharing subterranean secrets of two centuries' worth of racial and sexual nonconformists; and the shy, bespectacled Charles Hardin Holley, archetypal White Nerd, stumbling over his words and music as a way of pushing them into shape. Little Richard represented what happens to unspeakable desires after they've been dug out of the dirt where society buried them. Buddy Holly's singing embodied desire in formation: thoughts that seem unspeakable because they've never been spoken before. Elvis came off as wiser than Holly and more innocent than Little Richard. All of them had the same basic mandate—to turn fearful feelings into fun.

Richard Penniman was uncontainable from the beginning of his life in Macon, Georgia, a little queer boy whose penchant for dressing "beautiful" scared his father but whose precocious piano playing saved him from utter marginalization or an even worse fate. Inspired by gospel music and jump blues, he developed a vocal style that was, above all, loud. When a band touring through the South picked him up as a singer, his father finally granted approval of Richard's pompadour hairstyle—because that's how artists looked, after all. His early life as an entertainer included tours with drag queens, minstrel shows, and girls who would, as he said to his biographer Charles White in the early 1980s, "roll their bellies and stuff"—Little Egypt's granddaughters carrying exotica into the nuclear age.[21]

Unsurprisingly given the company he was keeping, Richard developed a wild act on the road and made a bunch of relatively successful rhythm and blues sides for labels like Peacock and RCA-Victor. But by the autumn of 1955 he was still mostly a Deep South sensation, and when he entered Cosimo Matassa's famous J&M Studios in New Orleans with producer Bumps Blackwell, nothing was working. Richard felt uptight. He couldn't get noisy enough. Only when he and the studio musicians took a break at the nearby Dew Drop Inn and Richard decided to show off by playing a very dirty number that made the queens go wild in the drag bars did Blackwell hear the lunacy he knew the singer could deliver.

But the song was obscene—all about "good booty" and what people did with it. Blackwell enlisted an ambitious young song-writer, Dorothy LaBostrie, to sub in some lyrics thin enough that Little Richard could saturate them with libidinal chaos while not breaking any censors' rules. What Little Richard did on "Tutti Frutti," as the song was called, was to eliminate double enten-dres and make matters much more direct. Most bawdy R&B songs pointed toward sex, albeit sometimes with a giant foam finger. Little Richard's vocalizations enacted sexual excitement itself. Richard spewed notes as if they were raging hormones, growling like a bluesman one minute, whooping like a gospel queen the next, shouting out nonsense words in a way that signified every-thing and nothing, entering a truly undone state. The historian W. T. Lhamon identified Richard's particular gift as promiscu-ity: "The ability to jumble multiple worlds seamlessly, white and black, straight and gay, gospel and blues and pop."[22] If the doo-wop groups cleared space for that sense of play preceding the moment of sexual engagement, and Elvis made such play charismatically personal, Richard grabbed on to the very moment the drive took over and rode it right into his fans' flailing arms.

This is not to say Little Richard was more primitive than his compatriots. He was just more committed to excitement. He knew what it bought him. After following "Tutti Frutti" with the equally ungovernable "Long Tall Sally" in 1956, Richard became a pop star with an equal number of black and white fans, and protected him-self by getting even more outrageous. "The white kids had to hide my records 'cos they daren't let their parents know they had them in the house," he told White. "We decided that my image should be crazy and way out so that the adults would think I was harmless. I'd appear in one show dressed as the Queen of England and the next dressed as the Pope." Literally embodying the mixed-up impulses that parents just didn't understand, Little Richard was happy to be the elephant in the room. He put a big smile on the face of depravity. Fans responded in kind. He was the first rock and roller to be barraged by women's underwear thrown by the crowd, and one of the first to have his shirts regularly ripped from his body into little pieces.

And depraved Richard was, by his own estimation. In his biography—which mostly consists of outrageous stories he told Charles White—he revealed himself as an omnisexual voyeur especially fond of dressing-room encounters. Richard likely knew that his refusal to play polite or to subdue the signifiers of his blackness would cost him the chance to be the king of rock and roll; and there is little doubt that homophobia, internalized and otherwise, contributed to him leaving the secular music business in 1959 to marry and become a preacher. (He would repeat the cycle of exit and return, minus the wife, many times throughout his career.) Yet the omnivorousness Richard represented both in live performance and on record also couldn't last beyond the first few years of the rock and roll era. By 1962, when he made a comeback that began with a tour of England, the promiscuous frenzy of the music's early years had died down, and the old orderly divisions reasserted themselves. Richard was then classified by many as a novelty act, selling outrageousness on talk shows. He continued to be a strong presence within rock, but his most important contribution during the 1960s was to insert a little chaos into the sound of the next big thing: the Beatles, who literally learned at his feet when they toured together in Germany, and included just enough of his squall in their sound to make the girls throw their panties again.

If Little Richard had a mirror image, it was Buddy Holly, the young oddball who came on the scene in 1957, just as Richard was exiting temporarily to hang out with the Lord. Both men were weird in a way that was cooked, not raw. Both came from edges of the rock and roll continent—Richard from the east, in Georgia, and Holly from the west, near the Texas–New Mexico border. And both made music that was primarily exploratory, though Richard rushed in while Holly delicately snuck around. The two men knew each other, and according to Richard, once even shared in a three-way sexual encounter after Holly walked in on Richard *en flagrante* with Lee Angel, the burlesque dancer who was his female soul mate during the height of his early fame. "He came and he went!" Richard quipped in his biography, sharing a filthy anecdote (that Angel fondly disputes).

Holly's own biography confirms that he was sometimes "a wild boy with the women" that Richard claims he was, but in his music, he was something different: the soul of tormented monogamy. Or at least monogamy as a teenager might feel it—more like fixation. Advice books for teens in Holly's era were filled with admonitions to hoist one's mind out of the gutter, usually directed at boys. "Boys who decorate their rooms with stimulating pictures, and who talk about sex subjects continually, usually experience frequent and strong desires," wrote the sex-education pioneer Lester A. Kirkendall in the guidebook *How to Be a Successful Teenager* in 1954. "Often they think this is because they have an unusually strong physical urge. Actually, it is the way they think about sex which produces a large measure of their physical desire. These same boys may go for a week's vacation, a hunting trip, or take a new job which requires all of their energy and attention. They often find during this period that their mind is so occupied with these new activities that they are hardly aware of sexual desires."[23]

Holly's songs expose what was really happening in boys' (and, in fact, girls') minds, even when they were hiking or hunting. His famous vocal technique involves worrying a lyric, taking words and syllables apart and reassembling them using hiccups and tics and pauses and halting breath, exactly the way a teenage boy would mentally rehearse asking a girl on a date, or a girl might go over that very same request in her own head later, until its meaning splintered into pieces. "You're gonna love me, too": so many of Holly's lyrics seem like both threats and promises. He's always sorting out whether emotion is going to complete his world or destroy it.

Charles Hardin Holley started playing country music as a high schooler in Lubbock, Texas, and briefly tried to make it in Nashville, but he became a rocker—and discovered himself as an artist—in Clovis, New Mexico. There he met Norman Petty, who recorded easy listening music on Columbia Records with his own trio (which included his wife), but invested in rock and roll's future by recording young artists in his state-of-the-art studio. Musicians liked Petty because he allowed sessions to run as long as the juices flowed. Petty liked Holly because he was ambitious. "He had the eagerness of someone who has something on his mind and who wants to do something about it," Petty reflected years later. "Really, he was unimpressive to look at, but impressive to hear."[24]

Holly was aware that his natural charisma was limited, and he'd need to use persuasion to become a star. Though known for his boundless energy onstage, he was never a pure teen idol, lacking both the undeniable pulchritude of Elvis and the sexual confidence of Little Richard (or of Chuck Berry, an older rock and roll pioneer who was both strikingly handsome and erotically experienced). Jerry Allison, drummer for Holly's band the Crickets, recalled that when girls seeking autographs backstage would see another act on the bill—say, the Everly Brothers—emerge from a dressing room, they would immediately swarm away and toward the better-looking star. He noted that boys seemed to like the Crickets better than other groups, perhaps because they weren't so worried that their own dates would run off with them.[25]

Giving voice to the awkwardness he couldn't help but embody,

Holly developed a unique way of singing. The high-end equipment in Petty's studio helped, allowing him to experiment with echo and overdubs. Instead of the raucous, endless party happening at Sun, the mood in Clovis was almost scientific. Holly and Petty would work their way through many different takes. The Crickets were able to develop an unusual level of synchronicity as a band, playing off Holly's odd guitar and vocal lines. These boys worked on their nonsense. Their songs explored why seemingly incomprehensible feelings take over in a lover's psyche as he pursues his beloved. And with his flexible, androgynous voice, Holly seemed to speak for the uncertainty of girls, too.

Musicologists and philosophers have pointed to Holly's singing as a revolutionary expression of how thoughts form in a desiring mind. Some have concluded that he was anti-sentimental, rejecting the soppy meaningfulness of the pop ballads that preceded rock and roll. Others hear the story of child development in his hiccups, oohs, well-a's, and other "baby talk." Dave Laing, an early Holly scholar, noticed how the "sudden changes of pitch" mirror "the breaking voice of a young teenager." The studied quality of Holly's music reveals him to be much more of a formalist than most early rockers, and while he probably wasn't thinking in psychoanalytical terms, songs like "That'll Be the Day" or "Words of Love" certainly can be heard as interior monologues, the fretful dreaming that comes before any encounter is attempted.[26]

Holly's alien sound didn't come out of nowhere. He was aware of doo-wop, and shared bills with doo-wop groups, playing the Apollo and even telling his mother, "We're Negroes, too!" after a mixed-race tour of the Southern states. His tone sometimes resembles that of Clyde McPhatter, the vocal group pioneer whose propensity for crying and howling at the climax of a song—melded with an elegance that made clear that every wild move was well-considered—formed a bridge between the gospel quartets and the secular styles of the 1950s. While Little Richard scooped up white and black sounds in his manic embrace, Buddy Holly made elaborate constructions from elements of both. His songs are like fetish objects, ritualizing the rampant musical amalgamations that characterized early rock and roll.

The nonmusical chatter going on between and around teenagers as that cohort's identity emerged also informed the sensibility Holly's music tapped. "This whole business of adolescents . . . is a complicated affair that often confuses and worries the adolescent himself and the adults who are part of his daily life," declared the social-worker authors of *Let's Listen to Youth,* one of the myriad navigational guides to youth's tricky waters published as rock and roll emerged.[27] The teen magazines that drew in girls with fashion tips and pinups elaborated on these complexities with articles like "Do You Know How to Flirt and Still Be Feminine?," "We Like Going Steady—But Why Do We Always Quarrel?," "Shyness—How to Beat the Problem," and "My Moment of Love, My Moment of Fear." These articles gave names to free-floating adolescent anxiety that may have helped or made things worse. They stressed the need for self-management. "Some days just don't seem worth it!" one declared. "But here're ways to understand and cope with your explosive emotions!"[28]

Holly's songs let kids know that even their new rock and roll idols could suffer from a nervousness that left them at a loss for words. Being a teenager was itself a public experiment in the 1950s, and the speculative sound of Holly's hits rang true to the young people caught in this unnatural pause in the life cycle. By the time he died in a plane crash in 1959, Holly was moving out of this phase: married to an older woman who led him toward Latin music and other new sources of inspiration (Maria Elena Santiago had been born in Puerto Rico, and worked in the music business before meeting her husband), Holly was on the road to becoming a sophisticated pop auteur. The loss that froze his music in time was, in a way, a gain for those trying to understand the unique ambiguities of self that afflicted teenagers and defined early rock and roll. Every day, Holly was getting closer to pinpointing the nuances of teens who felt caught in between—between childhood and adulthood, being eroticized and being sexually regulated, inventing their own freer world and recognizing that this world was a plastic bubble, and that their parents were watching every move.

In her history of the teenager, Grace Palladino crystallized the predicament youth during this era faced at the portal to adulthood. "Thanks to rock and roll and the rebel culture associated with the music, teenagers now had a choice of social identities, whatever their family background. They could see themselves as adults-in-training and use their high school years to hone their skills and discover their talents, as adults had been preaching for years. Or they could join the fast-paced teenager-only world of (loud) music, (fast) cars, and styles that mocked the very notion of adult guidance."[29] This was very confusing for most teenagers, who often vacillated dangerously between these two poles. Rock and roll encompassed the range of experience that characterized teenage life, with its most influential stars acting out different options, also familiar from the films, magazines, and pulp novels they consumed. With Little Richard as the violator of old norms and Elvis as the mediator presenting new ones, Buddy Holly stood for the teenager in process, becoming something no one—including himself or herself—quite understood.

SWEET LITTLE FOURTEEN

The truth, however, is that while Holly was creating a way to embody adolescent angst and hesitation, he was also getting laid on the regular by girls he met at the dances and all-night concerts the Crickets played. This reality reveals another crucial aspect of 1950s rock and roll. Like all popular musical styles, it embodied erotic ideals and fantasies alongside sexual fears and problems. But more than in previous eras, the makers of these dreams appeared right in front of the girls and boys who longed for them, in the flesh and ready to go. A unique combination of elements made early rock and rollers accessible in a different way than celebrities had been before. On the one hand, their charisma was mass-mediated and larger than life, thanks to the cheap 45 RPM singles introduced to the marketplace in 1949 and the new teen magazines and other merchandise that promoted them like movie stars. But they also quite literally moved within reach. Regional stars first, rock and rollers played teenagers' barn dances and local fairs. Instead of the Hollywood glamour that made even the original teen idol Frank Sinatra seem aloof, these boys were messy and rowdy and relatable. Hooking up with one, as a girlfriend or maybe just a meaningful fling, was not an impossible dream.

From the very start, rock and roll was a boys' game performed to stands full of females. Crucial women innovators like Ruth Brown and Etta James remained tied to rhythm and blues, and the few mostly Southern white women who tried to make a mark in the rockabilly scene, including Wanda Jackson and Janis Martin, had to really work to not be dismissed as novelties. Unlike sports, another male-dominated culture but one with a mostly male audience, rock and roll made its coin catering to females. It was a ritualized act of seduction framed within a heterosexual story line of boy-bowls-over-girl, and through its fourth-wall-breaking noisiness and visceral punch, it encouraged direct contact between fan and star. Rock and rollers always seemed out of place on television, like they were about to break through the screen. The live concert was their medium. And that medium was activated by the fans who screamed and ripped up their clothes and stormed the stage.

Feminist historians including Barbara Ehrenreich and Susan J. Douglas have long found the seeds of women's liberation in Beatlemania, the "sexually defiant consumer culture" formed by thousands, if not millions, of girls when the mop-topped pipers hit

American shores in 1964. "To abandon control—to scream, faint, dash about in mobs—was, in form if not conscious content, to protest the sexual repressiveness, the rigid double standard of female teen culture," wrote Ehrenreich and her coauthors in an influential 1997 essay, calling Beatlemania "the first and most dramatic uprising of *women's* sexual revolution."[30] These writers underestimate the fan girls of the 1950s. Media accounts from that time report just as much boldness from female rock and roll fans—and just as much concern from adults realizing that this new music and its subculture were breaking the bonds of conventional gendered behavior.

Rock and roll served as an activating agent for 1950s teens who recognized that the normal changes they were enduring had coupled with historic ones to push them toward new intimate realities, not just personally, but as a social group. Their moment was one in which racial divisions were being challenged and gender roles had been muddied as America rebuilt itself after the war. A photograph accompanying a *Pittsburgh Courier* account of a riot at a local show captured the change: it's the old scene of white observers discovering a new kind of erotic "somebodiness" while interacting with an African American performer whom they view as more liberated than themselves. "The fact is clearly in this photo that the rock and roll craze is not particularly restricted to one special group," the caption read. "Here a rabid bunch of white teen-agers 'get a message' but emphatically, as rock and roll ace Fats Domino 'turned them on' at a California dance."[31]

In the many hand-wringing newspaper articles published during its advent, rock and roll's young fans used the language of illogic and boundlessness to describe its effects. This language always defiantly stank of the erotic. The comments of seventeen-year-old Carole, interviewed by the *Washington Post* and *Times Herald* reporter Phyllis Battelle in 1956, were typical: "it moves me, man. Makes me want to jump. It's a feeling you get there with a person—

you're part of a big thing—you just don't wanta stand still. It's impossible to stand still. You get a lift, a real live charge."[32]

Parents feared and teenagers craved the real live charge rock and roll enacted. It turned the typical hormonal development of adolescents neon bright. In the presence of this music, teens performed the confusing transformation that struck terror in the hearts of their parents, sent alarms throughout society, and left teens in a limbo they could not successfully negotiate. "They get that wild look in their eyes, and they talk so funny, and when they're playing those awful roll and rock things," one mother told reporter Batelle. "You can't help thinking, 'Are these really children of MINE?'"

The long lens of history allows us to see that this behavior wasn't utterly foreign. Frank Sinatra's intimate-feeling performances had given rise to the bobby-soxers, hordes of young girls—real fans augmented by ones the singer's publicity agent hired—who swarmed outside theaters and, in hysterics and unwilling to give up their vantage points, famously wet the seats within. The Columbus Day riot of 1943, in which approximately thirty thousand young women overwhelmed Times Square the night Sinatra played the nearby Paramount, was, according to one observer, "a phenomenon of mass hysteria that is only seen two or three times in a century."[33] The floodgates were open: after Sinatra came Johnnie Ray, the half-deaf, flamboyant performer who openly wept while performing; Frankie Laine, Dean Martin, and other Italian neocrooners who blended emotionalism with a playful virility that appealed to youth; and those African American artists, like Clyde McPhatter, whose showmanship sneaked gospel's ecstasies into pop contexts.

What rock and roll added to the equation was a commitment to representing adolescence, not adulthood, and a unique combination of fantasy and accessibility. To teens, the stars of rock and roll were just like them and could very possibly become their friends—or even lovers. For teenage girls, the sense of intimate possibility within rock and roll blended with a growing social acknowledgment of their own sexuality to form a potent elixir. Going steady, necking, petting, car dates, and other social practices were designed for girls barely in their teens. Rock and rollers spoke to them directly, and created a space where they could answer back. But if the exchange had merely been symbolic it wouldn't have been effective. The young men of rock and roll—the musicians most of all, but also the male fans—were game to encounter these new girl-women. They weren't afraid of the ones who were, as Billy Lee Riley's famous Sun side put it in 1957, red hot.

Perusing the fan letters of one important rock and roller, Eddie Cochran, reveals just how toasty things could get between these musicians and their fans. Cochran is best remembered for his playful "Summertime Blues," which blended Holly's jumpy charm with the humor of vocal groups like the Coasters. He was a gifted guitarist and songwriter as well as a heartthrob, and would likely hold a higher place in the rock and roll pantheon if he hadn't perished at twenty-one in a car wreck while on tour in England. His mother lovingly preserved the voluminous correspondence from his fan club, now in the archive at the Rock and Roll Hall of Fame. These letters span the range of adulation, from a request for a group dinner from the Brooklyn chapter to ambitious attempts to connect professionally—several young women hawked their singing talents, while one male fan penned a slang-packed petition advising Cochran to liven up his lyrics with real teen lingo and offering to become his songwriting partner.

What jumps out from this collection are the letters from girls either seeking personal encounters with Cochran or reporting back on them. "Remember: Pennsville Memorial School June 6, 1957," wrote Nancy Griffith, from Pennsville, New Jersey. "When you were guest of Dick Clark. I was the one you held hand [sic] with and I've liked you ever since." Lorri Eggebraaten, who met the performer in St. Cloud, Minnesota, confided, "Even if you weren't the famous

Eddie Cochran I'd still love you for what you are." Betty Palmer, a fan club officer from Whittier, California, doled out advice as if she were an older sister: "Remember, Eddie; you can't win all by yourself—as it take [*sic*] a lot of little people working behind you— pushing you to the top. That's why we are here . . . " And a Dallas fan club president, in a letter marked PERSONAL PERSONAL PERSONAL— VERY PERSONAL, told Eddie of her recent split with his frequent tour mate, the rockabilly pioneer Gene Vincent, whom she'd discovered "had been two-timing me all along." She was turning her sights on Cochran, as a friend and professional investment, anyway: "Eddie I'll be eighteen in September, I'd like to come to California to live, it would be wonderful to handle your fan club there."[34]

Male artists' reliance on a support system of young female fans was (and is) part of the bedrock of rock and roll culture. Cochran seems to have been fairly typical. He was known more as a music nerd than as a wild man, and at the time of his death, he was en-gaged to the songwriter Sharon Sheeley, who was also in the car that crashed on that English back road. Living in Bell Gardens, a Los Angeles suburb, he had Hollywood connections and appeared in a couple of films. But as an independent musician playing all-ages venues in remote spots from Montana to Kentucky, Cochran also needed—and, judging from the intimacies mentioned in the letters, enjoyed—a close connection to fans who would buy his rec-ords and spread the word about his music throughout the halls of their high schools.

And the girls were not inhibited. "I'm 18, 5 ft. 4 in. 110 lb. dark auburn hair and dark brown eyes. Does that appeal to you?" wrote one named Diana Abbey. "If your [*sic*] ever in Lexington I'd really be honored if I had a date with you. I'll send a picture of myself if you want. Phone no. 30187. Love you loads." Another, Susie Shinsecki, expressed what would become the archetypal fantasy of a rock fan meeting a musician after seeing Cochran at the San Jose Civic Au-ditorium. "I was sitting in the very first row, and I had a long ponytail and a light green sweater on," she wrote. "When you first came out on the stage, my girlfriend yelled 'Hi Eddie!' and you looked our way. Then I waved my hand at you and you saw me and smiled at me. This got me 'all shook up.'"

Susie Shinshecki's dream was powerful because she could very easily see it coming true. The practice was sanctioned from the top of the rock and roll scene: in his early years of touring, Elvis Presley often dallied with fans backstage, allowing himself to be photographed kissing or lounging with them. One extraordinary account comes from Genie Wicker, who saw Presley perform at Atlanta's Paramount Theater in the summer of 1956. She was Genie Dettelbach then, and only thirteen.

Genie wrote a vivid account of her encounter with the King and sent it to her friends at summer camp; now a special acquisition of the Southern Folklore Collection at University of North Carolina, it has become known as "the Kiss Letter." Six pages long, it describes Presley's performance in detail—including a slow grind "after which my legs were shakin' kinda funny," Wicker writes—as well as the scene at the stage door where she and fifteen other fans lingered to obtain an autograph. They got all that and more:

A mob of girls leaned on the door + it came open. Then we rushed in. It was terribly hot. He was kissing some girl when the lights went off. There we were in a tiny little room with no lights. It was hot as hell. Policemen had by now cleared half of the screaming girls away but I hid in a sort of dark corner. There were just about 15 girls left I stuck my pen + paper in his face and asked him to please sign it. He made a few scratches on it. He couldn't see it was dark. Then he put his arms around my neck I did the same to him it was real dark with about 10 girls left. He kissed me. It was wonderful not sloppy just wonderful. It was just about 2 minutes long. I didn't hold my breath. It was so wonderful.

His hair smells like perfume. I had touched him about twice but I never dreamed of this then he did it again it was about the same amount of time. Then I went to sit down. I felt like I was gonna faint but I was determined not to. A police-man came up to me + told me to clear out I told him to wait til I got my breath I went up there again and said sort of loud to[?] Elvis do you have my pen?

He said yes kissed me and said I gotta go sugar.

Then he went out upstairs to change for his next show. A girl grabbed his shirt right before that + I got a big piece of it. The last time I kissed him he only had on half a shirt. He has a wonderful chest.[35]

The Kiss Letter is the most spectacular account of early rock and rollers rewarding their aggressive female fans with exactly what they wanted in the excited atmosphere following a show. The music answered this desire directly, with myriad songs about teenage queens finding freedom on the dance floor and becoming musicians' objects of desire. Some of this was marketing, but the enthusiasm in the songs rang true. Chuck Berry, who at twenty-nine became one of the most sophisticated and influential song-writers on the rock and roll scene, specialized in paeans to junior misses like "Little Queenie," who is "too cute to be a minute over seventeen." Johnny Cash's early single "Ballad of a Teenage Queen" told a conventional story of courtship and early marriage, but the chanted chorus—"dream on, dream on, teenage queen, pretti-est girl we've ever seen"—stimulated ambitions beyond the story's frame. "Only Sixteen," by the prototypical soul man Sam Cooke, told of romance between a girl who was "too young to fall in love" and a boy who was "too young to know"; the twenty-seven-year-old singer, with a long gospel career behind him and the suave moves of a notorious ladies' man, was the fantasy figure to which teenage listeners attached the story. Before the full onslaught of teen idols like Fabian and Frankie Avalon, who were carefully packaged and sold to magazine readers as potential prom dates, rock and rollers were much more forward, presenting musical propositions meant to sweep girls off the dance floor—or out of the crowd at a show— and into a tight squeeze.

There was a dark side to this exciting action. Many musicians did not hesitate to pursue the kinds of "crazy little mamas" their songs celebrated, and the girls often responded with little hesitation. Some were victimized. Sometimes the scenes were downright ugly. In his autobiography, Chuck Berry recounted a fan encounter after a concert at the Howard Theater in Washington, DC. "The Cleftones singing group scored a playmate from the audience who appeared overwhelmed by the spirit induced from the rock and roll songs," he wrote. "The next morning one of the Cleftones summoned me to show and boast about the girl, who they'd seen me speaking with the evening prior. At their room, I was shown her lying sprawled on her back upon a bed undignifiedly exposed and obviously drunk as a skunk. The male singing group, in their early twenties, were boasting that they'd all enjoyed the fruits of her femininity and could not resist offering a sample to someone else, namely me."[36]

Writing in 1987, Berry adopted a tone of moral superiority, describing how he helped the woman to put her clothes back on—after taking a look that he just couldn't resist. But thirty years before he published his book, he'd been embroiled in two of the most controversial cases involving the connection between male rock and rollers and female fans. Twice accused of violating the Mann Act, a 1910 law criminalizing an adult male's transportation of an underage female across state lines, Berry spent twenty months in prison in 1960 for bringing Janice Escalanti, a fourteen-year-old Native American runaway whom he'd met in a Mexican hotel, from the Southwest to St. Louis, where he'd employed her as a hatcheck girl in his nightclub. Escalanti testified that the two had been sexually involved. Berry tacitly denied this in his autobiography, writing that though they had shared a room as his tour made its way back to Missouri, he'd resisted her charms, only to be "sentenced to serve time for what I was convicted of just having the intention of doing."[37] In the other case, Joan Mathis, the Berry paramour involved, was a little older—seventeen, by most accounts—and declared herself in love with Berry when on the stand. He was acquitted of her corruption.

In the late 1950s, Chuck Berry challenged racist assumptions about what an African American man should be free to do. His Mann Act conviction has been viewed as a form of undue persecution of a gifted and outspoken African American entertainer crossing the same racial lines the civil rights movement would seek to eradicate. Joan Mathis was white, and clearly cared for Berry. The fact that she had been sixteen the first time she encountered the thirty-two-year-old Berry was the sticking point that put them both in a courtroom, but it's been overshadowed by legitimate outrage at the way the legal system has treated Berry throughout his career.

As for Janice Escalanti, a poor woman of color who was facing prostitution charges during Berry's trial and came across in court as petulant—and who, by her own admission, had traveled with Berry of her own free will—she never fit anyone's stereotype of pure femininity. Afflicted with what one Berry song dubbed "the grown-up blues" at a time when teenagers were often expected to be trouble, Mathis and Escalanti saw their stories swept up within a larger one about race, culture, and modernity, in which teenage girls are more metaphors for shifting attitudes than real people making complicated choices presented to them by men sometimes twice their age.

The shame of Berry's Mann Act conviction has faded over time, though it was vigorously debated upon his death in 2017. The general embarrassment surrounding Jerry Lee Lewis's 1958 marriage to his thirteen-year-old cousin, Myra Brown, endures. Myra herself has called the scandal that surrounded the union "the knife" that fatally injured early rock and roll, along with Berry's imprisonment, Presley's entry into the army, and Little Richard's temporary escape into the gospel world. These occurrences all preceded the more controlled era of teen idols and girl groups, when the forces of Top 40 attempted to reinscribe innocence onto teens. Myra was never that *American Bandstand* type. "I really, truly wasn't a typical teenager," a seventy-year-old Myra, by then long-divorced from Lewis and going by the surname Williams, told the journalist Alan Light in 2014. "My generation was taught to hide under our desk when the bomb came, so you always had in the back of your mind that any minute, any day, life could come to an end."[38]

In fact, Myra's feelings of deep instability, at once terrifying and full of an energy that made *do it now* a new mantra, were emblematic of the 1950s. The frequent retellings of her story have turned it into a Gothic allegory starring the tormented, demonic Lewis as an avatar of the ancient corruption of the Deep South; even in 1958, despite the prevalence of rock and rollers with underage girlfriends and tour companions, marriage between a twenty-two-year-old and his barely pubescent cousin struck most people as perverse. Myra was mouthy—she told reporters when the couple arrived in London, where the scandal first broke wide, that "age doesn't matter back home. You can marry at ten if you can find a husband." She was up for the publicity antics Lewis staged with her, including a widely viewed photograph of her feeding him peas (as if he were the baby) and another of the two sharing cotton candy, like two schoolkids, at Coney Island. Jerry Lee also disturbed gender stereotypes with his flamboyant stage act and long curly hair, which he would comb onstage, sometimes to cries of "faggot!" from the audience.

Yet at the same time, it's possible to see Myra as fulfilling the teenage fan girl's ultimate dream. She had come to know Lewis in the context of music making—her father was the bassist in his band. She was most visible as a tour companion, a support system and muse dressed in the latest teen styles. And she surfaced as Lewis's inspiration right when his hit "High School Confidential" was storming the charts. "Open up a-honey, it's your lover boy me that's a-knockin'," Lewis yelped in the tune's opening line. Myra was living the answer song.[39]

The family connection, more than Myra's age, may have been what repulsed the media and many fans. One British reporter who staked out the band's hotel made sure to provide details of what was going on in Myra's mother's adjacent room (not much) as well as the honeymoon suite. In addition, violence followed the pair after the collapse of Lewis's career; their son Steve drowned in a swimming pool as a toddler, and when Myra divorced Lewis, she claimed she had been abused. The sordid details make the Myra–Jerry Lee romance seem singular, when, in fact, it was not that far off from what was happening throughout rock and roll.

Learning a lesson from the way Lewis let those details fly, Elvis Presley kept his own fourteen-year-old object of fascination, Priscilla Beaulieu, under close guard until she could marry him without scandal. The pair met in Germany, where Elvis was stationed in the army and Priscilla lived with her career-military family. In her 1985 autobiography, *Elvis and Me,* Priscilla recalled that Elvis treated her like a fan when they first met at a 1959 dinner party. "What are the kids listening to?" he asked, peppering her with questions about his still-Stateside commercial rivals Frankie Avalon and Fabian. Priscilla cemented Elvis's interest in her by replying, "They're all listening to *you!*" A few days later, he would manage to get her alone, cuddle with her, and assure her that he'd "treat you like a sister." The pair proceeded to go steady as if they were a couple of high school students, exploring the edges of necking and petting, until the singer returned to the United States in 1960. Not long after that, Presley persuaded Priscilla's parents to allow her to move in with him in Memphis, where they lived "chastely" until marrying in 1967, when Priscilla turned twenty-one.[40]

Criminality and perversion, romance and ideal companionship— these are the paradoxical elements of the spectacular romances between teenage girls and adult rock and rollers in the 1950s. Little Richard had his own version, with Savannah high school student Audrey Robinson, whom he met when she was sixteen. Rechristened Lee Angel, Robinson became Richard's traveling companion and active other half. "We could read each other's mind," she once said about him, and most of what he thought about was sex. Under Richard's tutelage, the voluptuous Angel became an exotic dancer and, according to him, a voracious sexual adventurer. As he described it, she was the main player in the scenarios her voyeuristic rock and roller loved to watch, including that three-way encounter with Buddy Holly backstage at the New York Paramount. Angel later refuted most of Richard's claims, though lovingly. "I guess being in the same room where people were . . . doing things . . . means I was a part of that. But Richard," she told the British journalist Robert Chalmers in 2010, "would never let anybody touch me. What was going on across the room was a different story. Richard has a wonderful imagination."[41]

Like the other teenage queens living on the line between rock and roll fantasy and postwar American reality, Angel found quotidian ways to claim agency within the culture's highly sexualized and irrefutably male-dominated atmosphere. She continued to dance, became the lover of the eccentric R&B star Screamin' Jay Hawkins, and eventually moved to London. In 2010, she visited an ailing Richard in Nashville. He asked her to lie in bed with him. "I held him," she told Chalmers. "It was just like it was in the old days; he would never let me wear any clothes in bed, even though I had all these beautiful nightdresses. I held him close, while he went peacefully to sleep. It was as though we had traveled back in time fifty years."

This image of the lonely male rocker gaining strength from a younger woman whose vulnerability he's carefully maintained is both tender and damning. Such relationships between fully adult men and supposedly precocious girls set the template for rock and roll music, for its lore, and for its realities as it grew to become a worldwide mass phenomenon in the 1960s. Songs not merely naming girls' ages, but celebrating their jailbait status, form a seemingly endless playlist: they range from the Beatles' "I Saw Her Standing There" to Gary Puckett and the Union Gap's "Young Girl," from "Christine Sixteen" by KISS to Billy Idol's "Cradle of Love." In the 1970s and 1980s rock morphed into heavy metal, a scene notorious for "fresh meat" like Lori Mattix, the fourteen-year-old lover Led Zeppelin guitarist Jimmy Page kept hidden away in a hotel room, and Ted Nugent's seventeen-year-old road companion Pele Massa; in a particularly creepy move, Nugent persuaded Massa's parents to make him her legal guardian until they could marry. The hip-hop R&B titan R. Kelly nearly saw his career ruined when, after secretly marrying and then splitting from the fifteen-year-old vocalist Aaliyah in the 1990s, he faced charges on fourteen counts of child pornography after being accused of predatory behavior by multiple underage women in his hometown of Chicago. Acquitted in 2008, he still tours and records, supported by a devoted fan base. Even in a pop world growing more equitable in light of feminist activism, very youthful female sexuality remains a commodity. As has happened so many times within the realm of popular music, exploitation and the feeling of freedom merge in the troubling, celebrated figure of the teenage queen.

ALL I HAVE TO DO IS DREAM

Rock and roll girls and boys weren't always comfortable with the liberties the music promised. Sometimes they themselves felt like they were growing up too fast. These kids had an unspoken mandate, issued by experts in fields like psychology and sociology as well as by the dictates of an increasingly youth-oriented market-place, to define an ideal that was appropriate for more prosperous, forward-thinking times, but still able to accommodate traditional gender roles and life phases. "Tell me," Bo Diddley's 1956 song insisted, "who do you love?" It wasn't such an easy question to answer. "Today, custom dictates that young people must learn for themselves, through a variety of dates, just what kind of person they want to marry and live with," wrote the sociologist Paul H. Landis in the 1955 book *Understanding Teenagers*. "They have been given great freedom in dating and almost complete choice in developing the type of behavior that will characterize their dating relationships. It is expected that in some way, at the end of this period of trial and error, heartache and thrills, each will be better able to make the right decision concerning his own particular marital wants and needs."[42]

The practice of "going steady" encapsulated the hypocrisies of a time when teens could behave as "young adults" without openly enjoying the erotic self-possession adulthood promised. Girls were still expected to remain virginal until marriage, and boys, to want to marry a virgin. Boys and girls could spend private time, kiss, even go further into furtive embraces. But they had to check themselves. Boys were encouraged to channel their sexual urges into constructive activities, like sports; girls had to be both alluring and modest, encouraging boys *while* discouraging them. Gay teens, one guidebook suggested, could "make good citizens and good friends" as long as they learned how to control their impulses.

The freedom of adolescence sure came with a lot of rules. This made young people very fretful. A 1950 survey found that 41 percent of teens "often do things I later regret," while 35 percent "worry about little things" and "daydream a lot."[43] And sex, perhaps not surprisingly, was teenagers' main source of inner conflict. The crux of the problem was communication. Boys cited being bashful as their biggest problem. For girls, it was learning how to say no. Insecurity, shame, and regret hung like a misty cloud over the fun of adolescent freedom as the 1950s sped toward the 1960s. Often, young people felt confined within the giant test tube that was the adult idea of adolescence. They faced myriad confusing choices. Even worse, they were supposed to be able to express who they were. Artists like the Everly Brothers helped.

Though often viewed as a repressive phase spearheaded by music business executives who found well-groomed teen idols easier to manage than rockabillies and other troublemakers, the "taming" of rock and roll after Elvis went into the army in 1958 was equally motivated by the anxieties of youthful fans themselves. In the bedroom universe where young people listened to "rockaballads"—the slower or sweeter songs that still tapped into rock and roll's fervor—voices like their own spoke with forthright emotion and clarity from between the record grooves. Some were manufactured stars like Fabian Forte, a favorite of the *American Bandstand* mogul Dick Clark. Others, like the television star Rick Nelson and erstwhile doo-wopper Dion DiMucci, eventually rebelled against their own packaging. But if one sound exemplified teenage bedroom rock and roll, it was the harmony blend of the brothers Phil and Don Everly, the most popular, artistically ambitious, and influential dreamboats in a sea that swelled with them.

Child stars of country radio who loved the blues and could meld their voices like the members of the greatest gospel quartets, the Everly Brothers created something new out of pieces of different musical traditions. Their hits, including the playful "Wake Up Little Susie," the irresistibly fatalistic "Cathy's Clown," and "All I Have to Do Is Dream," the erotically charged rockaballad that simultaneously topped the *Billboard* pop, country, and R&B charts in 1958, showed how rock and roll could fit in with pop traditions without losing its deep pathos and integrity.

The Everly Brothers created songs that were metaphors for the unmoored feeling that defined the middle-class teenage experience in the 1950s and early 1960s. The duo's sound spoke to young boys feeling the pressure to man up, not only in the career counselor's office or among their male friends, but in the pursuit of girls who expected them to be assertive while also sensing limits: to know when the necking session should stop. "We took a special survey," wrote the editors of one teen girls' magazine in an article on necking. "A lot of boys admitted to us that they prefer girls who know how and when to prevent warmth from becoming heat! Otherwise there's too much of a strain on them . . . The honest truth is, they don't like a situation that puts too much of a strain on their new and awakening sex drives any more than you do."[44]

In the years after rock and roll's meteoric rise there was almost a panic, not just about teenagers, but also about the heavy burden of adulthood. It turned out that Jerry Lee Lewis and Chuck Berry weren't the only grown-ups attracted to teendom's allure. Mom and Dad were messed up that way, too. Between the pinups and the advertisements for deodorant, teen magazines regularly carried articles about parents in crisis, with titles like "Are Your Parents Delinquent?" and reports of thirtysomething mothers who embarrassed their children by wanting to go out dancing themselves. Many grown, married people felt lost—scattered from their childhood homes after the Great Depression, which made clear the fragility of prosperity, and then traumatized by war. This adult crisis had been brewing for most of the twentieth century. "Frequently a most serious element from the adolescent's point of view is that his parents are also groping," Katharine Whiteside Taylor wrote in the 1938 book *Do Adolescents Need Parents?* "For perhaps the first time in history, adolescents and parents alike are facing similar problems in adjusting to a rapidly changing world." Parents never really set themselves aright.[45]

Interactions with parents in Everly Brothers songs are often almost comical; the bounce of "Wake Up Little Susie," the quintessential story of two horny teens dodging parental observation, suggests a caper, not a walk of shame. Such lightheartedness symbolically diffused the very real tensions between parents and children that inevitably arose as teenagers fulfilled society's mandate to remake themselves. The music of the Everly Brothers showed listeners, young and older, that the most fraught moments of intimate conflict, whether internal or with family and other loved ones, could include grace and lightness. It suggested that sexual desire and its fulfillment could also be that way. This is one secret the Beatles borrowed from the Everly Brothers a few years later, when their international breakthrough secured rock and roll's position as a native tongue for both teens and young adults. In "Please Please Me," the band's first No. 1 hit, John Lennon and Paul McCartney borrowed the same static upper harmony style that made "Cathy's Clown" so special—one voice pulling back and staying still as the other tumbles into an oil slick of heartbreak—and, in doing so, added an element of ambiguity to what was otherwise a straight-up, aggressive seduction. That held note is the sound of a boy's uncertainty. It preserves all of the complicating emotions in the situation "Please Please Me" describes, the subtlety that might otherwise have vanished into the crash of Ringo Starr's drumbeat.

"Please Please Me" became an American hit in 1964, a decade after Elvis Presley first met Sam Phillips at Sun Studios and Frankie Lymon wondered why fools fell in love. With its direct if not utterly explicit demand for mutual erotic satisfaction, this key volley in the Beatles' invasion can be viewed as a kind of crowning point in rock and roll's confrontation with youthful sexuality. It addressed the desires and worries of youth in an immediate and serious way, facing sex in its troubling ugliness as well as its thrilling beauty. "Come on!" snarled John Lennon, and no one could mistake what he wanted. It was a tipping point.

The Beatles loved nonsense; they learned much from Little

Richard, who became their mentor when he traveled to England on his first comeback trail. They obsessed over the Everly Brothers, whose harmonies and intricate guitar tunings inspired the more reflective elements in their music. But the Beatles, of course, also built their music for girls, and their unique appeal was grounded in the fact that their songs had an extraordinary emotional range. In April 1964, when the Fab Four occupied every spot in the Top 5 of the *Billboard* Hot 100 chart and seven more in the Top 100, what they expressed beyond the particular complexities of "Please Please Me" included 1950s-style wildness in their covers of the Isley Brothers' "Twist and Shout" and Chuck Berry's "Roll Over Beethoven" and their own "I Want to Hold Your Hand"; Everly Brothers–style melancholy in "She Loves You"; rebellious antimaterialism in "Can't Buy Me Love"; bitter jealousy in "You Can't Do That"; chivalric faithfulness in "All My Loving"; roguish mystery in "Do You Want to Know a Secret." The desired subject described in "I Saw Her Standing There" might have been just seventeen, but she was wise to both romance's freeing aspects and its traps. And this was just the beginning of the expansion of youth music's language of love that happened as rock and roll became rock and soul in the 1960s.

Beatlemaniacs' knowing screams built the bridge between the struggle for coherence and acknowledgment that 1950s rock and roll represents and the full-blown youth movement, free in its thinking and its sense of the body, that flourished after the mid-1960s. In order to appeal to those girls who would become soul sisters and flower children, and to make the musical transition that would take rock and roll from its origins in the teenage heart into its adult phase, the Beatles learned not only from the male rock and rollers who'd set the stage for them, but from their own female peers—especially the girl groups springing up in cities like New York and Detroit, who connected rock and roll's nonsense firmly to real life and made way for the explicit erotic confrontations that would follow. "Will you still love me tomorrow?" That was the question the first great girl group, New Jersey's Shirelles, asked in 1960. No one knew then that it would set the tone for yet another phase of erotic revelation within music, one that would declare that love is free, even as it laid out its costs.

5

THE SEXUAL REVOLUTION AND ITS DISCONTENTS

NEW YORK, DETROIT, SAN FRANCISCO, LOS ANGELES, 1961–1970

The laws of physics and foreplay dictate that every action stimulates a reaction. This truism can be applied in reverse: major cultural permutations alter how we view what comes before them. The 1960s played host to what's now called the sexual revolution, a confluence of scientific, sociological, and legal shifts that pointed America toward greater permissiveness and dialogue about sex:

oral contraceptive pills, major surveys of Americans' sexual behavior by the scientists William Masters and Virginia Johnson (which became bestsellers), porn magazine publisher Hugh Hefner opening Playboy Clubs around the country, Helen Gurley Brown arguing for unmarried women's bedroom rights in her guidebook *Sex and the Single Girl* and as the editor of *Cosmopolitan* magazine. Intellectuals including psychiatrists Wilhelm Reich and R. D. Laing and social philosophers Herbert Marcuse and Norman O. Brown promoted a view of social progress grounded in loosening repression.

As young people in the cities came together to create what they viewed as whole new ways of being, even the settled folks in the middle-class suburbs began quietly experimenting with the new values of a "swinging society," with homemakers passing marijuana cigarettes at parties where one woman might end up wandering off with another's husband. Celebrating the new freedoms of the time, the historian Theodore Roszak wrote in 1969 of the gradual demise of social conformity and the kind of narrow thinking that "seeks to reconcile us to an existence without dreams, without fantasies . . . To speak of the ecstasies of life in such a somber environment is to risk folly. Here where all men trudge, none may dance. Dancing is . . . for later." In 1960s America, dancing was again for now—especially among the young.[1]

The nondancing squares who endured World War II and returned to the anxious orderliness of the 1950s had conformed so mightily to marital conventions that they produced an enormous generation that came of age in the 1960s and became known as the baby boom. These oppositional offspring produced what Roszak dubbed a "counter culture"—a world within the world, deliberately moving in opposition to the mainstream's values. Aided by a stable economy that made freedom convenient, new drugs that altered perceptions, and those early lessons in rebellion that rock and roll offered, the countercultural generation devoted itself to new ways of being that began in the body: new dress, new dance, new sex. By the end of the 1960s, these efforts would reveal themselves as life-altering for some, but limited.

OR JUST A MOMENT'S PLEASURE

At the dawn of the 1960s, pop's shifting subject matter gained new focus. Doo-wop and rock and roll nonsense had evoked what couldn't be said, but now it was joined by lyrics that unmistakably spoke about the longings of teenagers, especially girls. The hits emanating from New York's Brill Building and Detroit's Motown label established an ethics of sexual behavior for the adolescent set, directly confronting subjects like heavy petting, sexual frustration and jealousy, teen pregnancy, and romantic abandonment. Many of the best ones were written by young men and women who were going through the very struggles their catchy little dramas expressed.

Carol Klein and Gerry Goffin were two Jewish kids who met in the student lounge of Queens College in 1958 and discovered a mutual interest in telling teen tales. Goffin wanted to be a playwright, but Klein, who was already collaborating with friends like Paul Simon and Neil Sedaka and recording a little under the stage name Carole King, persuaded him to try writing lyrics. One thing led to another, professionally and personally. They had some luck selling songs to black vocal groups. Then Klein became pregnant. They had to marry, and to make ends meet.

The song that made the difference for them confronted the serious side of sexual exploration. They created "Will You Love Me Tomorrow" in their ground-floor apartment in Sheepshead Bay, with baby Louise right there; Gerry's day job testing polymers in a chemical plant meant they could only write at night. Klein came up with a melody that rose and fell like the female sexual response that sex doctors Masters and Johnson were busy analyzing. Goffin's lyric put the moment's pleasure in tension with the fear of consequences to come. Somber and majestic, not nonsensical at all, "Will You Love Me Tomorrow" expresses teenagers' awareness of the weight of erotic desire. The feeling wasn't entirely enjoyable, especially for girls—the decision to act on what Goffin's lyric called "the magic of your sighs" was no light thing. "Though now in his twenties, Gerry hadn't forgotten which three-letter word was foremost in the mind of every teen. It was s-e-x that kids thought about when they listened to lyrics about hearts full of love, hearts breaking, lovers longing, youth yearning, cars, stars, the moon, the sun," King wrote in her memoir.[2]

What makes "Will You Love Me Tomorrow" a pop turning point isn't simply the earnest lyric or the mounting melody. It's the vocal from Shirley Owens of the Shirelles, the group of New Jersey high schoolers who recorded it and took it to the top of the charts. Owens, who at first found the song too "country" for her taste, doesn't embellish Goffin's words. She just tells it like it is in her affectless alto, the only gesture toward virtuosity a quick, elegant drop into her lower register on the phrase "You say that I'm the only one." Listening, it's easy to imagine this plainspoken girl sitting up in a car's bench backseat and straightening her skirt before delivering the message. Her eyes are wide open, no stars.

Musicologist Jacqueline Warwick notes that the girl group sound of the Shirelles and other Brill Building–associated acts "was predicated on the sounds of adolescent female voices audibly going through hormonal development—most girl group singers really were *girls,* with ages ranging from 11 to 18 in most representative groups."[3] Employing this fluctuating register, they mirrored the boys of rock and roll and doo-wop in manifesting a truly teenage point of view, with an authority more studied voices couldn't match. The backing vocals in girl group songs carried over the stimulated rush of nonsense, using the syllables of playground games and mash-note margin scribbles. But at the center of these songs, Owens and her sisters didn't talk nonsense. They put an end to it.

An *Ebony* magazine article published in June 1960 asked "Are American Dating Customs Dangerous?" It focused on the courtship of model Lourdes "Lulu" Guerrero, a member of a large family from the Dominican Republic, and Clyde Otis, who, it happened, was an executive at the thriving New York record label Mercury. Guerrero and Otis practiced the Dominican custom of "duenna," or chaperonage. Every date the couple had included another family member, often Lulu's mother. (This old-fashioned approach worked for them: Otis and Guerrero wed and remained married until Otis's death in 2008.) Accompanied by a sidebar that noted the rapid rise in US illegitimate birth rates, the article portrayed Lulu as the winner in this relationship. "Her adherence to an ancient and honorable dating code throws into bold relief the freedom which Americans expect and almost always get."[4]

That freedom, according to *Ebony*, was perilous. By 1966, the magazine was reporting unwed motherhood among African Americans as a national crisis while noting that the men involved remained mostly unaffected. "The barbs are tossed at one-half of the duo responsible for illegitimacy—as if the sex had been a unilateral act."[5] Girl group music staged the conversations that a male-dominated larger culture refused, not only about pregnancy, but about abuse in relationships (the Crystals' controversial King-and-Goffin-penned 1962 track "He Hit Me [and It Felt Like a Kiss]"), male criminality (the Shangri-Las' "Out in the Streets"), early marriage ("Not Too Young to Get Married" by Bob B. Soxx and the Blue Jeans), and moral confusion (the Supremes' "Let Me Go the Right Way").

The Supremes were the signature female act of Detroit's Motown label, which transformed both black pop and African American entrepreneurship under label head Berry Gordy, a believer in the integrationist potential of crossover capitalism. Gordy's artists and the songwriters who fleshed out stories for them, like Smokey Robinson and the team of Holland-Dozier-Holland, aimed to accomplish this goal by blending unmistakably black sonic elements taken from gospel music and R&B with the supposedly white affects of modern recording studio production. Berry marketed their works as "The Sound of Young America"—an inherently political mainstream move that complemented the burgeoning civil rights movement led by Dr. Martin Luther King Jr. As the cultural critic Gerald Early notes, "Perhaps Motown, for the first time in American history, gave black kids a mythicized puberty of normal teenage angst."[6] It's arguable that doo-wop did something similar; Motown, however, more clearly expressed the agonies and ecstasies.

The moral and ethical conversations conducted in girl group records found further articulation in Motown music. Robinson's songs for the Miracles were more psychologically nuanced than virtually anything else on the pop charts, broaching subjects like sexual discernment ("Shop Around"), repression ("The Tears of a Clown"), and enthrallment ("You've Really Got a Hold on Me"). Marvin Gaye, who would create some of the richest countercultural albums of the early 1970s, began his career with the Gordy-penned defense of romantic fealty "Let Your Conscience Be Your Guide." The more impulsive, experiential side of eroticism also had a place at Motown—the Temptations pushed girls' limits with the early single "I Want a Love I Can See"—but as a whole this company, which advertised itself as sending its artists to charm school and providing chaperones on the road, made its mark by showing that rock and roll's youthful energy could serve culture that was "classy" and viable in the commercial mainstream. By 1964, when the Beatles invaded America, Motown artists were their chief rivals. Women reigned, at least momentarily. Motown's four No. 1 hits that year were all by women: Mary Wells's jaunty ode to monogamy, "My Guy," and three by the Supremes. These were all classic girl group laments about risky boys composed by Holland-Dozier-

Holland: "Baby Love," "Where Did Our Love Go," and "Come See About Me."

Though the Supremes' subject matter was familiar, the voice of Diana Ross made the Supremes a bridge into the next phase of pop eroticism. Ross is not often held up as a progressive force within popular music. For one thing, she favored old-fashioned Hollywood glamour and musical sheen over grit and earnestness, and for another, certain decisions she made seemed to betray the spirit of camaraderie fundamental to the appeal of the girl groups. The story of Ross usurping Florence Ballard as the Supremes' lead voice (the troubled Ballard was ousted from the group in 1967, and Gordy, then Ross's secret lover, helped orchestrate her exit) is one of pop's most celebrated tragedies, a tale of favoritism, greed, and, to some, misjudged talent that exposes the corrupt nature of the pop machine. There's even an award-winning musical, *Dreamgirls*, based on the saga. Yet no singer but Ross could have taken Motown into the late 1960s, when the nation's erotic idiosyncrasies increasingly permeated popular culture, including on the hit parade.

When the Supremes entered the studio to record "Where Did Our Love Go?," which would provide Ross with her breakthrough moment, they were cleaning up someone else's mess. The Marvelettes, whose lead singer Gladys Horton had one of those great plainspoken girl group voices, had turned down the composition. In a hurry to record, Lamont Dozier decided to keep it in the lower key that was not quite comfortable for Ross. He also had a brainstorm: the vocal hook could be a repetition of the word *baby*, in a long chain that might be a plea, a come-on, or a manifestation of erotic rapture. "The only way Diana could do it was to sing, 'baybeh, baybeh' in that low and sultry way," Dozier later told an interviewer. "All of a sudden, that was her sound, whereas previously she'd been up in the air."[7]

Ross's new sound wasn't about sex; like Little Richard's, it was *of* sex. And it expressed the core of a personality that connected

with an erotic archetype but also challenged it. The slender, androgynous Ross was a classic gamine, the neat and fashionable
Audrey Hepburn of black pop—yet she could also veer strangely
off-kilter within a song, her decorum unraveling in half coos and
pained cries. It was a paradoxical voice, as one admirer wrote,
"a combination of sex, temptation, little-girl coyness and breathy
Marilyn Monroe comeuppance."[8] And though Ross never truly
joined the coming counterculture, her voice fit in with its general
mood of immediacy and freakiness.

Motown would later align itself with the civil rights movement and, in the person of Marvin Gaye, find a champion of both
frank sexuality and broad political awareness. Yet even as its stars'
interests shifted, as far as romance went, black pop of the 1960s
remained relatively conservative. The seductive or self-protective
dynamics of romantic coupledom would remain at its center as it
matured. By the mid-1960s, though, on the wilder West Coast, a different musical contingent—the mostly white kids who were turning
rock and roll into Roszak's "counter culture"—was doing away with
a focus on the individual, providing a different kind of liberation
for kids who didn't want to save dancing for later. The leaders in
that scene replaced forthright ethical debates with minds blown
and bodies constantly whirling.

FREE LOVE MUSIC

When the guitarist Gary Duncan left his Central Valley hometown
for San Francisco in the late 1950s, he found a Beat scene full of poets, painters, and speed freaks. But it was evolving. The new hippie
houses grew ever more communal—especially after LSD, a halluci-
nogen psychiatrists had been using to treat alcoholics and patients
with minor personality disorders, became a leisure drug. The psychedelic experience broke down barriers among roommates so they
felt like family. Everyone was making art, and art was seductive.

"You'd go to, say, 1990 Page Street [in the Haight-Ashbury District], open up the door, and there'd be a fourteen-bedroom Victorian house with something different going on in every room: painters in one room talking to each other, musicians in another room," Duncan reminisced. "It was really cool, and to all outward appearances, there was nothing happening. It was like a secret society . . . There was a while when the place was just totally free."[9]

This feeling of ultimate freedom extended to erotic exploration. If earlier 1960s pop by the girl groups, Motown, and even the Beatles and Rolling Stones confronted desire as an ethical minefield to traverse, the countercultural rock played by Bay Area bands like Duncan's Quicksilver Messenger Service, the Jefferson Airplane, Big Brother and the Holding Company, and above all, the Grateful Dead, worked on principles of safe, open space. Music making created a zone where anything, including lovemaking, could happen. Dance, as much as hallucinogens, was the chemical agent that cleared the philosophical ground. "Everyone should dance every day," wrote novelist Tom Robbins, then a reporter for a Seattle hippie paper, in 1967. "Dance at a discotheque. Dance in your living room. Dance in bed. Stick flowers in your typewriter and dance at the office. Dance at the supermarket with a smoking banana in your teeth." Robbins assumed that this dance would involve multiple orgasms.[10]

Free love had roots in the utopian communities of the nineteenth century and in the writings of early feminist thinkers such as Victoria Woodhull and Emma Goldman. In mid-'60s rock, however, free love became an ideal expressed in music, as played by psychedelic bands at San Francisco's Fillmore and Avalon Ballroom. Historian Michael Kramer notes that in these halls where people gathered to trip and dance, several factors created a magical feeling. Wild light shows disoriented the senses. Posters on the walls invoked Eastern religions and pagan scenes, utopian-seeming alternatives to the strict Judeo-Christian propriety many revelers were trying to shake off. Simply being in these faded grand palaces of bygone eras made the bands and their audiences feel like they were creating a new city within the city, one more like Peter Pan's Neverland than like the boring neighborhoods where they'd been raised. Dancing called forth this new world. Kramer writes, "In the erotics of dancing bodies, participants engaged many issues key to public life: intimacy and collectivity, immediacy and distance, community and otherness, the supposedly mundane and the grand-historical. Their activities helped constitute a public sphere that seemed to flicker in and out of existence, much like they themselves did in the strobe lights of the psychedelic dance floor."[11]

Outside the ballrooms, old ways still lingered. Feminist reassessments of the 1960s counterculture, especially as it flowered in San Francisco's Haight-Ashbury district, have exposed the scene's sexism. "The women of the Haight were having sex with lots of different men and living in alternative families, but they were still expected, and many of them still wanted to be, pregnant and dependent," the historian Alice Echols wrote in 2002. And this was an almost entirely white scene, prone to casual racism. Brown-skinned goddesses with towering Afros adorned many psychedelic posters, and cartoons that came dangerously close to the minstrelsy era's "coon" imagery were common in underground newspapers that spread the news about the ballroom shows. Meanwhile, people of color were being pushed out of their own former neighborhoods by "urban renewal" that made available the very spaces countercultural youths used to liberate themselves.[12]

Despite these realities, within that ritualized realm of music and dancing people experienced some kind of erotic enlightenment. As Kramer points out, dancing free-form, not in couples, allowed women a kind of liberation, however momentary and contingent, from male harassment and the constraints of typical gender roles. Dancers engaged in symbolic free love as they grooved to the long, stoned jams that blew through so many doors in San

Francisco between 1965 and 1969. According to certain sensation-alistic reports, some participants took it to a literal level; an eyewit-ness account from a ballroom habitué known only as Peter stated, "After six hours of acid, pot and rock, the evening ended with virtu-ally the entire audience making love on the floor of the ballroom—a thousand-headed god with no cameras permitted."[13]

Oddly enough, this divine force was often stirred to life by a bunch of hairy hippies who loved old-timey music. To confront free love as a musical ideal is to come to terms with the eroticism of the Grateful Dead, a band that on its surface is as unsexy as rock and roll gets. Few artists—certainly none in the era of titanic hotness that was the 1960s—possessed less bottle-ready, market-able mojo. The band formed from the remnants of a jug band around 1965 and always retained that unwashed folkie vibe. Its unofficial sex symbol, Bob Weir, had the phlegmatic charm of a proto-slacker, while the most conventionally macho member was a very hairy scruff known as Pigpen. Leader Jerry Garcia owned up to his own sexual repression. "He would concede," writes his offi-cial biographer, Dennis McNally, "that sex and women were never his primary concern."[14] Yet the Dead embodied the free love energy that organized psychedelic rock, transforming its audiences and the concertgoing experience. The band's live performances made possible the turn from pop as a courtship facilitator to a more sen-sual, emotionally open-ended experience, and accomplished this precisely by not fulfilling the norms of pop allure.

The Dead found an identity as house band for the Acid Tests staged in the mid-'60s by writer Ken Kesey and his anarchist perfor-mance troupe the Merry Pranksters. These carnivalesque evenings included poetry, improvised theater, live art making, and whatever else anyone wanted to do while high. The Dead's players often took hallucinogens before performing; Garcia's nickname was Captain Trips. So it's fair to ask whether drugs, not music, enabled the poly-morphous release many experienced during San Francisco's long

Summer of Love. Anyone who has taken hallucinogens knows that, if anything, LSD startles people out of their customary routes to erotic satisfaction. New Age teacher Ram Dass, after a 1969 study on using LSD in sex therapy, concluded that the "perceptual-cognitive-affective re-organization" that the drug produced rearranged people's understanding of their objects of desire: "Our male subjects report over and over again that to look at one woman is to see 'woman'—the harlot, the virgin, the seductress, the juvenile, the matron, the mother and so on, with all feelings—lust, anger, love, kindness, protectiveness, vulnerability . . . and to look at any man is to see 'man.'" This change in perception could be erotic, terrifying, or profoundly distracting. Stars of the classic rock era reacted in different ways to the dissemination of these altered states. Mick Jagger of the Rolling Stones, for example, very consciously engaged codes of potency he'd picked up from the African American blues stars he admired and women he dated. (He learned his trademark strut and, arguably, much of his sexual bravado from Tina Turner, the incendiary R&B shouter who, with her then-husband Ike, toured with the Rolling Stones in 1966.) Jagger's pouty-lipped act became a portal for all kinds of fantasies of androgyny and racial amalgamation. Jimi Hendrix, conversely, challenged the stereotypes that haunted him by both leaning hard into them and declaring himself a free spirit who didn't believe in their boundaries. Both men used the widened perceptual field psychedelics created to build their hyper-potent images.[15]

The Grateful Dead never made such shows of altered masculinity. Garcia didn't consider the Dead to be playing for an audience—"Everywhere you looked you saw somebody you knew. We didn't start getting audiences until we started going out of town." He scorned Jagger's manipulation of his fans: "Well, see, the Rolling Stones never did have a cool audience. When they started playing, people were screaming. Then they knocked off for two or three years and now they come back, and it's back to screaming." Gar-

cia explicitly rejected star-fueled hysteria as a route to rock liberation. In the mutual exchange of an Acid Test, the performer doesn't
drive the crowd to a frenzy; everyone present finds his or her own
way, with the music serving as a net instead of a push.[16] Dancing
at Dead concerts was orgasmic, a full-body moment of jouissance.
The experience was polymorphous, enveloping the whole body; it
might be homoerotic, come in waves like a woman's orgasm, or
remain blissfully self-directed. This is how the thousand-headed
god manifests—not through stars' performed prowess but in a vast
circle where everyone is pleasuring and being pleasured.

Not long after the Acid Tests, the Dead began appearing in
Golden Gate Park, notably at the Gathering of the Tribes for a Human Be-In of January 1967. By making the choice to perform in the
beautiful green space adjoining their own neighborhood, the Dead
connected to a long history of encounters that brought private desires into the public sphere and took the scene beyond the realm of
the subcultural. In *Erotic City: Sexual Revolutions and the Making of
Modern San Francisco,* Josh Sides argues that Golden Gate Park was
destined to be rife with trysts as well as crime: "The very design
of the park—its winding roads, high shrubs and isolated dells—
allowed people to act out their human penchant for violence and
sex with anonymity and, usually, impunity." If sex already was key
to the park's legend before hippies arrived, the difference was that
the hippies performed their erotic acts in public. Nudity became
common in the Panhandle and on "Hippie Hill" at the eastern end
of the park, and it was normal for the audience to strip down and
dance. When that happened, the insular experience of free-love
music turned outward and became political.[17]

The hippie takeover of Golden Gate Park provided a template
for festivals like Monterey Pop and Woodstock, defining events
in the counterculture. The Dead endured for decades, even after
Garcia's death in 1995, and became the foundation of a subculture
that kept hippie ideals alive long after the counterculture itself lost

hold of history. For all the communality of this experience, countercultural rock was still entertainment, and the American pop
machinery demanded stars. There were many, and each claimed
a spot on the eternal wheel of erotic archetypes. English imports
like the Rolling Stones' Jagger and Keith Richards evoked both elegant exoticism and outlawry, selling their loving theft of American
blues music as a rogue's journey, with the Stones as modern-day
Candides chasing women and enlightenment. Protest music pinups like the erstwhile lovers Bob Dylan and Joan Baez connected
with the civil rights movements of the time, but also showed young
people how seriousness could be sexy. From within the African
American fight for equal rights, Aretha Franklin made secular gospel music showing how Martin Luther King Jr.'s governing principle of "somebodiness" applies to the love between a man and a
woman, uplifting the nation from every bedroom on out.

Among these idols, three stood out, all emerging from the Ar-
cadian, hedonistic West Coast and known for performances that
rode on each star's almost excessive sense of self, inspiring descriptions like "shamanistic," "primal," and, over and over again, "orgasmic." Jimi Hendrix, Janis Joplin, and Jim Morrison made being a
sex symbol psychedelic and nearly revolutionary. "Is everybody in?
Is everybody in? Is everybody *in*?" Morrison would shout to his fans
as each mesmerizing concert by his band, the Doors, began. These
countercultural sex symbols showed how individuals fleshing out
a generation's ideals could take both star and fan into realms of
bodily response and emotional insight that felt so new, they were
disorienting. That these artists were all dead by 1971 does not define them, though it speaks to the particular dangers of pushing
edges in a moment when the edges were collapsing—the critic Ellen
Willis's distinction in describing Joplin as "not so much a victim as
a casualty" applies to all three. What united Hendrix, Joplin, and
Morrison during the height of their fame was how each absorbed
the sexual revolution into their music, into their very bodies. That

this process remained incomplete reveals the restrictions of the counterculture.

THE ULTIMATE THREESOME

In the inverted world of the countercultural happening, things often got out of hand, but the evening of March 18, 1968, brought a possibly unmatchable moment of onstage mayhem. Jimi Hendrix, whose revolutionary guitar playing and stoned-sprite style was then redefining both rock and the blues, had found a pickup gig with the soul group the Chambers Brothers at a midtown New York club called the Scene. In the audience was Jim Morrison, singer for the LA proto-art-punk band the Doors and the media- and teenybopper-appointed "sexiest man in rock and roll." Janis Joplin, the biggest female star rock had yet produced—who like Hendrix was in town recording a new album—sat at a table drinking whiskey. It's unclear whether Morrison was invited onstage or simply stumbled up there, wasted on his own excess of alcohol. But a recording exists of him slurring about perverse sex acts while Hendrix tries gamely to respond with lascivious licks. At some point Morrison allegedly encircled Hendrix's slender hips with his arms and muttered, "I want to suck your cock." Joplin wasn't having that, say some accounts—she jumped onstage herself and hit Mr. Mojo Rising on the head with her Southern Comfort bottle. The three descended to the floor, brawling in a tangle of very valuable velvet- and leather-covered limbs.[18]

You could call Hendrix, Joplin, and Morrison "erotic politicians," the term applied to and used by the Doors singer during his late-1960s prime. At their peak, in the live performance settings that allowed them the most room to protest and to play, these stars tested the confines of identity with a forcefulness informed by musical restlessness and an acute awareness that at any moment they could become stuck within shrinking versions of the very archetypes they refreshed. Their performances also made clear how the confines of sexual convention persisted and pushed countercultural adventurers back into positions not that different from the ones they'd run from or rebelled against. "I tried to stimulate a few little riots, you know," Morrison said to an interviewer in 1968, a few months after he'd told his bandmates he thought he might be having a breakdown and wanted to quit, and two years before he expired in a Paris bathtub, still a member of the Doors. "After a few times, I realized it's such a joke . . . because it leads nowhere." The revolution in Morrison's head, in Hendrix's fingers, and in Joplin's scarred but miraculous throat remained incomplete. The arcs of their musical careers were tragedies not defined by the chemical misadventures that took their lives, but by the rage each was expressing by their final months, a frustration reflective of the darkening realization among many Americans that the promise of a sensual utopia was being smothered in the quagmire of racial and gender inequality.[19]

That was the story of the sexual revolution as enacted by hippies and freaks: floridly sweet-tempered idealism stagnated at key junctures by bad behavior accommodating the hierarchies the new generation was supposed to abolish. The era's beauty was typified by statements like this one, from a manifesto by Tuli Kupferberg, a member of the New York band the Fugs, known for boisterous pro-sex songs like "Boobs a Lot": "The world is an art form. He [the enlightened hippie] will decorate his body as a work of art. He will bead it, paint it, clothe it in rainbows and the idiosyncratic style or mixture of styles of all times all place; there is no CORRECT way to dress; there is no correct way to fuck. Let 1000 bodies bloom!" The stagnation stunk in accounts of sexual assault in neighborhoods like San Francisco's Haight-Ashbury, whose guardian angel group the Diggers posted a bulletin in 1967: "Pretty little 16-year-old middle-class chick comes to the Haight to see what it's all about and gets picked up by a 17-year-old street dealer who spends all day shooting her full of speed again and again, then feeds her 3000 mikes and raffles her temporarily unemployed body for the biggest Haight Street gang bang since the night before last." The flyer concluded, "Rape is common as bullshit on Haight Street," in stark contrast to Kupferberg's dream. Wonder and horror coexisted in the same erotic space.[20]

Hendrix, Joplin, and Morrison found notoriety as part of a larger pantheon of young musicians quickly elevated to the status of generational spokespeople, but were united by an aura of erotic challenge that few of their peers could match. They incarnated both the promise and the oppressive disappointments of the time. Beyond that night at the Scene, their biographies say Joplin had sex with each man on at least one occasion; Joplin and Hendrix enjoyed career breakthroughs with incendiary sets at the 1967 Monterey Pop Festival; each debuted with 1967 albums that remain central to the rock canon today, then died within a year of each other, at the same age, twenty-seven. Those final coincidences have led many to see more sorrow in their stories than anything else. What's less discussed is that fury each expressed at being pushed back into the confines of conventional self-expression, even as their performances showed, with humor and nuance, how constructed those categories were.

Jimi Hendrix's African American virility was conspicuous, but somehow translucently elusive. Janis Joplin survived the shame of an ugly adolescence to become the "first hippie pinup girl," but the lust she owned contained an oppressive note of ruefulness. Jim Morrison was her male counterpart—a highly unstable, aggressively strange drama club kid whose accounts of weird scenes inside the male subconscious became a mainstream turn-on; but also an out-of-control drunk partly driven to his excesses by denouncers who compared him to a stripper and a clown. The erotic breakthroughs of these culturally appointed savior-fools were doubled from the beginning by humiliation, censure, and defeat.[21]

JIMI HENDRIX:
AMBITION TO BE A MOVIE

Hendrix was, in the words of influential promoter Bill Graham, "the first black sex symbol in white America." He was Ralph Ellison's Invisible Man brought to light within a Pacific Northwest outlier's science-fiction dreams. But he also endured accusations of being a "psychedelic Uncle Tom" catering to the demands of white crowds who gathered round him as if he were a dancer in Congo Square.

"First, we had a music that was all body, then we had a music that was all mind, now we have a music that is mind and body." So an unidentified companion of Hendrix told the celebrity profiler Albert Goldman during the interview sessions for a 1968 *New York* magazine article. The quote must have triggered the literary pretensions of Goldman, who was an English professor before he began a long career digging up the lurid secrets of rock stars. It also echoed the pseudo-religious tone adopted by self-styled gurus such as LSD advocate Timothy Leary, whom Hendrix would soon meet while traveling in Morocco. Yet more subtly, the comment expressed Hendrix's fondest dream of overcoming a racism rooted in the way people viewed his own body. For though writers like Goldman often questioned the authenticity of Hendrix's blackness—dubbing him "SuperSpade" because of his "flash" performance, Goldman wrote, "Hendrix's blackness is only skin deep"—the guitarist lived the reality of oppression every day, struggling to both acknowledge and transcend it.[22]

Hendrix had been raised in a city, Seattle, with a small African American population based in the Central District, adjacent to and melding with the Pan-Asian International District. One grandmother was part Cherokee, and after Hendrix was grown, his father would marry a Japanese American woman. "There was all kinda soul there and Chinese, too," he told Goldman. Yet musically, Hendrix came of age in a different space: after first experiencing the brutality of the Jim Crow South as an enlisted army man stationed in Kentucky, Hendrix joined the touring circuit of African American musicians regularly barred from restrooms and diners and forced to drive fast through areas where the Ku Klux Klan still ruled. Settling briefly in Nashville, Hendrix played in an integrated band, the Continentals, whose gigs would sometimes be canceled when white patrons called the police in protest. It's well known that Hendrix's chitlin' circuit experience, supporting the likes of Little Richard and the Isley Brothers, taught him that "flash" he so perfected; the hip grinds and guitar-mouthing that astounded white New York and London fashionistas were common feats among black entertainers on this most demanding musical route. But even as he learned, he stood apart. "He wasn't a black act," Nashville singer Jimmy Church once said. "He was left-handed and had a little effeminate thing about him: soft-spoken, smiled a lot. And when he was onstage and flicked his tongue out, the girls really went for that."[23]

Knocking women over with a flick of his tongue, Hendrix found a way to give the sometimes overbearing lasciviousness of the R&B performer a light touch. His "explicit mime of cunnilingus," the critic Charles Shaar Murray notes, invoked what "was still considered an exotic activity that only wicked, depraved men would perform and even wickeder and more depraved women would want." But it was also fun and funny, a sign that he would be an enthusiastic and engaging lover, not an overbearing one. "I think about sex a lot; it's part of my nature," Hendrix told AP reporter Mary Campbell in 1969. "I cry easy," he told another reporter, gilding his allure with emotional vulnerability.[24]

Both African American and white women played significant

roles in bringing Hendrix to fame. His first serious lover upon leaving Nashville for New York was Lithofayne Pridgon, a supremely well-connected Harlem-based paramour to stars like Little Willie John and James Brown. Linda Keith, an English blues connoisseur who was then dating Keith Richards of the Rolling Stones, discovered Hendrix playing in Greenwich Village's Cafe Wha? and introduced him to his future manager, Chas Chandler. The day he moved to London, he met Kathy Etchingham, who became his longtime companion and social connection to the rock glitterati who would soon pack rooms and gape at his performances. After fame, when he became known for the mixed-race female entourages accompanying him everywhere, Hendrix would tell reporters that his erotic color blindness (and sense of entitlement about crossing those lines) originated in adolescence. He was kicked out of high school, he said, because "I had a girlfriend in art class and we used to hold hands all the time. The art teacher didn't dig that at all. She [the teacher] was very prejudiced."[25]

As a performer and a personality, Hendrix practiced what's now known as code-switching: alternating between black and white idioms in ways that both engaged with and confounded stereotypes. His early admiration for Bob Dylan, whose Semitic Afro inspired Hendrix's "bush" hairstyle and whose path he followed to Greenwich Village at the urging of fellow code-switching black folksinger Richie Havens, makes utter sense in this context. ("We called him 'Dylan Black' because of his hair," one New York friend told Hendrix biographer Charles R. Cross.)[26] Dylan, too, grew up an ethnic outsider in a supposedly less-racist-than-most state, Minnesota; he didn't hide his Jewishness, but neither did he dwell firmly within it. And like Hendrix, Dylan had a strangely delicate air. "Pallid and soft, he seemed childlike, almost feminine," Dylan biographer David Hajdu described the former Robert Zimmerman in his early Village days, quoting his first manager, Terri Thal. "He looked like he could really use some help around the house."[27] Hendrix cultivated a similar, arguably passive-aggressive spaciness in rambling conversation and through a messily pretty sartorial style. Manager Chandler tried to get him to wear the mohair suits favored by macho bluesmen like Hendrix favorite Albert King; declaring himself done with that, he adopted a flouncy layered look that had other musicians calling him "that guy walking around looking like he walked into a girl's closet and put everything on."[28]

Upon his arrival in London in 1966, Hendrix quickly worked to blur the lines between the bluesman self he'd established when touring the South and the rocker persona that he'd begun developing in Greenwich Village. Forming the Experience with Chandler's help, he chose Mitch Mitchell as a drummer because of his chops, but the inexperienced bassist Noel Redding got in because of his hair. What made Hendrix different from other masterful showmen was a technical gift that allowed him to roam among musical signifiers (and, in doing so, among identities) with seeming effortlessness. The guitarist John Perry, who saw one of the Experience's first London shows, described it in athletic terms: "His technique was so assured he had time to play brilliantly and do all this other stuff with his arms. Sometimes he only had one hand on the guitar, and it still sounded great. It was similar to that quality seen in those rare sportsmen who come along once or twice in a decade: they seem to have fractionally more time than their peers, time in which they can choose their shot, or adjust it without ever looking hurried, time which makes their play seem effortless and their companions or opponents look clumsy."[29]

Hendrix's skill, according to Perry, made his technique transparent, causing his playing "to become a direct expression of personality rather than a brilliantly executed performance." It's a small word change, but really, Hendrix was translucent. Traces of Hendrix's blues schooling were clear in his licks and chord changes, his tendency to brandish the guitar as if it were a large appendage, and to dance with it. Yet that illusion of naturalness was key. It caused observers not only to gape, but also to meet some looseness in themselves. Fitting a moment when the performance of sexuality, too, was being loosed from its primary signifiers, Hendrix's musical mastery became a metaphor for polyvalent pleasures that broke down the barriers separating people racially and in other ways. An incident involving Hendrix's rivals and admirers Eric Clapton and Pete Townshend illustrates this. Charles R. Cross writes, "The two developed a friendship that winter based almost solely on discussing Hendrix and what they might do in response to him. During [one] particular show, as they watched Jimi play an intense version of 'Red House,' their fingers accidentally brushed. Clapton grabbed Townshend's hand, and they clasped them together the way two schoolgirls might while watching a particularly gripping film."[30]

Heterosexual male fans were not embarrassed to become rapt within Hendrix's sensual spell. His physically free playing could feel like a guide to the wide open sexuality the counterculture idealized. The influential German philosopher Herbert Marcuse wrote in the 1966 edition of his Freudian critique *Eros and Civilization* that the era's most relevant battle was "the body against the machine." Sensually pleasuring his machine, the guitar, and becoming one with it, Hendrix seemed to de-mechanize rock. His comfortable oneness with the instrument signaled his ability to inhabit the state of full-body bliss that Marcuse puts forth as the only one adequate to the revolution the counterculture attempted. Marcuse thought that people could transcend mere genital stimulation while engaging consciously in sex, their awareness expanding beyond those hot spots to encompass the whole body and psyche and even recast the world around them as wholly erotic. In this experience, he saw the potential for a new kind of enlightenment. "This process almost naturally, by its inner logic, suggests the conceptual transformation of sexuality into Eros."[31]

Marcuse's heady language trickled into countercultural rhetoric through manifestos like Kupferberg's or another by poet and

Digger Chester Anderson, addressing the sensory overload of the San Francisco ballroom scene in the *Oracle* newspaper in 1967: "The things a really imaginative [lighting and sound] engineer could accomplish by working on our many senses, singly and in orchestrated combinations, are staggering. Imagine: sensory counterpoint—the senses registering contradictory stimuli and the brain having fun trying to integrate them. Imagine *tasting* G-Minor! The incredible synaesthesia!"[32] For many, psychedelic drugs allowed for such beneficial sensory confusion, pulling the lines of desire and sensuality off track and making fingers, ears, or toes as enjoyable to touch and explore as were genitals. Anderson identified rock music as the ideal conduit for this experience, as an "essentially synthesizing art, an art of amazing relationships." The extreme amplification and distortion electric instruments made possible also contributed to rock's decentering power, allowing, for example, bass to be "experienced in the abdomen as localized vibrations, an amazingly private sensation impossible to resist."

Hendrix did more than provide this experience for concertgoers; he enacted it. "His body language was impossible to separate from his technique," notes Perry. The feedback Hendrix created by playing at top volume and moving his guitar over his head, around his back, or, yes, between his legs was the product of his embodiment of Marcuse's theory of Eros. Using the whole stage as an instrument and every part of his body to play it, Hendrix cultivated a wide field of pleasure, penetrating it and being penetrated by it. The field included the audience: "People make sounds when they clap. So we make sounds back. I like electric sounds, feedback and so forth, static," he once told a journalist.[33]

Insistently nonchalant, Hendrix gained a remarkable amount of mobility for a black popular musician within a pop world that, even in its most progressive corners, remained mostly segregated. But he kept running into roadblocks that prevented him from inhabiting a truly blended identity. He encountered legal problems, as when Linda Keith's father, horrified by their relationship, made her a ward of the court and shipped her back to England. He accepted minstrelsy-level nicknames like Wild Man of Borneo and Mau Mau from insensitive friends and supporters. His recorded attempts to forge a new musical form akin to John Coltrane's jazz suites were severely edited to accommodate the requirements set forth for pop songs. And Hendrix rarely if ever received airplay on black radio, though he had African American fans and, after disbanding the Experience, played with black musicians.

In his personal life, he dealt with the unspoken taboo the white Austrian artist Alfreda Benge expressed in a lustful recollection of the guitarist in 1991: "He was the first black performer of whom you can say, 'PWOOORRRRRGH, I FANCY you.' I don't know what it was about him, but he was incredibly important for that . . . I had shared houses with black people, I wasn't distant from black people, but it had never occurred to me to fancy someone black." Pete Townshend exhibited similar shock at Hendrix's interracial appeal when he puzzled aloud about his wife's interest in Hendrix: "'What was it like? Was it sexual?' She said, 'What a fucking stupid question.'"[34]

To be the only black man white women could desire was to become a new kind of invisible man, accepted as a cipher, not a real person born into a black community. As the historian Lauren Onkey notes in her analysis of Hendrix and 1960s race relations, by the time the guitarist disbanded the Experience in 1969, "he had come to realize that the hybridity of his act wasn't communicating what he wanted it to either to counterculture or mainstream audiences." Hendrix, whose instrument was the stage, never found acceptance among African American live audiences—he was greeted by thrown eggs and an admonition by a black activist to "come home" when he played a street festival in Harlem three weeks after his triumphant sunrise set at the 1969 Woodstock Festival. Yet among the hippies and hipsters who became his fan base in both England and the United States, he faced a kind of blinkered idealism, wrapped in unacknowledged prejudice. Though he occasionally spoke in positive terms about the militant nationalism of the Black Panthers, Hendrix did not actively join the black power movements that arose during his career, either literally, the way Muhammad Ali did when he refused to be drafted in 1967, or in song, as James Brown would with "Say It Loud, I'm Black and I'm Proud" in 1968. As an artist, he longed for the kind of erotic liquescence Herbert Marcuse had proposed as a harbinger of change, a way of becoming a new being—a merman, he said in one song. But these dreams of transcending the body he'd been given also contained Hendrix's fear of losing himself; his songs acknowledged Ralph Ellison's assertion that "to be unaware of one's form is to live a death."[35]

Depression was the counterpart to Hendrix's athletic ease. Evoking that mental state was central to his persona and his artistic process from the beginning of the Experience. He made it explicit in songs like "Manic Depression" and "I Don't Live Today," with its traditional blues lyric, "Feels like I'm livin' at the bottom of a grave." His love affair with the guitar was a tragic one; the poem he wrote on the back of one of the first instruments he smashed invoked "frustration, wracked feelings of not being able to make true physical love to the universal gypsy queen of true free expressed music."[36] Known for humor and gentility in most situations, Hendrix was occasionally prone to violent, hotel-wrecking outbursts that frightened his girlfriends and bandmates. He had grown up in a chaotic, extremely impoverished household, a past he hinted at to English journalist Jane de Mendelssohn (in an interview he gave, probably to disarm his interlocutor, in the nude). She had asked his opinion of the burning of warehouses by radical US activists. He thought more should burn: "If I wasn't a guitar player I probably would [burn down buildings]," he said. "I'd probably be in jail, 'cos I get very stubborn, like with the police. I used to get into arguments with them millions of times, they used to tell me to be quiet and

I just CAN'T be quiet, there's no reason to be, especially if I have something to say. So I'd probably wind up getting killed."[37] In his performances, when others saw and felt sex, Hendrix experienced a catharsis meant to dissipate simmering rage. "It's best to have violence on stage and watch it through TV than do it yourself," he told de Mendelssohn. "So many people would dig it, would really be turned on by it, and they don't bother their old ladies as much when they get home. They don't beat their old ladies up as much, because there's hardly anything left in them. We try to drain all the violence out of their system."

Countercultural chroniclers echoed white hippie leaders in often dismissing racial discord within the new polymorphous utopia. In fact, black artists found themselves still trapped within stereotypes even as they tried to dissipate them. "I want to see you down there looking like a bunch of *wild niggers!*" an inner-city black radical named Chaser advises his fellow ambassadors to the white liberal elite in journalist Tom Wolfe's 1970 account of interracial de-activism, *Radical Chic & Mau-Mauing the Flak Catchers.* (Wolfe's widely read satires skewered people across racial lines, but should be read with an awareness of his own white Yalie background.) Looking wild was a safe bet for African Americans whose usurpations of authority went deeper than most whites could accept. In his fantasies, Hendrix imagined himself dissolving: in a 1967 interview, he described his professional ambition as "to be a movie and caress the screen with my shining light." Yet he remained alive within cocoa skin, the audience's inability to really see him eventually suffocating him.[38]

Near the end of his life, Hendrix's performances became strangely lackluster. Realizing that his audience was having trouble identifying with his polymorphous vision of lust and satiation as an aspect of a larger spiritual evolution—a very science-fiction scenario, reflecting Hendrix's immersion in that genre—he retreated more and more into his Electric Lady Studios, where he could, as the historian Steve Waksman has observed, "enact his wildest fantasies of sound, and . . . work to exert the greatest amount of control."[39] His death came during a European tour, when, exhausted and behaving erratically, he overdosed on sleeping pills while in the company of a woman he barely knew. The man who had so nimbly moved through sexual stereotypes in hopes of rendering them obsolete had found the counterculture's unceasing craving for them too much to overcome.

JANIS JOPLIN:
TOO MUCH IS NOT ENOUGH

Like many countercultural sensualists, Hendrix found little need to separate the enjoyment of sex from the experience of taking drugs, blending references to the two in his lyrics and in interviews. Janis Joplin, in many ways his female counterpart, similarly mixed metaphors in a 1968 *Time* interview. "I'm on an audience trip," she said. "When I go onstage to sing, it's like the rush that people experience when they take heavy dope. I talk to the audience, look into their eyes. I need them and they need me. Sex is the closest I can come to explaining it, but it's more than sex. I get stoned from happiness. I want to do it until it isn't there anymore."[40] Joplin, naked and bead-strewn in a poster on her former tormenters' walls, despite her acne and unfashionably soft flesh, was "the first major girl sex symbol in rock."[41] But like the classic blues queens she emulated, Joplin demanded that her audience recognize the costs of the libertine stance she took. "Women is losers," she repeated over and over again in one song, exposing sexism but also centering her story on the experience of being sunk under its weight.

If Hendrix's allure was fed by a perceived miraculous mobility—that flicking tongue on the guitar strings—Joplin's was tied up in appetite. "She swoops around the stage like some kind of female bat about to get a kinky thrill from drinking your blood," wrote

one reporter in a profile titled "Lock Up Your Sons."[42] An image
of her with a Southern Comfort bottle, ready to take more swigs,
was central to her eroticism, which was as categorically transcendent as was Hendrix's, but aggressive and enveloping where his was
elusive and ego-dissolving. Famous for her keening, thick soprano,
which she pushed so hard that her vocal cords produced multinote
overtones, Joplin presented womanhood as a form of excess—a performance of the state of being "too much" that defies rules made
by men, but which also presents feminine desires as dangerously,
irresistibly insatiable. (Feminists, much later, would theorize such
perceived excess as the product of society's inability to process experience outside a male paradigm.) Deeply ambitious, Joplin chose
this path to both fit in and stand out within a male scene. She
played the bawd and she bawled her eyes out, though better known
for her wild cackle. That laugh was her native tongue—a sound too
loud to be ignored.

The critic Ellen Willis, whose crucial work brought explicit
gender politics into the arena of rock criticism, once described Joplin's performance as the quintessential "prefeminist" response to
the false (for women) freedoms of the counterculture. "The male-
dominated counterculture defined freedom for women almost ex-
clusively in sexual terms," Willis wrote in her essay on Joplin in *The
Rolling Stone Illustrated History of Rock & Roll.* "As a result, women
endowed the idea of sexual liberation with immense symbolic importance; it became charged with all the secret energy of an as yet
suppressed larger rebellion. Yet to express one's rebellion in that
limited way was a painfully literal form of submission. Whether or
not Janis understood that, her dual persona—lusty hedonist and
suffering victim—suggested that she felt it."[43]

Joplin was a messy person. Willis noted that seeing Joplin in
concert, wild locks flying, inspired her to stop ironing her own
curly hair. The star made herself an eyeful, consulting her hippie boutique–owning female intimates (some were lovers) to de-

vise a layered look featuring bangle bracelets, feathers, scarves, and capes—none of which prevented slips revealing her nipples or dimpled backside. Scholar Lisa Rhodes has suggested that journalists' focus on Joplin's clothing signified a double standard in music writing; in truth, mentions of clothing almost always figured into accounts of Hendrix and Jim Morrison. But there was more to take in with Joplin. "Her wild brown hair, touched with gold, hung in untamed waves down her back and over her lavender silk shirt and blue velvet vest," the journalist Michael Lydon wrote in a profile. "Gold sandals and bright blue stockings were on her feet, on her wrists dozens of bracelets in flaming acrylic colors; a blue and red kerchief was tied loosely into her immense fur hat; silver Indian bell rings were on every finger, and she was laughing, dancing, singing, her eyes, mouth, and body never still." Lydon witnessed Joplin playing eight-ball pool with a barfly in San Francisco's B & G club; the main personality trait he identified was what said barfly described as "pep."[44]

One person's "pep" is another's mania. Myra Friedman was Joplin's publicist and first chronicler, author of the tortured 1973 elegy-cum-biography *Buried Alive,* where she quotes a former psychiatric counselor who says of the singer, "She was . . . 'diffused'—spewing, splattering, spraying all over, without a center to hold." The older Friedman was trying to process Joplin's drug use and her bisexuality, which Friedman found distressing. But the shrink's reductive description actually applies fairly well to Joplin's onstage style, which was purposefully disordered, grating one minute and soulfully warm the next.[45]

Joplin early on proved able to absorb many different musical influences, from pristine folk singing to gutbucket blues belting. By the time she tried out for Big Brother, the noisy psychedelic blues band that would bring her the fame she craved, she'd developed a lot of vocal options. "She had about three different voices when we first knew her, see. When she sang rock and roll, that was one particular kind of voice," her bandmate Peter Albin told another early Joplin biographer, Deborah Landau. "When we lived over in Lagunitas together, one night I remember we were listening—I was up in my room with my old lady—and I heard this Joan Baez record singing songs I never heard before, and I went down and it was her! It was this Joan Baez voice, exactly like the record. And then she had a Bessie Smith voice . . . a deep growl, the kind of voice that she couldn't get on stage with a rock and roll band, because the volume was too loud . . . when we first started doing stuff with her she tried to use that voice and it just couldn't work. Times changed and the music grew louder than her voice. She had to gradually change herself."[46] To fit in with the boys of Big Brother, Joplin learned to bellow. "To try and get out in front of that heavy sound, the only thing that she could apparently think of to do was just to scream, which she did," another friend of Joplin's told Landau. "Just screamed, oh man. It was really hard to stay in the same room with her."[47]

But people did stay, because Joplin turned that scream into something fluid, and even joyful. "To sing the blues is a way of transcending pain by confronting it with dignity, but Janis wanted nothing less than to scream it out of existence," Willis wrote. Joplin did something else when she basically invented the singing style that came to signify hard rock. She screamed old notions of dignity out of existence—screamed away the social hierarchies that demanded women be deferential and self-contained, using not only noise but ribald humor and an embrace of ugliness that employed nuance to make it seductive, even beautiful.

Joplin's outrageousness had a paradoxical effect often experienced by women who fulfill the time-honored role of the good-time girl. Excessively female, she could no longer fit a proper definition of the feminine, and so she became "one of the guys." That phrase has been used by countless male associates of the singer, from the high school friends in Beaumont, Texas, who climbed the towering Rainbow Bridge with her, to Paul Rothchild, the producer of her final album, *Pearl*. "How can I say this without being sexist? Janis was one of the guys. When I was with her, there was no sense of she's female, I'm male," Rothchild told Joplin's sister and biographer, Laura, twenty years after the star's death. He recalled her taunting her session players in a recording studio parking lot with boasts like, "Who's got the biggest balls? I DO!" One way Joplin bonded with her high school buddies was to gossip with them about their classmates' sex lives, though she didn't have many stories of her own to share. In the free-love environment of her hippie days, she'd create those stories by frequently enjoying one-night stands with men who were, before and after, primarily friends.[48]

Her occasional partners included several members of Big Brother, but her main accommodation to them was adapting her singing style to their frenetic playing. Inspired by free jazz and acid trips, the group tended to play very quickly and very loud, "much faster than the punk rock that came later," in the words of guitarist Sam Andrew. When the band made room for Joplin, she felt an overwhelming need to fill the space. "See, there's this big hole in the song that's mine, and I've got to fill it with something," she told journalist Richard Goldstein. "It really tires me out." As part of Big Brother, Joplin stepped away from the big, open phrasing she'd borrowed from Bessie Smith and cultivated a kind of blues glossolalia, informed by gospel music and Tina Turner (whom she once declared "the best chick ever"), but also by that polymorphous feeling prevalent at San Francisco's psychedelic parties, where babbling made sense.[49]

Babbling—repeating words until they became run-on sentences, or squalling like Aretha Franklin, but with rawness instead of the gospel soul queen's clarity, or moving into a yowl and then pulling it back into a murmur, only to push it past its limit again—Joplin made the blues, a music about life's limits, into a body of water constantly overflowing its banks. This reflected her own version of Hendrix's manic depression, a performance of pain that was in part authentic and in part a playing out of false presumptions about the African Americans who'd invented the music she loved, not disconnected to the "coon"-style images of African Americans within the R. Crumb cartoon that famously graces the cover of Big Brother's first album, *Cheap Thrills*. (These were exactly the kinds of images that hippies thought their idealism rendered acceptable, but which in fact embodied the casual racism Jimi Hendrix regularly faced.) Jae Whitaker, a fellow musician who is black and was one of Joplin's early San Francisco lovers, remarked to Alice Echols that she felt Joplin used drugs in part "to put herself on the lower rung." Yet if she courted pain partly to fulfill her debt to heroines like Bessie Smith, whom she viewed on some level as courting trouble, she also recognized the importance of those forebears' humor. At her best Joplin slipped past the racially charged caricatures she courted, on the power of a confrontational smile.[50]

Even when communicating sorrow, Joplin retained that spirit of "pep," reveling in her vocal power and making it clear that constructing these blood-and-guts stories was fun for her. Her comparisons of singing to sex were blunt—she often used the word *orgasm*—and her remark to one reporter that she often asked her lovers, "Do I ball like I sing?" suggested that singing might have been the greater pleasure for her. One way in which Joplin was "prefeminist" was in her bold public image, which anticipated the early street protests of women's liberation groups like Willis's Redstockings, who protested the 1968 Miss America pageant by marching with placards emblazoned with phrases that could have been in blues songs ("If you want meat, go to the butcher") and a giant, big-breasted puppet that looked something like an R. Crumb drawing.[51]

Eventually, Joplin's pep became a trap very similar to the one Hendrix felt stifling him. After leaving Big Brother, she sought out more conventionally competent musicians in an attempt to match the soul-revue stylings of her idols Aretha Franklin and Otis Redding. Playing with musicians who could competently roll out blues and soul clichés instead of making a happy mess of them, Joplin still sang powerfully, and perhaps more legibly. But audiences now dwelled on the role she was playing instead of the ways in which she constantly exceeded it. Reviewers began referring to her approach as "brassy burlesque" and "showboating."[52] A disastrous performance in front of African American music-industry insiders in Memphis in 1969 made her wonder if she could ever perform the music she loved without slipping into parody. Her best songs on *Pearl*, unfinished at the time of her accidental heroin overdose, saw her exerting more control over her vocals, if not exactly toning them down. Perhaps she'd begun to question her own immersion in glorious excess, realizing the ways in which it stopped her from developing personally, even as it offered so much to her fans—especially the female ones.

JIM MORRISON:
LAMENT FOR THE DEATH OF MY COCK

While Janis Joplin was entertaining hippies with jokes about her private parts, Jim Morrison and the Doors were courting teenagers via gossipy rock publications like *Hullabaloo*. "See how well *you* match with the Doors!" read the introductory text to a 1967 quiz in that publication, peppered with questions about keyboardist Ray Manzarek's favorite seafood dish (snails, oysters) and bassist Robby Krieger's screen idol (Marlon Brando). Mixed in with the typical fan mag material, however, were a couple of seriously eyebrow-raising answers from the band's ultimate pinup. "Jim is attracted to ideas about . . . ANSWER: revolt against authority." And, "Jim's music is concerned with . . . ANSWER: chaos (that means disorder, kids!)."[53]

Serving an audience eager to experience and explore, the counterculture's musical avatars embodied irreverence for established gender roles and patterns of behavior. Yet they operated within mass media, where sex was often still sold in old-fashioned ways. Hendrix and Joplin inhabited and exploded roles that were both marginalized and fetishized within the counterculture. They were sex symbols who, sometimes consciously and sometimes in frustration, showed how the experience of embodying desire was empowering and alienating all at once. "There was a real vengeance there," Pete Townshend said of Hendrix's performances; the rival guitarist saw the black one's rage as a form of reclamation, but it was also an expression of Hendrix's awareness that in order to even begin to communicate eroticism in a new way, he had to still offer up the old ones, which were ultimately degrading. Joplin expressed this conundrum, too. In 1970, in the midst of the fame whirlwind that ultimately placed her in an LA hotel room to perish alone, an old friend at a show asked if she enjoyed what she was doing. "I wrote the part," she answered testily.[54]

For Jim Morrison, a former film student who'd been raised by a very traditionally masculine military father, sex symbolism was easier to access but no less complicated. Committed to wreaking havoc upon orthodoxies of desire, he couldn't help but fit within them. He wanted to be love's terrorist, but he looked, moved, and sounded like a teen idol. Wielding his penis as a weapon—to a brutal extent that sometimes led to real violence against individual women, and against the teen-girl audience that was always his most loyal fan base—he always realized how flabby that sword inevitably became. In 1970, not long before he would slink off to Paris to overindulge himself before dying, he wrote a poem:

> Lament for my cock
> Sore & crucified
> I seek to know you
> acquiring soulful wisdom
> You can open walls of

mystery

strip-show[55]

This work, both the apex and the denouement of Morrison's lifelong attempt to become a serious writer, continues for nine brutally self-deflating stanzas before ending with the phrase "I sacrifice my cock on the altar of silence." It encapsulates what makes the Doors singer such a compelling and ridiculous figure. An unstable firebrand whom the critic Richard Goldstein, who wrote about him frequently, called "a borderline personality," and an alcoholic who justified inebriated incoherence as a way of accessing old gods (he regularly invoked his Celtic forebears, as well as the Greek sacrificial figure Dionysus), Morrison also expressed, in moments of clarity, a pitch-black absurdity that dismantled the very myths he used to fuel his charisma. In his own memoir, Goldstein recalled asking Morrison if he'd planned his satyr image; his reply that it "just sort of happened . . . unconsciously" implied that he'd lost control of it. What he'd lost, most of all, was humor. Goldstein writes: "He shot me his famous half-smile. 'I'm beginning to think it's easier to scare people than to make them laugh.'"[56]

The counterculture granted rock stars, figures once considered nonsensically preliterate, a cultural authority never before thrust upon musical entertainers. They could be gurus, members of the literati, political activists, and experts on everything from race relations to the fine details of the sexual revolution. Yet they also had to be clowns. Talk show hosts treated them like comic relief; in one appearance by Joplin on Dick Cavett's program, her host and good friend ribbed her about singing so hard she pulled a muscle "somewhere around Maryland," and she shot back with a classic punch line, "It was a lot closer to home than that!" The rock press took them much more seriously, but used them as sounding boards for their own (often chemically) high theories and explicit fantasies. One writer for *Jazz & Pop* magazine chronicled his own orgasm while listening to the Doors' "Horse Latitudes," sweatily concluding, "I broke on through the other side."[57] Between poles of uncomfortably intimate hero worship and barely tolerant derision, the new stars tried to communicate.

Morrison, like Joplin a childhood devotee of *Mad* magazine, first hit upon his life's work of exploring and disrupting the phallic paradigm by creating junior high school cartoons of figures with outrageously distended penises and collages that showed Donald Duck penetrating his paramour Daisy. Though his posthumous reputation is as the counterculture's most pretentious wild man, who intensified the rock game with what the critic Greil Marcus describes as "a seriousness of intent that was thrilling on its own terms," during his life, Morrison always undercut his elaborate dramas with deliberate buffoonery. Apparently, this was his way in private, too; a college girlfriend recalled asking him why he didn't brush his hair, and Morrison replying, batting his eyelashes, "Because I want it to look like a bird's wing." Later that night, he threatened her with a kitchen knife. This was the borderline nature of his game; possibly suffering from bipolar disorder, Morrison couldn't control his drama or his jokes. But by making music at the needle point where a joke turns serious, or seriousness becomes so intense only manic laughter can relieve it, Morrison attempted to unravel the white masculine authority he found as oppressive as it was powerful.[58]

The counterculture was a great place to be a white male. The new permissiveness and pursuit of self-realization (social progress, hippie heroes argued) through sensual self-exploration allowed men to wear their hair long, dress like dandies, and lecherously pursue conquests. "The plumage and the punch in the last three years has remained in the province of men," columnist Howard Smith wrote in a 1968 paean to Joplin as the new foil for (who else but) Hendrix and Morrison. Throwing off their ties, countercultural men enjoyed a psychedelic version of what *Playboy* magnate Hugh

Hefner was selling less revolution-minded men. "[Underground] magazines and newspapers increasingly became littered with personal sex ads, caricatures of naked women, and jibes at women's liberation," writes musicologist Nadya Zimmerman. "Photographs of women showed their breasts, often without the rest of their bodies, portraying them as disembodied objects." In houses where these publications caused coffee tables to sag, women were expected to offer up their bodies for the cause of free love. White guy hippies liked boobs a lot, and they grabbed them often, too.[59]

This permissiveness was not only top-down; it was also tacitly homophobic. Although men like Hendrix were known to indulge in group sex with multiple women and trade partners with male bandmates as a form of homosocial bonding, aggressive heterosexuality obscured most traces of physical love among the scene's male peacocks. Though a nascent movement burst forth in the riots at the Stonewall bar in New York in 1969, and produced small hippie collectives like San Francisco's Cockettes, the dominant attitude toward queer sexuality within the counterculture was suspicion: some progressives suspected gay liberation was a conservative conspiracy meant to disrupt their communities.[60]

Hippies who felt they might be gay often suppressed their longings. "Openly gay writers were expected to be bitchy, fucked-up, or geniuses, and I was none of those things," writes Goldstein, who would later marry a longtime male partner after first wedding and divorcing a woman. "Instead I went with the orthodoxy of the time and told myself that everyone was basically bisexual."[61] Bisexuality was mostly considered a hobby, though; Joplin was widely viewed as a man-loving chick who just ran through women as a stopgap, despite the fact that her longest relationships were with female companions like Jae Whitaker and Peggy Caserta. (Joplin herself was ambivalent on this subject; her biographer Alice Echols calls her "a throwback to an earlier bohemian model of sexual ambiguity.")[62] It would have been even more difficult for Morrison to clearly articulate an erotic connection to men, and though rumors have surfaced that he had some undergraduate same-sex encounters, his main romantic and sexual pursuits involved women.

Yet as a performer, Morrison trod the same perverse, darkly comical, proto-queer ground his New York counterpart Lou Reed was exploring with the Velvet Underground in New York, lending credence to desire in ways that challenged the straight paradigm. The echo of the line he drunkenly hurled at Hendrix—"I want to suck your cock!"—resonates throughout his life and work.

"Grab your fucking friend and love him!" Morrison shouted before allegedly exposing his penis at Miami's Dinner Key Auditorium on March 1, 1969, not the first but the most consequential occasion of him tussling with police onstage. Morrison harbored a lifelong animosity toward police, and the homophobia of the state was built into the censure he received. Photographs of him being arrested and dragged from the stage evoke those of the men hustled into paddy wagons outside gay bars across America during the same time period. His ritualistic acts of self-love and self-exposure went beyond Mick Jagger's preening or even Hendrix's gyrations, because they weren't clearly directed or ultimately beautiful. If the hippie ideal of sex elevated "the worship that it is to fuck" without fully acknowledging the power relations defining such encounters, Morrison focused on the interruptions, the limitations, and the violence that compromised the dream of free love. Morrison would stand stock-still onstage for long stretches of his performance, or collapse so quickly some thought he was having a seizure. "[The Doors] don't extend themselves to please an audience in the usual sugary, entertainer way," declared a writer for *Freakout*. "That's Jim Morrison—mysterious, unreachable."[63]

For Morrison, this led to a long struggle with an image that he initially cultivated—he famously asked Hollywood stylist Jay Sebring to make his curls look like those of Alexander the Great— but which he soon rubbed aggressively against. In their first year playing Hollywood clubs, the Doors employed an amateur army of pubescent girls to pack their shows. Morrison's treatment of those girls was, from the beginning, highly questionable. Leading band courtesan Pamela Des Barres had an interlude with Morrison; later, during his show, he reached out and slapped her in the face while shouting, "Get it on!" Her diary entry said she found this abusive behavior fascinating and framed it as the realization of an animal spirit most people repressed. "How perfectly he has reached his insanity! Can insanity be perfect I wonder? He took a full bottle of beer and threw it into [fellow groupie] Miss Lucy's face tonight, and when she screamed, 'That wasn't very nice!' he looked up painfully and said, 'I know.'" For Des Barres, Morrison's brutality revealed a truth about sexual freedom: "How wonderful to do what your body tells you to do." What he did to others' bodies, however, wasn't always so liberating.[64]

Morrison's love-hate relationship with his teenage fans (groupies or not) reflected a deep ambivalence about his own erotic power. It manifested in abuse rooted in his mental instability and misogynistic tendencies, and possibly his resentment about having to perform heterosexual heroics when his own desires ran across a wider spectrum. But his overdetermined boorishness, coupled with unabashed displays of deep vulnerability, also unraveled conventional masculinity in powerful ways. "Over and over, as he performed these songs in concert, Morrison at the dramatic high points cupped his hands over his genitals," novelist Bernard Wolfe wrote in *Esquire*. "The gesture was as ambiguous as the words: was he featuring these organs in carnalizing revelry or protecting them for one last moment from the imminent and urgently solicited smash-up?"[65]

His stance confused people. Many rhapsodized about his allure. "On his face, there was the look of suffering of someone who knows he is too beautiful to ever enjoy true love," Al Aronowitz wrote in the *New York Times*. Other accounts revealed the prejudices of the time: Jerry Hopkins, who would befriend Morrison and write the most successful of his biographies, claimed in *Rolling Stone* that "Jim Morrison looks as if he were . . . made up on the phone by two fags." Morrison also earned comparisons to "the tinsel heat of a hooker," "the bumps and grinds of a burlesque dancer," and (from San Francisco eminence Ralph J. Gleason) Shirley Temple. "The only catharsis I received came from paroxysms of uncontrollable laughter," allowed Marxist jazz writer Frank Kofsky. "The result of watching Jim Morrison's ludicrous antics onstage." *Saturday Review*'s Ellen Sander came up with perhaps the pithiest put-down of Morrison's pretensions: she labeled him "Mickey Mouse de Sade."[66]

Morrison was acutely aware of this mixed reception, and like Hendrix, if not Joplin, expressed frustration about the failure of critics and fans to comprehend the intellectual framework behind his music. He spoke of reading psychoanalyst Melanie Klein and social philosopher Norman O. Brown, whose book *Love's Body* promoted a notion of "body mysticism" that highly influenced the singer's more portentous ideas of ritualistic self-sacrifice within live rock. Like many of his peers (including Joplin and Hendrix), Morrison was also smitten with the pessimistic vision of the counterculture presented in *Easy Rider,* Dennis Hopper's film about two motorcycle-riding bohemians who set out to explore "straight" America and are ultimately murdered by a gang of Southern good old boys. The script for Morrison's own short film *HWY* predated Hopper's hit by two years, but resembled it in many ways; the crucial difference was that in *HWY,* murderous masculinity inhabited the soul of Morrison's protagonist himself, who was a serial killer.

The sense of failure within Morrison's work—of self-defeat at the hand of the internal father, who is everywhere, despite the Oedipal murder enacted in the Doors' most notorious set piece, "The End"—is present from the beginning, rooted in his psychological issues and bookish preoccupations. It's difficult to know how in control this alcoholic, who may never have been sober for a show, was of his actions or words onstage. Yet Morrison's determination to continually reenact the moment when counterculture dreams collide with the hand of the law—the literal law, and those patriarchal values embedded within would-be revolutionaries' psyches—made the Doors, even at their most laughable, truly oppositional. Morrison's antagonistic stance was all the more affected because it was directed at himself: a military son, a heterosexual ideal, a man who would slap a woman and then express sorrow at the act. Was he laughing inside? At whom?

The thread that ran through Morrison's life that best illustrates his position as both an archetype and an enemy of the male-defined law was his battle with the police over obscenity. Other rock stars risked being shut down—Hendrix for his lascivious movements, Joplin for curse words she threw out carelessly—but few made the moment of potential arrest the climax of the show. Once he'd written "The End," an opus whose whole meaning rested in the forbidden utterance "Mother, I want to fuck you," Morrison guaranteed that anywhere his band went, the police would be nearby. This was a literary move on his part. As a fan of the Beats and other writers whose books had been banned, Morrison knew that openly courting censorship would elevate his transgressions and make his lyrics part of a lineage he valued. But whenever Morrison was led from the stage in handcuffs or the sound was shut down on the Doors, the effect was more visceral. That the voice silenced was a deep baritone, and the body part hidden, a penis, created an ouroborous effect: this was masculinity devouring itself.

Morrison's self-imposed mandate in such moments was to not seem like a martyr. He relished the absurdity of his position. "It's pretty playful, really. We have fun, the kids have fun, the cops have fun. It's kind of a weird triangle," he told *Rolling Stone* a few months after the Miami incident, which led to his conviction on charges of indecent exposure and profanity. He elaborated: "You see cops today, walking around with their guns and uniforms and the cop is setting himself up like the toughest man on the block, and everyone's curious about exactly what would happen if you challenged him." Morrison was not a political activist, but he clearly saw the disruptions he staged in concert as an attempt to disrupt a legally defined balance of power framed within a conversation about obscenity. "Why don't we have a little revolution here?" he uttered before reaching into his pants in Miami. Morrison recognized that it was just a little revolution—just a momentary crack in the continuum of language, which he could make with his body, but which the subsequent containment of his body in handcuffs would erase.[67]

It was a failed revolution. By most accounts, and certainly all the official reports, the audience in Miami was more disgusted by Morrison's slurred words and gestures than they were incensed. The star's previous encounters with the legal system had all ended relatively calmly, but this trial dragged on and elicited little public sympathy. Morrison himself seemed to have realized that the sloppiness of his action rendered it ineffective, and perhaps that it was overblown. In a thoughtful interview a year after the event, he spoke of the privileged position that made him not much of an outlaw at all. A fan of and borrower from the blues, Morrison admitted that the African American world from which much of his source material originated had far worse problems as a criminalized community than he ever would: "My eyes have been opened up a bit. There were guys down there [in the courthouse], black guys, that would go on each day before I went on. It took about five minutes and they would get twenty or twenty-five years in jail."[68]

The Miami incident isn't generally remembered as a closing bell on the 1960s; that dubious honor goes to the deaths of Hendrix, Joplin, and Morrison, or to Altamont, the Northern California festival where a Hells Angels member killed an African American concertgoer as the Rolling Stones played. Yet Morrison's sacrifice of his cock on the altar of silence did strike like a final blow, to both the idealism that imagined erotic freedom as a magic force erasing inequity and the implicit body-centered critiques of that simplistic thinking that the era's "sexiest" rock stars carried out. Next would come a wave of explicitly sexual mass media that left hippies in the dust of their body paint, and the advent of identity-centered politics that would bring fully to the surface the issues Hendrix, Joplin, and Morrison raised in their music. It was the 1970s, the age of porn, heavy metal, and disco, and the sound of sex rang everywhere.

6

HARD AND SOFT REALITIES

LONDON, LOS ANGELES,
NEW YORK, 1971–1979

In 1971, after an acoustically flavored performance in a former air raid shelter in Haverstock Hill, London, twenty-four-year-old singer-songwriter David Bowie encountered America. America came to him in the form of a threesome: Cherry Vanilla, a rock groupie who liked to flash her tits; Leee Black Childers, an underground photographer with Magic Marker in his hair; and Wayne County, one of New York's leading drag queens. They'd hoped Bow-

ie's rumored freakiness would match their own, but were not im-
pressed. "We just looked over at him and said, 'Look at that folky
old hippie!'" County later recalled.[1]

Vanilla, Childers, and County were denizens of the Factory, the
New York art studio and decadence wormhole where high society,
commercial art, and the low life came together under the cool gaze
of pop art pioneer Andy Warhol. They were in town to perform a
play called *Pork* that involved the cast exchanging obscenities on
white prop telephones. "It really was all very wild, vicious cheap,
perverted, boring, all those Warholian things," Bowie's then-wife
and chief image strategist, Angie, wrote in her memoir.[2] Bowie had
already visited the Factory once and begun aligning himself with
its house band, the Velvet Underground, whom Jim Morrison had
also checked out a few years earlier. The Lizard King was more
troubled than intrigued by the bondage and street prostitution
scenarios favored by songwriter Lou Reed. Bowie was open to what
Morrison found depraved, striving to move beyond the hippie longing for an Eden in which men and women still assumed "natural"
roles. He needed what drag and kinky sex practices offered: theater
and in-your-face individualism.

"We all had blue and multicolored hair; we were wearing big
blond wigs and huge platform boots and purple stockings," County
remembered. "And he was wearing those floppy hats and the long,
stringy hair, and he took one look at us and you could see that this
was what he wanted to do."[3] Within three years, Bowie was living in
America, transformed into Ziggy Stardust, a bisexual space alien
who blended Little Richard's whoop-it-up with the Velvets' hard-
edged sensibility. He wallowed in futurism. "What frightens me . . .
is that people are holding on to a century that is fast dying," he told
an interviewer. "That includes a lot of young people as well."[4]

Bowie's jeremiad captured a prevalent mood: the counterculture and its sexual revolution had hit a barricade of old ideas
that could not be cleared away by peace-and-love fantasy. Women

and homosexuals were in open rebellion, forming consciousness-raising groups and marching in the streets. At the other end politically, a "silent majority" identified and mobilized by President Richard Nixon embraced more traditional values. Caught in the middle were Vietnam veterans radicalized by the war but distressed by a moral collapse that, some felt, was embodied by women who had defied, sexually betrayed, or simply become unrecognizable to them.[5]

Unsettled and sometimes disappointed, people turned inward, intimate. They explored the new self-help psychology surfacing from the dust of drug-fueled psychological explorations, communal cults, and health fads. Many turned away from any thought of a vast common ground and focused on building resplendent identities that distinguished them within subcultures. The vision of a united hippie front "half a million strong," as the folk singer turned auteur Joni Mitchell had sung about Woodstock, was being replaced by these smaller insurgencies. "It's a gay Woodstock!" a participant in New York's first gay pride march declared, but the marchers only managed to go five blocks. The revolution, as the political soul man Gil Scott-Heron sang in 1971, would not be televised. Change would come from special-interest groups or evolve in private, through community, consumerism, and leisure.[6]

One private activity that surged in public visibility was pornography. Soft-core publications like *Playboy* and underground stag films had existed for decades within homes or clubs, and burlesque had taken up residence in red-light districts since the days of Little Egypt. But new decisions changed what was permissible. A presidential commission found (to Nixon's horror) that pornography had no measurable detrimental effects on society. The definition of "hard core" by the Supreme Court established a separate sphere for explicit content, exemplified by the Triple-XXX theaters that surfaced in every major city. Porn producers, emboldened by nudity-splashed European art films, created narratives instead of stags' plotless, soundless "beaver" loops. By 1972, when *Deep Throat* became a national phenomenon, porn chic drew both elites and average Americans. The details of sex became much more visible, audible—and enticing. As one scholar writes, "When the pursuit of quality sex, of proper orgasms, began to loom as a large part of the carnal story, so hard-core arrived, speaking not just of sex and fucking, but of better sex."[7]

It was this fractured, changing America that David Bowie entered during the 1970s. His music and performances touched all the era's bases: he questioned gender roles, explored sexual reenactments onstage, and experimented with the different forms—hard rock, glam rock, and disco—that most directly engaged with this nascent sexual openness. A traveler in a brave new world, Bowie soaked it all up.

QUEENS OF THE SUNSET STRIP

By 1972, as David Bowie and his band the Spiders from Mars spent a working holiday at the Beverly Hills Hotel, teenage energy permeated the night close by on Los Angeles's Sunset Strip. "Kids who can't be more than twelve years old, boys with lipstick smeared on their faces, girls with all those kitschy, klutzy shoes, hot pants, and feathers," rock scribe and trend spotter Lisa Robinson wrote about the scene on the Strip that year. "Like some kind of fungus, it's slowly creeping across the country, but it's at its best in LA. I'm talking about *sleeeeeeze.*"[8] Bowie and crew partied nightly alongside other satin-clad purveyors of arena rock in clubs like Rodney Bingenheimer's English Disco.

One evening, they connected with two star groupies. These high school burnouts had turned scene queens by being utterly forward and adopting personae suiting their illegal ID–worthy names: Sable Starr and Lori Lightning. Both made it clear that Bowie was their conquest, and a competition ensued. He had eyes for Lori, whose real last name is Mattix. The next time he was in town, Bowie took her to his hotel bungalow, where he donned a Japanese kimono, a hallucinogenic version of the bathrobe *Playboy* publisher Hugh Hefner famously wore. He had Mattix wash him in the tub. The evening proceeded—according to Mattix, anyway—as one might expect.

Mattix recalls this night as a beautiful and happy one, not least because she'd bested her rival. "Two hours later, I went to check on Sable. She was all fucked up in the living room, walking around, fogging up the windows and writing, *I WANT TO FUCK DAVID.*" Others recall Mattix's initial encounters with Mr. Stardust differently. Another teen then, Nancy McCrado, later told Bowie's biographer Paul Trynka that Starr and another teenage girl initially broke into Mick Ronson's room and were rejected by the focused guitarist, seeking solace with Bowie later. Lori joined them at that point. "David was tired, but eventually proved more obliging than his lieutenant," Trynka writes.

Both accounts likely contain some truth: adult male rockers regularly had relations with underage girls in this particularly depraved phase of the rock and roll lifestyle. Those girls often relentlessly pursued the men, and displayed their sexual allure as a source of power, yet doing so ultimately disempowered them—for example, when they were passed to another in the band or on the road crew. Among rockers, this was what you did in the 1970s: ask for action, and ye shall receive.[9]

When Bowie died in 2016, the wave of reverential remembrances was broken by assertions that his encounter with Mattix made him a statutory rapist. Led Zeppelin guitarist Jimmy Page was intimate with Mattix from 1972 to 1974; her mother gave him permission to pursue that relationship. This didn't prevent Page from keeping Mattix hidden in his room at the Sunset Strip rock hotel the Hyatt House (fondly known as the "Riot House") on nights he went carousing. Mattix's "romantic" imprisonment, which she accepted as a protective measure, at least spared her public humiliation, unlike the Hyatt House groupie who on one night, according to a *Time* magazine article on the hotel, "was propped up in the corner of an elevator and rode up and down for 90 minutes before her presence was reported."[10]

"Attracted by the concentrated power of the performing artist, the groupie wants to get as close as possible, into the eye of the hurricane, and she doesn't mind getting a bit storm-tossed along the way," read a definition of "groupie" in the hard rock–oriented teen magazine *Circus* in June 1974.[11] The highly visible presence of groupies in a milieu where women rarely found a lead role is a major reason feminists and conservatives alike developed a view of hard rock in particular as irredeemably misogynist. More recently, some female memoirists, journalists, and scholars have reclaimed the groupie role as strategically empowering. Academic Lisa Rhodes concluded after interviewing numerous groupies that they typically had few regrets about their time on the rock scene. "The groupies were not stereotypes, they were not pornographic tropes, they were not just mindless starfuckers," Rhodes writes.[12]

The figure of the groupie remains a vector for anxiety about music's ability to both dissolve protective rules of behavior and reinforce a paradigm that limits women's freedom. Groupie tales are sometimes celebrated as a sign of more open times, before the clampdown of feminist-driven identity politics in the 1980s. (Though groupies still operate in every popular music milieu, their presence always seems to signify the past, whether idealized or frightening "dark ages.") Horror stories—most famously, the Led Zeppelin "shark incident," in which members of Led Zeppelin's road crew allegedly molested a woman using a fish they'd caught from the window of Seattle's Edgewater hotel—vie with adventure tales like the ones Pamela Des Barres recounts in her 1987 bestseller *I'm with the Band: Confessions of a Groupie*, which rehabilitated the term for a "post-feminist" generation. Discussions always turn on the issue of individual agency, the notion that one or the other party possesses the power of choice. In some accounts, male musicians are cast as predators; in others, female groupies are extolled as autodidact liberationists.

Too much stress on individual agency within hard rock's sexual milieu obscures the larger forces that affected libertine attitudes. "Bands are power," groupie Sweet Connie told one of her conquests, Michael Bruce of the Alice Cooper band. Within the 1970s rock scene, sex was a force that became systematized, and all had to find their place within that system. "It's like I'm just a prostitute, right, but if I'm okay, maybe they'll give me a Lincoln and make me a pimp," David Johansen of glam-punk pioneers the New York Dolls said of auditioning for record labels, the entry into the hard rock hierarchy. With music becoming a major industry, its makers felt they were doing a job, and since the content sold was eroticized, it felt like sex work. This sense of obligation, even entrapment, extended to the touring life lasciviously chronicled by the rock press.[13]

The slippage between rock as pleasure and as labor connected its sex scenes to other realms: hard-core pornography, the gay nightlife of the bathhouse and the hookers' pier, suburban swingers' culture, and body-centered therapy styles like those illustrated in the bedside coffee table book *The Joy of Sex*. Now mostly remembered as chaotic—either liberating or criminal—these spheres were in fact systems, enabled by capitalism and maintained because they offered order as the boundaries of eroticism seemed to be irrevocably changing.

Many of the youngest participants in the Sunset Strip scene were from homes made newly unstable by changes in the family structure. In California in 1970, governor Ronald Reagan signed a "no fault" divorce law that created what one historian describes as a "divorce deluge." Sunset Strip *sleeeeeeze* chronicler Robinson assumed the tarted-up kids she found there were children of moth-

ers trying to negotiate the newly expanded terrain of single parenthood. "They were probably better off before they left Mommy,
except that Mommy herself came to Hollywood to be a STAR.
After all, Mommy is perhaps only 33 (unless those girls aren't really 14) and she's schlepping drinks in some cocktail bar on Hollywood Boulevard all day in a pair of high heeled wedges," Robinson
wrote.[14]

THE SOUND OF SOMEONE COMING

One avenue leading to fame for the hungry young women of 1970s
Hollywood was hard-core pornography. Until the 1970s, few
feature-length porn films existed. Most had vaguely instructional
titles like *Africanus Sexualis* and *Man & Wife* and depicted "demon-
strations" interrupted by professorial commentary. *Deep Throat*
changed that, though cheaply made by people with little film experience. It possessed a coherent story line, a breakout star in perky
Linda Lovelace, and sound. In New York, celebrities and ordinary
folk mingled in the lobby before watching Lovelace discover pleasure through oral sex. They marveled at sights they'd never previously seen while eating popcorn.

   Deep Throat made porn ordinary. Lovelace became a celebrity,
securing a book contract and a magazine column and appearing
on television talk shows. Although later she would allege that she
was being severely abused by her husband and manager, Chuck
Traynor, at the time she seemed as wholesome as any starlet.
Equally rosy Marilyn Chambers had actually been an Ivory soap
girl before making 1972's *Behind the Green Door*. Constance Money,
star of the witty romp *The Opening of Misty Beethoven,* resembled a so-
rority girl, while at thirty-six, Georgina Spelvin in *The Devil in Miss
Jones* was every would-be swinger's wife gone wild. Moustachioed
Harry Reems and teen-idol type Jamie Gillis also seemed like ordinary folk. They possessed less glamour than the average Holly-

wood actor, and the stories structured around their sex scenes were amusingly accessible. No matter how much it might be still seen as a "pariah," the new porn was no longer exactly an outsider art form—it was, as its leading theorist, Linda Williams, has noted, a genre among other film genres.[15]

The rise of hard core in the 1970s coincided with a surge of sexual explicitness in virtually every other popular art form, continuing to the end of the decade. The titillating television comedy came into vogue. Art films like *Last Tango in Paris* and *Midnight Cowboy*, the first X-rated film to win an Oscar, entered the canon. Grade schoolers passed around grubby copies of books like *Jaws* (the "wet panties" scene!) and Jacqueline Susann's many bestsellers with the pages of the sexy passages earmarked. And sex sounds moved up front in music, too, years before disco: Barry White in soul, one-hit wonders the Jimmy Castor Bunch ("Troglodyte") and the Chaka-chas ("Jungle Fever") in funk, orgasmic Deep Purple and the sex gods Led Zeppelin in hard rock.

Sound was a key element that made the new porn different, signifying sex itself. Stag films, the cheap loops of women undressing or people engaging in coitus that circulated privately in earlier eras, were silent or added a tacky soundtrack. Narrative porn, aspiring to be like "straight" cinema, included dialogue, but the sex scenes used overdubs of the actors moaning and crying out, to enhance the erotic experience. Williams suggests that in this way hard-core pornos resemble musicals: the sensual impact of a song bursting through a story line. She notes that the sounds of pleasure and the sounds of music have similar rhythmic and melodic features. That *Deep Throat* fetishized the bodily region also crucial for singers seems less coincidental if you consider that sexual pleasure is also expressed through the voice.[16]

Before porn became audible, music was the only place where erotic noises regularly surfaced. They ran through the blues into doo-wop, within Elvis's stutter and the Beatles' squeals, echoed by

their own teenage fans. But the stakes became higher once Linda
Lovelace unleashed her moan. That assertion of sexual authenticity had to be answered. By mid-decade heavy breathing left its
steamy imprint upon virtually every corner of pop. Significantly,
however, the first voice to be deeply associated with a newly pornographic musical eroticism came from hard rock. It belonged to
Robert Plant, the golden god of LA's Riot House, one of the most
elusive prizes on the *sleeeeeeze* scene.

With his signature curly mane, dimpled chin, and penchant
for exposing his slender chest in cutaway jackets, Robert Plant was
one half of '70s hard rock's most notorious sex-god duo, the Apol-
lonian hero to guitarist Jimmy Page's Dionysian/Satanic mage.
Page's onstage histrionics suggested a mastery that, rumor had it,
he deployed with whips and chains in the bedroom. But if Page set
Led Zeppelin's erotic scenes, Plant provided the ejaculatory money
shots; his signature moans and yelps, often strung together in
improvised arcs that lasted for minutes at a time, did the pornographic work of authenticating his own arousal. "The raunchiness
is in everybody; that below-the-belt surge that everybody gets at
some time or another," he told a journalist.[17]

Indeed, Led Zeppelin may be the band most associated by rock
writers with not just arousal but orgasm. "Robert Plant gives me
orgasms," Donna Gaines recalls telling boyfriends who didn't understand her dedication to the group when they first toured the
United States. Des Barres, who dated Jimmy Page on and off, writes:
"When you saw Led Zeppelin play, it was all over but the orgasm."
Brad Tolinski, like Gaines a suburban teen whose life was turned
around by Zep's many US tours, employs cinematic terms. "'Dazed
and Confused' [the centerpiece of the group's live performances]
turned the sexual act into something very Cecil B. DeMille: orgasm
as mystical experience. It sounded super dangerous. A Led Zeppelin orgasm wasn't pulling a girl's pants down in some alley." When
the musicologist Susan Fast interviewed female fans for her 2001

book on the band, the word came up over and over. "I swear that man has a hard-on at every concert," one fan gushes. "Orgasmic."[18]

Plant readily admits that he borrowed his jouissance from the blues. He also insists that his voice had certain insurmountable limits that made actually imitating artists like Muddy Waters impossible. Led Zeppelin's thefts were particularly blatant, and the group has been sued several times for plagiarism. Yet the very strictures Plant acknowledges made Led Zeppelin original and tightened up the erotic tension they generated. Unlike many white musicians, he and his bandmates foregrounded differences of race rather than trying to overcome them. They decorated their heavy blues with pastoral flourishes borrowed from Romantic poetry and Celtic myth. Plant, most of all, sang in a keening tenor instead of the deeper ranges where Mick Jagger and Jim Morrison dwelled. He didn't sound like a smooth soul crooner or a growling bluesman. Violating, violated whiteness made Led Zeppelin stand apart in ways that other blues-based rock bands rarely did. The erotic effect this distancing had on its nearly all-white fan base was profound: its catharsis both exposed and blew apart the discomfort many still felt toward overt black sexuality while tapping into the release that the sexually forthright blues lineage provided.

Robert Plant did, arguably, sometimes sound like a black man—or a black woman, Tina Turner, for example, as channeled by a white one, specifically Janis Joplin. In early reviews of Led Zeppelin, Joplin was the most often cited vocal influence. Even Plant's fashion choices, his flowing curly locks, his scarves and bangles, were extremely Joplinesque. Plant's lithe quality, his determination from the start to master the dynamics of the soft push as well as the hard thrust, mitigated the band's force and allowed women fans a way into Led Zeppelin's music. It also reflected Joplin's gender-bending: if she sometimes tipped into masculine excess, he risked the feminine kind.[19] Joplin, of course, loved to imitate the sound of orgasm, and this may be the most significant vocal trick

Plant learned from her. The moans about two minutes into "Dazed and Confused" are gentle, but soon grow more aggressive, intermingling with Page's distorted guitar effects. While Joplin would decenter the sound of her already loose bands with her libidinal cries, Plant remained locked in with his. The last thirty seconds of "Dazed and Confused" pound to a climax that's almost cartoonishly linear.

Plant understood what he was doing: "I was playing into character with the songs."[20] Focusing on the rhythmic aspects of the wordless passages in Led Zeppelin songs, groaning in sync with the players surrounding him, Plant engaged pleasure in ways that resembled porn performance. What happened in the musical margins was central, in that it disrupted the stories Led Zeppelin's songs told, via moments of driven release. This is what sex scenes do in porn. Like a porn star, Plant was playing a role, but also genuinely feeling its effects; there wasn't a sense that he could stop once he was swept up in a song. Everyone in the clubs and, eventually, the arenas where Led Zeppelin played believed that what was happening onstage was real. Though not visibly "jizzing," as male porn stars did, Plant made sounds that went beyond conventional musicality, and he did so not as a novelty, but as the core of his vocal performance. Another way Robert Plant blended the feminine into his machismo was this repetition; every night onstage, he came multiple times.

Just as straight men saw other men's erect penises for the first time in hard-core films, so Led Zeppelin's white male rock fans heard a new expressiveness about sex emerging from an ideal version of themselves. The loose structures and commitment to noise that hard rock borrowed from psychedelia made room for a capaciousness that singles-oriented rock and roll artists like Elvis, or even the pre-1970s Rolling Stones or Beatles, rarely accessed. In that space, a singer like Plant could roll around, get hard, go soft, come back, and take his time blowing his wad.

But this new heavy rock was not freeform; like porn itself, it was programmatic. Jimmy Page, a hardworking professional who'd reached a plateau with his previous band, the Yardbirds, carefully assembled Led Zeppelin as a commercial enterprise. Undeniably creative, Led Zeppelin was also functional; the band's practice of "rewriting" tried-and-true blues songs further illustrated how much Page wanted this band to hit its mark. Reviewing the first Led Zeppelin album in *Rolling Stone,* John Mendelsohn found it formulaic. (He also called Robert Plant "prissy.")[21] That formula was just what American rock audiences craved—it ordered the drives and emotions the sexual revolution had unleashed. By the time the second album's moan-infused "Whole Lotta Love" had hit the Top 5, 21,000 people had showed up to see them in a 10,000-capacity venue in New York, and Mendelsohn was eating his words. "Hey man! I take it all back!" he wrote, sarcastic but resigned. "You've got to admit that the Zeppelin has their distinctive and enchanting formula down stone-cold, man." This band wasn't going away.

THE GROUPIE SYSTEM

Offstage, Led Zeppelin defined the top tier in the groupie system. Page, Plant, and Bonham represented a more accessible fast-life ideal than glam rockers like Bowie, whose theatrical freakishness never grabbed the heartland. A new way of talking about rock was brewing in the media and among fans, and the blatant but contained sexuality of Led Zeppelin fit it perfectly. Meanwhile, back on the Sunset Strip, groupie hierarchies were hardening. Des Barres noticed a change from the free-love vibe she'd enjoyed in her early days, as the mood of camaraderie dissipated. She and Sable Starr especially tousled, with Starr once screaming, "Give it up, you old bag!" in her direction at a party for Elton John. Des Barres was then twenty-five.[22]

Such rude rejoinders made sense in a rock scene that had aban-

doned the hippie pretense of sex as the foundation of loving community for a more individualistic, hedonistic, and adolescent erotic
vocabulary. For some, this felt freeing—guitarist Kid Congo Powers fondly recalled Rodney's English Disco as the place where he,
as a gay teen, could safely explore: "The older men were trying to
get girls, while the younger boys were just there to be gay, fashionable and dancing around music and musicians and excitement. The
girls were all necking with each other. I was in heaven. I had found
a home."[23] Others were horribly betrayed. Kim Fowley, the manager
of the all-female teenage band the Runaways, allegedly assaulted at
least two women connected to the group, including Runaways bass
player Jackie Fox. He committed these acts at parties, in front of
many bystanders. "We all watched. We were all high," one member
of the scene later remembered. "It's that haze and not knowing what
to do. It was all about drugs, rock and roll, and sex back then."[24]

Sex, drugs, and rock and roll were expected to solve problems in
the 1970s, not create them. Anyone thinking otherwise was a kill-
joy. This attitude could be seen all over the rock press, increasingly
full of blatant sex jokes and images of seminaked women . . . and
men. Rock bands loved (or were persuaded by their management) to
pose shirtless, and bottomless, too, in ads that lent a pornographic
aura to music magazines. Grand Funk Railroad, the catchy Michigan blues-rock outfit whose massive 1973 single "We're an American Band" paid lyrical tribute to hotel-crashing groupies, showed
off hairy chests in several ad campaigns and, surrounded by tiny
flags, in the gatefold photo of the album named after their biggest
hit. Other bands who bared flesh included Southern rockers the
Allman Brothers, David Bowie's pal Iggy Pop, and jokers Dr. Hook,
who posed in the low-rent porno magazine *Zipper*. Alice Cooper
took his nudie session to another level, wrapping a boa constrictor
around his private parts.[25]

While some images still evoked pastoral hippiedom (the Allman Brothers frolicked in a picturesque river), often these naked

efforts came off as more comical than alluring—the sex joke as a marketable commodity. Ads like the one for Rolling Stones bassist Bill Wyman's solo debut *Monkey Grip,* which showed a manicured female hand firmly stimulating a banana, or the one celebrating the name of the progressive rock band Wishbone Ash by showing a vagina-shaped chicken bone being licked by a feminine tongue, fit in not only in music magazines but in the pornographic ones—not just *Playboy,* but *Penthouse* and *Screw*—where rock bands were beginning to seek new audiences. Album cover artists also aimed for raunch, with the 1972 illustration for the forgotten boogie band Mom's Apple Pie taking the pastry for the most lurid. Referencing Grant Wood's classic painting of tight-lipped farmers *American Gothic,* Nick Caruso's illustration shows a buttoned-up country maid licking her lips and holding a pie with a slice removed, dripping, looking just like a wet vagina.

Editors and writers at music magazines happily engaged in the increasingly pornographic repartee. San Francisco's underground newspapers had highlighted the Rabelaisian work of cartoonists like R. Crumb, whose images of massively endowed women had also appealed to Janis Joplin. Now, cartoons were more in league with fart jokes than fantasias—direct and often confrontational. *Creem,* the Detroit magazine that best captured the emerging 1970s zeitgeist, often used photographs to make crude asides: an image of Raquel Welch, half-clothed, with a caption about "hot tortillas"; a topless shot of a female J. Geils Band fan, a backstage pass affixed to her nipple. *Creem* had several female editors, and its own promotional campaigns—like the "CREEM Mate of the Month" centerfolds who were usually pudgy comics or hirsute rockers instead of airbrushed girls-next-door—poked fun at the ubiquity of porn. When *Deep Throat* went nationwide, the publication's star critic Lester Bangs wrote a highly critical review of the film, finding its imagery dull and belabored: "If *porn*'s an effort for Chrissake, then sex as a national pastime is doomed," he wrote.[26]

At that point, sex in America hardly felt doomed, but it did sometimes seem to scream out for a little order. This is what the groupie system provided. A hardworking band could pull into a new town and expect to be greeted by young women who, like wartime nurses, would offer them succor. In return, those women would gain status in a world where few other roles were available—there were barely any females onstage, on the road crew, in management, or working in positions of power at the venues. Becoming a groupie placed women in rock on a kind of solid ground, however imaginary it ultimately proved. The simulated sex at the core of early-1970s rock could be made tangible within encounters that took place in in-between environments like hotels and backstage areas, where the moral codes women were questioning via the emerging women's movement—and which men found incompatible with life on the road—were temporarily suspended. The stable element in this dizzying milieu was the conventional double standard in which men had power and women gained power through them.

The suspension of codes was enticing; so was the temporary nature of that suspension. No terms would have to be radically redefined, because everyone had a place. Old terms could even be carried over, if they felt comforting. One account of backstage life during this period mentions a groupie "chastely" sleeping her way through the Rolling Stones' entourage in order to finally get to Mick Jagger, taking liberties with that term to describe a woman using sex not for her immediate pleasure but to reach an admirable goal. Another anecdote had Ken Hensley, keyboardist for hard rockers Uriah Heep, begging one virtuous-seeming groupie to "take me away from all this" on a particularly abandoned night at the Whisky. "She did, and today she's his old lady," *Circus* magazine reported. These anecdotes about women who played by certain unspoken rules to get their men, avoiding profligacy and self-centeredness, exemplify how the groupie system valued order and its own kind of propriety.[27] So do guides to the groupie world like "How to Meet Rock Stars," published in *Circus* in 1973—a feature that echoed 1950s advice columns, except that instead of marriage to the boy next door, a wild night with a passing hitmaker was the goal, and strategies like "friendships with the older men who manage the stage or the security" were suggested.[28]

Reality was often not so rosy. Many young women were violated. The mere presence of underage girls required a web of adult complicity. Club owners and promoters, like Rodney Bingenheimer, made sure plenty of teenage cuties were available to entertain touring musicians. Hotel staff overlooked the semiclad women slumped in their hallways. Police apparently looked askance, or worse: in her memoir of teenage groupiedom, Robin Maltz recalls being nearly molested by a cop in exchange for his not hauling her in. Des Barres recalled seeing Led Zeppelin tour manager Richard Cole kick in a fan's teeth for simply approaching Robert Plant from behind and startling him at LA's groupie hangout the Rainbow Bar and Grill. "They thought they could get away with anything, and they could, because everybody wanted to be near them . . . It got to be incredibly sick," she said of the scene around the band.[29]

The competition among the groupies also often took ugly turns. "Groupies groom groupies," writes Robin Maltz. "Groupies hang out in cliques." The system had definite winners and losers. The short-lived teen magazine *Star* served and promoted the Sunset Strip scene, offering advice to would-be teen seducers in articles like "Quiz: Are You Ready for an Older Guy?" and "The Black Foxy Lady: Can You Hold Your Own Against Her?" In a feature on the alpha kids of the Sunset Strip, Sable Starr consistently badmouthed her rivals, recounting one night when she wanted to pair up with Mick Ronson: "He was going with this ugly girl named Leslie and I can't stand her . . . It just made me so mad that she was with him. Anyway she made faces at me so I went up to her and splashed her gin gimlet right in her face! After that, Mick came over to me and left Leslie sitting by herself with her runny makeup and sopping wet hair."[30]

That adults would observe and take part in blood sport waged by drunk high school sophomores raises not only the obvious questions about agency and power, but more complicated ones about the way people avoid responsibility within situations that seem predetermined by established positions and rituals. As in pornography, the groupie system was both authentic and simulated—celebrated in song, made hip through fashion spreads, providing color in magazine features, eventually rendered nostalgic in films like Cameron Crowe's *Almost Famous,* from 2000. As in a "money shot" orgasm scene, rockers and their conquering conquests did what was expected to achieve the outcome everyone agreed was most desirable. Is a game consensual if the rules prove exploitative? Some male rockers found the situation difficult to sustain, too. "Everyone felt pressure to live up to this previously unknown ideal of perfect sexual freedom," one musician active in this era, who wishes to remain anonymous, wrote in a recent e-mail exchange. "It was quite common to feel like one was not living up to the modern ideal, that one simply was not fucking enough. The idea that sex necessarily involved a power relation that had to be thought about was completely foreign. I knew hundreds (yes) of young girls and many young men who put on false bravado about their sexual exploits and not only claimed more action than they had, but had more action than they wanted."

GIRLS WILL BE BOYS AND
BOYS WILL BE GIRLS

What Sable Starr didn't realize about Pamela Des Barres when she called her an old bag in a room full of rockers decked out in satin, spangles, and feathers is that Des Barres had helped invent the personae of the guys Starr was trying to steal from her. In 1968 Des

Barres was in a band called the GTOs; a performance art troupe, really, with little musical experience, but all the flower-power swagger five groupies making free-rock noise could produce. Avant-pop star Frank Zappa had assembled the GTOs when he realized the women backstage at his shows had as much, if not more, creative energy than the men they hotly pursued. The music never gelled, but as a style unit Miss Pamela and her peers had significant influence, most directly on a band recently relocated from Phoenix that went by the drag name of their male lead singer—Alice Cooper.[31]

Free love hadn't opened Alice Cooper, the singer, to bisexuality; born Vincent Furnier, he was an avowed heterosexual who liked old Hollywood movies and considered Bette Davis's Gothic-camp performance in *Whatever Happened to Baby Jane?* primary source material. But like many artists at the turn of the 1970s, Furnier was beginning to think that the impetus for cultural change might not be communal effort, but individual revolt. He wanted to inhabit the new role of the rock star: not envoy of a larger movement but hero within a ritual space where outrageous dreams and encroaching nightmares could be enacted. Theatrically kicking aside the anxieties that haunted Joplin, Hendrix, and Morrison, 1970s rock stars like Alice Cooper took on the decade's challenges by turning them into stories told on their own constantly reconstituting bodies.

In his academic analysis of glam rock, Philip Auslander invokes fellow theorist Richard Schechner to posit that rock stars specialize in "showing doing": not just letting an expressive act flow forth in a seemingly natural way, as Hendrix or even Morrison did, but theatrically "pointing to, underlying, and displaying" every move. To show doing, properly, you need a costume. The porn star's costume is nakedness. Alice Cooper knew a musician going naked would be arrested—and besides, he was homely. His solution came when he met GTOs member Christine Frka one day in Hollywood. The extremely slender, giantly Afroed Miss Christine was a magical wraith, a dream girl whose look invoked Storyville and the graveyard in one fell swoop. She and Alice became lovers, and he convinced his bandmates to let her work some sartorial wonder on them.

"Alice got in deep with Miss Christine," Alice Cooper bassist Dennis Dunaway wrote in his 2015 memoir. "They became hand-holding fashion clones. They not only wore each other's clothes, but you might say they wore each other." Cooper himself described the style Frka developed for him—one that would help make him one of the biggest rock stars of the early 1970s—as "a pair of black leather pants worn underneath a torn black lace slip with some GTO lingerie, smeared Bette Davis makeup, unusually long hair, and black lace gloves. It was shocking even to the hippies."[32]

Other artists in Los Angeles and elsewhere were making equally outrageous moves. David Bowie was rethinking his own hippie drag, getting ready to go alien. In New York, there was the Velvet Underground, whose leader, Lou Reed, favored motorcycle-boy leathers, and whose drummer, Moe Tucker, was a boyish woman who was Reed's twin just as Miss Christine was Cooper's. And in San Francisco, most outrageously of all, there were the Cockettes, a mixed-gender, communally oriented, predominantly gay collective that began doing weird variety shows in North Beach venues. On New Year's Eve 1969, the Cockettes staged one such "Nocturnal Dream Show" at a run-down Chinese-deco theater called the Palace, wearing lampshades and coconut bras, the women among them going topless, the men forming chorus-girl kick lines as the Rolling Stones' "Honky Tonk Women" played on repeat. One Cockette told entertainment reporter Rex Reed that the goal was "sexual role confusion." It was the spirit of the day.[33]

Within a year, the Cockettes would gain another member, perhaps the most glorious androgyne of that early gender-fucking period and, indeed, of the whole 1970s. Around the time Vincent Furnier was transforming into Alice Cooper, Sylvester James, then a high schooler known as Dooni, was tiring of his own drag scene in South Central Los Angeles, where he'd perfected a 1920s blues queen look as part of a party-circuit gang called the Disquotays. He'd soon relocate to San Francisco and join the Cockettes. His pristine look, modeled on Josephine Baker, was a striking contrast to the chaotic countercultural mess his fellow Cockettes made. So was his voice: a burnished-chrome falsetto he'd first cultivated in the gospel church and perfected listening to old Billie Holiday sides. Sylvester would eventually emerge as a star in his own right, an out gay man who came to embody the spirit of a different 1970s phenomenon, disco. Sylvester certainly got Bowie's attention. When the Spiders from Mars failed to sell out San Francisco's Winterland in 1972, the glam king explained away the failure by saying, "They don't need me—they have Sylvester." Opening for him, Sylvester had flown through the former ice rink, hitched up to a cable "like a big-boned, glittering brown Tinkerbell." Androgyny had truly taken flight.[34]

The omnisexual mood of the early- to mid-1970s was generated by messy gender-fuckery that, in 1973, *Creem* magazine called "the most conspicuous trend in rock and roll" in its introduction to an "Androgyny Hall of Fame." The corners of the counterculture sympathetic to such things—like the Cockettes' San Francisco and Warhol's New York—eventually pushed rock's closet open, in a way. As *Creem* noted, a Londoner, Ray Davies of the Kinks, "brought the question to American airwaves" with "Lola," his 1970 love song to a transvestite; then Bowie became the beautiful face of this "magical uncertainty tour." Rock's legacy of gender and sexual code-switching stretched back to "Queen Bitch" Little Richard, and included everyone from Bob Dylan, who allegedly wore rouge on the cover of his album *Highway 61 Revisited,* to Bowie compatriots like the lipsticked and feather-boaed New York Dolls and the "possibly post-sexual" Iggy Pop. *Creem*'s guide was undershot with a certain nervousness. Noting that many of the day's leading gender-benders, including Bowie, were men married to women, the article's introduction ended, "Will the real homosexuals please stand up?"[35]

Creem's distress at the "ungay gay" showed how difficult it was for even open-minded rock-scene habitués to grasp that sexuality could be anything other than cast along a straight-gay binary. Auslander argues that what made 1970s androgyny so powerful was that its constructed nature—hobbled together, as Alice Cooper said, with bits of pilfered lingerie and ripped motorcycle gear— challenged the deep presumption that gender was ultimately a stable, biologically determined human trait. Rock and pop stars struggled with how to best represent the moment. The most interesting ones expressed ambiguities in ways that opened fans' minds but acknowledged that such inner unrest could feel violent, and even like a violation. "I'll suggest certain things: maybe that I'm gay or super-macho," Cooper said then. "Those are all lies. But that's Alice. Alice is a liar."[36]

Many people wondered if they might, too, be liars in the 1970s. Wives and husbands were questioning their vows. Bisexuality was in. Dubbed a trend, the orientation earned cover stories in *Newsweek* and *Time*. At West Coast "sex farm" retreats (to use journalist Tom Wolfe's term) like Sandstone, which blended New Age religion, self-help, and erotic exploration, individuals and couples combined in every formation possible. Open marriage became popular. Feminists critiquing patriarchy turned from heterosexuality as a political gesture that, for many, uncovered hidden same-sex desires. Via Warhol's factory, popular texts like Gore Vidal's 1968 sex-change saga *Myra Breckinridge* and John Schlesinger's 1969 male-hustler film romance *Midnight Cowboy,* the trans musical *The Rocky Horror Picture Show,* and the subversive drag star Divine, Americans were expanding their definitions of the ideal man, woman, or whichever.

Alice Cooper was one of the first and most all-American peddlers of this unsettled self. Like Iggy Pop's band the Stooges, who emerged from the Detroit psychedelic scene around the same time, Cooper recast the counterculture's societal questioning in terms that were both individualistic and highly confrontational. "We looked right into the eyes of our audience with arrogance about who and what we were," Cooper writes about the group's early gigs with hippie bands like Blue Cheer. Unlike David Bowie, who adopted the icy cool of a literal (space) alien, Alice Cooper was an unkempt everyfreak: plain, hairy, with amateurish makeup and a stage show that borrowed from horror movies instead of Bowie's favored literary sources. His voice was artless, creaky; his drag persona felt lumpen, not elegant. Too gross for LA, the band relocated to Michigan in 1970, and it was there that it found its lumbering groove in songs like "I'm Eighteen," an anthem of what Steve Waksman calls adolescent "terminal confusion." The dirge-like chord progressions of "I'm Eighteen" explode into cacophonous, almost unpleasant but irresistible release, expressing the more tortured aspects of ambiguous identity: the alienation, fear, and loathing that the half-metamorphosed caterpillar experiences in the cocoon. Like many Americans trying desperately to evolve to fit new sexual ideals, Alice Cooper never got his wings. If he had, he would have smashed them anyway.[37]

Fracture, a floating turmoil, the creeping sense felt on both the right and the left that society was veering out of control—these were the moods of the 1970s. The era confirmed what the 1960s counterculture had revealed to the parents and kids of the baby boom: that self-transformation inevitably generated both inner and social turmoil. Writing of a "Me" Decade, Tom Wolfe perceived a narcissistic turn that "smacked of vanity," an aristocratic impulse to buff up one's personality "like a high-class piece of psychological cabinetry," newly available to the masses through a mix of loosened morals and greater general wealth.[38]

This is not how many people experienced the 1970s, however. Gay men put their bodies on the line in the street protests that began with Stonewall. Feminists also struggled with street confrontation and risked rejection by family members. Many in communities of color had grown deeply cynical of the integrationist ideal and were struggling to retain a sense of their own lineages. Heterosexual white men, still dominant, felt destabilized, too—uncertain of what authority still resonated. "I know what I am, what I am is a man!" screamed Ray Davies at the climax of "Lola." What did that even mean anymore?

"What have I got that makes you want to love me?" Alice Cooper asked in "Is It My Body," an agonized yowl of a song that was the B-side to "I'm Eighteen." "Is it my body, or someone I might be? Something inside me?" Iggy Pop asked the same question using the shards of a broken whiskey glass when he cut himself onstage during Stooges performances, howling about wanting to be a dog or having no fun. "He rubs his body, he contorts, bending over backwards until his head nearly touches the floor," wrote Mike Jahn in the *New York Times* after witnessing the Stooges at a Cincinnati festival. "He rolls his tongue around. He makes grotesque shapes with his lips. He is very ugly and precociously sexual. The audiences love it. They don't understand it. Neither does he, most likely. But they are drawn to watch him with mouths agape." David Bowie loved Iggy Pop, too. Once he tried to kiss the Detroit singer during a press conference, and Pop punched him in the face.[39]

"Personality crisis! You got it while it was hot!" David Johansen of the New York Dolls yelled in that band's signature riff-ripped tirade. "But now frustration and heartache is what you got." Like kids who'd followed Bowie's glitter trail out of the American hinterland but then slipped on Alice Cooper's grease and stayed in the gutter, the Dolls anticipated New York punk's "rip it up and start again" ethos five years before that movement coalesced. Like Iggy Pop, they put the glop in glamorous: Johansen was a habitué of Andy Warhol's art world, but like his bandmates, he was from the outer boroughs, not Manhattan, and he retained a street-tough sensibility. "I would be a sex murderer if I didn't wear these pumps," he once told Lisa Robinson while sporting spangled women's heels. "You know you could be in fatigues, and put on pumps, and look totally queer." Such aggressive and tacitly homophobic language was common among 1970s hard rockers, who found energy in the disarray of the period, including the profoundly mixed signals androgyny chic created. Guitarist Mick Ronson of David Bowie's Spiders from Mars made a similar, if more benign, comment to a journalist in 1973: "I'm gay inasmuch as I wear girls' shoes and have bangles on my wrist. I get offers to—but I don't accept them."[40]

For homosexuals in the 1970s, the glam world of hard rock could be a shelter or a source of frustration. Music critic Jim Farber, then a teenager, experienced the era as a time when he could show outrageousness without necessarily making its essence clear: "With my attachment to glitter, as a nervous, virginal mid-teen, I wasn't announcing my coming out but ensuring my staying in," he wrote in 1998. "Pledging allegiance to glitter rock awarded me a safety zone in which I could both sidestep all definitions of what it meant to be a boy and stave off a commitment to what it would eventually mean for me to be a gay man." But to *Creem* writer Vince Aletti, who as an out gay adult in 1972 was already turning toward the more openly homosexual scene that would become disco, the patina of androgyny chic was "bullshit . . . Just another restriction of the straitjacket. Or, in this case, straight jacket." Noting that for all of the air kissing and lipstick application Bowie and Pop and Johansen did, "there are no songs about homosexual love," he demanded that songs come out of the closet, too.[41]

Rock audiences were not ready to embrace straightforward homosexual desire. (Though Rob Halford of Judas Priest came out long after he rose to fame, and Adam Lambert crossed over from the pop realm to front a new version of the progressive rock band Queen in the mid-2010s, mainstream rock has still not produced a male star who was out from the beginning of his career.) The

dazzle of glam and the Grand Guignol spectacle of rockers like Alice Cooper and Iggy Pop differed from the actual gay liberation
movement taking hold in cities like New York and San Francisco.
That was deeply confrontational, too. "I don't like the word 'gay'—
aside from being a dumb, weak word and a part of that 'positive'
stereotype, it seems like a cover-up," Aletti wrote, voicing the determination to be wholly acknowledged. "I prefer the word faggot
'cause it has a harder, nastier sound that has nothing to do with
the cocktail party and drawing room definition of the 'acceptable'
homosexual."

What Aletti demanded was a far cry from the "swishy," ambiguous, ultimately hetero-affirmative teasing of David Bowie or
his fellow glam pioneers. "They're not a fag band," an editors' note
read above an early New York Dolls profile in *Creem*. David Johansen did more than flirt with homophobia in the ensuing interview.
"'A lot of people thought that we were the band that was gonna
camp on the Sixties for the old queens,' spits David with a look of
disgust, 'but you can tell 'em that I said "those used-up queens can
all go screw!"'" The rest of the band loudly voices their support
of this motion."[42] Bowie's connections to the emergent gay culture
were more intimate; in the late 1970s, he was lovers with the Dutch
transgender cabaret artist Romy Haag and performed on American
television with the pioneering queer performance artists Joey Arias
and Klaus Nomi. Yet Bowie was also famous for bedding hundreds
of women. His relationship with wife Angie Bowie was perhaps the
most visible of the era embodying the "open marriage" trend, and
for most of the 1970s it allowed Bowie to remain an ally and a dab-
bler, but not, as Aletti might say, a faggot.

Rock's moment of androgyny chic did produce one bona fide
gay liberationist: Jobriath, a twenty-six-year-old former theater
kid whom the high-powered music-biz entrepreneur Jerry Brandt
molded to be the next Bowie. Signed to a huge Elektra Records
contract, Jobriath and Brandt planned a tour intended to be the

spectacle to end all spectacles, involving a "Kama Sutra altar" and a reenactment of the death scene in *King Kong*. The press went wild, publishing extensive interviews with both Brandt and Jobriath, in which the men (who claimed to have met in a gay bar) made grand pronouncements about bringing popular music into the next decade: "The drug culture is dead, Broadway is dead. The only thing that's keeping us alive is sex. I'm selling sex. Sex and professionalism," said Jobriath, while he kindly dismissed Bowie: "David Bowie is a good lad. I become a true fairy onstage."

Brandt invested huge hopes and capital into Jobriath, but two albums in Elektra executives pulled the plug. Brandt and Jobriath fell out. Jobriath's only tour ended fabulously but smokily on September 20, 1974, in Tuscaloosa, Alabama, of all places. Jobriath French-kissed his guitarist onstage in front of a crowd full of students and drag queens, and received four encores, even after a malfunctioning motor in the hall's cooling system caused the room to fill up with smoke. Jobriath returned to New York, adopted the stage name Cole Berlin, and became a cabaret singer. He was an early casualty of the AIDS epidemic, dying in 1983.[43]

That the most committedly gay transgressor in 1970s rock ended his brief career in a conservative Southern college town says much about the craze for sexual and gender openness that overtook America in the 1970s. The semester before Jobriath performed in Tuscaloosa, the University of Alabama's alternative-minded New College sponsored a "Sex Week" featuring appearances by Linda Lovelace and *Screw* magazine editor Al Goldstein, a standing-room-only lecture by a male-to-female transsexual, and a student play about homosexuality entitled (hello, Ray Davies) *Boys Will Be Girls, Girls Will Be Boys*. Jobriath was able to find momentary support, even adulation, in outposts where people were hungry to enact the fantasies popular culture was presenting them. But the era's true stars only occupied those fantasies provisionally. In his 1971 anthem, "Changes," Bowie demanded that his fans face the strange.

He kept turning toward something new, a strategy that served his own restless muse but also made his music a better sell to a mainstream perhaps not ready to accept some of those "strange" ways of being as normal. "In the mix of male and female friends making up my glitter coterie," Farber wrote, "I was the only one who was gay (and the only one who knew that I was gay)." Farber noted that one of the most flamboyantly "swish" artists of the 1970s, Freddie Mercury of Queen, remained closeted in his fans' eyes, even though during concerts he did things like address his male fans as "my little bathing beauties." Only after he died from complications of AIDS in 1991 was Mercury's bisexuality openly discussed by those close to him.[44]

As identity-based activism increased in the early 1970s, gay liberationists and feminists (occasionally together) increasingly demanded larger social change. Turning politics into rock and roll theater, activists played rough with stereotypes of sexual allure. The 1968 Miss America pageant protest co-organized by rock critic Ellen Willis saw women parading a sheep on the Atlantic City boardwalk and throwing high heels, makeup, and lingerie into a "Freedom Trash Can." Gay activists staged bold displays of pleasure like dance-ins in Central Park, which also served as ways for men and some women to cruise potential sex partners.

And there were pride parades, the first of which took place in 1970: joyful, carnivalesque moving actions in which politically minded organizers mingled with participants costumed in their own preferences—leathermen, drag queens, radical fairies, butch dykes on bikes. This was Sylvester's home base. He participated in a proto–pride parade not long after moving to San Francisco in 1970, honoring the newly concocted Aquarius Day. The event amalgamated "a countercultural hodgepodge of queens, flower children, and rock-and-rollers, where the lead float was the band Black Sabbath," according to his biographer Joshua Gamson. Sylvester encouraged the Cockettes to scream from the float instead of just waving and batting their eyelashes. "The crowd screamed back," Gamson writes.[45]

In a few years, Sylvester would realize that his path did not lie within this undifferentiated mass of sensual searchers and embark upon his own career, separate from the Cockettes, moving from soulful rock to the new, gay-led subculture of disco. An ad for Sylvester and the Hot Band, his funky new group, adorned the back cover of *Creem* in 1973 and made his allegiance to gay pride clear: "All men are created equal," the copy read above a picture of Sylvester in sequined blouse, leggings, and platform sandals.

Sylvester was not the only African American artist to participate in androgyny chic in the early 1970s. Labelle, a Philadelphia trio that began as a 1960s girl group led by the gospel-fired vocalist Patti LaBelle, found itself at a career crossroads in 1970, when Dusty Springfield's English manager, Vicki Wickham, approached them with a rejuvenation plan. Wickham saw potential in LaBelle's charisma, Sarah Dash's purity of voice, and Nona Hendryx's musical curiosity. Taking the group to England, Wickham helped them immerse in the rock world that had transformed Jimi Hendrix. Encouraging the then-Bluebelles to change its name to the more rock-flavored Labelle, and to begin recording the genre-defying songs penned by the also newly renamed Hendryx, Wickham guided Labelle into a previously unexplored space where glam met funk and soul via strictly female interplay. She connected the trio with costume designer Larry LeGaspi, who'd worked with the majestic drag queen Divine, and who would later design the famous costumes for the horror-glam band KISS.

Labelle was as connected to funk as it was to glam. Funk was psychedelic soul, pioneered by James Brown and brought into the 1970s by Parliament-Funkadelic. Led by seasoned doo-wop veteran George Clinton, P-Funk, like Bowie, set its music within elaborately staged scenarios that explored existential alienation using science-fiction story lines. The collective also developed its own style of carnivalesque sartorial androgyny. Albums like Funkadelic's *Maggot Brain* and Parliament's *Mothership Connection* form a core part of the Afro-Futurist lineage also shaped by jazz great Sun Ra and Jamaican innovator Lee "Scratch" Perry. P-Funk's music was sexy and hilarious, and also experimental and mind-expanding, tackling themes of societal corruption, racism, and freedom through mind expansion alongside lustier topics in songs like "Standing on the Verge of Getting It On." "Alice Cooper and David Bowie, they were doing their thing," George Clinton said later. "That whole period, everybody was going for theatrical rock. So we just said, 'Let's go all the way with it. Let's do it all.'"⁴⁶

Nona Hendryx soon found that the permission rock artists had to experiment—not often afforded women in soul or pop, although male funk artists enjoyed it—freed her mind. Her writing followed. Her compositions for Labelle confronted world politics, the strictures of the entertainment industry, and, though in a somewhat metaphorical way, lesbian sex. "We are not afraid to sing revolutionary songs," she told *Billboard*. "That sets us apart from other female groups."⁴⁷

The group's high point came on October 6, 1974, when it played the Metropolitan Opera House. "Wear Something Silver!" the posters advertising the event read, and the crowd obliged—the even mix of gay men and mostly African American heterosexual couples dressed in tinseled finery were documented with a spread in *People* magazine. Labelle wore LeGaspi's space costumes that night, their garb reflecting the title of the group's latest album, *Nightbirds*. At one point Patti LaBelle was lowered from the ceiling by a wire while wearing huge yellow wings. "There can rarely have been so many bearded gentlemen in dresses, razzle-dazzle sequins and arched eyebrows at a Met performance before," a bemused John Rockwell wrote in the *Times*. For Aletti, however, the show was a triumph—a performance that openly connected with a gay audience while refusing those "polite" stereotypes he abhorred.⁴⁸

Labelle only had one major hit, "Lady Marmalade," a stomper written by Bob Crewe and Kenny Nolan about a fiercely empowered sex worker in New Orleans. Hendryx's songs tended to be too experimental for radio, taking sinuous shapes inspired by Funkadelic's long jams and the urban pop symphonies of singer-songwriter Laura Nyro, a sometime collaborator. While male rock and funk stars like Bowie or Clinton were extolled for pushing musical boundaries, Labelle left mainstream audiences puzzled. Like Janis Joplin, these women were considered excessive: too stylized, too weird, too loud. The group did not reach the fame of its male counterparts. In New York, however, it was a sensation, especially among gay men and black and Latin audiences.

"Lady Marmalade" was a hit propelled, in part, by the disco craze that followed glam rock's brief interlude. Disco allowed for outliers like Labelle and Sylvester, who enjoyed his biggest hits as part of its whirlwind, to flourish. With few exceptions—notably the Runaways, Suzi Quatro, and Fanny, the first all-female band to record a major-label album, in 1970—hard rock remained the provenance of white males, no matter how much mascara its practitioners applied. To appeal to a mainstream audience with as many women as men, rock would have to do what male porn stars never did: go soft.

DO THAT TO ME ONE MORE TIME

In 1975, the writer Jane DeLynn hadn't yet had an orgasm. She'd tried analysis, consciousness raising, the usual tools of the Me Decade, but nothing had worked. So she signed up to attend a workshop by Betty Dodson. A women's health advocate whose 1972 polemic/guide *Liberating Masturbation: A Meditation on Self Love* had become a sensation in feminist circles, Dodson believed strongly that claiming pleasure could be a radical and transformative act. She gathered activists and homemakers, professional women and

bohemians like DeLynn in her New York apartment, to share stories and massage, play with sex toys, and come.

"I felt odd as I walked through the living room, for on the deep
brown wall-to-wall carpeting sat fourteen naked women, my classmates," DeLynn wrote in an account she published in *Crawdaddy*
magazine that December. "They were mainly suburban housewives
in their thirties and forties. At twenty-seven I was clearly the youngest. Most of them sat hunched over, arms around drawn-up knees,
embarrassed at the nudity that revealed stretch marks, moles, sag-
ging breasts, cesarean section scars. They were surrounded by the
accoutrements of slick American sex—stereo speaker, large pillows,
bowls of fruit, handcrafted pottery mugs of herbal tea. I slowly got
undressed in the bedroom where a second set of speakers was softly
playing Elton John."[49]

It's telling that the only male element in a room full of women
stripped down and eager for optimal genital excitement was a pop
star few would have called a paragon of 1970s virility. The flamboyant, cuddly Elton John was a ubiquitous and flexible presence
on American radio throughout the decade, an Englishman who'd
become an adult-contemporary music favorite with a sound that
veered from glam rock to country stylings to barrelhouse rock
and roll. Closeted until coming out as bisexual in *Rolling Stone*
in 1976, John was briefly a teen idol, but mostly a translator of
riskier artists' ideas for the masses. He and lyricist Bernie Tau-
pin even penned a more accessible take on David Bowie's alien
imagery with the astronaut love song "Rocket Man (I Think It's
Going to Be a Long, Long Time)." In DeLynn's story, though, John
wasn't a harbinger of glamour. His background presence signified
something else: the healing and gently stimulating presence of
soft rock.

Soft rock was the understanding yin to the arrogant yang
clanging through American arenas in the 1970s, a ballad-based
form that strove for the immediacy and frankness of hard rock but

set aside its cocky noise. "It's meaningful, a lot of the songs in soft rock are meaningful, and you can get into the words," said Grand Funk's singer Mark Farner when asked about its growing popularity in 1970. "But I like to express myself, through my guitar, I like to scream when I feel like it."[50] Many women got off on the wails of Farner and his peers, but at times a gentler touch appealed to both genders. This was especially true during private moments—not only in masturbation workshops but on any given night where a couple, triad, or solo adventurer stayed home in search of a little euphoria.

If arena rockers put their genderfuckery in fans' faces, soft rockers took them by the hand and encouraged them to explore their own potential. Early on, self-defined poets like Leonard Cohen and expressionist troubadours like Tim Hardin—both arty sophisticates—were linked to the form. But so was Kris Kristofferson, the Nashville songwriter who'd written "Me and Bobby McGee," a heartrending tale of love and loss Janis Joplin made famous, as well as the groundbreaking country seduction "Help Me Make It Through the Night." Handsome enough to be the movie star he became, known for a murmuring but resonant drawl that he couldn't have pushed to a scream if he wanted to, Kristofferson stood at the other end of the spectrum from glam's big show. "He is possessed of a deep, roughly hewn voice with tinges of country and western that draws out every last drop of emotion and feeling from the songs he performs," an admiring male critic wrote in 1971. Though plainspoken, Kristofferson and his ilk were certainly expressive: regular guys getting in touch with their feelings.[51]

This was the mandate of domestic life in the 1970s: become your best, most communicative, and erotically engaged self. As in the 1920s, when women's newfound desire for freedom pushed men, too, toward companionate marriage, 1970s women's liberation threatened to leave uncaring men in the dust. The decade gave rise to a new stereotype—the sensitive male, "a man ambitious and successful in his professional life who is also intensely concerned about his emotional and personal life." Those words described the actor Alan Alda in a 1976 feature from the women's magazine *Redbook*, which enthused about Alda's vocal support for an International Women's Day and willingness to do household chores. They could have also applied to confessional singer-songwriters like James Taylor and Jackson Browne.[52]

With women demanding reproductive freedom, voicing radical critiques of the family structure, and telling men all those previous decades of orgasms hadn't been genuine, men felt lost. Women who were courting enlightenment but not yet ready to step into a wholly feminist milieu also craved guidance. Many wanted to repair marriages they now could admit were flawed, but did not want to abandon. "I think that a lot of the so-called feminists—single women, professional women—don't feel they need help, or that they have other things to occupy themselves," Dodson told DeLynn about her orgasm students. "It's the suburban housewife who knows she wants to make changes." These average people needed guidebooks, and capitalism obliged. Explicit how-to books flooded the publishing market.

The most famous is *The Joy of Sex,* a "gourmet guide to love-making" written by English physician Alex Comfort. Topping the bestseller list for eleven weeks in 1972, it remained in the top five for a year and a half longer. The book's tone is jovial, extending the cookbook metaphor to chapters that recast terms like "feuille de rose" (anal stimulation) as "sauces and pickles." Its lavish illustrations were pornographic, yet somehow as cuddly as Winnie the Pooh. They showed a very hairy man and a short-coiffed woman, distilling the moment's aura of gender-role reversal into one smiling couple, coupling in every way imaginable. Comfort adopted a tone of kindly authority, noting that "this is a book about valid sexual behaviors" and that "sex is the most important sort of adult play." He cast sex as the only arena where problems couples might be trying to overcome in therapy or consciousness-raising could truly be resolved; his naturally androgynous couple had returned to a private Eden to remake the world anew.[53]

A surfeit of manuals, polemics, and detailed confessions emerged to shepherd people through the realm of "adult play." The Boston Women's Health Book Collective, a consciousness-raising group, issued *Our Bodies, Ourselves,* an overall guide to feminist well-being with explicit sexual content that also became a bestseller. Its polar opposite was psychologist David M. Reuben's breezy tome *Everything You Always Wanted to Know About Sex But Were Afraid to Ask,* which betrayed extremely old-fashioned values, condemning homosexuality and suggesting that nonorgasmic women might simply be resentful of their husbands.[54] *Making Love: How to Be Your Own Sex Therapist,* written by a woman, included feminist-inspired relationship advice, addressed homosexual men and women as well as straight couples, and acknowledged controversial subjects like rape and pornography. *The Art of Sensual Massage* offered what its title advertised and included an interracial couple among its photographed subjects. Pseudonymous memoirs like *Loving Free* and *The Couple* brought readers into real Americans' bedrooms. *Open Marriage* offered a how-to for nonmonogamy grounded in the experience of its authors, anthropologists Nena and George O'Neill. There was even a diet book, *How Sex Can Keep You Slim*: "Reach for your mate instead of your plate."[55]

Something had to play on the stereo while readers enacted the lessons at their fingertips. For many, soft rock variants did the trick. Throughout the 1970s, lyrics grew ever more directly focused on sex acts, exploring their potential variety and revelatory power. If hard rock took self-expression into freaky new territory, soft rock focused on relationships. "Hey, have you ever tried really reaching out for the other side?" crooned David Gates, the Oklahoma-born lead singer for the pioneering soft-rock band Bread, in a voice as light as one of the feathers Alex Comfort suggested couples use as a sex toy. A 1972 Valentine's Day television special sponsored by the Hallmark card company featured couples reading Bread's lyrics to each other as the music wafted through the background.[56]

Some soft rock was more assertive, especially by women singer-songwriters. On one of the most enduring albums of the decade, 1971's *Tapestry*, Carole King updated the teen revelations she and then-husband Gerry Goffin had staged within girl group pop for the feminist era. Its opening song, "I Feel the Earth Move," was a gospel shout-out to the feminist cause of orgasms for all. Joni Mitchell, the most sophisticated songwriter of the era, generally stayed away from explicit content but released one of her most overtly sexy hits, "You Turn Me On, I'm a Radio," in 1972; it blended images of the hit parade with provocative lines like "Kick off the sandflies, honey, the love's still flowing." Carly Simon, whose marriage to soft rock kingpin James Taylor received unending scrutiny from an admiring public, showed off her lanky body on her album covers and found success with the foreplay anthem "Anticipation" in 1971. These women, all of whom had very public relationships with male peers, presented an image of liberated womanhood that was also glamorous and appealed to men.

Though soft rock was dominated by male voices, other women found a place in its satin sheets with messages of sexually game self-awareness. Merrilee Rush and Diana Ross (no longer a Supreme) sang of gaining strength from breakup sex in the similarly titled "Angel of the Morning" and "Touch Me in the Morning." Roberta Flack's expansive version of Ewan MacColl's folkie ballad "The First Time Ever I Saw Your Face" stretched out the phrase "the first time ever you lay with me" for the length of a languid orgasm. Karen Carpenter, shackled to a squeaky-clean image in the brother-sister act the Carpenters, had her own steamy moment singing Bonnie Bramlett and Leon Russell's ode to groupiedom, "Superstar," in 1971. And as part of the married duo the Captain and Tennille, Toni Tennille made connubial bliss explicit in "Do That to Me One More Time" and "The Way I Want to Touch You."

Radical feminists, meanwhile, began creating a separate sphere in which gentle music presented an alternative to the aggressiveness of "cock rock." Expressing what activists believed was a "universal female sensibility," women's music, as the subgenre was called, eschewed big drum parts and amplification, tended toward the confessional, and espoused a compassionate eroticism that was often explicitly lesbian. Women's music was "a little different than David Bowie playing with androgyny," said one of its first stars, Holly Near, noting songs that addressed political issues like income disparity and the rights of children. What many fans loved, however, was its opulent celebration of women's love for each other. Artists like Near and the sultry Cris Williamson were sex symbols as well as role models.[57]

Radical softness served different purposes for different constituencies. For feminists, it allowed an escape from the pounding phallocentricity of rock. In country music, a realm as traditional as the women's movement was revolutionary, soft rock's intimacies created a way into modern mores. Dolly Parton and Loretta Lynn had brought feminist consciousness into the genre with witty protest songs like "Dumb Blonde" and "One's On the Way." Male songwriters responded as their nonmusical counterparts did: by going behind closed doors, as Charlie Rich sang in one of the great ballads of the era, and trying to make themselves and their lovers glad that they were men. "Whatever the precise motivation, country music today stands as the most sensuous form of American popular music," *Chicago Tribune* columnist Gary Deeb wrote in 1973. Deeb held up Conway Twitty's single "You've Never Been This Far Before," then No. 1 on Chicago's country station WJJD, as an example of country's daring stroll from the family room to the bedroom.[58]

The African American recording industry developed its own

version of soft rock, eventually known as "quiet storm," in league with what became known as the "Ebony lifestyle." That term applied to a radio format that favored mood music and light talk over the soul sounds and political dialogues of the civil rights and black power eras. But it also invoked the magazine *Ebony,* the favorite among middle-class blacks, which was full of couples' relationship advice. Proto-quiet-storm artists like Barry White and the Isley Brothers, with songs like the moaning "I'm Gonna Love You Just a Little More Baby" and the soft-core "Sensuality," simultaneously catered to women's fantasies of an attentive lover and men's need for sexual role models.

Many African Americans responded equivocally to the pornographic openness of the 1970s. Burdened by stereotypes that cast them as hypersexual, they often clung to a stricter moral code. The writer Nelson George, then a teenager, recalls in an essay about the action-packed "blaxploitation" movies of the era that the cartoonish sexuality of stars like Richard Roundtree in the cop flick *Shaft* embodied a fantasy that felt forbidden. "The white girl he picks up in a bar is just another conquest he can't be bothered with the next morning. Shaft not only gave it to the man, but to his woman too; with his black leather battle gear and ever ready sneer, Shaft was our black id unleashed, realizing the worst nightmares of the NAACP and the KKK."[59] Artists like White, who described his own sexual technique in a signature *basso profundo* murmur over a lush string section, adjusted the Shaft stereotype in ways that still enticed, but also argued for elegance. Isaac Hayes, whose theme for *Shaft* captured the tensions of this moment with a chorus of soft female voices telling him to "shut your mouth" when his bragging turned profane, explored similar ground with his radiant covers of mellow pop hits like Burt Bacharach's "Walk On By."

Sensualizing soul or tenderizing country and rock, pop's shapers of radical softness shared allegiance to a fairly formulaic songwriting approach. Tempos were slowed, electric guitars muted; the focus of arrangements often shifted to other instruments, such as Daryl Dragon's keyboards in the Captain and Tennille or the oboe in the Carpenters' version of "Superstar." Harmonies became key, standing in for the thrill of relationships. Starland Vocal Band's ode to daytime coitus "Afternoon Delight" featured two couples intertwining their voices in ways that mirrored the illustrations in *The Joy of Sex*. Male harmonies showed delicate prowess; in the Eagles' "Peaceful Easy Feeling," from 1972, Glenn Frey offers the key line of the first verse, "I want to sleep with you in the desert tonight," in solo voice, shored up in later verses by a building three-part harmony that takes the lyric from proposition to artfully realized union.

Jazz was the best mood music for Hugh Hefner acolytes of an earlier era, but soft rock suited sophisticates who liked their dreams a little more naked. Just as the "showing doing" of glam rockers exposed how gender roles were constructed and could be reimagined, narratives of radical softness mirrored the experience of better sex. As a product, soft rock and quiet storm complement the leisure toys of swinging 1970s consumers, sounding great on the pricey stereo systems extensively advertised in *Playboy* and other porn magazines and in tricked-out rides where fantasies like the one detailed in Sammy Johns's 1973 hit "Chevy Van"—he picks up a hitchhiker, she obliges him with mind-blowing lovemaking, she gets off at the next town—could possibly be realized.

There was much pop-cultural evidence that men of the 1970s were getting down to soft rock. In Hal Ashby's 1975 film *Shampoo,* promiscuous hairdresser Warren Beatty beds his female clients to a soft rock soundtrack; the style could signify sexiness in grittier movies, too, such as *Midnight Cowboy,* which shows Jon Voight plying his "stud" wares with Manhattan housewives as Harry Nilsson's version of "Everybody's Talkin'" echoes in the background. A profile of former *Playboy* marketing director Steve Byer presented him as the ideal sexy man: "The stereo is purring soft rock, the

Tiffany lamp is glowing over the tournament-sized pool table, and the neon sculpture on one wall pulses a blue 'hello' to the Gallo bas-relief across the room while a 6-foot, soft-pine dude leans like a gunman on an opposite wall." Frank Gallo was "the Nabokov of epoxy resin," sculpting voluptuous nude Lolitas in a vaguely Italianate style; Byer's mood-lit apartment, so adorned, was a love lair where he could wrap his lanky form around a companion while enjoying a little Bread.[60]

Radically soft music worked best in private environments partly because it was, like sex manuals and pornography, designed for intimate consumption. The music's feeling of privacy also suited a time when Americans, if eager to buy sex-oriented goods, were deeply divided over the social impact of more open eroticism. The family values agenda that remains central to the New Right today emerged in the 1970s. With its less confrontational "adult" sound, soft music was aimed at the over-eighteen set, whose sex-plorations, adventurous as they became, were contained compared to the teenage riots of the 1950s and the countercultural freaki-ness of the 1960s.

LOVE SAVES THE DAY

The spirit of radical softness did have a public counterpart: disco, which became the signal music craze of the later 1970s. Before it was a musical genre, disco was an environment where members of marginalized groups awakening to their own power could gather and interact freely. Earlier, discothèques were French record clubs, then they became venues focused on dancing. David Bowie's early-adult musical education took place at one such disco. Catering to the fashion industry, the Sombrero was, in the words of Bowie's then-wife Angie, "visual, dance oriented, and gay. David loved it, and so did I. It was the first club we'd ever seen with the dance floor lit from below, so it had a new edge of atmospheric excitement.

It was set up for watching and being watched, too: a wide, curving staircase for making grand entrances, plenty of perches from which you could see the whole dance floor, and—very important—enough square-footage. You had room to move and breathe and circulate."[61]

At the Sombrero, Bowie discovered that the spectacles he admired in rock and theater could belong fully to the audience. With no musical performer present, the dancers were the show. There was Freddie Burretti, a dashing gay dandy who would become Bowie's personal designer; Mickey King, a club kid with wild red hair whose name Bowie briefly adopted as a pseudonym; Daniella Parmar, Burretti's platonic teenage girlfriend, who changed her hair color from blue to pink to red on a weekly basis and helped convince Bowie to adopt his own neon hues. These self-made beauties danced to "hard American R&B—not a note of rock or anything British" and flaunted desires that the establishment might label perversions. "They were wilder than college kids, and more direct, and they cared a lot more about dancing and looking hot and flaunting their sex, and—the bottom line—they were the majority," Angie Bowie writes about the working people getting loose in the Sombrero, whom Bowie always kept in his mind as an ideal audience.

The United States had its own Sombreros by the dawn of the 1970s. The prototypical early New York disco was the Loft, actual domicile of DJ David Mancuso, who threw "Love Saves the Day" parties with no alcohol but plenty of punch laced with LSD where he blended deep soul into hard rock into Latin jazz. Under the scattered light of a mirror ball, dancers at the Loft—as at the Sombrero, mixed racially and in sexual orientation, though mostly gay—engaged in a sensual round robin. "You could be on the dance floor and the most beautiful woman that you had ever seen in your life would come and dance right on top of you," recalled Frankie Knuckles, later a leading New York DJ, of those early parties. "Then the minute you turned around a man who looked just as good would do the same thing. Or you would be sandwiched between the two of them, or between two women, or between two men, and you would feel completely comfortable."[62]

At the Loft and other nascent discos like the Gallery and the Tenth Floor, New Yorkers explored a polymorphous pleasure principle similar to what therapists encouraged at woodsy self-help retreats like Esalen and Sandstone in California. In *Thy Neighbor's Wife*, the epic tale of his ten-year immersion in America's sexual subcultures, Gay Talese noted that carefully programmed stereo music was crucial to the mood at Sandstone, which founders John and Barbara Williamson envisioned as a sort of nude, orgasmic private club. There was even an area called the Ballroom where couples or groups could make love while up-tempo songs and ballads, carefully arranged on ninety-minute cassettes to enhance the rise and fall of libidos, played in the background.[63] Early disco DJs like Mancuso and the Gallery's Nicky Siano similarly strove to whet the loins of dancers, but with more nonlinear goals. On the dance floor, the release was more communal, even for couples moving together.

Being on a disco dance floor could feel like a public display and a private indulgence at the same time. For gay men, who embraced discos en masse, they allowed for privacy without the stifling claustrophobia of the closet. Women (gay, straight, and elsewhere on the spectrum) and people of color also felt freer to be expressive within discos, which often catered to particular clienteles; the harassment and even violence they faced on the street ran counter to the utopian mood disco sought to preserve. As the phenomenon spread, discos took over abandoned spaces or newly designed adult playgrounds. "We started at the Sanctuary, a deconsecrated church in Hell's Kitchen, then proceeded to the Anvil, a raunchy backroom bar . . . and finally ended up at Le Jardin, a disco in the Hotel Diplomat," recalled Patrick Pacheco, editor of the decade's unofficial gay nightlife bible *After Dark,* of a typical disco night. "My own personal favorite during those years, however, was G.G. Barnum's, a wild, Mafia-owned dance palace with a two-story-high dance floor over which 'disco bats'—transsexuals and humpty Puerto Rican boys on trapezes—would fly."[64] Feeling protected by the music, Americans accustomed to walking with one eye peeled for harassers tripped through this fantastical cityscape without fear.

The music created for discos took similar risks. In 1975, Robert Plant's improvised sex sounds were superseded by the moans of Donna Summer, an American stage actor who teamed up with Italian producer Giorgio Moroder in Germany to record the epochal "Love to Love You Baby." Inspired by expansive Philadelphia soul hits like Eddie Kendricks's nearly eight-minute-long "Girl You Need a Change of Mind," and by "Je T'aime . . . Moi Non Plus," the pornographic duet between actress Jane Birkin and singer Serge Gainsbourg, Moroder persuaded Summer to suggest the sounds of orgasm, which he set to pulsing music. Summer had the room darkened when she recorded, picturing herself as Marilyn Monroe . . . and as quiet storm progenitor White. "Barry White was the epitome of masculinity, voice-wise," she later said, "and I just figured men needed something that was comparable to that. There were people singing ballads, but there was nobody singing erotic music for men." Summer's vocals are seductive, but also confrontational. Just as foregrounding women's pleasure in pornography touched the intimate core of women's liberation, Donna Summer's love cries made clear that liberated females considered equality to be a full-body experience.[65]

The sound of women coming and going—enjoying sex or, in anthems like Gloria Gaynor's "I Will Survive," testifying gospel-style that they would remain strong and independent in this new world of unconventional partnering—dominated disco, as men's ecstasies and anxieties drove hard and soft rock. Some songs were explicitly lascivious, like porn star Andrea True's good-natured

"More, More, More"; others, like Chic's "I Want Your Love," dressed up erotic assertiveness in sophisticated sounds that reflected the glitter and satin women donned to go out dancing, their birth control pills in their evening bags. Sending messages that the changes wrought by sexual liberation wouldn't utterly undo the power of the feminine—including the feminine as expressed by a biological male like Sylvester—disco's soundtrack was daring, but also reassuring. Like the television heroines of the hugely popular prime time "jiggle" detective show *Charlie's Angels,* who could wield guns while wearing Spandex and high heels, disco proved that "the New Woman was still a woman." At the same time, the expressiveness of disco divas appealed to gay men, who saw in their insistence on dignity a mirror of their own desire to be openly themselves.[66]

Disco did have male stars, including its most successful Top 40 act, the Bee Gees, an Australian brother trio that rejuvenated its folk-rock-based career by immersing in the disco coming out of Miami. In 1977, the Bee Gees released the soundtrack to *Saturday Night Fever,* starring a strutting John Travolta as Tony Manero, a Brooklyn Italian gangster of love; the movie and its songs remain disco's most familiar—and straightest—artifacts. Sylvester also found within disco the success that had eluded him in rock. The sublime "You Make Me Feel (Mighty Real)," one long shot of ecstasy peaking like Mahalia Jackson on poppers, was Sylvester's signature song. Its remixer, Patrick Cowley, also wrote electronic music for gay porn films. In 1978, Sylvester and Cowley were contemplating taking sex sounds in music to a new level; he told a writer that "blatant sex disco music" would be their next move. "Sex disco music will be fabulous," he said. "I want to have someone fuck on the record and record it, the sounds. Not moaning or groaning, but the sounds of sex, the sounds of touching, the actual sounds of penetration. Nice music and close miking. It's not gonna be a record for sex, it's a record for dancing, with sex." Alas, it never came to pass. Both Sylvester and Cowley would die from complications of AIDS in just a few years.[67]

Perhaps David Bowie was thinking of Sylvester, his onetime rival, when he too turned to disco on his 1975 album *Young Americans*. Bored with rock, his open marriage with Angie foundering, he'd moved to New York in 1974 and was keeping company with two different African American singers, Ava Cherry and Claudia Lennear. With Cherry, he went to Harlem's famed Apollo Theater, catching a multi-artist bill that included the Main Ingredient, a big soul band David Mancuso favored in his Loft sets. With Lennear, he attended a Los Angeles club show by the soulful bluesman Bobby "Blue" Bland and sang along from his table when passed the microphone. In Philadelphia, he entered Sigma Sound Studios with the guitarist Carlos Alomar, who'd played with the Main Ingredient as well as James Brown; Alomar's wife, the singer Robin Clark; and his best friend, Luther Vandross, who ended up doing all the album's vocal arrangements.[68]

Bowie's underlying goal with *Young Americans* was to unravel his relationship with race the way he had done with gender on earlier albums. "He was working in a studio run by black entrepreneurs, with mostly black musicians, on music that was inspired by the sound of black America," notes critic Peter Doggett in his book on Bowie in the 1970s. "As a kid, that had been the most seductive part of the myth, before he knew what it meant to be black in this land. Now after the official end of segregation, the supposed death of discrimination, what was black America, the youngest America of them all?"[69] But black America is also the oldest America. Connecting with soul in the disco age, Bowie finally challenged himself to face the core conundrum of the music he'd loved since his teenage years: the way racial anxiety, the desire to mix, and the long legacy of whites observing and exploiting African American culture created unbearable tensions made accessible, though never resolved, in popular music.

Bowie honed in on the centuries-old predicament behind the many blendings in disco, and, beyond that, the hopeful attempts to expand and order sexual experience in the 1970s. Unleashing emotionalism and eroticism within interracial music that reflected his own desires but which also spoke to a long history of white appropriation—he himself would later call *Young Americans* "plastic soul" and "the phoniest R&B I've ever heard," only to take back those criticisms later—Bowie confronted the limits of individuals' potential to transform themselves, erotically or otherwise. The album is overwrought, tragic, and beautiful. It carries an air of finality, anticipating disco's own fall, after it had infiltrated the mainstream, in a backlash that obliterated its commercial and cultural presence.

By the time of the backlash—in 1979, when thousands of hard-rock-loving fans blew up disco records and rioted on Chicago's Comiskey Park during a radio station–sponsored Disco Demolition Night—Bowie was long gone from America, living in Berlin and making experimental albums with little overt erotic appeal. The culture he'd mined and mirrored on his stateside journey had moved on, too. A new puritan mood was just beginning to emerge in the stringent sounds of punk, the raw rock style rising out of gutter clubs in New York and Los Angeles. American sex would go through many changes in the ensuing decades: a plague; an increasingly conservative political mood; in entertainment, the full emergence of a corporate culture that found its biggest sensual thrills within mass-mediated spectacles. The erotic heroines and heroes of the next pop era would no longer be preoccupied with intimate self-improvement. Instead, their major statements would throw into question the meaning and value of sex itself.

OH NO, IT HURTS

AIDS, REAGAN, AND THE BACKLASH

NEW YORK, SAN FRANCISCO, SEATTLE, 1977–1997

The Disco Demolition Night of 1979 now seems ridiculously wrongheaded, but it did effectively end the music's commercial reign. Organized by the rock radio DJ Steve Dahl and sportscaster and White Sox scion Mike Veeck, it was the sputtering war cry of

classic-rock-loving dudes who felt backed into a corner by the vi-
brant identity movements of the 1970s. And it worked. Suddenly,
in straight white America, it wasn't cool to like disco anymore.
Stations nationwide dropped their disco formats and returned to
rock; record labels, not seeing profits from DJ-favored twelve-inch
singles anyway, welcomed the backlash. Yet the demolition hardly
killed dance music. That lived on in the inferno's embers, mutating into new forms like the house remixes pulsing through the gay
clubs of Chicago and New York and the New Wave synth-pop bubbling up to form a seedbed for what would become mainstream
pop in the 1980s.

As the trends turned, a nearly six-foot-tall black woman with
a jawline like a battleship stood on the bridge between disco and
what would come next. The Jamaican-born, Syracuse-raised Grace
Jones was a supermodel in Paris and an "It" girl on every chic guest
list in New York before becoming a disco diva with "I Need a Man,"
produced by the genre's standard-bearer Tom Moulton, in 1977.
An early *Ebony* magazine profile described the habitual provocateur as "a question mark followed by an exclamation point." Especially adored by the gay male fans who loved to sweat to Moulton's
beats, the impossibly angular, deep-voiced Jones cultivated an image that, like Bowie's, cast androgyny as the chosen response to
the era's ruling notion that gender, even the sexual urge itself, was
constructed and mutable. For the covers of her pioneering 1980s
recordings, Jones's French lover and collaborator Jean-Paul Goude
manipulated her image until she looked like a cat-human, a cubist
sculpture, or a fearsomely alive mannequin. "So much of Jones's
aesthetic seems bound up with the eroticization of alienation," the
music critic team of Simon Reynolds and Joy Press reflected in their
1995 book on gender and pop, *The Sex Revolts*. By that time, Jones
had become an icon of the technologically obsessed, art-damaged
New Wave underground. From the ashes of disco's inferno, she rose

as a symbol of a new day, when desire would be melted down and reshaped as something sleeker, harder, perhaps unreal.[1]

A regular at discos like the Paradise Garage, whose DJ Larry Levan was moving disco forward using synthesizers and drum machines, Jones participated in the creation of safe spaces where the music's exhortational, highly sexualized feeling of freedom could survive both its commercialization and those attacks by hard-rock-loving homophobes. She held the baby shower for her soon-to-be-born son with Goude at the club in October 1979, surrounded by male dancers dressed as toy soldiers. "The Garage was the kind of place where this kind of thing could happen," Jones wrote in her memoir. "A world unto itself embedded in but separate from the surrounding city." Like the crowd of devotees who, one reporter said, screamed for her to "show us the stomach, honey," Jones felt the need for such sheltering. Alongside its report on her shower, *Jet* magazine ran an item about Jones almost being run out of the women's room at Bloomingdale's for "being a man"—until she flashed that stomach and proved her biological bona fides.[2]

The world was already beginning to close in on the sensual playground of the 1970s. The nation's political mood continued to darken as the decade wound down, with two energy crises, a stock market crash, and massive unemployment feeding a pervasive mood of scarcity among average citizens. After an international hostage crisis his administration could not resolve, President Jimmy Carter, once a symbol of easy times who featured Southern rockers like the Allman Brothers on his campaign stops, lost his second-term bid to a new patriarch: Ronald Reagan, the former governor of California, a hippie-hating, Communist-baiting social conservative who by 1984 was promising a new "morning in America." Economically, Reagan's policies favored the wealthy and attacked social programs for the poor; culturally, they were grounded in a conservative Christian framework that assumed "shared values" rooted in the Bible and a Puritan clarity about right and wrong. "The era of self-doubt is over," Reagan declared in an address at the West Point military academy in 1981. "We've stopped looking at our warts and rediscovered how much there is to love in this blessed land." For this president and his acolytes, the critiques raised by countercultural freaks or by milder folk who'd simply enjoyed trying new positions, erotic and otherwise, were like a disease, one that required forceful suppression.[3]

Few suspected then that an actual virus, its spread abetted by Reagan's cruel refusal to acknowledge it, would devastate multiple communities in the 1980s and the 1990s and do more to undermine erotic freedoms than any government policy could manage. The summer after Reagan's inauguration, the first national reports of a strange "gay cancer" began appearing in the media. As early as 1979, the newly uncloseted men who'd flocked to the "gay ghettoes" of New York, San Francisco, and Los Angeles had begun noticing that a rising number of them were falling prey to strange afflictions that went beyond the usual syphilis and herpes that resulted from highly promiscuous lifestyles. By 1982, people were starting to call it a plague, and to use the acronym that would change America's erotic life profoundly: AIDs, or Acquired Immune Deficiency Syndrome.

That year, Grace Jones found herself at another party dubbed "Showers": the first major benefit for victims of this new epidemic, held at the Paradise Garage on April 8, 1982. She attended to support her friends, though the entertainment was provided by other disco acts, including Evelyn "Champagne" King and the Ritchie Family. The posters for the event, organized by the nascent activist group Gay Men's Health Crisis (GMHC), screamed out the aversion many men felt at curtailing their pursuit of pleasure. The line drawing on one showed a well-endowed man from neck to thighs, holding a hose in one hand and an umbrella in the other, apparently torn between getting wet and protecting himself. The playwright and GMHC cofounder Larry Kramer objected to the image, but it helped attract 2,500 people for the event. The crowd laughed and yelled, "NO WAY!" when one of the female singers in the Ritchie Family sweetly lectured dancers to keep to "one lover at a time." No one was yet ready for the future speeding toward them, when lovers would drop like the wounded during a massacre.[4]

As the 1980s became the 1990s, the AIDS pandemic and the cultural chill encouraged by the Reagan administration's social policies would greatly undermine the openness and sense of liberation that characterized the sexual revolution and its aftermath. Explicit sounds and images still abounded in popular culture, but they became increasingly embattled. Spectacle and confrontation replaced the attempts to invoke feeling at the heart of both 1970s arena rock and disco. In some corners, where a rock style called "punk" was mutating, the critique of sexual excess eventually tilted toward the puritanical. The great pop stars of the 1980s— especially Madonna, Prince, and Michael Jackson—played freely within the dreamscape of eroticized fantasy, aided by the rise of the music video; yet their epic sound-visions still reflected the era's fears and unresolved debates about normality and the perverse. A new musical style, "hip-hop," became pop's paradigm; its relationship to the erotic was conflicted from the first.

Through all these changes, a long arc of reaction and reformation that began to shift only when new medications made AIDS a chronic illness instead of a death sentence, popular music retained its central focus on the erotic. But the innocence that had always really been more mythical than maintainable was fading, replaced by a self-awareness tinged with both sorrow and rage.

BLOOD ON THE DANCE FLOOR

On June 23, 1983, the *Washington Post* ran an obituary for the sixth man to succumb to a new virus surfacing in the capital's gay neighborhoods. "William (Dirk) Diefenbach was one of the most well-

known figures on the homosexual nightclub scene here in the
mid-1970s," reported John Mintz. "A professional disc jockey, he was
said to be able to 'make or break' disco records locally with the play
he gave them at clubs and private parties. In some circles, he was
known as 'the king of disco in Washington.'"[5]

Diefenbach had held court at Lost and Found, one of DC's
disco palaces, with an 1,800-dancer capacity, seven bars, a restau-
rant, and two decks for summer nights. The club was emblematic of both the promise and the problems of post-Stonewall gay
male nightlife, which had begun to develop its own confining
roles, notably the highly muscled, mustached yet clean-cut white
"clone" ideal, the action-movie opposite of the multicultural gender bending of the Cockettes era. Early on, the club was accused of
discriminating against clubgoers of color and drag queens, a not-
uncommon violation in an increasingly segregated gay America.
Yet Lost and Found was also key in raising gay visibility in the DC
area, winning prizes for its spectacular parade floats and hosting
parties that fed the movement toward gay pride.

"Dirk was so talented," his roommate, R. J. Quinn, told Mintz.
"We were all drawn by his talent, his charm, his wit." After he became ill, though, Diefenbach's friends avoided him. They feared
the mystery infection that so many young men had suddenly contracted. Quinn, who refused to leave Diefenbach, admitted that he
hadn't eaten in their shared apartment for months. "We feel like
ticking time bombs," he said of himself and David Brown, Diefenbach's lover and fellow roommate. "I may be a dead man."

What was it like to go dancing surrounded by bombs, knowing
that you yourself might harbor a burning fuse inside? "Something
we have done to our bodies—and we still don't know what it is—has
brought us closer to death," said the GMHC's board president Paul
Popham from the stage of the Paradise Garage during the "Showers" fundraiser in 1982. AIDS was a wasting disease with hideous

symptoms, covering its victims in the purple blotches of Kaposi's sarcoma, hollowing their faces into death skulls because they couldn't keep food down. Until 1984, no one knew what caused it; until 1987, no drug was available to treat it. During that time, more than fifty thousand AIDS cases were reported to the Centers for Disease Control, and the syndrome's public face, though not the path of its actual epidemiology, was white and gay. The same men who had united in joy and hope during the liberatory 1970s were now carrying each other's emaciated bodies into hospitals, begging for help—and being rejected by many medical and social workers, who were as afraid as they themselves were. The Reagan administration enforced the public's fears by first refusing to acknowledge AIDS at all, and then perpetuating myths that marked its most visible victims as transgressors deserving of God's wrath. "You are not to touch other flesh / without a police permit," wrote the poet Essex Hemphill, an early leader in raising AIDS awareness among African American men, in 1987. From the early mystery years through the days of rage that invigorated AIDS activism, and into the 1990s, the AIDS pandemic spread as if it were a complicated terror campaign heightened by misinformed politicians and a prejudiced general public eager to believe incendiary headlines like the infamous 1985 *Life* magazine cover story that declared, in red block letters, *NOW NO ONE IS SAFE FROM AIDS.*[6]

Most heterosexual Americans had little risk of contracting the blood-borne human immunovirus that causes AIDS at that time. In the music world, however, the polysexual adventuring of the previous decade did leave all kinds of people wondering about their own health. "There was this world where friends and friends close enough to be family were disappearing all around you, leaving you feeling very vulnerable," wrote Grace Jones, who got tested after her friend, the model Tina Chow, discovered she'd contracted it from a bisexual male lover. "AIDS was a dreadful, chaotic amplification of the deathless facts of mortality that we evaded while we partied in the '70s." Her closest friends had "suddenly dropped out of sight."[7]

In the 1970s, music helped unfurl a rainbow of erotic desires and identities; and that rainbow became a flag, a symbol of a new openness. Now a sickness inextricably linked to music threatened to drive liberation back underground. The virus spread within groups of men who congregated at clubs like Lost and Found, the Stud in San Francisco, and New York's Paradise Garage and the Saint, as well as in the bathhouses where beloved divas like Jones and Bette Midler regularly performed. Some of the first known cases were music makers: local celebrity DJs like Diefenbach and nationally known artists like Sylvester's producer Patrick Cowley, who died in 1982. The singer and songwriter Michael Callen was diagnosed with what was then called Gay Related Immune Deficiency in 1982 and lived on for a remarkable eleven more years; he became a prominent activist, making music that confronted the crisis with humor and pathos. "Living in Wartime," "Love Worth Fighting For," and "Two Men Dance the Tango" became anthems of both the epidemic and of gay pride. Callen understood his affliction as a motivating gift as well as a harsh reality. "I'm happier now than I've ever been," he said to a *New York Times* reporter in 1987. "Though everything I write seems somehow to be informed by living with disease and death."[8]

The paper of record, like most of the mainstream press, lagged behind in its coverage of AIDS. *Rolling Stone,* remarkably, ran a feature on the new "sexual cancer" in February 1983, illustrated with a moody portrait of Callen and his lover and musical collaborator, drummer Richard Dworkin.[9] For the most part, the media and the music industry responded hesitantly. The Dionne Warwick–led charity single "That's What Friends Are For," with its oblique message of support, was an early fundraiser in 1985, and the New Wave innovator Cyndi Lauper wrote and recorded her memorial to a lost friend, "Boy Blue," in 1987; beyond that, music confronting AIDS was mostly segregated within the gay community before the 1990s.

Fear and homophobia explained pop's slow response to the epidemic. Even some gay men hesitated to acknowledge its reality, not wanting to curtail the sexual freedoms they'd achieved. Callen was an outlier, discussing his illness from the beginning, the opposite of bigger stars like Queen's singer Freddie Mercury, who only confirmed that he had AIDS the day before he died in 1991. Hollywood also mostly kept quiet until the screen idol Rock Hudson "gave AIDS a face" just months before his death in 1985, though a few independent films did take on the subject, including the next year's *Parting Glances,* which features future star Steve Buscemi as a musician struggling to come to terms with the illness and its disastrous effects on his career. With big budgets at stake and mainstream audiences to please, record labels and studios alike hesitated to explore the controversial subject of a "gay" disease.

The American Top 40 certainly wasn't ready to hear frank accounts of life with AIDS, even as English New Wave acts like Frankie Goes to Hollywood and the Pet Shop Boys created danceable pop hits deeply informed by gay culture and eventually infused with knowledge of the epidemic. The musicologist Paul Attinello has pointed out that nearly all mainstream songs written about AIDS in the syndrome's early years present the singer addressing a dead or dying friend. Even "The Last Song" by Elton John, who had finally come out as gay in 1988 after decades of living in a glass closet, is structured to make clear that John is assuming a character in order to deliver its first-person narrative. Attinello points out that this approach helped foster widespread empathy and make greater tolerance of homosexuality possible. Yet it also kept gay men silent and motionless, relegated to the safe space of the memorial. The fact that outside of dance music, AIDS memorial songs stood in for songs about queerness in general also obscured lesbian visibility; not until the country-pop singer k.d. lang and the rocker Melissa Etheridge emerged in the late 1980s as the most visible "dyke hopes" outside the women's music community would that sensibility reach the mainstream.[10]

The epidemic's realities did increasingly inform the music of scenes where gay men were more audible, from dance music to Broadway and classical. Men's choruses, a fixture in gay communities since the early 1970s, focused their energies on both fundraising and memorializing. "I sing for two" became the informal motto of San Francisco's famous touring choir, which lost 257 members to the epidemic. The theater world saw the confrontational *AIDS! The Musical* debut in Los Angeles in 1991; William Finn's Tony Award–winning *Falsettos* trilogy took Broadway in 1992, and the blockbuster rock musical *Rent,* which showed the effects of AIDS on a mixed-race community of gay and straight East Village bohemians, had its first staged reading in 1993. Classical composers like John Corigliano and jazz musicians like Fred Hersch took on AIDS as a subject. Dying musicians pioneered a stark new practice: self-memorializing. "It was as if he were determined to tell the world about life and *this* was the way he wrote music and *this* was the way he could play the piano—a conscious culmination of the years of practice, the long hours of meditation, the genetic predisposition and family relations, the friendship, love affairs, joys and sufferings that sometimes, mysteriously, combine to make an artist," critic Tim Page wrote of a concerto performed by its composer, Kevin Oldham, who would die two months after the event described. "It should have been Oldham's first great triumph; it may well have been his last."[11]

These works told the story of the epidemic. They were complemented by rituals of the dance floor, which remained a haven for those in the thick of the fight. People's need to stay in touch with what made being alive matter to them pushed music into hyperdrive even as death pressed close. Disco had shifted toward electronics in the late 1970s, when Patrick Cowley and a handful of other producers took the synthesizer sounds popularized by European producers such as Giorgio Moroder to new levels, creating a sped-up wash of soundwaves that became known as Hi-NRG. While Larry Levan's balance of the organic and the electronic in DJ sets that blended soul, funk, salsa, and New Wave into a new hybrid defined one 1980s approach, Hi-NRG dominated another, especially in clubs like the Saint, patronized by the white "clone" crowd.

The Saint, with its domed interior and a giant lighting rig that loomed like a spaceship over the dance floor, played a heightened role in the AIDS story—the syndrome was even known as "Saint's disease" for a moment because so many regulars had contracted it. At the Saint, Hi-NRG music, which paired relentless electronic rhythms with processed versions of the warm African American vocals always prevalent in disco, sponsored a kind of mass ecstasy. Dancers retreated to the balconies and corners to have sex during DJ sets; others remained in plain sight, providing informal sex shows. Dance historian Tim Lawrence called the Saint's dance floor formations "amoeba-like": a seemingly interlocked mass of bodies cultivating synchronicity instead of the individualistic expressiveness on display at clubs like Levan's Paradise Garage. "The goal was the moment of unity, the moment when everything disappeared, when time and space disappeared," Saint regular Jorge La Torre said. "It was just pure energy. It was extremely welcoming and extremely powerful. Within it, everything seemed possible."[12]

The shift from organic-sounding to mechanically driven dance music enhanced its role in providing gay men with a sense of order amidst chaos, just as the groupie system had helped heterosexual rock fans navigate erotic confusion in the early 1970s. Songs like Miquel Brown's "So Many Men, So Little Time" and Hazell Dean's "Searchin' (I Gotta Find a Man)" expressed the unruliness of desire via gospel- and rock-based vocals provided by female singers. But the hard beats and repetitive sound effects transforming this human element created patterns and restrictions that made those "amoeba-like" dancers respond. Walter Hughes, who in 1992 wrote the first academic defense of disco, argued that submitting to disco's rhythms guided men into a particular post-Stonewall gay identity—to accept their sexual outsiderness "with pleasure, rather than suffering." Post-AIDS, Hughes argued, dancing to increasingly machine-dominated dance tracks helped men process the ways in which the epidemic had changed their lives. "The music that once taught some men to be gay can now teach them what all gay men must learn: how to live with AIDS. Like safe sex or ACT UP or the concept of sexual identity itself, this indispensable discipline enables them to submit without acquiescing," he wrote. Hughes, a Princeton professor, died from complications of AIDS in 1994.[13]

The discipline of the beat engendered a prophylactic way of being gay. The young men of the AIDS generation weren't always practicing safe sex, but many did project a more distanced and overtly puritan attitude toward desire. *Mother Jones* writer William Hayes noted the shift in 1990 at the legendary San Francisco club the Stud: "The lead dogs of the new generation are easy to spot. Tom Cruise and Charlie Sheen are their icons: clean-cut, clean-shaven, straight-jawed, white, all-American boys, wearing ripped and bleached Levi's, t-shirts or starched shirts, tennis shoes or loafers, blue blazers or stressed leather jackets. These pristine boys, who appear to possess an inbred, heterosexual strength and immunity, are the clones of the new order. There are no more red bandannas, signifying that they are into fisting or fucking, in their back pockets. The *look* is antidrug, safe sex, perhaps even monogamous relationships, whether boys today believe in them or not."[14]

Throughout the 1980s, this cleansed, streamlined version of eroticism would infiltrate the mainstream, especially within Madonna's songs and videos. But within a gay scene becoming activist and, in a new vernacular, queer, it had a more openly confrontational counterpart. A queer punk aesthetic arose in league with AIDS street activism: performers, writers, and visual artists like David Wojnarowicz, Ron Athey, Vaginal Creme Davis, Dennis Cooper, and Kathy Acker expressed the far more in-your-face spirit of street movements like ACT UP and Queer Nation. These activists weren't throwing fundraisers in fancy discos; they were threatening to dump the bodies of AIDS sufferers on the steps of federal buildings until the state responded full force to the threat.

ACT UP's most resonant slogan—SILENCE=DEATH—was a call to clamor that echoed into the 1990s and changed the course of the epidemic. Its celebration of noise reflected a musical movement that challenged the long-established languages of eroticism. The music called "punk" exposed bodies as conduits of pain, disgust, and extreme vulnerability. It made room for pleasure, too, but that always came as a shock, like a boy's first wet dream or a girl's shiver as she rubbed against a rough sponge in the shower. If 1980s dance music helped gay men—and through them, the pop mainstream— relearn adult sex in the harsh light of AIDS, punk responded to the era's sexual crisis with the inherent impropriety and moral certainty of a child. Punk reformed sex and rock and roll by making them dirty again, spitting on them, and wiping them clean.

LOVE COMES IN SPURTS

On an ordinary East Village night in 1976, Stiv Bators of Cleveland's Dead Boys got a blow job onstage at CBGB. Unlike the all-male sexual explorations occurring blocks away at the baths on St. Mark's Place, Bators's oral trip was an act, not destined for completion. The Dead Boys were new in town and had recently met Genya Ravan, a pioneering female rocker of the 1960s, then breaking into production. The Dead Boys had a song called "Caught with the Meat in Your Mouth," and Ravan saw it as an opportunity for the group to up its showmanship. She goaded a waitress to jump on-

stage, extract Bators's member, cover it with whipped cream, and
suck. "The waitress didn't fellate Stiv to the point of coming, because the guy had to sing," Ravan later said. "I didn't want him to
go off-key. So I said, 'Don't go *that* far.' Poor guy."[15]

An unfinished blow job: in many ways, that was the spirit of
punk. This subculture's erotic energy was fitful, frustrated, and
deliberately crude. Originating on both sides of the Atlantic in the
mid-1970s as a grittier take on glam and art rock, punk stood in
opposition to the excesses of both disco and hard rock. Its main
stated target was "pathetic hippie crap," the idealistic haze that had
obscured not only the sexism and racism that no amount of free
love could overcome, but also the frustration, awkwardness, and
pain endemic to human intimacy.[16] Often punks actually seemed
to resent sex. "I don't believe in sexuality at all," said Sid Vicious of
the Sex Pistols, the British band that made punk an international
sensation, in 1976. "People are very unsexy. I don't enjoy that side
of life. Being sexy is just a fat arse and tits that will do anything
you want."

From its bloody 1970s birth onward, and even within the
commercialized versions sold today in mall stores like Hot Topic
or on the annual Warped Tour, punk's take on sex has remained
committedly awkward, even resistant. "It wasn't about hot-wiring
the body," remarked the essayist James Wolcott, who hung out at
CBGB at the club's height, though he did note that "there was a
sex chart in the ladies' room peter-metering [that is, measuring the
penis sizes of] the top contenders on the scene." Sex Pistols road
manager Nils Stevenson echoed Wolcott's unromantic view from
the English side: "Sex was often sordid, not particularly good, just
lots of it," he once told oral historian John Robb. "In club toilets
in London, Birmingham, Manchester. We weren't getting into
the pervy, interesting sex—the masks and that sort of stuff. There
wasn't time. It was a biological function."[17]

Yet punk was also one of popular music's most sexually explicit genres, going well beyond the pleasure sounds of Donna Summer and Robert Plant to incorporate every unappetizing squish, sticky slap, and stifled fart that issued from bodies *en flagrante*. "Love comes in spurts," yelped Richard Hell, one of punk's first frontmen, and, with his pouty lips sneering beneath dark-circled eyes, its emblematic sex symbol. "Oh no, it hurts!" He sounded like he was masturbating, possibly for the first time. Punks like Hell uttered what was both obvious and improper, and, onstage, did what was both indecent and irresistible. Sex Pistols manager Malcolm McLaren's famous manifesto for punk began with the phrase "Be childish," continuing, "be disrespectful, be irresponsible, be everything this society hates." The irresponsibility of the child is different than that of the criminal or even the morally questionable adult: it denotes a certain clarity of vision and an uncorrupted heart, the ability to see the basic preexisting truths that social niceties obscure.

Making those noises that people are taught from babyhood to keep private, not prettying them up the way porn stars might but including ugly grunts and creepy shouted fantasies, punks declared that 1970s music had gone far enough in its sensual pursuits. This music stripped everything down to the basic urge; "I just can't get wise to those tragical lies," Hell sang, spitting on old ideas of romance. Though there is such a thing as punk crooning, usually performed off-key with an eye roll, punks generally hated that lovey-dovey stuff and the glorification of privacy that went with it. Like kids walking in on their parents fucking and flipping on the light, these truth seekers demanded that sex be naked and exposed.

Also like children, punks would put anything in their mouths. Dead Boys guitarist Cheetah Chrome complained decades after the group's glory days that most people didn't recall how tight and melodic the group's high-octane rock could be, but they'd always mention the onstage head that became the band's shtick, or "Stiv blowing his nose on bologna and eating it." Marky Ramone, the original drummer for early punk's best-known quartet, was no-torious for taking dares to scarf down anything from roaches to cat food. The Ramones also had a singer with a weirdly distended mouth, Joey (born Jeffrey Ross Hyman to a very nice Queens cou-ple), who crooned in a style derived from the girl groups—except his dreamy dreams were about eating refried beans. "Handsome" Dick Manitoba of the Dictators preferred burgers, even though, as he sang in the satirical "Master Race Rock," they made him throw up every day. The binge and purge was "the best part of growing up," he claimed. Taking in whatever came next, punks also made a show of getting it out: gobbing, as it became known, was the trade-mark of punks and proto-punks from Patti Smith to the Sex Pis-tols' Johnny Rotten to Manitoba, who perfected a drawn-out saliva ball–expulsion technique he called "the spit trick."[18]

Punks were also famous for exposing themselves—especially their mooned derrières—and wearing ripped, stained, or otherwise trashed clothing, often bearing confrontational slogans written in indelible felt pen. The movement intersected with fashion in New York boutiques like Trash and Vaudeville, and in the London shop called Sex, run by the Sex Pistols' manager Malcolm McLaren and his partner, the designer Vivienne Westwood. Sex was where the Sex Pistols originated; the store sold gear favored by bikers, gay cruis-ers, and bondage fetishists. Punk fashion wasn't childlike, but it did have an unmistakable aura of dress-up—not the cute kind that parents catalog in photographs, but the kind that feels just wrong, inappropriate, aesthetically displeasing. In his topography of punk, Lipstick Traces, which connects the music to other art movements such as Dada, critic Greil Marcus wrote: "Today, it's hard to remem-ber just how ugly the first punks were. They were ugly. There were no mediations. A ten-inch safety pin cutting through a lower lip into a swastika tattooed onto a cheek was not a fashion statement."[19]

Punks cultivated immaturity as a method of refusal. They practiced what Marcus has called "negation": not the narcissistic blackout of the nihilist, but the truth teller's curtain pull, revealing that the world is not as it seems. When it came to sexuality, punk childishness was textbook Freud—a celebration of oral and anal fixations that spread scat and cum all over those pretty line drawings in the 1970s sex manuals. The groupie system had encouraged young girls and some boys to behave as if they were adults; as punks, they could reclaim their bodies as their own juvenile domain. Writer Carola Dibbell captured punk's gift to young women in her description of what one of its founding mothers, Patti Smith, presented to her fans: "What this skinny weirdo offered wasn't androgyny per se but a new use for it: to cut a niche in the music that was neither sexual invitation nor sexual confrontation, like, 'Hi, I'm Patti Smith. I'm going to be charismatic. But not sexually charismatic! That way we can be friends.'"

Some prominent punk women competed with each other for time with men in bands—there were still groupies, the most tragic being Sid Vicious's girlfriend, Nancy Spungen, whom he stabbed to death in 1978. But for the first time in any number, women were also *in* bands. In New York, there was boyish Tina Weymouth, playing bass in the Talking Heads, and womanly Debbie Harry, a former Playboy bunny who made sex symbolism comical as Blondie's frontwoman. The West Coast had Alice Bag and Exene Cervenka in Los Angeles and Penelope Houston in San Francisco—"violence girls," as Bag called herself, in thrift-store rags and combat boots, determined antidotes to the tanned, willing California beach baby. Southern anti-belles in bands like Pylon and the B-52s entered the scene and introduced an accented and regionally rich vocabulary into rock singing. Punk women managed bands, put together fanzines, ran clubs. "Punk was the right metaphor for us, with its emphasis on meaningless threats, on weakness and chutzpah and the relativity of size," Dibbell writes. "We were the right metaphor for punk, with our ungaugeable ability, our nerve, and our joy at just being there at all."[20]

The idea that women could be loud, aggressive, and even dis-
gusting contradicted both conventional views of femininity and
the common feminist notion that women were essentially peace-
loving and gentle. How could punks acknowledge gender difference without reinforcing inequality? Mostly, they didn't. Instead of
taking glam's femme-leaning androgyny fix, punks insisted they
could breach the gendered divide by stalling the processes that fed
it. In the punk filmmaker Alex Cox's 1984 comedy *Repo Man,* two
petty thieves, Duke and Debbi, struggle to define their relationship; at one point, Duke says, "Don't you think it's time we settle
down? Get a little house. I want you to have my baby . . . Everybody
does it." Debbi replies, "Asshole!" and the two continue on their
trail of mayhem. Duke's daydream of ordinary family life is presented as the most ridiculous idea either has ever entertained.[21]

Punk's rejection of adulthood had little to do with the hippie
cult of innocence that surfaced in songs like Buffalo Springfield's
"I Am a Child," which updated Victorian notions of youth as closer
to nature and spiritual wholeness. Instead, it responded to realities about children coalescing since the 1970s. The phenomenon
of the "latchkey kid," left unsupervised with no adequate day care
while parents worked, had become a matter of national concern; at
a 1983 Congressional hearing, researchers reported that nearly 15
million minors returned to an empty house every day. Next came
"milk carton kids"—the missing children, whose faces adorned domestic dairy products starting in 1985. Most of these kids were ab-
ducted by aggrieved divorced parents, and others were runaways,
but the carton campaign inspired widespread terror of pedophiliac
perversity. "There are child pornographers out there," a police officer commented in one report on the campaign. "Others just want
a child of their own. Sometimes children are sold in baby-selling
rings. It happens all the time."[22]

A more tangible threat was domestic abuse—something several stars of the punk scene themselves had experienced. Los

Angeles punk pioneer Alice Bag writes in her memoir about her father's abuse of her mother. When her boyfriend, also a punk, once slapped her in the early days of her band, Bag found her own furious child energy resurging. "My 6-year-old self is taking control, and she only sees one way to go," Bag writes. "*'You are either a tyrant or a victim . . . .'* little Alicia whispers to me in the darkness. *'. . . and you will never be a victim.'*" It was this rage and determination that Alice poured into her snarling vocals.[23]

Punk was the sound of kids telling adults to cut the bullshit and assuring each other they wouldn't repeat their parents' mistakes. In Bret Easton Ellis's emblematic, punk-influenced 1985 novel *Less Than Zero,* which depicts a group of rich teenagers descending into unobserved mayhem (and occasional prostitution) in Southern California, the standard answer one kid gives to another when asked about an absent parent is, "They don't care." The novel's only moral presence is an image—a poster hanging in the bedroom of the novel's antihero, Clay, showing the punk-influenced English singer-songwriter Elvis Costello on the cover of his 1981 album, *Trust.* (The novel's title also derives from a Costello song.) Like the eyes of Dr. T. J. Eckleburg presiding over F. Scott Fitzgerald's desolate modern landscape in *The Great Gatsby,* Elvis Costello's peer out over pink-tinted sunglasses, witnessing his audience of lost boys and girls gradually abandoning hope.[24]

Costello loved words too much to remain in punk's childhood; his witty, complicated songs heralded the mainstreaming of the music within the more pop-friendly packages of 1980s New Wave, a style that also welcomed back androgyny via code-switchers like Annie Lennox of Eurythmics and Culture Club's Boy George. Costello's early music did show some of the childlike discomfort with sex that other punks so gleefully declared; more to the point was his appearance, skinny and pimpled, as he sang about sneaky feelings and the "paper striptease" of failed monogamy. Harder-sounding punk bands provided endless examples of punk's childish mix of repulsion and base desire. A few choice titles from both England and the United States: "Bodies" by the Sex Pistols; "Orgasm Addict" by Buzzcocks; "Carcass" by Siouxsie and the Banshees; "Germfree Adolescents" by X-Ray Spex; "What Does Sex Mean to Me?" by Human Sexual Response; "Love Lies Limp" by Alternative TV; "Come Again" by the Au Pairs; "Asexuality in the 80's" by the Tools; "Sex Bomb" by Flipper; "Family Fodder" by Debbie Harry; "Stained Sheets" by James White and the Blacks with Lydia Lunch; "Anthrax" by Gang of Four; "Code Blue," an ode to necrophilia, by T.S.O.L.; "53rd & 3rd," about male prostitution, by the Ramones; "Johnny Hit and Run Paulene," about rape, by X; "Slip It In" by Black Flag; "Too Drunk to Fuck" by Dead Kennedys; "I Can't Come" by the Snivelling Shits.

These songs vary in sophistication and political awareness. Some songwriters borrowed from a literary legacy that included French outsiders like Arthur Rimbaud and American barflies like Charles Bukowski; John Doe and Exene Cervenka of X, the artiest of LA punks, had actually met at a poetry reading. Others, like the explicitly Marxist Gang of Four and feminists the Raincoats and the Au Pairs, were openly critical of social norms. Andy Warhol's favorite punk band, the Talking Heads, were New Wave before the term was invented and didn't scorn sex so much as infuse it with anxiety; David Byrne's idiot-savant valentines like "Uh-Oh, Love Comes to Town" were both neurotic and sweet. Despite these many variations, what punk's originators and early antecedents shared was a determined and often gleeful refusal to view sex as either romantic or sophisticated. Marcus calls this "banishing the love song," though punk didn't banish the love song so much as smash it, finger it, strangle it, and make it into a nasty nursery rhyme. With a bang, early punks started the process of building a genuinely new approach to sex and gender within rock. It flowered thornily in many different ways: in the more puritanical, aggressively male California and New Jersey hardcore scenes; the politically radical subcultures of clean-living "straight edge" and feminist "riot grrrl"; and in a new generation of mainstream rock musicians who didn't identify with the spangly satyrs punk first called ridiculous.

That new cohort had matured in the shadow of AIDS. By the mid-1980s, because of the common practice of intravenous drug use and because its own gay and lesbian members were becoming more visible, AIDS had come to affect the punk scene. Partly in response, a strong queer punk community emerged, though mostly centered in the visual and literary arts rather than in music. Drag artists like Vaginal Creme Davis and Joey Arias, writers including Wojnarowicz and Acker, performance artists like Karen Finley and Athey, and filmmakers like Nick Zedd and Richard Kern faced both social approbation and, in some cases, government censure in the face of social pressure from the religious right. The fun of sexual childishness was fading in light of so many new threats. "It's a strange world full of frivolity on one hand and people dropping dead of starvation, AIDS and murder on the other," wrote the queer punk novelist Steve Abbott in 1989.[25] He died from complications of AIDS in 1992, but his peers continued to hug romance 'til it hurt at least until the end of the century. In the meantime, pop would deal with the issues of the age in a different way.

MATERIAL GIRL, UNUSUAL BOYS

In 1989, after half a decade as the premier pop star of the 1980s and, according to her adoring fans and the press, the most famous woman in the world, Madonna answered an interviewer's question about how she ever managed to get any sleep. "You know what I do?" she said. "I think of a very specific moment in my life, like when I was nine years old and I was the fourth-grade hall monitor, and everyone in class was all lined up to go to the bathroom. I remember every detail—what people were wearing, what I felt like, what I was wearing, the smell of the school. It works my mind and tires me out. Then I find myself drifting into sleep."[26]

This seemingly trivial anecdote struck at the heart of what made Madonna not only a superstar but the defining spirit of mainstream America's erotic redefinitions: not her beguiling if admittedly thin voice or her highly trained dancer's body, but her steely, highly utilitarian imagination. Beginning in 1983, when she became the first major star of the music video age, and well into the 1990s, Madonna embodied the nation's quest for new paths toward sexual freedom. As AIDS became a devastating fact of life for millions and the Reagan administration continued to "just say no" to civil liberties conservatives found sinful, Madonna created a spectacular music universe where female pleasure and self-determination ruled. She came to stand for a style of liberal, sex-positive feminism that was less idealistic and openly radical than 1970s women's liberation but better served the tastes of women entering the corporate sphere or trying to bring awareness into their otherwise conventional marriages. She championed a multicultural vision of the erotic, grounded in her own experiences with lovers and close friends of color. And though Madonna herself identified as heterosexual with only an occasional queer roving eye, she helped bring the sensibilities of lesbian, gay, bisexual, transgender, and queer communities into the light. Madonna did all this within a swirl of controversy arising from her insistence on having the final say about which fantasies her songs and image would sell to the public—and how they would do so.

Madonna's waking dreams ranged from reenactments of Marilyn Monroe's movies to a solo dance, broadcast nationally on the new cable network MTV, depicting a bride having an orgasm. They offered hints of bondage and other unconventional sexual practices that became full-fledged explorations as Madonna's fame and power increased. In the first years of her career, she was labeled a slut and a tart by social conservatives and dismissed as vapid by many (mostly male) music writers. Madonna nonetheless rapidly found her public: gay men and teenage girls, two demographics whose own erotic explorations had long represented risk and impropriety, and young adult women, who saw in her blend of independence and glamorous femininity a way to move beyond the incomplete transformations of the sexual revolution. Each of these groups found their own forms of solace and inspiration in the dream worlds Madonna and her collaborators constructed in songs, dance-based live performances, and a new form, the music video, which now had its own television network, MTV.

Born Madonna Louise Cicconne in Bay City, Michigan, in 1958, Madonna willed herself into being as a singularly named, voraciously ambitious young adult. Though she had peers, including fellow MTV favorites Cyndi Lauper and Debbie Harry, Madonna's aura of utter self-sufficiency—some would say selfishness—made her unusual among female stars in the 1980s, if not wholly unprecedented among women in American pop. Most women in the rock and soul era emerged either within bands or as part of tight-knit communities; few presented themselves as the instruments of their own destinies with the force and clarity that Madonna did. Aretha Franklin was tethered to the church and to her powerful father; Janis Joplin first found success with her Big Brother brothers. Joni Mitchell stood out in the 1970s as a chronicler of female independence, yet spent her early years intimately collaborating with (and struggling to not be overshadowed by) lovers like Graham Nash and James Taylor. Whitney Houston, the biggest female R&B star of the 1980s, had a very visible mentor in Arista Records chief Clive Davis. In punk, the band was the basic unit and few solo artists emerged at all, while the divas of disco were nearly always associated with their male producers. Outliers like Nina Simone, a jazz artist who hadn't yet been reclaimed by younger generations as the High Priestess of Soul, and Kate Bush, who was forging a highly unusual path within art rock but remained obscure beyond her native England, had little influence on the general presumption that in popular music, women did not stand alone.

Not so Madonna. From the beginning of her rapid rise from New York club kid to megastar, she presented herself as singular and self-directed. An assertive teenager who felt like a misfit, Madonna had begun her artistic life as a dancer, mentored by her teacher, Christopher Flynn, who would take her to black and gay clubs after ballet class. "Just as Madonna's adult self was emerging at the age of sixteen, she found a gay man to make sense of her world," her biographer Lucy O'Brien writes. In dance class, Madonna learned how to manage time and take calculated risks with her body. In the clubs, she discovered how dancers' erotic display could signal their desires to potential partners or provide satisfaction in and of itself. At Menjo's, Detroit's flashiest gay nightspot, Madonna would sip soda and dance to Earth, Wind & Fire, reveling in the room's amoeba energy while always keeping her wits about her, assessing how she fit in.[27]

Madonna absorbed the look and energy of punk, ripping the leotards she'd wear to class and reassembling them with safety pins. Arriving in New York in 1978, she split her time among dance classes, discos, and punk clubs. In a mid-1980s interview with her friend, the actor Harry Dean Stanton, she would cite early punk-pop pioneers Debbie Harry and Chrissie Hynde of the Pretenders, who sang openly about their own sexual adventures and desires, as among her chief inspirations. "They gave me courage," she said.[28] They also gave her a vocal style. If dancing helped her learn musical structure—to "understand musicality and rhythm and coordination," as she told Stanton—and the mostly African American sounds she heard in dance clubs informed her ideas about emotiveness, punk and its more commercial cousin New Wave helped her structure the aggressiveness that had been a defining personality trait since her childhood.

Demos of her early band, first called Breakfast Club, then Emmy and the Emmys, show Madonna trying on the punk techniques of vocal overdrive and word distortion in songs like "On the Ground" and "Burning Up." (The latter, transformed into a club track, became one of her first hits.) She namechecked R&B singers like Patrice Rushen (also a major early influence on Madonna's male counterpart, Prince) as inspiration for the demos she shopped to clubs, but punk's impulsiveness continued to play into Madonna's vocal approach. This was the sound of a young woman trying out what singing is like, having fun "like a kid on a carnival ride," as an early review put it, and seemingly not noticing who's listening. A childish sound, rapidly coming into new knowledge. Young women, especially, could relate.[29]

Madonna's female fans cherished her self-presentation as a modern "material girl" who also felt the pull of old-fashioned romance, if not the values of monogamy and the subservience attached to them. As she aimed for fame, the singer polished up her look to be less punk and more Betty Boop, in a comical reappropriation of classic glamour that was also popular among New Wave artists like Lauper. Her acting ambitions (her first featured role was in the 1985 screwball comedy *Desperately Seeking Susan*) cemented her connection to Hollywood, and several of her videos replayed classic romances like *West Side Story* and *Gentlemen Prefer Blondes*. Yet unlike Marilyn Monroe or Natalie Wood, who'd both died tragically, Madonna consistently projected a resilience that felt very conventionally male. She identified as much with gay men as with other women; like drag, her femininity was obviously constructed. And even as she mined many histories' worth of erotic imagery, both in her self-presentation and in dance, Madonna retained the spontaneity she'd learned from punk. The constant interplay of masculine and feminine signals within her own performances offered a new kind of energy that was highly adaptable to different interpretations of sensuality and romance. At a time when earlier erotic models were failing, Madonna presented a way to dance through the landmines.

"When sexual freedom was tried out on a large scale, many

women began to discover that it created a whole new set of problems," wrote Erica Jong, whose 1973 soft-core pornographic novel
Fear of Flying had helped take that revolution to the masses, in a
1986 op-ed entitled "Women and the Fear of AIDS." "There didn't
seem to be much freedom in waking up in bed with someone with
whom you didn't want to share breakfast." Once the great advocate
of the commitment-free "zipless fuck," Jong found herself harbor-
ing cautious hope that fear of AIDS might cause people to "make
sex a little more mysterious and precious again." Such sentiments
revealed a certain blinkered callousness among white heterosexuals, far less at risk (Jong did acknowledge) than gay men or people
of color. Yet with so little still known about the syndrome, AIDS
anxiety remained very real for everyone in the mid-1980s, com-
pounded by new heterosexual scares about less lethal STDs such
as herpes.[30]

If the fear of sex was rising among those who once welcomed
freer mores, among moral conservatives it began to reach a fever
pitch. The religious right was not a new force in American politics,
but it surged, a strange mirror to the video fantasy realm of MTV,
as televangelists such as Pat Robertson and Jerry Falwell raged
against sensuality on their daily cable broadcasts. Falwell founded
the Moral Majority political action committee in 1979, then found
a partner in the Reagan administration. Reagan's attacks on social
services were grounded in demonizing the poor, especially African American and Latino "welfare queens" who allegedly became
pregnant as teens to gain a federally funded free ride. Abstinence-
only education grew in popularity among conservatives, reviving
the Cold War–era notion that unwed sex threatened national security by dissipating the futures of the nation's youngest citizens.
"Babies having babies" became the catchwords for young female
lives squandered. Gay men and teenage girls found themselves in
a strange (and mostly metaphorical) alliance as the demonized
figures of a values-driven backlash that viewed their sexual lives

as sick and potentially catastrophic for the whole nation. While many popular musicians stood up against the religious right, only one managed to embody both the resilient joy of gay life and the eager sense of exploration teenage girls inevitably still embraced— Madonna, the woman whose hits spoke in nonjudgmental ways about "physical attraction" and "going over the borderline" and even, in "Papa Don't Preach," teen pregnancy.

"She is living out our fantasies," a sixteen-year-old "Madonna wannabe" told *Los Angeles Times* music writer Robert Hilburn at a 1985 concert. "She's able to be something that our parents would never let us get away with . . . that whole 'slut' image. I'd never really want to be like that, but it's fun seeing someone else do it on stage. It's usually just the guys who get a chance to do that." Madonna played up her own girlishness to appeal to these fans, but she also sent them a message serving her original community of artists and bohemians, one highly populated by gay men. Recalling a youth spent going to gay clubs in her native Michigan, she explained to a reporter the awakening she felt in those thrilling environments, her "introduction to glamour and sophistication": "Men were going crazy and doing poppers," she said. "They were all dressed really well and were more free about themselves than all the blockhead football players I met in high school."[31]

Having lost close friends (including her former roommate and style advisor, the artist Martin Burgoyne) to AIDS, Madonna championed awareness of the pandemic. In 1985, as a host on *Saturday Night Live*, she appeared in a skit lampooning straight people who feared they could contract the infection through skin-to-skin contact. She participated in AIDS fundraisers throughout the 1980s and recorded a safe-sex public service announcement in 1988. Her 1989 album *Like a Prayer* included an insert instructing readers about safe sex and declaring, "People with AIDS—regardless of their sexual orientation—deserve compassion and support, not violence and bigotry." In 1992, on her multimedia foray into soft-core pornography—the album *Erotica* and the book *Sex*—she paid tribute to Burgoyne with the tender ballad "In This Life." The song concluded with Madonna quietly intoning, "Someday I pray it will end. I hope it's in this lifetime."

Madonna offered those affected by AIDS—anyone sexually active in the 1980s—a gift: she cleared a space where eroticism could run free. That space was in the mind. She established this safe zone in the video for her breakthrough hit, "Lucky Star," a simple clip of two performances, one solo and another accompanied by two other dancers, against a white background that looked like infinity. While the group shots establish Madonna's athleticism and unique girlish androgyny, the images of the singer alone, gazing seductively but most of all knowingly at the unidentified recipient of her advances, are key; they make the viewer think of Madonna thinking, dreaming, feeling herself. The girl group–style lyrics—"you must be my lucky star, 'cos you shine on me wherever you are"—reinforce the message that Madonna can enjoy this love light without the physical presence of her lover, by imagining him (or her). It was the first of countless erotic performances where Madonna showed she needed only herself to be satisfied.[32]

Soon, this self-pleasuring power would become explicit and central to Madonna's version of sexual liberation. Her 1984 performance at MTV's first-ever Video Music Awards ceremony, in which a flowing but translucent wedding gown covered her white corset as she sang her latest love song, "Like a Virgin," while gyrating across the floor, climaxed with a series of floor humps that were unmistakably onanistic. Masturbation was the centerpiece of her 1990 Blond Ambition Tour, in which she mounted a bed while singing the same song and, caressed by male dancers in conical bras, gestured herself to feigned climax. Her most famous video of the 1980s, for the gospel-inspired "Like a Prayer" (a song that seemed to many to be about oral sex, with its catchphrase, "I'm down on my knees, I wanna take you there"), was an elaborate and surreal sequence in which Madonna fantasized about carnal relations with a statue of St. Martin de Porres (the patron saint of mixed-race people, played by the actor Leon Robinson) come to life. By the time she embarked upon the *Erotica/Sex* project of 1992, preceded by the explicit (and banned from MTV) video for "Justify My Love," Madonna was stating the obvious: "These are my fantasies," she wrote in the introduction to *Sex*. "My fantasies take place in a perfect world, a world without AIDS."[33]

Madonna's safe-sex imaginary, as it evolved from the come-ons of "Lucky Star" to the interracial, polymorphously perverse bondage fantasies of *Erotica/Sex,* was much more redolent of music video than of Golden Age pornography. Everything is sleekly posed and informed by a dancer's sense of telegraphed gestures. As the most significant superstar borne to greatness by MTV, Madonna's aesthetic defined the network and, in many ways, the medium, at least until hip-hop and alternative rock became more prominent at the turn of the 1990s. More than the early New Wavers who preened and posed through their clips and the heavy metal stars who enthusiastically eyed strippers in theirs, Madonna was a fully realized subject and agent of this new form.

And what was music video? As its pioneering scholar, Andrew Goodwin, wrote, it was television *made musical*: "Television is made to succumb to new rhythms, in the pulses of rock, rap and dance music . . . [M]usic has invaded television as [much] as it is true that video has 'taken over' music." In music video, the logic of the song, not of cinematic narrative, takes over. Conflict and resolution can occur simultaneously. The performer's identity merges with that of the song's main character, and the main "action" involves the viewer's physical and emotional engagement with stimulating musical hooks, complemented by visual ones, instead of with an unfolding story line. Finally—and this is even more evident today, as youths grow up making their own video tributes and posting them on social media platforms like YouTube—music video encourages imitation, the living fan fiction of learning stars' moves and styles by watching them on repeat. Ultimately, music video is a fantasy realm, creating a feeling of privacy in viewers and listeners who experience through these clips the nonlinear barrage of sensation they otherwise create in their own daydreams.[34]

It was the perfect form for an era whose great erotic metaphor was, by necessity of the epidemic, self-pleasuring. Music video was also a great foil for the moral arbiters of the religious right, whose desire to keep sex neatly within the bonds of marriage made the awakening of women, gay people, and the young a particularly vivid terror. The songs that video made popular, with their appeal to the erotic imagination, deeply disturbed many parents. In 1985, when the religious right found strange allies in the Congressional wives of the Parents Music Resource Center led by liberal Democrat Al Gore's spouse Tipper, the view was firmly established that video made music a threat in children's own homes—where they might, as moms say, get ideas. The PMRC's most memorable battle was the attempt to label albums with "explicit content" stickers. According to Gore's cofounder, Susan Baker, her seven-year-old daughter's interest in Madonna's song "Like a Virgin" inspired the censorious campaign.[35]

That's one historical account; others credit Tipper Gore's discovery that a song on the soundtrack to the film *Purple Rain*, "Darling Nikki," included a line about its heroine "masturbating with a magazine." That song was by Prince, Madonna's chief rival, brief lover, and onetime collaborator in cultivating Reagan-era safe-sex outrageousness. Born Prince Rogers Nelson in Minneapolis the same year Madonna was born in Detroit, the African American multi-instrumentalist and songwriter was also inspired by Joni Mitchell, 1970s dance music, and, if not punk, New Wave. He released two albums in the late 1970s, but it was 1980's *Dirty Mind* that established his winning persona. On the front cover, he wore an overcoat and black bikini underwear, while the back cover showed him lounging on a bed, revealing that he also wore thigh-high stockings. His glam look and his blend of rock hooks, funk rhythms, and synthesizers defied musical categorization and led *New York Times* critic Robert Palmer to ask, in 1981, "Is Prince Leading Music to a True Biracism?" Noting Prince's isolation outside any musical milieu, Palmer also heard in his explicit but also often spiritually tinged lyrics the idea that "sexual liberation is both a political program and a religion." In fact, like Madonna, Prince was most interested in cultivating a sexual utopia within his listeners' minds and bodies.[36]

Simultaneously androgynous, worshipful of women, and boisterously heterosexual, Prince reconnected the dots between Little Richard and glam rock to enact a sly critique of heterosexuality. Like Led Zeppelin, he incorporated elements of pornography into his act.[37] His trick was to rewrite porn's story lines. Songs like "Little Red Corvette" and the notorious "Darling Nikki," both released at the peak of his fame in the mid-1980s, recount sexual encounters in which women fully run the show. "I guess you could say she was a sex fiend," Prince snarls appreciatively about the self-pleasuring exhibitionist he meets in a hotel lobby in the latter song. Throughout his music, Prince depicts himself as both pursuer and pursued, an experienced alpha male and a virginal, androgynous beta. His songs about more sustained relationships—"When You Were Mine," which has Prince accepting a threesome with another man to please his lady, or "If I Was Your Girlfriend," one of many fantasies in which he imagines himself as a woman's soft and wet plaything—invoke a utopian ideal in which a conventionally aggressive masculine principle and a receptive feminine one can be cultivated within one person. In Prince's ideal couple, a man and a woman interchange roles with ease. When, in "Uptown," Prince and a potential female lover each ask if the other is gay, both are recognizing an innate androgyny that disrupts the straight paradigm.

In a 2009 interview with *Out* magazine, Lisa Coleman, a key-
board player in Prince's most notable band, the Revolution, called
Prince "a fancy lesbian." Her musical partner and former girlfriend,
the guitarist Wendy Melvoin, corroborated the description: "He's a
girl, for sure, but he's not gay. He looked at me like a gay woman
would look at another woman." She added, "It doesn't matter what
sexuality, gender you are. You're in the room with him and he gives
you that look and you're like, 'Okay, I'm done. It's over.'" Dez Dickerson, also a guitarist for the Revolution, once said that Prince
devised archetypes for each member of the band to embody. The
bandleader's was "pure sex. Those were his exact words." Prince's
pure sex either transcended or preceded designations of gender or
orientation, but it always released a feminine perfume.[38]

Prince imagined heterosexual love as a mirror in which the
male reflects the original female. This was deeply appealing to
female fans, especially. It reflected the artist's comfort with his
own feminine side and suggested that "women, not girls, rule my
world," as he sang in "Kiss." Funk and glam rock had played at
boys being girls; Prince played with the idea of putting the girls
in charge. In *Purple Rain*, he pays homage to David Bowie with a
scene that reflects his own nonbinary vision. During a nightclub
performance by the Revolution, the menacing synth riff of the
song "Computer Blue" fills the room. As the band plays, Melvoin,
dressed and coiffed to identically resemble Prince, strides over
and drops to her knees before him, miming fellatio on his guitar
as she continues to play her own. It's a clear reference to Bowie's
early 1970s habit of putting his mouth on Mick Ronson's Gibson
Les Paul during Spiders from Mars shows. "The total effect is un-
nerving," the *Purple Rain* script reads. "Prince is going down on
himself." Is this an autoerotic moment, or one in which Prince
reveals his true self as the "fancy lesbian" of Coleman's description? Traces of the male homoeroticism of Bowie's electric blow
job remain in this scene of a lesbian woman who struts like a man

servicing a man who looks like a woman. The signals blur until it becomes Prince's ideal: pure sex.

Madonna employed image and voice to cultivate sexuality; Prince found equally strong tools in lyrics and instrumentation. His songs incorporate a multiplicity of styles and effects, overtake the senses, and make the stories he tells—of every taboo-breaking subject from transvestitism and oral sex to public masturbation and even sibling incest—clearly fantastic and even utopian. In an early interview revealing his porn roots, Prince made clear that his tall tales came strictly from within: "As far as the sexuality and explicitness goes, when I was a kid, the only books that I read were my mother's pornography books. And when I got tired of reading them, I would write my own stories. That was at an early age and that sort of warped my mind."[39]

This likely apocryphal origin story, told when Prince was twenty-one, reflects Prince's love of blurring all kinds of categories— his particularly idealistic spin on mixing, the erotic underpinning of American popular music. By suggesting that his mother was the porn connoisseur in the family, he upended assumptions about the family structure and proper female desire. His songs did the same, voicing sexuality in vividly hued psychedelic language. Only highly deluded people could possibly view Prince's fancies as posing as any kind of actual moral agenda; they're outrageous, the stuff of play. Though in later years he himself became a Jehovah's Witness and questioned the worth of his early material, Prince in the 1980s delighted in being the trickster the religious right loved to hate. The great film critic Pauline Kael recognized the service Prince provided in showing up the Moral Majority's prudery: "I'm disposed to like Prince," she wrote in her review of *Purple Rain*, "because he is, as a friend of mine put it, 'the fulfillment of everything that people like Jerry Falwell say rock and roll will do to the youth of America.'"[40]

The third great star of the music-video era also dealt in fantasy, but was far less frank when it came to sexual expression. Michael Jackson, who eventually claimed the self-generated title of King of Pop in order to rival Madonna and Prince, was a child prodigy who grew up to be a prodigiously talented but troubled man. At the height of his stardom, in the 1980s, Jackson's appeal crossed all boundaries, including moral ones. "Jackson, unlike Prince, appeals to the innocent child in all of us," wrote one conservative commentator in 1984. "He keeps us in touch with our better selves."[41] Jackson was actually as much a fabulist as Prince and as much a provocateur as Madonna. His 1983 video for the song "Thriller," the most popular and influential music video of all time, may have been inspired by a childlike sensibility—"everything that happened on 'Thriller' happened because Michael wanted to turn into a monster," director John Landis said of the hugely elaborate thirteen-minute film, which cost a record $500,000 to produce—but within his Eden lurked the specter of erotic inner conflict. As great a dancer as pop has ever known, Jackson "exploded" in performance, often thrusting his pelvis in ways that seemed not just masturbatory but multiply orgasmic. In "Thriller," desire transforms him into a beast—a werewolf, who stalks the pretty ingénue that human Michael simply wants to take to the movies. In his other great 1980s videos, for "Billie Jean," "Beat It," and "Bad," Jackson plays similar roles: whether noir gumshoe or gangland street fighter, he is always a hero driven into action by baser desires. Jackson's eroticism was soaked in the sexual anxiety of the 1980s, presenting a potent, troubling counterpart to Prince's antic utopianism and Madonna's messages of self-love.

Madonna, Prince, and Michael Jackson remained pop household names into the 1990s, as the conservative presidencies of Reagan and his successor, George Herbert Walker Bush, gave way to the more liberal era of Bill Clinton. In the 2000s, each responded differently to the waning commercial success of their recordings, a seemingly inevitable reality for American pop stars over age forty.

Jackson became increasingly eccentric, modifying his appearance through plastic surgery and leading a semi-cloistered life, especially after he faced multiple accusations of child molestation from young men who had worked with him or served as companions as boys. Jackson died of a prescription drug overdose in 2009 while preparing for a comeback tour. His death was mourned by fans worldwide, and his artistic legacy remains indisputable despite the deeply troubling and still unresolved claims made against him. His sister Janet, also a favorite of the MTV age, upheld his memory and established her own way with musical erotica on albums like *The Velvet Rope*.

Prince transformed himself numerous times after his 1980s glory days. In an effort to wrest control of his music from his record label, Warner Bros., he changed his name to a "love symbol" in 1993—a combination of the alchemical symbols for male and female combined with a cross. This flamboyant iconography served Prince's serious intention to produce as much music as humanly possible; his output never slowed, and his reputation as one of the most astounding live acts of the rock and soul era only grew. His fluid body did not prove immortal, however; after enduring years of chronic pain in the joints he'd destroyed executing backflips and floor drops on stages across the globe, Prince died of an overdose of painkillers in 2016.

As for Madonna, during her 2015 Rebel Heart Tour, the fifty-seven-year-old staged elaborate tableaux celebrating oral sex, queer sex, and sex on staircases, still declaring herself the queen of postmodern burlesque. Showing off a body honed by a strict exercise and diet regimen, she danced solo to "Like a Virgin" on a runway shaped like a cross. Her fans continued to rave at these displays—that tour was one of the top three grossing of the year—but others questioned her attempts to maintain the visage and body of a twenty-five-year-old as she neared sixty. Celebrity branding consultant Jeetendr Sehdev, a professor at the University of Southern California, claimed to have conducted a survey of one thousand millennials and found that the youngest adult generation now found Madonna "toxic" and "irrelevant."[42] Having shown her own generation how erotic freedom might work even during a plague linked to sex, Madonna could not seem to escape the trap of America's conventional attitudes about aging. Instead of using midlife as an opportunity to develop a new vision of mature sexuality, she still sought to be that material girl whose pleasure in feeling herself stimulated lust in others. That many found this stance implausible indicated that even Madonna's dares had their limits when it came to redefining American eroticism.

Much has happened since Madonna first imagined herself a sex symbol. A new genre, hip-hop, came to dominate and change how music sounded and what it said. Rock fragmented into many different forms and reclaimed the mainstream for a brief and difficult moment. The generation coming of age during hip-hop's rise and rock's resurgence had grown up with AIDS, with the furious eye of the Moral Majority upon it. Their musical movements carried with them a spirit of reform, particularly in their most lauded and scorned manifestations: grunge and gangsta rap.

KOOL THINGS

On a summer day in 1989, Kim Gordon found herself sitting uncomfortably in a corner in a New York rehearsal studio, wondering what the man she was there to meet had in mind when he glanced toward her. The bassist and singer was used to being around sullen rock boys who didn't always make things clear; playing in the art-punk band Sonic Youth, she'd been living around various kinds of obnoxious attitude for nearly a decade. But she hadn't spent much time around rappers, the kingpins of another rapidly mutating musical form, hip-hop. She was a fan, had in fact borrowed from rap songs in her own music. But she would have been the first to admit that within this black-made-and-nurtured genre, she was an interloper. Someone at *Spin* thought it would be cute to put the thirty-seven-year-old Gordon in the ancient hot seat held by white observers who step into African American music making's circle, so they'd sent her to interview LL Cool J, the nineteen-year-old rapper who was then considered by many to be the best (and by virtually all to be the sexiest) in the game, and who was one of Gordon's favorites. But he was busy, keeping her waiting. "Occasionally he shoots a look my way," she later wrote in the interview's introduction. "I have no idea if he's expecting me or he's just looking at my out-of-place bleached blonde hair."[43]

We don't have an account of the interview from LL Cool J himself, but it's clear that neither party ever settled into a groove. Gordon, the underground rock star, pushed back when LL revealed his favorite band was the hair metal-ish Bon Jovi. LL, raised Christian and still relatively devout, got a terse "good luck with that" from Gordon when he said he hoped "that God gives me strength to crush everything in my path." Gordon ultimately concluded that their differences at least partly lay in the racialized hierarchies that make whites into consumers of black culture while leaving blacks largely isolated. "I have more access to his world—even if it is superficial . . . than L.L. will ever have to mine," she wrote in *Spin*.

Time eventually has proven Gordon wrong about LL Cool J's access to a world beyond hip-hop. After his reign as a rap sex symbol faded, he continued to be one of its biggest crossover stars, hosting the Grammy Awards telecast for years, collaborating with the country artist Brad Paisley, and starring in a prime-time detective show aimed largely at white senior citizens. Gordon, conversely, stuck with the art world, a smaller sphere. She became an exhibiting visual artist and a writer and continued to make experimental rock within and outside of Sonic Youth. Only a brief go at a fashion line and the minor fame that came with Sonic Youth's two early-1990s Top 10 *Billboard* Modern Rock hits had her "crushing" in a way LL Cool J would have recognized.

At a certain point in the late 1980s and early 1990s, hip-hop and post-punk rock seemed like equal forces within popular music, but their trajectories soon diverged. Hip-hop became a massive commercial force, shifting the axis of global popular music. Its rise restructured pop, its samplers and synthesizers replacing rock's guitar, bass, and drums as the basic tools of youthful music making. Hip-hop recast the rock star as a rapper, reclaiming for African American men the central charismatic role usurped by white performers since the age of minstrelsy. Within hip-hop's complicated ecosystem of instrumentation, style, dance, and historical knowledge, rappers became envoys and icons. And most did so without compromising. Rappers said no to the assumption that they would have to outgrow their origins to make it in the mainstream. Their slang, their dress style, the things they found sensual or sentimental, all came from deep within African American urban experience. Rap required listeners to either get these references or do the work.

From the birth of the genre in the disco era, rappers had always been eloquent—the life and the voice of the party. Their thickly witty rhymes contradicted the racist view, newly reinvigorated in the Reagan era, that young black men were illiterate thugs. "Stereotypes of a black male misunderstood / and it's still all good / If you don't know, now you know, nigga," Brooklyn's the Notorious B.I.G. (also known as "Biggie Smalls") spit in his 1994 breakthrough single, "Juicy." He proved his point in the rest of the song, with dazzling internal rhymes and Shakespearean scene-building. Rappers didn't run from stereotypes; they confronted them directly and imbued them with humor, psychological depth, and, sometimes, revolutionary spirit. The one-armed bandit Bras-Coupé of old New Orleans lived again in the voices of these rappers. Finally, he spoke for himself.

The most charismatic '90s rappers included Tupac Shakur, the California son of black nationalists whose lyrics examined the psy-

chic wounds of racism, and who became a matinee idol as well as
the genre's creative standard bearer; and Smalls, his rival, an enormous man with an incomparably deft lyrical touch. Both Shakur
and Smalls fell victim to the real gang violence that intersected
with hip-hop's gangster dreams, murdered within six months of
each other in the mid-1990s. Their short lives showed that rappers' affected swagger could sometimes have real consequences.
Another self-made ghetto don, Jay Z survived his own past as a
Brooklyn drug dealer to become a legitimate mogul, running the
multimillion-dollar Roc Nation company; in time, he married the
R&B queen Beyoncé Knowles and formed a friendship with President Barack Obama, becoming rap's ultimate patriarch. His career was paralleled by that of Sean Combs—the rapper alternately
known as "Puffy," "Puff Daddy," and "P. Diddy"—who, like Jay Z,
mentored a carefully constructed family of protégés while expanding his empire to include fashion, alcohol brands, and ventures
connected to virtually every other aspect of popular entertainment.
Producer Dr. Dre did the same thing on the West Coast, inventing a new hip-hop style grounded in marijuana-steeped slow beats
and parlaying that "G-Funk" sound (and the careers of superstars
like Snoop Dogg and the white rapper Eminem) to a multimillion-
dollar empire.

"We do dirt like worms, produce G's like sperm," Jay Z said on
his 1996 debut album *Reasonable Doubt,* connecting the grime of
his criminal past with the dream of his executive future (the "G"
stands for a grand, or a thousand dollars) and milking both images
as signs of his virility. An assertion of African Americans' right to
excel within both shadow and mainstream capitalism, rap made
money sexy—sometimes sexier than sex itself.

As hip-hop expanded its empire and rap became the new lin-
gua franca, rock got smaller. Its devotees tried on new names like
"indie," "modern," "alternative," and the much-derided "grunge,"
but, after one confusing, glorious, ultimately inconclusive moment

in the early 1990s, the scene itself remained relatively contained. (For this reason, "indie," a term that designates modesty, remains the most resonant.) Yet Gordon had been onto something when she went in search of commonalities between hip-hop and rock. In the ways each engaged with popular music's ongoing conversation about desire, eroticism, and identity, both became catalysts for reformation. This was the music of the generation who'd inherited the AIDS crisis along with many other sobering realities: the urban decay resulting from the Reagan administration's gutting of social services; feminism's uncovering of the realities of rape and sexual abuse; the rise of street drugs, especially crack and heroin, that could turn the body from a source of pleasure into a site of self-destruction; the religious right's campaign to stigmatize any but the narrowest definitions of sexual fulfillment. Rap brought the noise, a confrontational, highly masculine sonic barrage based on the inorganic art of sampling, which rendered its warrior voices fully armored and ready to battle. Indie rock reveled in the dirt of amateurism, rejecting pop's polish and sentimentality in favor of rougher approaches. Practitioners of both styles believed in the power of refusal.

"I don't think so," LL Cool J muttered in his hit, "Goin' Back to Cali," which satirized the superficiality of sunny Top 40 pop. "I don't wanna, I don't think so," murmured Gordon in Sonic Youth's "Kool Thing," which she wrote after her frustrated attempt to connect with LL Cool J. The phrase suits both parties. What rappers and indie rockers shared was a need to say no: sometimes to each other, but mostly to a status quo they experienced as a threat.

Pleasure did soften the boundaries set by hip-hop and indie rock's young zealots. In their earliest years, both genres made room for sex, often using humor. "He can't satisfy you with his little worm, but I can bust you out with my super-sperm!" rapper Big Bank Hank boasted in the genre's first national smash, "Rapper's Delight," in 1979. The Southern California hardcore scene that was one bridge from punk to indie rock traded in similar broad strokes, as it were, though these white kids from LA's poorer suburbs tended to be more crude and openly misogynist than their rapper counterparts. Songs like Nig-Heist's "Hot Muff" and Black Flag's "Slip It In" made fun of their male protagonist's Neanderthal tendencies even as they reinforced them. Though certainly offensive to women, these cartoonish efforts also ridiculed the peacocks and superstuds who'd dominated rock and soul discourse throughout the sexual revolution and its aftermath.

Those superstuds did matter to rappers, especially comical ones who played on the image of the pimp, the flashy inner-city entrepreneur who made his living by managing a "stable" of female sex workers. The pimp had long been a folk hero known for his verbal dexterity; in the 1960s, celebrated by comedians like Redd Foxx and Richard Pryor and militant writers like Eldridge Cleaver and H. Rap Brown, the figure had become heroic.[44] Pimps traded in sex, and ostensibly enjoyed it, but in rap, the trade—an exchange between men—became the focal point. Male rappers talked about women incessantly, but they were talking to each other, absorbed in each other's technical prowess and power plays. The essence of rap, as it developed, became male competition. In a 1980 interview with the longtime music journalist Nelson George, a then-twenty-year-old Kurtis Blow told of discovering rap's potential at a Midtown New York disco where the DJ spun tales over song breaks. Blow said he was something different: a "coordinated rapper," more precise and keyed in to an audience. One way to view this tightening up of skills is as a reaction against the looseness of a previous era. The free mood of disco and the hallucinogenic fancies of funk weren't as relevant to this new generation, steeling itself to face welfare cutbacks and the rising impact of drug use and disease—problems they experienced as a legacy from more open-ended times.[45]

The proto-indie rockers of hardcore punk were even more uptight. (*Hardcore,* in this subculture, didn't signal anything pornographic; the word was more evocative of the sweat of military training or a punishing gym routine.) In the late 1970s and 1980s, punk took hold in outposts across America because kids were disgusted with their parents' excesses, which, in their view, had led to broken marriages, chemical dependencies, and the general bloat of mainstream pop, rife with arena rock excess and vapid novelty singles like "Disco Duck." "We were fed up with all the crap of the seventies, with disco, with country rock, with posy glam bands and people like Jeff Lynne of ELO [the Beatlesque Electric Light Orchestra] saying he looked forward to the day when they could send holograms of themselves to arenas to 'play' all over the world," Jello Biafra, singer for the San Francisco hardcore band the Dead Kennedys, told writer Gina Arnold. "Something drastic needed to be done about these people, and punk was it."[46]

Unlike early punks, who were mostly in their twenties or thirties, most hardcore kids were still close enough to their parents to really despise them. *Damaged,* the first album by Southern California hardcore favorite Black Flag, came with a sticker attached, containing a quote from a horrified record executive who'd tried to keep it from stores. It read: AS A PARENT I FOUND THIS TO BE AN ANTI-PARENT RECORD. "It was then that I knew that I had to have it because I didn't want to be anything like my parents," said one devoted fan.[47]

These hardcore kids felt let down by their parents, whose own coming of age in the easy-living post-countercultural era often left them ill-equipped to deal with their children's needs. In a 1985 profile of a seventeen-year-old female punk DJ named Shaggy, *Texas Monthly* reporter David Seeley noted that she'd left her suburban home not merely due to the usual mother-daughter squabbles, but because her disabled dad and working mom had let the house fill up with trash; the stove didn't work, and everyone fended for themselves, living on fast food. "Sometimes I think my dad's really messed up a lot," she told Seeley, holding a photograph of him helping her take her first toddler steps. "He didn't save any money or buy much insurance, didn't plan in case something happened, and so he can't put me through college. But I look at that picture, and I know he taught me to walk, you know? It means a lot to me."[48]

As the 1980s wore on, rap and indie rock reflected the disappointment and frustration of a generation toddling amidst the wadded-up waste their parents left behind. Reagan's policies were hard on white working-class families, and even harder on most families of color. The music industry reflected America's income gap. Major labels and a few massively popular blockbuster artists were earning millions and spending them as quickly as they could ingest the cocaine their dollars bought. (The 1980s "hair metal" bands who emerged in glam's wake epitomized this hedonistic spirit on MTV and in teen fans' hearts.) Hip-hop and indie rock presented alternatives to corporate music industry bloat. These lean youths made themselves mobile with portable DJ setups or "jammed econo" (as indie band the Minutemen put it) in broken-down touring vans, aiming to succeed on their own terms. Artists and their independent managers formed their own labels, booked their own shows, and cultivated an oppositional attitude. The indie ideal was to avoid excess, though people certainly still indulged in all kinds of it. Rappers welcomed excess, but presented themselves as keeping cool in the midst of it: "Never let me slip, cos if I slip, then I'm slippin'," in the words of Dr. Dre.

Sex was problematic because it was an occasion to slip. "I wasn't anti-sex, but if everybody spent all their time trying to get laid, we'd never be able to build anything," Ian MacKaye of the foundational DC hardcore band Minor Threat told scene documentarian Steven Blush. "Sex was a diversion every teen did, so I thought it was stupid." Attitudes like MacKaye's, however deeply felt, masked the fact that people were still having sex, often in great quantities. Hardcore musicians would grab assignations where they could, often in the vans they drove from town to town. "Many nights I had sex in that van, sometimes next to another guy having sex in the van," Henry Rollins told the journalist Michael Azerrad about his glory days fronting Black Flag. "And you have to have a very understanding or very enthusiastic partner to get together with you in such close proximity."[49]

Unlike in earlier punk scenes, in hardcore, women remained hidden in plain sight, often organizing shows, hosting visiting bands, and providing that sweet one-night succor, but keeping their sensibilities largely to themselves. As the scene grew broader and became indie rock, many more women would participate, but overt femininity remained an uncomfortable subject. This repression would bubble under until the mid-1990s, when a counterreformation led by female punks through with being marginalized would emerge.

Rap, meanwhile, did acknowledge women—as objects of its boasting rhymes, anyway—but also remained an overwhelmingly masculine enclave. Female-friendly lover men like LL Cool J were rarities. This was partly because rap's creators desperately needed a cultural space of their own. "Hip-hop will always be remembered as that bittersweet moment when young black men captured the ears of America and defined themselves on their own terms," wrote the critic Joan Morgan, who would play a major role in the music's late-1990s reckoning with the feminine. "Regenerating themselves as seemingly invincible bass gods, gangsta griots, and rhythm warriors, they turned a defiant middle finger to a history that racistly ignored or misrepresented them." As for the women of color who loved rap and tried to find their own place in it, Morgan wrote: "Selfishly we chose to ignore the dangers of rappers believing their own myths."[50]

These celebrations of the masculine had little room for gay men (or, needless to say, queer women). Both rap and hardcore punk were openly homophobic. On both coasts, 1970s punk had a strong gay element, with the transgender performer Jayne (Wayne) County playing a major role in New York, and LA's Masque club owner Brendan Mullen serving as the central spoke in a scene that, he once estimated, was "thirty to thirty-five percent gay, maybe even more." But few punk songs celebrated same-sex love until a joyfully defiant "queercore" scene surfaced in the early 1990s, led by bands like the pop-loving Pansy Division and the astounding Tribe 8, whose dyke (now trans) leader, Lynn Breedlove, wore leather chaps and a dildo during performances. Mostly, LGBTQ people in punk kept their desires private, both before and after AIDS became a threat. Grant Hart of the Minneapolis indie-punk band Hüsker Dü compared his and bandmate Bob Mould's closeted homosexuality to the discipline of warriors: "It was a superiority type of thing, like the Spartans of ancient days or something."[51]

In rap, an antigay bias was woven into lyrics from the beginning. Early singles "Rapper's Delight" and "The Message" included references to "fags" and "fairies." In time these toss-offs would grow more virulent, sometimes focusing directly on AIDS, as in the pop-rapper (and later movie star) Will Smith's 1988 demand that "all the homeboys that got AIDS be quiet" or the otherwise politically progressive and musically groundbreaking Public Enemy's fearful "Meet the G That Killed Me," which contained the lines "Man to man / I don't know if they can / From what I know / The parts don't fit." African American culture in general had grown more openly homophobic since the days when semi-closeted "angels" had flourished in the gospel world, partly because the black church became more conservative, and partly due to fear. As the epidemic developed, AIDS wreaked havoc in the African American community, proliferating through shared needles as well as sexual transmission, affecting heterosexual women most of all. These factors all fed the misperception that homosexuality, and even any kind of open acknowledgment of sexual activity, was a threat to African American values. "In the black community, we host panel discussions, town hall meetings, and forums about acquiring wealth, politics, and community service, but we never openly discuss sex, sexuality, or HIV/AIDS," wrote the scholar Terrance Dean—himself a gay man trying to reconcile his sexuality with his love of rap—in his 2008 memoir. "We live by the 'don't air your dirty laundry in the street' code."[52]

Most male rap stars didn't participate in AIDS activism or even awareness-raising. But they did lose one of their own when Eric "Eazy-E" Wright, a founding member of Dr. Dre's group N.W.A, succumbed to the disease not long after being diagnosed in 1995. "I've learned in the last week that this thing is real, and it doesn't discriminate," Eazy-E wrote in a letter to fans while on his deathbed. By then AIDS had become the leading cause of death for young African American men and the second for young black women. This rise was inextricably linked to the subject of many of Wright's drug-dealer glamorizing lyrics: crack.

A concentrated, highly addictive form of cocaine, crack had overtaken many inner-city neighborhoods. As it devastated more and more lives, laws like Reagan's Anti-Drug Abuse Act of 1986 reinforced a "war on drugs" that put users in jail instead of offering them help. This tightened the noose of criminalization around the neck of anyone caught even experimenting with drugs. It established a vicious cycle that, as Nelson George writes, was the true source of the hard-heartedness reflected in what had come to be called gangsta rap: "There is an elemental nihilism in the most controversial crack-era hip hop that wasn't concocted by the rappers but reflects the mentality and fears of young Americans of every color and class living an exhausting, edgy existence, in and out of big cities."[53]

With the genre's biggest male stars both embodying the gangsta role and struggling with the emotional (and real-life) constrictions it created, it was left to women rappers to employ the music as a tool to educate listeners about the blights overtaking their communities, including AIDS. Few in number compared to their

male counterparts, women rappers often found themselves playing the role of conscience in a milieu that didn't have room for
much open, mature talk about eroticism. The New York trio of
rappers Salt-N-Pepa and DJ Spinderella enjoyed a breakthrough
with 1991's "Let's Talk About Sex," a playful invective against both
conservative censorship and men's hesitancy to be clear with their
partners about their expectations. The trio rerecorded the song
as "Let's Talk About AIDS," releasing an all-star video that included a few pop-friendly male rappers alongside other minor celebrities like MTV VJ Dave Kendall. In 1992, the R&B group TLC
attracted national attention with its slinky sound, distinguished
by the crafty rapping of Lisa "Left Eye" Lopes. Lopes adorned
her costumes with condoms; the gimmick also served as a public
service announcement. "We wanted something eye-catching, so
when kids see the condoms, they ask why do we wear condoms
and talk about condoms? That brings up the issue of safe sex," she
explained.[54]

Those "sex packets," as the Bay Area group Digital Underground wryly called them, were affixed to Lopes's colorful, baggy
jackets and pants when TLC entered the pop scene. But by the mid-
1990s, women in hip-hop were working a different look and style:
the "hard-edged black girl MC glam" of rappers like Lil' Kim and
Foxy Brown, associates of male rap stars like Biggie Smalls and
Sean "Puffy" Combs. These women shot out rhymes recalling the
dirty verses of 1920s blues queens. As Imani Perry has explained,
they looked feminine, but "occupied male spaces linguistically,"
matching their male counterparts in bluntness and mercenary
attitude. Articulating desire for sex itself as well as the material
goods sex often earns women in a patriarchal society, hard female
rappers engaged in the time-honored tradition of battle rhyming—
only now it was the battle of the sexes, not a strictly masculine
game, that preoccupied and titillated audiences. The male-female
relationship in rap continued to be played out within the resur-

gent narrative of the pimp and his whore. Eithne Quinn has argued that this story partly made a comeback in the 1990s because women were making economic gains, securing more power in the American system than black men, ever more criminalized, could muster. "The pimp was about registering as well as repudiating the power of women," she writes.[55]

Hip-hop in the late 1990s was not merely about hard men and the women who fulfilled their fantasies (and occasionally stood up to them). A strong alternative scene focused on groups like A Tribe Called Quest and De La Soul represented more bohemian styles and self-consciously progressive values. In this world, women like Queen Latifah, Lauryn Hill of the Fugees, and Mary Ann "Ladybug Mecca" Vieira of Digable Planets did sometimes speak women's truths. Hill in particular made a powerful statement with her 1998 solo debut *The Miseducation of Lauryn Hill,* eloquently considering the responsibilities of young motherhood in the poignant "To Zion" and cautioning her female fans against predatory boys in the girl-group throwback "That Thing." Hip-hop would continue to blossom in countless ways, providing a foundation for an increasingly diverse array of artists, including, in the 2000s, major women pop stars like Beyoncé and Rihanna.

Yet gangsta rap, with its nihilistic overtones and strangely puritan streak, held a strong grip on the mainstream imagination, crossing over to a large white audience whose motivations for embracing its stereotypes were highly questionable. Its influence reached a nadir in 1999, via a rock-rap fusion that became hugely popular, pioneered by bands like Limp Bizkit and Korn, who blended hard rock's most depressive elements with gangsta rap's misogyny. That year, at a festival in upstate New York meant to carry on the countercultural spirit of Woodstock, four women were raped, one near the stage as Limp Bizkit performed. "This was an orgy of lewdness tinged with hate," one reporter wrote.[56]

DOWN IN IT

When Kim Gordon wrote "Kool Thing" for LL Cool J, she included a question for him: "Are you going to liberate us girls from male white corporate oppression?" In the song's verses, she made fun of herself, playing the clueless fangirl as Chuck D of Public Enemy, fully in on the joke, leered, "Oh, yeahhhh," in the background. That was in 1990, long before rap-rock's cretinous pretenders in backward baseball caps made their own horrible joke of the genre. Hip-hop would recover. Mainstream rock had a harder time; its cultural impact has continued to diminish. But indie rock would be redeemed in the 1990s by a counter-reformation led by furious young women, the spiritual younger sisters of Gordon, who said "I don't think so" to the scene's sexism and then kept talking until it changed.

As rap responded to tough realities, indie rockers sought some solace by looking to the past. By the mid-1990s a highly diverse form rooted more in the economic practices of running a label, publishing low-cost fanzines, and touring at a club level than in any one sound or even attitude, indie rock had always welcomed some heavy metal parking-lot long-hairs into its mix. The Replacements, one of the 1980s bands that developed the scene in ways that diverged from hardcore punk, regularly covered songs by metal progenitors Black Sabbath and KISS. Starting around 1989 more players and fans began to show allegiance to those roots. Rockers grew their hair long and stretched out their guitar explorations, replacing the short sharp shock of punk with heavy riffs and even, sometimes, guitar solos—once the ultimate symbol of arena-sized overindulgence. Seattle became the emblematic town generating this heavier sound. It was an industrial city then, known for shipping and airplane building, with a working-class soul that suited this expressively earthy, self-consciously unpretentious trend.

"Grunge," as the Pacific Northwest sound came to be called by the media, held on to punk's suspiciousness of the mainstream even as its stars crafted arena-worthy anthems. It was hard rock in a thrift-store plaid shirt instead of Spandex.

Grunge sounded like a giant male moan; the critics Simon Reynolds and Joy Press called it "castration blues, the flailing sound of failed masculinity."[57] Its creators styled themselves as sensual refuseniks. As one star of the indie rock scene adjacent to grunge, Sean Nelson of the band Harvey Danger, described it, "The idea, I thought, was not to deny your sexual urges—that would be folly—but to keep them to yourself, to mute them, to deplore the fact that any expression of them was bound to be either vulgar or predictable or, worst of all, male."[58] Even the name "grunge" was a self-deprecating term that Mark Arm, the singer from Mudhoney, devised as a joke against alpha-male ambition: "Pure noise! Pure grunge! Pure shit!" he wrote in a letter about his own band to the Seattle zine *Desperate Times* in 1981, a decade before it became common parlance.[59]

Viewed by many as the last commercial gasp of mainstream rock, grunge's legacy is tinged with sorrow, both because its most beloved figure, Nirvana singer Kurt Cobain, committed suicide in 1994, and due to the heroin habits of many other key players, several of whom died of overdoses. Yet grunge was also openly progressive, and it was the first mainstream American rock milieu to embrace feminist politics, with Seattle band Pearl Jam regularly playing benefits for pro-choice and anti-rape organizations and Cobain famously writing in the liner notes to Nirvana's 1992 compilation album *Incesticide*, "If you're a racist, a sexist, a homophobe, we don't want you to buy our records."

Cobain's politics were locally rooted. Before forming Nirvana in 1987, he briefly lived in the college town of Olympia, Washington, where he became close to Tobi Vail, a young feminist whose own band, Bikini Kill, would become the central voice of a new take on women's liberation known as riot grrrl. A major factor in the generational shift within feminism starting to become known as the Third Wave, riot grrrl was a movement as noisy and confrontational as hardcore punk, but with sexism—and specifically, the sexism young women experienced within the indie rock scene—as its main target. The very young women who invented riot grrrl wanted to raise up what they saw as the ghost of feminism, drained dry by academic entrapment in women's studies programs or diluted to death by neoliberal corporate culture's surface gestures toward diversity, and make it scream as it had in the streets in the 1970s. The scream blended rage with pleasure. Declaring "this society isn't my society cuz this society hates women and I don't," the photocopied manifesto Bikini Kill distributed at shows read, "The revolution is about going to the playground with your best girlfriends. You are hanging upside down on the bars and all the blood is rushing to your head. It's a euphoric feeling. The boys can see our underwear and we don't really care."[60]

The young punks whose lives were changed by riot grrrl formed consciousness-raising groups; they published zines like Vail's *Jigsaw*, to share stories of rape and resistance; they formed bands with furious, funny names like Bratmobile, Heavens to Betsy, and the Frumpies. Their numbers grew. The new guard of Third Wave feminism found leaders in writers like Susan Faludi, Naomi Wolf, and Rebecca Walker and rekindled grassroots activism by learning self-defense skills and protecting abortion clinics from pro-life picketers. Riot grrrl turned its reformist energies on rock itself. Watching Bikini Kill's charismatic vocalist and songwriter Kathleen Hanna snarl "Here are my ruby red lips, better to suck you dry" at the band's very first show, Seattle journalist Emily White comprehended riot grrrl's strategy, which was to shove the energy of rock and roll misogyny back in the music's face. "Such acts probably confuse and terrify the teenage boys in the audience who've been waiting for this moment, but they make more and more sense to a generation of young women who are coming to understand that contradiction might be the most powerful feminist tool yet, creating a kind of paralysis, or night blindness, in the man/boy imagination," she wrote.[61]

Feminist rock in the 1990s extended far beyond the borders of riot grrrl. All-female bands began to proliferate: L7 in Los Angeles, Babes in Toyland in Minneapolis, 7 Year Bitch in Seattle. Solo performers like Liz Phair, whose 1993 album *Exile in Guyville* wryly identified male micro-aggressions in explicit songs like "Fuck and Run," and PJ Harvey, who flipped the switch on rock clichés with declarations like "you leave me dry," went where countercultural heroines like Janis Joplin hadn't dared. In "Me and a Gun," the singer-songwriter Tori Amos recounted her own rape with utter clarity; she would go on to help establish RAINN, the Rape, Abuse and Incest National Network, which continues to provide services to victims across America. Out lesbian duo the Indigo Girls and solo balladeer Melissa Etheridge forged a link between the folksy sounds of 1970s women's music and contemporary rock. Focusing on music industry inequities, the singer-songwriter Sarah McLachlan founded the female-dominated Lilith Fair Tour in 1997, which, over three summers, included performers from across genres and generations. Lilith Fair drew so many women that it became 1997's highest-grossing package tour, grossing $16.5 million for thirty-eight shows. Its popularity even raised Reagan-era televangelists from their slumber—an editor at the newspaper run by the Reverend Jerry Falwell declared it demonic because the name invoked the biblical Adam's apocryphal first wife. Other men, less scripturally motivated, simply dismissed it as "Lesbopalooza" and "Breastfest."[62]

The shots fired toward Lilith Fair remind us that while feminist rock did signal a new consciousness about gender entering the rock mainstream, plenty of backlash greeted its rise and threatened its stability. The phenomenon produced polarizing figures, none more controversial than Courtney Love, leader of the band Hole. Love was not a movement type. She despised the activists of riot grrrl, ending Hole's second album *Live Through This* with a tirade against what she viewed as their lockstep conformity: "We look the same, we talk the same, we even fuck the same." As Kurt Cobain's wife, then widow, and one of grunge's most charismatic performers, Love occupied a privileged position within the scene. Yet she was also highly stigmatized. Accusations that she had victimized Cobain, using him for fame, dogged her, reaching a fever pitch after his death, for which some rumor-mongers went so far as to blame her. Love's aggressive personality and blatant ambition to become a pop star only fed her image as a dangerous succubus, a particularly unattractive role in a punk-based scene that valued independence above all.

Yet Cobain and Love, who had one child, Frances Bean, in 1993, did form a significant artistic partnership in the brief years when both Nirvana and Hole thrived. Their music speaks powerfully in tandem with the physical and psychic struggles of being in bodies oppressed by impossible standards of masculine strength or feminine beauty, and of trying to connect with another body across the minefield of gendered limitations and stereotypes. The fury and darkness in Nirvana's songs, especially those Cobain wrote after uniting with Love, emanate from a man who feels trapped inside his body, because of its weaknesses (Cobain had multiple afflictions, including addiction to opiates, chronic stomach pain, and likely bipolar disorder), but also because others expect him to fulfill the masculine ideals of virility and physical strength. Love's songs are equally visceral, spilling the milk of her new-mother's breasts and smearing walls with obscenities written in the lipstick of a beauty queen. Had Cobain lived, perhaps the pair would have eventually reached for more coherence in their music and silenced their naysayers. As it was, the music they made while together is a powerful document of the confusion of a moment that, for many, felt both open-ended and oppressive.

"Grunge is the one good thing that AIDS gave us," the comedian Hal Sparks joked in a radio interview in 2010. "Nothing explains the biggest left turn in the history of music, but AIDS . . . You tell a generation of thirteen-year-olds that sex equals death, you're gonna have them going—*A DENIAL!*" Sparks screamed the notorious concluding words of Nirvana's most significant hit, "Smells Like Teen Spirit," as evidence of the music's fatalism. Though crude, his humor hit a nerve. The music's incessant focus on sexual politics and on the pain, even horror, that could come of erotic desire did often dwell in a place that, for popular music, was uniquely uneasy. "I was up above it . . . now I'm down in it!" wailed Trent Reznor of the industrial rock group Nine Inch Nails in 1989. In 1994, he'd make the dreck specific in what would become his signature song, "Closer." Over a thorny bed of dissonant electronics, Reznor moaned: "I broke apart my insides . . . I want to fuck you like an animal . . . My whole existence is flawed. You get me closer to God." Sex still might sanctify individuals, in the view of the grunge generation, but not before it devastated them.[63]

As the AIDS pandemic entered a different phase, with new prescription drug cocktails finally promising to make the syndrome chronic instead of fatal for those lucky enough to afford them, the reformist and sometimes nihilistic spirit of the previous decade seemed to devolve into a mood of aggression devoid of pleasure, much less love. The twentieth century was ending in a dark place for popular music. A new generation would need to emerge to turn the tide. And it did, in an emerging environment called cyberspace.

8

HUNGRY CYBORGS
BRITNEY, BEYONCÉ, AND
THE VIRTUAL FRONTIER

CYBERSPACE, 1999–2016

As the new millennium began, Americans found ways to reinvent themselves as erotic beings. The fear of AIDS was manageable for many once life-sustaining drugs became available, though the epidemic continued to worsen worldwide. By 2000, American attitudes about physicality itself were shifting as people spent more and more time within the virtual realm made possible by a new phenomenon called the World Wide Web. This electronically enabled computer screen world, where people could interact with both stars and each other across time and space instead of just passively consuming, was a prime environment for imaginative play—a place where regular folk could reimagine themselves as airbrushed superpeople, and where cyborgs, those enhanced creatures of science fiction, were real. And inhabiting it increasingly *felt* real. Physical reality, inversely, seemed more and more like that screen world—a place where impossible goals could be realized. Women's bodies acted as maps for these new explorations. But men were not exempt. Viagra, the anti-impotence drug, became the fastest-selling drug in history upon FDA approval in 1998, extending male potency past the age when most accepted it would become a fond memory. High school jocks might be hiding a stash of their own supplements, participating in the "creatine craze" after the well-built baseball player Mark McGwire confessed to taking such performance-enhancing drugs in 1998.

So the virtual world wasn't the only place where people played at sexual perfection; the privileged and their children could do so in the material world, too. The late 1990s and early 2000s saw a dramatic increase in plastic surgery within mainstream America, with minimally invasive techniques such as laser surgery and Botox becoming commonplace. In 1999, the *Washington Post* reported that twenty-five thousand teens had cosmetic procedures, up 100 percent since 1992. Many pop stars of the 2000s also reportedly got plastic surgery, even as adolescents. Journalists fretted that celebrities were inspiring young girls to reject their natural bodies too young, yet also were obliged to report that 50 percent of such girls had mothers who underwent the surgery, too.[1]

These developments in the mainstream collided with a long-building wave of intellectual interest in "the post-human." In 1985, the philosopher of science Donna Haraway published her influential "A Cyborg Manifesto," a feminist analysis of technology's ability to make "thoroughly ambiguous the difference between natural and artificial, mind and body, self-developing and externally designed, and many other distinctions that used to apply to organisms and machines."[2] Haraway argued that women could engage this new reality to free themselves from the confines of essentialism: being more than human might be liberating, sexually and otherwise. Haraway's ideas found a complement in the cyberpunk science fiction of the 1980s, which often featured street-smart heroines who negotiated multiple realms of reality. Writers like William Gibson, Lewis Shiner, and the explicitly feminist Pat Cadigan and Octavia Butler imagined worlds that were postapocalyptic but also pretty sexy. Theorists produced enough books on cyberspace, cyberculture, and cybersex to fill a warp-speed spaceship. These futuristic thinkers captured the mood of people moving beyond bodily limits on a worldwide scale. The philosopher Sadie Plant enthused in her essay "Coming Across the Future," "You make the connections, access the zone. Whatever avatar you select for your scene, you cannot resist becoming cyborg as well. Some human locks on, but a replicant stirs. Depending on the state of your time-tract's art, the cyborg you become will be more or less sophisticated and extensive; more or less hooked up to its own abstraction and the phase space in which you are both drawn out. But it will be post-human, whatever it is."[3]

LOLITA ON AEROBICS

In the summer of 1998, music journalists and radio programmers received a back-to-school package from the cyber frontier: an inflatable bubble backpack holding a pot of sparkly silver-and-blue lip gloss, a compact, stickers, and a cassette previewing a hot new fall release. The featured artist was seventeen-year-old Kentwood, Louisiana, native Britney Spears. The photograph accompanying the press release ("From a small town to the big time!") showed this latest teen-pop contender in down-home denim shorts and a tank top, with a subtle red tint in her hair, wearing just a bit of lip gloss—pink, not blue. Gazing into the camera, she looked natural, not highly processed like the backpack.

Few who received this lagniappe sensed the impact Spears would make within the year. She had come up the traditional way, doing theater (she was an understudy in a play called *Ruthless,* about a murderously motivated would-be child star) before securing a spot as a tween on Disney's *New Mickey Mouse Club,* a revival of the show that launched rock and roll beach babe Annette Funicello back in the 1950s. But Britney was something new: the first American sweetheart of the Internet. Those who popped in that cassette and listened to Spears's first single, an aggressively catchy electro-pop come-on called ". . . Baby One More Time," produced by an emerging studio superpower named Max Martin in a hit factory in Sweden, heard a voice equally redolent of girlish vulnerability and super-heroic aggressiveness, perfectly calibrated for a moment when robot dreams were becoming increasingly immediate.

Spears, raised on Michael Jackson's *Thriller* and the cosmetically obsessed beauty pageant culture of her native South, heralded a new era in which music's body-bound pleasures would be framed by ethereal tones and mechanized beats produced in fully digitized recording studios. With her gorgeous flesh and tiny voice—its metallic tone perfectly suited for manipulation—Spears presented from the beginning as a hybrid: half shopping mall American, half creature from another planet. Her body, voice, and projected emotions were youthful but washed clean of any adolescent awkwardness. In performance, Spears tapped a sexual maturity that seemed almost perverse in its effective power. Observers weren't sure what to call her—an "adult teen," a "baby babe." In an early profile, the celebrity-oriented *People* magazine sought the opinion of the popular sex theorist Camille Paglia, who commented, "She is a glorified 1950s high school cheerleader with an undertone of perverse 1990s sexuality . . . Britney is simultaneously wholesome and ripely sensual. She's Lolita on aerobics."[4]

That last phrase nicely sums up Spears's erotic but cold evocation of bodily perfection, achieved through endless exercise routines. Though she dutifully performed vulnerable ballads—an early one was called "E-mail My Heart"—Spears became famous for her more aggressive synthesizer-driven dance hits, which addressed romance as a sometimes violent game. ". . . Baby One More Time" disturbed many feminists because of its possible endorsement of domestic violence: Spears was asking her potential lover to "give me a sign, hit me, baby, one more time." But as Neil Strauss of the *New York Times* pointed out, the reference could just as easily be connected to DJ E-Z Rock's call to "hit it," pushing the button on the mechanized beat that drives the hip-hop classic "It Takes Two." Spears was the beat, her voice as instrumental as a synth-drum.[5] In her breakthrough video she was a dance machine in pigtails, more human than human, to quote the description of android replicants in the prototypical cyberpunk movie *Bladerunner.*

The business plan made Spears a virtual-reality sensation before she became a physical one: Spears's label created a World Wide Web page displaying images, videotaped chats, and more musical nuggets. "The response was tremendous, without even having a single in the market," Jive Records executive Kim Kaiman told *Billboard.* "Kids were intrigued by Britney."[6] Spears's emergence as a solo star built upon a new style of prefab pop, led by groups like England's Spice Girls and the harmonizing "boy bands" *NSync and the Backstreet Boys. The Spice Girls, a mid-1990s phenomenon, even had doll names: Sporty, Baby, Ginger, Posh, and Scary. Spears was one shade more accessible: a girl actually born with a name that sounded like it came from a comic book, or a porn movie.

She was the product of two factories, one for her sound and the other concocting her image. O Town, located just miles from Disney World, specialized in pop prepackaging aimed at where the youngest listening generation lived: the mall and the Internet. She and *NSync, whose de facto leader Justin Timberlake (also a former Mickey Mouser) became her tabloid-endorsed sweetheart, toured shopping centers together, singing to prerecorded backing tracks, and engaged in newfangled fan interactions like Web chats.

The other factory where Spears's stardom was assembled was in Stockholm, where she recorded much of her first album under the guidance of producer Max Martin, a former heavy metal musician who'd become obsessed with crafting hits. On singles for both the Backstreet Boys and *NSync as well as for international stars Celine Dion and Ace of Base, Martin had exhibited a knack for irresistibly repetitive melodies and hard-driving hooks. In Britney, he found his foil: a self-styled successor to Madonna and Michael Jackson, who sang in a style similar to her idols', with a dancer's precise attention to rhythm and a child star's deeply ensconced sense of life as a show. Martin and Spears also shared an intense work ethic. Their approach was the opposite of the punk-inspired spontaneity and slack embraced by 1990s rock stars like Kurt Cobain. A 2001 *Time* magazine profile of Martin described his recording studio technique as an exhausting process designed to produce something "direct, effective, we don't show off"—like a Volvo rolling off an assembly line. Spears appreciated Martin's taskmaster side: "'He's hard on you with the vocals,' Spears reports. 'Then when you hear it, you're like, *Oh, damn! I'm so glad.*'"[7]

A notion of the new teen stars as almost genetically predesigned cogs in a hit-making machine ran throughout the media's coverage of Spears and her contemporaries. Consumed by teens alongside video game heroines like the princess in *The Legend of Zelda* or *Tomb Raider*'s Lara Croft (herself to become a movie star in 2001, embodied by actress Angelina Jolie, whose unusually voluptuous lips and eyes made her look like an animated character), these idols learned early to transcend limitation. In 1999, *Rolling Stone* complained: "Today's little troopers are showbiz lifers, pros since the minute they made it down to the hospital lobby, sporting cell phones and production deals while rattling on glibly in interviews about merch and market saturation." The image of a cell phone as both dehumanizing and empowering reflected prevalent anxieties: "Teens don't have an attention span anymore," said Carson Daly, host of MTV's update on *American Bandstand, Total Request Live.* "They just want to feel good for those four minutes, then go hit the Internet . . . Britney is a poster child for them."[8]

What teens did on the relatively new Internet mystified adults, and as before those fears often focused on sexuality. "Call up Britney Spears on the Web and you'll get something like 120 porn sites before you hit even one that's clean enough to be viewed by an eleven-year-old girl," wrote one critic. Teens were skilled participants in this new realm; the Internet was their automobile and sometimes they hopped into the backseat. Looking at Spears-themed websites (including pornographic ones), one Internet executive noted: "Some of the Britney sites are really high-quality, professional stuff, yet they have been created by computer-literate children."[9]

The new millennium's sensations both resisted and played into the idea that they represented something dangerous. The Backstreet Boys, nominally the elders on the scene, greeted the year 2000 with the futuristically packaged album *Millennium* and a song called "Larger Than Life," which slyly came on sexually to young fans. Its video featured the Boys as mildly lecherous cyborgs in a phallic spaceship. *NSync went for a different more-human-than-human image, outselling its big brother band that year with an album, *No Strings Attached,* whose cover portrayed the band as puppets freed from their strings, suddenly animate, and which included a song, "Digital Get Down," about the relatively new phenomenon of cybersex. Performing it live, the group appeared in cyborg guise, humping the floor after apparently being generated within a display of frisky computer code.

These robot dreamboats had nothing on Spears. She worked her magic mostly without resorting to science-fiction metaphors, although she did appear as a comely space alien in the video for the title track of her second album, "Oops! . . . I Did It Again." Spears's android soul was grounded in her music itself, and in the self-regulation behind the image she projected—a steely extreme of youthful femininity that was commanding and invulnerable, her doe eyes locked in a thousand-yard stare. She claimed to be a virgin when she first gained fame. "I have no feelings at all," she said to one reporter, quizzed about possible boyfriends. "All those feelings," she said to another. "It's too much stress."[10]

Making this resistance to emotion musical, Spears, Martin, and her other producers structured her singles around the idea of control. She pushed out the chorus of ". . . Baby One More Time" with the steely spit of a sparring partner, not the vulnerability of a victim. "Oops! . . . I Did It Again" also framed romance within metaphors of manipulation and resistance; the "oops" signified Spears losing herself in love, but then walking away with a self-possessed sneer. "I'm not that innocent," she growled as Martin's synthesizers created a huge, door-slamming *whomp!* behind her. Other explorations of control and its absence followed: "(You Drive Me) Crazy"; "Stronger"; "Toxic," with its metaphor of being poisoned; her duet with Madonna, "Me Against the Music," in which the elder pop siren nearly begs Spears to "lose control." Perhaps the most blatant song in this vein was "I'm a Slave 4 U," written and produced by the hip-hop team the Neptunes: over layers of breathy release and enraptured murmuring, Spears utters the title line like a self-deflating sigh, followed by the words "I cannot hold it / I cannot control it." The song is supposedly about loving music, but there's no mistaking the erotic mood of submissiveness. The video showed a dance floor dissolving into an orgy.

The artists who most influenced Spears also connected a focus on the dynamics of dominance and submission with the plastic new world of cyborgs and cyberspace. Janet Jackson's 1986 breakthrough album was called *Control,* and, like Spears, she possessed a vocal instrument that was more synth than saxophone. Working with Prince associates Terry Lewis and Jimmy Jam, Jackson pioneered the connection between the erotic and the electronic, rejecting usual diva displays in favor of a delicate, conversational style that was also highly percussive—a robotic siren call. Her brother, of course, was the master of the funky melody. Spears's love of staccato utterances clearly came from Michael. Spears also found vocal inspiration in the 1990s R&B queen Aaliyah, whose career was cut short by a 2001 plane crash, when she was just twenty-two. In an appreciation after her death, *New York Times* critic Kelefa Sanneh extolled Aaliyah as "a digital diva who wove a spell with ones and zeroes," insinuating her gentle voice into the deep digital soundscapes of her producer Timbaland. Comparing Aaliyah's singing in her last single—the tellingly titled "More Than a Woman"—to the spirit of the android boy David in 2001's popular science-fiction film *AI,* Sanneh called her "a real person chasing an ideal of electronic perfection."[11]

As her career progressed, Spears became immersed more deeply within the sphere of the electronic. Music writers whose ears were accustomed to music made by fleshy, ego-assertive rockers and rappers found this troubling. "It's hard to visualize real live musicians picking up real live instruments and actually making these songs," complained critic David Segal. By 2003, when she released the frankly erotic album *In the Zone,* critics were bemoaning the veritable absence of Spears within her own songs. "Her voice is so processed, her physicality almost disappears," wrote critic Jon Pareles. Sanneh himself argued that the album was "almost perversely devoid of personality." Whatever he'd heard in Aaliyah's music—a deeper soul resonance reflective of African American legacies, perhaps—he didn't hear in Spears's.

Spears's voice represented a prime example of the rise of what the Scottish philosopher Andy Clark called "the soft self": a melding of human and post-human "processes—some neural, some bodily, some technological—and an ongoing drive to tell a story, to paint a picture in which 'I' am the central player."[12] Small-voiced women vocalists like Jennifer Lopez, Ciara, and Ashanti topped the charts in the early 2000s, upholding the legacy of Janet Jackson and Madonna more than the one forged by lung-power-driven vocalists like Whitney Houston and Mariah Carey. These manipulable voices blended well with the electronic elements of dance music and hip-hop; Ciara and Lopez often worked with rappers on their hits. Meanwhile, Spears continued to pursue a sound that was ever more synthetic, attached to lyrics that were increasingly sexual.

It was no accident that Spears's sexy new material conjured thoughts of work. "Spears is slapping on a headlamp and heading into the mines," wrote Caryn Ganz in a *Spin* review of *In the Zone*. Nearly every early profile described her life as a glittery indentured servitude, with twelve-hour rehearsals, painful dance injuries, and isolation on tour buses and in hotel rooms punctuated only by management-sanctioned shopping sprees. Her self-sexualization, Spears maintained, was simply an element of this work ethic, put on to please her audience. In interviews, she consistently described herself as "playing a part" when behaving provocatively: "That's not me" was her standard line. Detractors called Spears a "cynical cyborg" and "blank screen" for her ability to both project intense sexuality and stand apart from it. Most public discussions of

Spears began by expressing familiar divisions employed to question female sexuality: girl versus woman, virgin versus whore. But increasingly, "product" versus "person" became the dichotomy that most troubled Spears's detractors. Was she real, or was she a replicant?[13]

During Spears's heyday, cyber fantasies were settling in as a staple within popular culture. Television showed a preference for the supernatural, with shows like *The X-Files* and *Buffy the Vampire Slayer* providing narratives about shape-shifting that harkened back to classic science fiction and fairy tales. Video games like *Halo* and *Final Fantasy* told cyber stories and offered a cyber experience, allowing players to assume idealized (usually muscular, perfectly fit, hypersexual) forms and even switch gender at will. The *Matrix* trilogy, which launched in 1999, became the era's definitive cinematic science-fiction adventure by reimagining the world as a game. The films featured the sleek couple Neo and Trinity, played by mirror-image androgynes Keanu Reeves and Carrie-Anne Moss, kicking ass and coupling within alternate realities that rendered them superhuman and superhot. Nerds in the flesh, Neo and Trinity found their ideal forms by jacking into the Matrix, a computer platform which, though they were forced to be there, made them into the dreamboats audiences loved to watch. Blending Eastern ruminations on the world as illusion with Japanese anime style and an epic through line that both questioned technology's dominance and made it irresistible, *The Matrix* marked the moment when the post-human became an ideal state for the average multiplex popcorn chomper.

Writer Chuck Klosterman made the connection between Spears and *The Matrix* explicit: "Britney is almost like the little kid who freaks out Keanu Reeves in *The Matrix*. You say you want to bend a spoon? Well, the first thing you need to realize is there is no spoon."[14] Spears's ability to inhabit multiple identities—

teenybopper queen and hard-core vixen, or, to put it in classic sexist terms, virgin and whore—lifted her beyond those categories, or
even negated them. Within her music and persona, sexuality was
Britney's spoon, something she generated and could manipulate,
but which was not natural to her and therefore not confining. In
this, she resembled the cyborg ideal Donna Haraway had imagined, simply without the feminist framework. Her stardom was a
warped fulfillment of the cyber-feminist ideal of erasing the limits
culture placed upon the flesh.

Many musicians explored this interface between meat, machine, and network as the 2000s progressed and everything from
smart phones to implants rendered it more present in the everyday.
An interesting hybrid of cyborg identity and a naturalistic, soulful sound surfaced when the Atlanta-based singer Janelle Monáe
burst upon the scene in 2007, entrancing critics and a cult audience with her highly conceptual, retro-flavored music. Working
with a team of likeminded producers and multimedia artists who
called themselves the Wondaland Arts Society, Monáe created an
alternate world in her music, influenced by the Afro-Futurism of
science-fiction writers like Octavia Butler and funk pioneers like
George Clinton. In her first few releases, Monáe actually took on a
post-human alter ego named Cindi Mayweather to tell a dystopian,
Bladerunner-like tale of rebellion motivated by transgressive love
between this cyborg and a human. Monáe and other alternative-
pop favorites like the Swedish dance music innovator Robyn and
the English duo Goldfrapp conceptualized the erotics of the cyborg in their songs. But their embodiments of the role were limited
compared to what Spears managed: a fusion of the real and the
robotic that seemed instinctual.

Yet as her music became more electronic and lyrically explicit,
the breezy Britney who laughed off her own contradictions collapsed beneath their weight. A 2004 quickie marriage to her backup
dancer Kevin Federline produced two sons but ended acrimoni-

ously in 2006. The next year, Spears suffered a very public nervous breakdown, including an episode where she shaved her own head in a San Fernando Valley salon—an attempt, perhaps, to erase the allure that was so fluid within her music but had become a trap in her everyday life. She was hospitalized, entered and exited drug rehab several times, and lost custody of her children. At age twenty-six, in what seemed like a subplot from a cyberpunk paperback, Spears actually lost custodianship of herself—her financial self, at least—when her father was appointed her conservator, managing all of her money and property. This arrangement is still in force today.[15]

This "tragedy," as one *Rolling Stone* cover story described it, did not interfere with Spears's stardom. Ever the cyborgian slave to her pop career, Spears barely stopped working, and in her darkest personal hour she became a darling of many who had long questioned her value and impact. *Blackout,* her fourth album, was released in the midst of her personal struggles. Her production was more experimental than ever, but her voice was so processed and blended into its background vocals that her actual human involvement seemed questionable. Spears the artist wasn't simply e-mailing her heart; she had herself become code. The machine had become the matrix, as Sadie Plant had predicted in a 1996 essay: in Latin, *matrix* means "womb," and pop's electronic space of reproduction allowed female artists like Spears to endlessly replicate themselves.[16]

Within a few years, any controversy about embracing these strategies within pop stardom had fallen away, at least for women. Lady Gaga openly wore prosthetics in her videos. Rihanna mimed sex with a robot during her arena tours. Katy Perry went for a vintage vibe that recalled Britney's "Oops" video in her song about mating with an alien, "E.T." And in the video for her 2008 hit "Single Ladies," which signaled her usurpation of Spears as pop's definitive female star, Beyoncé Knowles figured out her own way to be more human than human: she danced and sang with naturalistic fervor while brandishing a *Matrix*-style "cyberglove."

Spears continued to have hit singles and tour, did a stint as a judge on the singing competition *X Factor*, and maintained a less hectic if still lonely-seeming personal life, with multiple marriage engagements and the continued conservatorship of her father. In the mid-2010s, she settled into a Las Vegas residency, which many pop stars considered a crowning achievement. Her 2013 single, "Work, Bitch," was a Top 20 single though it plummeted fast. In it, she tied together the themes of her life's work: bodily perfection, human being as self-production, and the labor of the inexhaustible post-human pop star. "You want a hot body? You want a Bugatti? You want a Maserati? You better work, bitch!" she intoned in the flat, even tone of the GPS that came standard on the luxury cars named in the song. The body, the machine, the work: for Britney Spears, as for her listeners, it was increasingly all one.

ALL THE SINGLE CYBORGS

By 2008, though she continued to sell records and occupy the tabloids, Britney Spears no longer held the center of the spotlight where eroticism and popular music commingled. A phalanx of rivals had developed their own styles of uncanny pop allure. The main one was a multitalent who'd been active in pop for as long as Britney herself. Beyoncé Knowles first gained fame in the late 1990s in the girl group Destiny's Child. Going by just Beyoncé, she released her first solo album in 2003, at age twenty-one. She immediately became the leading voice marrying hip-hop rhythms to R&B melodic theatrics. By 2008 she was one of the top-selling artists in the world and a celebrity in a career-enhancing though well-guarded relationship with the rapper and record executive Jay Z. But she still needed a breakthrough moment. To use a then-new term describing what happens when something spreads like crazy on the Web, Beyoncé needed to go viral.

She did it with the video for "Single Ladies," a B-side from her third album, *I Am . . . Sasha Fierce*. The clip, directed by Jake Nava, was an afterthought made during the same session that produced a much more expensive one for the ballad "If I Were a Boy." The song "Single Ladies" is a hip-hop romp characteristic of Beyoncé's up-tempo style, a dance-floor confrontation between a skittish boyfriend and the woman he won't marry that taps into gospel's call-and-response tradition by way of cheerleader routines and the playground chants used by 1960s girl groups. The message is socially conservative—"If you like it then you shoulda put a ring on it"—and the video is simple. But the performance Beyoncé and her two dancers gave ended up being the perfect conduit for the increasingly fluid sense of self and erotic life online it granted.

In the video, the trio enacts an intensely physical dance routine within what photographers call an infinity cove: a cornerless, all-white space that makes them seem to exist somewhere otherworldly. (Madonna used the same effect in her "Lucky Star" video.) Their leotards and jazz-hands moves take inspiration from the late Bob Fosse, a choreographer who represented the Broadway aspirations long harbored by Beyoncé, a fan of both Barbra Streisand and Diana Ross. But the routine also borrowed from a street style known as J-setting, which originated with Southern college drum majorettes and had been taken up by young gay men within the world of nightclub drag competitions. J-setting is a bodily form of call-and-response in which the lead dancer initiates moves that her seconds quickly imitate to create the effect of an endless movement loop. Beyoncé's dance, a reflection in a queer mirror, exists in a kind of metaphorical infinity cove, where a star is imitating queer club kids imitating college girls imitating Broadway stars. It's a replicant dance, ready to be imprinted on any viewer's DNA.

Beyoncé connected her retro-futuristic dance routine to the fluctuations of cyberspace by way of a striking piece of jewelry. The three-piece accessory, made of titanium by jewelry designer Lorraine Schwartz, was alternately known as the roboglove, the cyberglove, and the gling. Beyoncé conceived it as an emblem of the "superpower" possessed by her alter ego Sasha Fierce—the confident, sexually forthright, drag-androgynous force who took over when shy Miss Knowles took the stage. The roboglove transformed Sasha Fierce into an avatar, a creature brought to life by technology. Invoking the gloves worn by users of the first iterations of virtual reality, who could prosthetically "feel" and manipulate their experience in a computer world, Beyoncé's roboglove defined the "Single Ladies" video as a product of cyberspace, infinitely reproducing itself there, and accessible to anyone who logged on and found it.

It didn't take long for "Single Ladies" to attract responses on YouTube, the video-sharing website that since 2005 had become the visual hub and leveling ground for megastars and amateurs, diarists and parodists alike. The first known "Single Ladies" imitation came from twenty-seven-year-old dancer Shane Mercado only five days after the video was released. The forcefully flamboyant Mercado brought the routine back into the queer vernacular, stressing its bumps and grinds as he performed in his bedroom in a strategically disassembled, nipple-baring leotard. Beyoncé approved, and Mercado had a brief moment on the talk-show circuit. "I locked the door and just went for it," he told daytime host Bonnie Hunt, explaining that he shared an apartment with his mother and didn't want her walking in. "I had a blast. And one website actually nicknamed me 'Heyoncé.'" Mercado held the spotlight as "Heyoncé" for only a moment. He had a rival the very next day: Chris McMillon, aka Angel Pariz, executed the routine with even more androgynous aplomb as a caption flashed across his video screen: "I AM A BOY!! A BOY!" McMillon never gained even the small amount of mainstream attention Mercado enjoyed, but the two videos together added up to something: a claim on the "Single Ladies" dance as an open route to the multiple identities being online could offer.[17]

Soon, seemingly every Beyoncé admirer was using "Single Ladies" as a portal to a new way of being: one 2009 list of tributes includes a trio of plus-sized, self-described "big girls," an Asian American a cappella group, a baby, a male comedian diapered like a baby, a Barack Obama impressionist, the teen idol Joe Jonas, a football team, and Justin Timberlake, who performed the routine along with comedian Andy Samberg and Beyoncé herself on *Saturday Night Live*.[18] Writing about one of the many flash mobs of dancers who recorded "Single Ladies" videos in public—this one was in London's Piccadilly Square, and involved one hundred participants—the blogger Alex Watson declared the phenomenon to be a triumph of virtual reality. "It is, essentially, VR," he wrote. "Actions in reality that are targeted at, and only make sense when experienced virtually." Beyoncé had always been a forward-thinking pop star who'd marketed herself through whatever new technology was available: ringtones, iTunes, exclusive deals with game companies like Nintendo. But with "Single Ladies" she gracefully stumbled onto the central nerve in the rapidly evolving system of synapses connecting people online, across old boundaries of being.

Viral connection was the new reality for Beyoncé's fans, the first generation to grow up connected via the Internet. "Our neurochemical response to every ping and ring tone seems to be the one elicited by the 'seeking' drive, a deep motivation of the human psyche," wrote the social scientist Sherry Turkle in 2011. "Connectivity becomes a craving; when we receive a text or an email, our nervous system responds by giving us a shot of dopamine. We are stimulated by connectivity itself."[19] Turkle, who in her influential 1984 book *The Second Self* celebrated forging new identities via computers, had become cautious. Like the adults who wrote teen advice books in the 1950s, she recognized the freedoms offered by new technologies, especially in identity building and erotic intimacy; but she also feared that these changes would prove damaging, pushing youths, especially, too far away from healthy, normative behavior.

Young people were at the vanguard, but everyone was rapidly becoming wired and trying to figure out how to negotiate the Matrix. John Palfrey and Urs Gasser noted several threats in their 2008 book *Born Digital: Understanding the First Generation of Digital Natives*. These included the insecurity of online information, which could make people victims of crimes ranging from online stalking to identity theft; the fact that online games produce the same biological responses in players as does pornography in viewers; and the risk-inducing pressure young people felt from peers to put forth an impressive online persona. Online life was shaking identity to its core and rewriting the rules of intimacy as it did so. Andy Clark's idea of "the soft self," of human experience enhanced by devices (like smart phones) that do not penetrate the skin but still fundamentally extend or at least change the possibilities of what we can do as biological beings, complements Turkle's description of "the collaborative self," negotiating reality as a "life mix" of online and offline encounters: "These days always-on connection leads us to reconsider the virtues of a more collaborative self," Turkle wrote. "All questions about autonomy look different if, on a daily basis, we are together even when we are alone."[20]

Though the "Single Ladies" video parodies were generally good clean fun, countless people were also using the Internet to create and share explicit erotic material. Whether having fully realized sexual encounters or simply posting cute photographs on MySpace to attract virtual friends, online adventurers were always engaging some level of risk. Palfrey and Gasser cited "instability and insecurity" as the two major elements in these new online ways of being, warning that "one's identity in the digital age changes frequently, and not always through the volitional acts of the person whose identity is at stake." Sounding like worried suburban fathers handing their teens the keys to the car, they continued, "Just as the digital identity of a Digital Native is at once rich and interesting and easy to create, it is also fragile and vulnerable to manipulation and falsification."[21] As experts had done before, they singled out youths as the most at risk from societal changes no one could stop, facing their biggest challenges within the realm of the erotic.

Young people dominated the "Single Ladies" parodies. In 2010, the video of a dance team of eight- and nine-year-olds performing "Single Ladies" in midriff tops and spangled boy shorts caused nationwide outrage at the sexualization of grade schoolers, but also garnered more than two million views. The ensuing conversation was as much about the fetishization of children as it was about YouTube, yet the virality of the video that went far beyond the obscure arena of amateur dance made the girls seem particularly threatened. "The girls weren't meant to be viewed by millions of people," one dancer's father said during an interview on *Good Morning America*. Behavior that might not seem overtly sexual in context, parents feared, could be used against these children, exploited by those seeking erotic stimulation without permission.

The Dance Precisions troupe performance of "Single Ladies" entered a world in which sex tapes stolen from or secretly leaked by celebrities (many of them rock or pop stars) were being traded for money; where Web-based communities like the rapid-fire sharing platform Chatroulette allowed participants to surprise visitors with scenes of them masturbating or performing other lewd acts; and where young women, particularly, faced threats from stalkers and predators within social media environments with increasingly unstable borders. At the same time, the chance to transform on the Internet, to develop sexual and emotional confidence and forge relationships otherwise made impossible by

distance and other meat-world limitations, was impossible to resist. Negotiating this risky territory became the number one preoccupation within many Americans' private lives. How could a
person enjoy the possibilities of online dating, social media connections, and erotic self-display on sites like YouTube without
utterly giving herself away? No other question haunted desire so
powerfully in the mid-2000s.

It was Beyoncé who gradually evolved a way of being public in
private that could serve as the ultimate guide to this new, volatile
erotic realm. Always a perfectionist deeply concerned with control,
the singer developed an approach to social media that seemed revelatory while maintaining strict borders around both her day-
to-day life and her creative process. After "Single Ladies," Beyoncé
became the standard-bearer for twenty-first-century pop stardom,
even in a crowded field that included many equally commercially
successful pop divas. She did so by developing a persona artfully
balancing the conflicting elements of life as a collaborative self: experimentation with self-preservation; connection to the many with
strong ties to the very few; exhibitionism with modesty; openness
to fantasy with dedication to keeping it real.

What had "keeping it real" become in the twenty-first-century
imaginarium? For Beyoncé, that question was grounded in a
sense of the performing self as both distinct from and evocative
of her day-to-day ways of being. The biography she shared with
reporters was of a shy child who "just . . . *changed*" when she began
performing at talent shows in grade school. "I don't have a split
personality," she told one in 2004. "But I'm really very country
and would rather have no shoes on and have my hair in a bun
and no makeup. And when I perform, this confidence and this
sexiness and this whatever it is that I'm completely not just happens."[22] Beyoncé often said the most important quality she'd
learned from the women who taught her to perform—the nuns at
her grade school, and her mother, who was also her career men-

tor and costume designer—was discipline. Self-control allowed her to become free in performance while maintaining distance from that wild behavior offstage. This was a shift from the rockstar behavior expected from musical celebrities since at least the 1950s; it also distinguished Beyoncé from her early rival Spears, whose inability to manage her personal life contributed to her self-diminishment within her own music. Beyoncé could wear the virtual reality glove while maintaining an even-keeled naturalness that identified her as relatable. Her pop stardom was not unlike that of the superheroes who resurged in popularity during the video game–dominated 2000s: Spider-Man, Batman, and Iron Man, donning costumes to perform daring deeds and then vanishing as much as possible into normal lives.

The ability to divide herself into persona and person and retain an aura of health, deliberately projecting stability in a private life dominated by close family members and her longtime beau and eventual husband Jay Z, distinguished Beyoncé from her other female digital-age pop stars like Rihanna and Taylor Swift, who struggled with scandals or at least an ongoing barrage of gossip. The one who came closest to matching her example was Lady Gaga, a glam-rock-loving, punk-baptized former New York prep school girl born Stefani Germanotta, who borrowed directly from drag artists and cyberpunk in songs and videos that dwelled on the artifice of romance and the perversity of fame. Beyoncé turned to Gaga as a collaborator when the latter was at her early peak as the David Bowie of cyborgian divas. The 2010 video for "Telephone," a duet from Gaga's album *The Fame Monster,* got the most immediate attention: a nearly ten-minute-long tribute to trash-culture film, music, and fashion directed by frequent Madonna collaborator Jonas Åkerlund. Its exploitation-movie narrative involved a women's prison, a murder spree in a diner, and its two stars playing at testy lesbian intimacy in a Chevy Silverado with the words "Pussy Wagon" airbrushed on the back.

Their collaboration on Beyoncé's "Video Phone" more power-fully served her project of becoming the leading pop presence in an age of avatars. The video was directed by Hype Williams, whose pioneering 1990s clips introduced high-tech Afro-Futurism to MTV. Until Gaga enters near the end, Beyoncé is the only female figure in it. Male dancers occasionally surround her, but their faces are obscured; sometimes they wear giant cameras on their heads, reduced to voyeuristic machines. As she goes through a series of porn-suggestive poses, including stripper bends, gun play, and bumps and grinds, more than a dozen variations on her signature leotard seem to change themselves, the way outfits did on paper-doll figures in the dress-up-oriented video games that girls played on their smart phones. Beyoncé fully enters into virtual reality in "Video Phone," taking control of the fantasies others project upon her, reaching through the lens of celebrity and declaring, "I can handle you."

"Video Phone" was released as a single in November 2009, mere months after Apple announced sales of one million iPhone 3Gs within three days of the model's launch. A year later, the song's scenario of real-time intimate engagement via hand-held touch-screens became widely available through the iPhone's FaceTime function. For decades, fans had gazed at pop stars through the screens of television or film, heard their whispers through radio, or dreamed using images carefully framed within the pages of a magazine. Now lovers could perform for each other as pop stars did for them, and become each other's audiences in acts of disclo-sure only limited by data plans. Beyoncé was the ideal star for this time of pondering what personhood, and relationships, meant within high-resolution retina displays. Her evolving use of social media came to define best practices—or at least, the most effec-tive strategies—within that realm. She and Jay Z occasionally faced scandals, including rumors of his infidelity. But they reined in the gossip, always returning to social media to ask for respectful dis-

tance from fans and in exchange offering carefully curated images
or words from the world behind the transparent curtain.

Between 2008 and 2012, when she became the top-earning
woman in popular music according to *Forbes,* Beyoncé gave up her
Sasha Fierce persona and fulfilled her conventional dream of whole
womanhood, marrying Jay Z and birthing daughter Blue Ivy. When
she announced that pregnancy on the MTV Video Music Awards in
2011, the news broke Twitter's record for most tweets per second—
nearly nine thousand. Ten months later, she shared photos of her
child on a relatively new social media platform, Tumblr. Her use
of Tumblr boosted its success, and it was eventually sold to the
tech conglomerate Yahoo for $1.1 billion.[23] A confidential tone, the
media critic Anne-Helen Petersen wrote, is what made Beyoncé's
social media use so powerful. "Whether Beyoncé herself is 'old-
fashioned' or even a naturally private person is really beyond the
point. Her image has acquired a gloss of privacy, and in today's
media environment, saturated with celebrity disclosure, it renders
her unique," Peterson wrote.[24]

Beyoncé's Tumblr overflowed with images that embodied the
phrase "far away, so close": Beyoncé carrying Blue Ivy, both of their
backs to the camera; Bey and Jay in a crowd at the music festival
Coachella, the rapper wearing a bandana to hide his still instantly
recognizable face. Scattered in these shots were high-fashion poses,
including some of Beyoncé in superhero costumes. The Tumblr
balanced exposure and concealment, becoming a work of art in itself: it felt more like a lovingly tended diary than the product of
the chaotic openness of the Web. In Beyoncé's hands, social media
became a true medium: the substance through which raw material
is rendered into art.

Beyoncé's use of social media as art hit a peak with the release of her self-titled fifth album in the wee hours of December
13, 2013. The world learned of *Beyoncé* via a simple post reading
"Surprise!" on the photo-sharing platform Instagram, and could

immediately download its fourteen tracks and accompanying videos via iTunes. Beyoncé was not the first major star to suddenly unleash an album via the Internet, but there had never been one so well orchestrated as an event. Within twenty-four hours, *Beyoncé* had produced 1.2 million Twitter responses, more than 25,000 Tumblr posts, 7,000 Instagram photo reactions, and, according to one search engine, 600 GIFs, or animated images, connected to Beyoncé's name. Most important, it also sold 828,773 copies through the iTunes store in its first week. "In other words, the album has created a social media class of its own, generating a sort of ripple effect that is keeping the album front and center in the Web's ephemeral consciousness," wrote the media critic Jenna Wortham in the *New York Times*.[25]

Beyoncé was uniquely qualified to create this kind of response. It contained the most experimental music Beyoncé had ever made, heavily connected to regional rap styles like the sloweddown screw music of the singer's native Houston; it also showed the mark of her explorations of cutting-edge electronic sounds and art rock. It wasn't meant for radio, but for more open-minded listeners who got their music searching online. While about half of its songs dealt with themes familiar to any Beyoncé fan—female empowerment and camaraderie, emotional vulnerability, the costs and pleasures of fame—the others were bluntly pornographic fantasies and confessions, far raunchier than anything Beyoncé had previously done or what most of her peers were willing to try. These songs, Beyoncé told interviewers, were inspired by thoughts she indulged during the months after her pregnancy, when actual sex was more difficult for her and Jay Z. Conjuring scenes of a sizzling hot married life, these songs penetrated the nerve of privacy, yet impeccably supported the distanced intimacy at the center of Beyoncé's art.

"Partition," the album's most successful single, is an account of

sex in a limousine whose details—torn party clothes and a chauf-
feur averting his eyes—fused glamour and tawdriness. "Drunk in
Love" became notorious for naming the position Beyoncé prefers
for bathtub sex—"surfboard"—alongside an image of the couple
waking up in the kitchen after a night of debauchery. "Rocket"
combines explicit lines such as "let me sit this ass on you" with mus-
ings about Beyoncé's and Jay Z's blended personal and professional
lives, culminating in the declaration, "Goddammit I'm comfortable in my skin / and you're comfortable in my skin." Throughout
Beyoncé, the domestic scene becomes a pornographic one, a sequestered stage for sex.

If, as one critic noted, *Beyoncé* was "the rudest mainstream album since Madonna's *Erotica*," it was also in some ways diamet-
rically opposed to that work.[26] While Madonna's songs and the
accompanying book *Sex* branded her as an extroverted explorer,
engaging in random encounters, exhibitionism, and group sex, Beyoncé's established her as the raunchy queen of an inner sanctum
whose sensual electricity would serve as inspiration and guidepost
to fans, but would ultimately remain Beyoncé's and Jay Z's alone.
She was solving the problem of the celebrity sex tape, feeding the
insatiable demand for public knowledge of famous people's lives
with divulgences that satisfied but remained in her grasp. Beyond
that, for the average listener or viewer, *Beyoncé* fought back against
the assumption that to live online was to surrender any real control over one's private life. It showed how a person could reveal herself without being violated.

"Only a mama can do that, and only a wife can do that. That's
your strength," the producer Pharrell declared to the singer in a
promotional video for *Beyoncé*, reminding viewers that in these
songs, Beyoncé was not merely performing sexuality but presenting it as a gift for her husband. The "mama" and "wife" behind this
material reasserted her social and economic position constantly, in

the luxurious settings of the videos and the emotional details of the songs, which contextualized the pornographic lines as uttered between powerful equals for whom love and partnership, not sexual performance, mattered most. "We're so much more than pointless fixtures, Instagram pictures, consumers," Beyoncé sang on "Rocket." "Home is where the heart is." And in these songs, home remained inviolable. What Beyoncé shared could be enjoyed, even embraced, but not entered by anyone except the confessor herself and her mate.

Beyoncé also pointed toward a new way for an artist to confront the shadow world of pornography that had haunted mainstream entertainment since the nineteenth-century days of burlesque. While the album's music abounds in juicy details, the videos tend to be more conventional, showing Beyoncé in high-fashion versions of stripper or dominatrix gear dancing or teasingly touching herself in ways anyone who'd ever watched a porn video would recognize. Others show Beyoncé and mostly female friends (and fellow dancers) in nostalgic leisure scenes: roller skating, riding the Cyclone roller coaster on Coney Island, or rehearsing moves before a mirror at home. The songs' explicit content contrasted with these images, but combined they offered a sense of how erotic thoughts run through a woman's mind even when she is not in the midst of an encounter. Certain songs, like the melodramatic ballad "Pretty Hurts," also acknowledge that erotic ideals can be confining and even oppressive to women. It all adds up to an exquisitely well-balanced view of sexuality, one that elevates the pornographic through high production values, difficult choreography, and the constant reassertion of Beyoncé's personality. Acting erotically, she actively fights against being reduced to the status of object. The insistence on sexual subjectivity, which generates sexual power, is *Beyoncé*'s ultimate message.

In a much-circulated videotaped panel discussion after the

album's release, the venerable feminist writer bell hooks said that "part" of Beyoncé was "a terrorist" because, despite her ostensible frankness, she still upheld a standard of beauty and sexual allure that most women could not achieve.[27] Yet if *Beyoncé* can be considered as a direct response to the rise of both social media and pornography online, it does seem different than most pop stars' attempts to exploit their own attractiveness for profit. Porn has always been big business on the Internet. In 2009, however, reports began circulating that social media sites had superseded porn to become the number one reason people visited the Web. The next logical question—is the future of porn social?—was quickly answered in the affirmative with the rise of sites like Pinsex and Pornstagram, where amateurs trade explicit images while avoiding the fees commercial porn demands. Beyoncé's favorite social platform, Tumblr, was a home for porn from the beginning. At the same time, online dating was veering toward one-night stands or afternoon hookups through mobile apps like Grindr (for gay men) and Tinder (mostly for heterosexuals). In this context, *Beyoncé,* with its spicy but contained fantasies of monogamous love and female self-possession, stands out as a kind of protest, conservative in some ways and determinedly centered on female self-respect. For those attempting to locate their own desires within the fast-paced, bafflingly varied, and often near-anonymous realm of online sex, Beyoncé's assertion of strength and positive containment suggested that sex could be fully enjoyed, and even shared, online in healthy and even loving ways.

"My first album came out when I was fifteen. I was a child," Beyoncé said in one of the promotional videos she released in tandem with *Beyoncé.* "But now I'm in my thirties and those children that grew up listening to me have grown up." Her self-described "journey" into sexually explicit content was the final step in her becoming fully adult as an artist, and as an embodiment of the

soft self, fully inhabiting a mobile online world that complemented and enhanced her physical-world assertions of identity
and power. In a time increasingly dominated by virtual experiences, her nimble advances and self-preserving retreats made her
the queen of pop.

BLURRING THE LINES

Britney and Beyoncé, the cyborg and the avatar, embodied new
ways of being—and being sexual—within the twenty-first-century
life mix. But they didn't emerge in a vacuum. In the 2000s, pop in
general grappled with new modes of human behavior enabled by
the Internet, and the moral codes, often linked to sexual behavior, that arose to accommodate them. If pop seemed to get cruder
and cruder as the new century wore on, this was largely a response
to the new sexual openness that online living made possible. In
an atmosphere where pornography, sexual hookups, and gender
switching were all available at the click of a hyperlink, pop yet
again staged Americans' conversations about the blurred lines of
behavior within their most private lives. Music led the way into a
new sexual mode in which every act of flirtation potentially could
be shared across multiple platforms, and even in the most furtive
moments of connection and climax, lovers were aware of themselves as being watched, presenting personae, acting out sexual
scripts.

At the same time, the most fundamental questions of right and
wrong, evoking the biblical commandments *Thou shalt not steal* and
Thou shalt not bear false witness, arose at the center of the pop world.
Computer programs that could alter vocal sounds, especially the
ubiquitous pitch-correction program Auto-Tune, threw into question the very definitions of authentic expression and identity. And
the shift toward digital music distribution—the ease with which

MP3 files could be illegally shared on peer-to-peer networks like Napster—caused a genuine panic within the recording industry, as ordinary citizens were tracked down and sometimes prosecuted as music thieves.

These broader moral debates often zeroed in on sexuality. Though computerized pitch correction was everywhere in pop by the mid-2000s, a particular strain of R&B and hip-hop that originated largely in strip clubs became a primary target of critics decrying the loss of musical authenticity. At the same time, questions about the corrosive effects of music downloading mirrored concerns about the rise of online pornography; the two realms were even linked in legislation, as congressmen tried to regulate file-sharing services that facilitated the distribution of both. As the music industry changed, its veterans expressed longing for more innocent times. "You can't watch modern stars like Britney Spears or Lady Gaga with a two-year-old," the 1980s British hitmaker Mike Stock said during a one-man campaign against the sluttification of American pop in 2010. "Ninety-nine percent of the charts is R&B, and ninety-nine percent of that is soft-core pornography."[28]

Stock's comments were racist, overlooking the intense sexualization of women in white-dominated subgenres like heavy metal and even his own home turf of British New Wave, where models dressed as animals cavorted in Duran Duran videos. Yet he wasn't wrong to associate R&B (and, implicitly, its sibling, hip-hop) with the business of sex. At the beginning of the twenty-first century new musical forms were being developed in rooms where women danced and men mostly watched. There was an echo of nineteenth-century New Orleans and the ten-cents-a-dance palaces of New York in the strip clubs of what had come to be known as the Dirty South.

"Magic City, Blue Flame, Cheetah, Diamonds of Atlanta, Follies: the way some cities are known for their restaurants or their museums or their turn-of-the-century architecture, Atlanta's landmarks are strip clubs," the *New York Times* writer Jon Caramanica reported. The first wave of influence lasted from the late 1980s through the mid-1990s; it then receded for a decade, only to return when America's black entertainment industry essentially relocated to Atlanta in the mid-2000s. Several elements influenced the turn back, Caramanica noted: "The city's arrival as the center of hip-hop innovation, its rising black celebrity class and the pernicious influence of the crime syndicate BMF, which was known for its flamboyant and extravagant strip club outings. These were huge transactional scrums—rappers, dancers, criminals, bottles of alcohol, tens of thousands of dollars in the air."[29]

Strip clubs made for good places to try out new sounds because they were de facto dancing arenas. The way women moved to a track's heavy beats and ear-catching samples told songwriters and music industry executives if it would be a hit. And, once again, new dances emerged from the clubs. As early as 2000, *New York Times* style reporter Julia Chaplin noted one dance called "rear-ending"—the Funky Butt of the cyber age. "Me and my friends joke that going out now is like being in an interactive strip club," Chaplin quoted one young promoter as saying. "As he spoke at the club near Union Square, a woman with a silver thong peeking above her tight leopard-print hip-huggers pressed her backside against his leg to the rally of Jay-Z's 'Give It to Me.'"

The connection between Beyoncé's then–future husband Jay Z and strip-club culture shows how mainstream it had become as a hip-hop reference point. The Florida rapper and entrepreneur Luther "Uncle Luke" Campbell had brought strip club dancers into his videos in the late 1980s; his very public struggles with censorship culminated in a high-profile trial and acquittal in his native Florida, and his 2 Live Crew's subsequent fame made their jiggle a national phenomenon. By 2000, New York–based video directors like Diane Martel were looking to the clubs for dancers. "The strippers are playing regular girls [in her videos]," Martel told Chaplin. "I just like to use them because they are amazing freestyle dancers."

In 2005, a Tallahassee "rappa ternt sanga" (Jamaican-style patois for "rapper turned singer") named Faheem Rashad Najm, but better known by his stage name of T-Pain, helped the romance of the strip club cross over to a massive pop audience. He was also the first performer to fully show off the novel possibilities of the otherwise controversial Auto-Tune. Auto-Tune was invented by engineer Andy Hildebrand in the late 1990s strictly as a tool to help perfect the sound of the recorded voice. The singer and actress Cher had a dance club hit in 1998, "Believe," in which her producers used it as an effect, to make her sound like an angelic cyborg. T-Pain, inspired by the use of the more primitive vocoder in 1980s R&B, took Auto-Tune to extremes, bending and morphing his vocals until they were sometimes almost unintelligible. Though many described T-Pain's music as robotic—one 2007 review compared him to a "horny, alcoholic android"—the *New Yorker* magazine critic Sasha Frere-Jones came closest to capturing its uncanniness: "In his hands, the program becomes pop music's rose-colored glasses, or a balloon's worth of helium inhaled . . . His vocals hang, flickering, and suggest not a technological intervention but a chemical one."[30]

T-Pain's accomplishment was the creation of giddy confusion between the flesh and mechanics, calculation and emotion: he was the soft self, celebrating. He found the ideal balance in his signature song, "I'm 'n Luv (wit a Stripper)," which became a Top 5 hit in 2005. In it, T-Pain, along with the rapper Mike Jones, sings the praises of a performer who convinces her customers that she feels more than professional obligation toward them. It's an update of the tender, chilling Temptations soul classic "Just My Imagination," in which the male narrator imagines a whole life with a woman who walks by his window every day, only to reveal, in the song's last line, that "she doesn't even know me." The object of T-Pain's affection does at least know her would-be paramour is looking at her, and she looks back—"right in my eyes," T-Pain sings, thinking this means he'll have her home and in his bed in no time. In the end, though, he's left guessing if her interest is feigned or genuine. "She don't even know me," he sings, echoing Eddie Kendricks's earlier dreamer-cum-stalker. After using Auto-Tune to twist and buoy his singing throughout the song, T-Pain murmurs that line in his vulnerable natural voice.

In 2005, the New Orleans–based writer Alison Fensterstock noted that the more upscale gentlemen's clubs of the early 2000s created "a fantasy dating zone . . . where women way out of your league would approach you, reaffirm your heterosexuality, let you relax outside the confusing and changing world of gender relations and then basically disappear from your life until you choose to return."[31] In his song, T-Pain longs to break the barrier between this comfortable but expensive construction and real life, all the while knowing how unlikely it is that this will happen. His subject matter is the distortion of reality that takes place when erotic performance explicitly involves money. The form the song takes—the unstable Auto-Tuned vocal—mirrors this predicament. It's unclear whether the listener can really know T-Pain as a singer, just as he doesn't really know the woman whose direct look is likely for show.

In the couple of years following T-Pain's breakthrough, his Auto-Tuned voice became ubiquitous on hit singles: he collaborated on seven Hot 100 singles in 2007, and showed up nine times on *Billboard*'s club-oriented Rhythmic Top 10 chart. Many other artists explored Auto-Tune on their own, usually within songs that described seduction and sex acts. Rapper Lil Wayne used it to enhance his double entendres on "Lollipop," a No. 1 song about oral sex. Snoop Dogg, whose laconic rhyming style defined cool in gangsta rap, employed it on his highly explicit hit "Sexual Eruption." Some artists also employed Auto-Tune to communicate vulnerability in a way that hip-hop's swagger usually didn't accommodate. Most notably, Kanye West used it throughout his 2008 album *808s & Heartbreak*, inspired by the death of his mother (in a grim twist for this cyber age, during plastic surgery) and his breakup with his fiancée, the fashion designer Alexis Phifer. The album, West said at its launch party, was about "emotional nakedness"—something he could achieve, apparently, only while wearing the costume of Auto-Tune.

The rise of Auto-Tune coincided with the rise of a new kind of "raunch culture" that differed in tone from the sexual experimentation of previous eras. Young women were embracing not just erotic freedom, but the aspects of the sexual economy that feminism had once taught them were sexually oppressive: pornography, obscenity, and, within limits, sex work. Some feminists had long argued that sex work could be liberating if women remained in control of their labor; a side gig in a strip club was fairly common among young bohemian women (and even feminist academics) starting in the 1980s. Life online accelerated the mainstreaming of these attitudes. Amateur pornography was becoming ever more common, and for those who wanted to be less explicit, strippers offered an example of forthright sexual behavior that seemed powerful and fun. YouTube abounded with videos of women trying out routines on self-installed stripper poles. Health clubs began offering Strippercise classes. The general tone behind these developments was celebratory, but also somewhat cynical. Raunch culture focused on sex as a power game, and suggested that softer feelings about romance—represented by the red roses offered to contestants on the television dating show *The Bachelor*— were, though enjoyable, just a form of artifice. Tenderness, this version of the stripper sensibility suggested, was as fake as a crooning vocal processed through Auto-Tune.[32]

If love couldn't be trusted in this new era, neither could music. Auto-Tune was just one of many computer tools that played up the manipulated nature of voices, and indeed of all musical elements held up as authentic, within recorded music. Critics of these methods of enhancement, many themselves musicians, considered them to be cheater's tools and feared for the loss of real human presence. Defenders argued that innovation, not some notion of "the real," was the genuine article that made pop special. The embrace of Auto-Tune shared something with raunch culture: it presupposed that a certain basic inauthenticity was at the heart of human self-expression. Everything was a performance, even within our most intimate experiences of voice and flesh and the human heart.

The sociologist Elizabeth Bernstein came up with the term "bounded authenticity" to describe a shift in sex work in the 2000s, away from brief encounters and toward the "girlfriend experience," in which men would purchase not only carnal contact but emotional support and companionship, if only for a night.[33] Her term also well describes music like T-Pain's, in which a voice is twisted by machines, yet somehow wrung out more thoroughly by the manipulation—the computerized elements reshape and heighten emotion in these songs, rather than deadening it. "Bounded authenticity" also accurately defines sexual encounters online, where lovers who have often never met in person dare each other to go further and reveal more, precisely because their interactions are contained within the glowing screen.

In a culture increasingly dominated by online interactions, the "bounded authenticity" of sex work, typified by the figure of the stripper, becomes more appealing because it recalls the highly performed identities each of us cultivates when we log on. The same is true of music that blends human and electronic elements. "Increasingly, the identity of just about anyone living in a digital era is a synthesis of real-space and online expressions of self," wrote

Palfrey and Gasser in *Born Digital*.[34] In this hybrid way of being, old ideas about pure experience—whether sexual, musical, or emotional—were falling away. The show that is sex work started to seem a lot like the one women, and men too, put on whenever they entered social media. The sound of T-Pain's altered voice echoed the chopped-and-screwed selves people constructed constantly, fingers caressing keyboards as they became something more or less than what they they could be offline.

Such enormous changes could not occur without moral panic. The Internet was reassembling humanity itself; on a more specific yet still startling level, it was also taking the recording industry apart. The creation of the MP3 audio-coding format made it possible to easily distribute music online. Next came Napster: the original peer-to-peer file-sharing program, created by college kids Sean Parker and Shawn Fanning in their dorm room, that freed songs from the confines of bought-and-sold CDs and made them as exchangeable as imaginary spit in an erotic chat room. It wasn't long before the Recording Industry Association of America, the trade group representing labels and distributors, sought legal action against downloaders, many of whom were just kids. The narratives of these lawsuits resembled those that formed around juvenile delinquency in the 1950s. Many of the cases that caught the media's interest were brought against women and even young girls; in 2003, for example, twelve-year-old Brianna LaHara of New York was charged with storing more than one thousand songs illegally on her computer. "According to news reports, Brianna believed that she was allowed to download the music from the Internet—partly because her mother paid a monthly subscription fee to be connected to the Web," noted Palfrey and Gasser.

Congressmen determined to stem the tide of online file sharing linked the act of downloading MP3s to another, more old-fashioned "sinful" activity: viewing pornography. Children seeking to download the latest hit by a favorite rapper could stumble across the Triple-XXX videos that rolled like tumble-weeds across the landscape. Peer-to-peer (P2P) systems, California Democrat Henry Waxman said, "give children access to the vilest hard-core pornography." "P2P stands for piracy-to-pornography," Andrew Lack, the chief executive of Sony Music Entertainment, told a *New York Times* reporter in 2003.[35] The panic surrounding music downloading was sexualized, in part, because a real connection existed between acquiring music and viewing pornography. Anyone who has copped a new album via a BitTorrent site has likely been assaulted by jiggling, butt-slapping women in the video ads for porn that keep these shadow systems funded. In general, though, the link between downloading music and pornography addiction was more projected than proven.

It was definitely true, however, that young people were exploring sex in cyberspace. Once P2P networks evolved into social media platforms like MySpace, Facebook, and Twitter, young people were accustomed to being outrageous within these fluid communities. The same environment that transformed them into music-sharing lawbreakers turned out to also be a safe-feeling space where they could share their bodies—or at least the images, sounds, and thoughts their bodies made possible—in selfies, videos, and erotic chat. "Teenagers may not own much, but they develop a very early and clever sense of the most important thing they will ever own: their bodies," wrote the educator S. Craig Watkins in his 2009 portrait of online youth, *The Young & the Digital.*[36]

For all the boisterousness with which a new generation embraced social interactivity online, questions remained. What limits should or could be drawn around sex and emotional intimacy when the physical couldn't be separated from the virtual? The Internet lover thinks differently about the limitations of her own body, which can be cleaned up with a filter in a photograph, or done away with altogether while sharing a fantasy with someone via texts. Perhaps this increasingly common experience of being multiple and, if not unlimited, at least unfettered, is what has made the experience of pushing limits a central subject within twenty-first-century popular music.

Some major artists explored the complexity of this bounded/unbound state via their own biographies. Rihanna, for example, who started her career as an adolescent Jay Z protégée instinctively bolder than most pop stars her age, faced a crisis when her boyfriend, the singer Chris Brown, brutally assaulted her in his car following a Grammy Awards week party in 2009. After that incident, for which Brown was sentenced to five years' probation, Rihanna frequently used her songs to confront violence within relationships. Hits like "Russian Roulette" and her duet with the rapper Eminem, "Love the Way You Lie," suggested that she felt that both victim and victimizer were complicit in violent relationships; like a modern-day version of the daring dancers of the Jazz Age, she examined the choreography between victim and brutalizer as a complex and seemingly irresistible series of dangerous moves. Rihanna also favored increasingly bawdy lyrics in her up-tempo songs, presenting herself as a sexual aggressor who considered love a game and herself a daring player. Three years after Brown beat her face in, Rihanna even reunited with him for the X-rated song "Birthday Cake"—as if to say that no story, even one so brutal, is simple when sex is involved.

Many listeners were repulsed by Rihanna's choice to record "Birthday Cake" with Brown and puzzled by the raunchy image she constructed instead of embracing one more redolent of female empowerment. Such seemingly willful perversity abounded in pop during these years. Women artists ruled the charts, but their ascent did not achieve what the feminists of either the 1970s or the riot grrrl '90s might have hoped. Each new star assumed a slightly different spot within a cartoonish card deck of sexualized female archetypes. Katy Perry played a vintage pinup girl, shooting whipped cream out of her candy-colored bra and singing about losing her virginity in various ways—with a man in "Teenage Dream," with a woman in "I Kissed a Girl." Lady Gaga played the perverse imp in vinyl fetish wear; she turned that role into one of liberation with her anthem "Born This Way," which became a signature song for a new generation of LGBTQ liberationists. Nicki Minaj, the leading female rapper of the era, focused fetish seekers on her prodigious backside, celebrated in her songs like "Anaconda," which climaxes with the chant: "This one is for my bitches with a fat ass in the fucking club!" The one millennial pop star who didn't engage with explicit material was Taylor Swift, whose roots in the more conservative country music world allowed her to become famous without foregrounding sex. Yet even Swift was shaking her booty (comically, at least) in her videos by 2014, when she made a decisive jump out of country into mainstream pop.

What really preoccupied the pop world in the new era was the view from the edge, and it was confused and contested, changing all the time. The greatest strides came in LGBTQ equality: same-sex couples were free to marry in a majority of states by 2014, and for the first time, musicians like the *American Idol* singing contest finalist Adam Lambert, the indie-pop duo Tegan and Sara, and the viral-video maven Troye Sivan were beginning their careers as openly gay or bisexual. Yet other rights were threatened. In several states, abortion became nearly inaccessible due to legislative restrictions placed on providers and on women themselves. Was this a time of greater acceptance of diversity when it came to sex, or of increasing restrictions? In the physical realm, both seemed true. In cyberspace, both realities also manifested simultaneously. Sexual conservatives, often religiously motivated, gathered together within diffuse communities like Quiverfull, a fundamentalist movement arguing for a strict biblical interpretation of gender roles and family life. People seeking sexual freedom congregated on hookup apps like Tinder and Grindr.

There wasn't even a general agreement about what sex might be anymore. Those mobile apps that could lead to an afternoon of play with a stranger were also often simply used as titillation, as users scrolled through available dates and swiped left or right to signal approval or rejection. That activity itself became an erotic act for many—what one famous Tinder user, the alternative rock singer Adam Duritz, called "the freakiest video game EVER." The widespread phenomenon of sexting, or sending pornographic texts from one's phone, further confused the definition of the carnal. "Our only way of being alone was to do it over the phone," one young woman told the journalist Hanna Rosin about her relationship with a trusted boyfriend in her semirural community, when Rosin investigated the rise of sexting among teens for the *Atlantic* in 2014. "It was a way of kind of dating without getting in trouble. A way of being sexual without being sexual, you know?"[37]

Being sexual without being sexual. This was different than pushing the limits of necking in the 1950s or rubbing close during a dance marathon in 1919. The flesh could no longer be relied upon as a guide to resolving the ambiguities of desire. In cyberspace, you were safe but also vulnerable in new ways: to photographs being distributed by your partner, to the harassment that became known as "slut-shaming," or to simply being misinterpreted, being failed by the vagaries of language and code.

In 2013, a song entered this confusing space that seemed to encapsulate its contradictions. Its very title—"Blurred Lines"—evoked a state of radical uncertainty. The music itself didn't sound futuristic at all. Based on the 1977 Marvin Gaye song "Got to Give It Up," it was a nostalgic party anthem sung by a male protagonist trying to convince a "good girl" to get loose with him, on the dance floor and, presumably, in the bedroom. Though it was composed by the producer Pharrell Williams, the name attached to the single belonged to Robin Thicke, a white singer who'd been kicking around the middle of the R&B charts for a decade with sensitive ballads attracting a mostly female audience. This was an about-face for Thicke: a dance-floor burner full of double entendres and attempts at persuasion that bordered on harassment.

If the lechery of "Blurred Lines" could have ever been in doubt, its video was explicit. Three topless female models wearing nude panties and white sneakers appear alongside a fully clothed Thicke, Williams, and T.I., the rapper who provides the song's middle break. The men cajole the women, who dance and flirt but ultimately stave off their advances. The presence of whimsical props, including a goat, an oversized bicycle, a plush dog, and a giant foam finger, adds an element of the surreal. Thicke's last name—a phallic double entendre in and of itself—flashes, recast as a Twitter hashtag, across the screen. So does the phrase "Robin Thicke has a big dick." The shoot was helmed by Diane Martel, the same director who had extolled the "amazing freestyle" talent of strippers more than a decade earlier. Martel often played with explicit imagery in her work, and it was her idea that the women in "Blurred Lines" be so exposed. She secured an all-female crew for the day, to ensure "zero sexual tension," as she told one reporter. The pink-lit blank backdrop was Thicke's idea. The props, Martel said, came from "the creative graveyard where the ideas that are too crazy go and wait for the right project," and indeed they have the feel of a trash bucket on a hard drive—weird, stray thoughts manifest as abandoned toys. The video doesn't have a linear narrative; it's just a lot of prancing, flirting, and rebuffing. No one takes off any clothes, or puts them on. This is seduction stalled in an artificial safe zone, where men can be voyeurs and women, exhibitionists, and nobody gets hurt.[38]

That's what Martel and the artists imagined, perhaps, but it's not how women viewing the video responded. "Blurred Lines"

was an instant hit; even though it was quickly banned from You-
Tube because of the nudity, one million people viewed it within its
first few days online. Yet within weeks the video and the song had
engendered a groundswell of angry responses. Many women felt
that the song was an apology for harassment and even rape. "Has
anyone heard Robin Thicke's new rape song?" wrote the feminist
blogger Lisa Huynh shortly after the video's release. "Basically, the
majority of the song (creepily named 'Blurred Lines') has the R&B
singer murmuring 'I know you want it' over and over into a girl's
ear. Call me a cynic, but that phrase does not exactly encompass
the notion of consent in sexual activity." Another blog post jux-
taposed lyrics from the song with images from an online photo
exhibit of rape victims holding up signs inscribed with their assail-
ants' words; they often matched. Rare among women, prominent
music critic Maura Johnston wrote a defense of the song that cited
its humor and the way its lyrics unspooled not like a harangue but
as one half of a dialogue, concluding in a musical fade-out signifying that the situation remained unresolved. A fan of R&B familiar
with the prevalence of come-ons in the genre, Johnston found the
song alluring.[39]

One person with an interesting view of "Blurred Lines" was
Robin Thicke himself, who called the video "existential" in an interview. The singer proved to be an untrustworthy source—a year
after his hit charted, he admitted that though he received a writing
credit, he didn't contribute anything to its composition because
he was drunk and high on painkillers in the studio. "Existential"
applies, however: as transformed within the video, "Blurred Lines"
effectively evokes the indeterminate experience of engaging erotically online. Its blank background is actually a white cyclorama,
a cinematic cousin to Beyoncé's "Single Ladies" infinity cove; it
creates a "limbo effect," where action seems to run on a loop. The
strange props add to the dreamlike atmosphere. The clothed men
and nude women seem like porn actors but without any notable

physical contact—there's not so much as a kiss—this is the opposite of hard-core pornography. Instead, it's an endless, circular tease, as is the song itself, with its highly repetitive lyrics, its looped groove, and the disembodied whoops that punctuate the melody like movements toward orgasm that never reach a peak.

Pharrell Williams borrowed those whoops, and much else in "Blurred Lines," from Marvin Gaye, whose soul recordings in the late 1960s and 1970s set the bar for seductive R&B. Gaye was a master of ambience and indirection, riding tidal rhythms that signified pleasure directed by a woman's undulating desire rather than a man's linear release. In "Blurred Lines," Williams took that organic feel and made it shiny, plasticene. The beat is tight; the sound, compressed. Thicke's vocals are mostly a mumble. Johnston wrote, "'Blurred Lines' is sensual in a way that isn't wholly reliant on any sort of consummating act." In fact, it's not sensual at all, in the conventional sense; it unfolds light and airy, free of the bottom that bodies provide. This is the sound of online sex, where a mild-mannered man might risk the language of aggression, and a self-respecting woman might even accept it, entertaining possibilities she wouldn't tolerate in the flesh. Or perhaps she would just ignore it. "Blurred Lines" is a one-way conversation, it turns out. Thicke could be talking to an empty avatar.

The controversy over this song's content raged on for much of 2013, but the following year it was superseded by new questions about the song. A series of suits and countersuits between Williams and Thicke and the Marvin Gaye estate exposed just how much the producer had relied on the earlier song within his compositional process. A judge eventually ruled that enough similarities existed between "Blurred Lines" and "Got to Give It Up" for the family's lawsuit to proceed, and a jury found the songwriters guilty of copyright infringement. A song risking images of sexual violation turned out to be grounded in artistic trespassing. And though the song's true author, Williams, is African American, the fact that

Thicke, a white interpreter of a black style, was its frontman connects "Blurred Lines" to the questions of self-possession and miscegenation at the historic core of American popular music. Cultural miscegenation yet again provoked anxieties framed as sexual.

"I know you want it": the mantra of "Blurred Lines" encapsulates the risk and possibility of popular music, its frequent violations and its freeing encouragement to unleash unrecognized desires. Americans have so often wondered, alone and together, what they want erotically. Songs and dancing and all the talk surrounding music can never answer that question clearly or definitively. The answer shifts and shimmies like rhythm itself, like a body in the throes of pleasure.

EPILOGUE

On April 23, 2016, two and a half years after Beyoncé rode to pop supremacy on her sexified surfboard, she debuted another surprise album, this time not via the porn-soaked Internet but on the relatively dignified cable network HBO, home of award-winning "event television" programs like *The Wire*. *Lemonade* is to *Beyoncé* what a marriage counseling session is to make-up sex: highly emotional but purposeful, focused on issues instead of sensual impressions, meant to foster dialogue that builds toward a future. Superseding the intimate, fantasy-filled inner monologue represented by *Beyoncé*, *Lemonade* reaches out with a strong undertone of feminist solidarity.

Unfaithfulness is its most obvious subject. By the time of their 2014 On the Run World Tour, the rumors of his cheating that Jay Z and Beyoncé had long quietly fought back were beginning to tarnish their celebrity role-model marriage; in these songs, the singer stands strong as "the wife" who reminds the rapper, "I give you life," presenting herself as a take-no-guff truth teller and taking control of her publicly displayed private realm once again. In songs like "Don't Hurt Yourself" and "Sorry" (catchline: *not sorry*),

Beyoncé takes her place in music's long line of blues queens, confronting the ways love can lay a woman low without compromising an ounce of her pride.

Lemonade is also a political album. Like the classic blues, its lyrics locate intimate stories within a larger framework of African American marginalization and displacement. In the companion piece that made the HBO *Lemonade* debut so powerful, six video directors created tableaux evoking the quadroons and other Creole women of New Orleans, that city's recent struggles after the federal government's tepid response to 2005's Hurricane Katrina, and the hardships faced by Southern African Americans after Reconstruction—all historic reference points that related to Beyoncé's own life as the Houston-born "Texas Bama" daughter of a mother from Louisiana and father from Alabama. The black feminist poetry of Warsan Shire, read in voiceover by Beyoncé, links these images in menstrual-bloodstained confessionals about the ties binding African American daughters to the crises their mothers and grandmothers endured: "You find the black tube inside her beauty case where she keeps your father's old prison letters. You desperately want to look like her. You look nothing like your mother. You look everything like your mother."[1]

Received ecstatically by music critics and fans alike as a gift to Beyoncé's strong base of African American female fans, *Lemonade* also continued the artist's open alliance with a new activist movement founded by women of color. That loose coalition had been building across America via the Internet, arguably since Katrina and definitely since the death of Trayvon Martin, an unarmed seventeen-year-old shot by a neighborhood watch volunteer in 2012. It coalesced on social media and in the streets after the subsequent police killings of two unarmed African American men, Michael Brown and Eric Garner. In Ferguson, Missouri, Brown was shot multiple times by a police officer he encountered in the street, and his body left on the ground for hours. People gathered in protests that spread nationwide, often anchored by the chant "Hands Up, Don't Shoot." The same swell of protest occurred in Staten Island, where the cry was "I Can't Breathe," commemorating the fact that Garner, who had asthma, died in a chokehold. Garner's arrest on suspicion of selling loose cigarettes—a misdemeanor—was captured on video via a bystander's phone, and went viral. So did a cell phone video of witnesses discussing the killing of Brown as his body lay nearby.

The movement is called Black Lives Matter, but it could have been Black Bodies Matter. Its impact had everything to do with the way technology allowed people to see and hear how people's bodies were affected by violence in real time. As people realized they could record and distribute these encounters, images proliferated of African Americans being shot at close range, held to the ground, and otherwise restrained by police. Some videos came from security cameras near the sites of the altercations, but most came from witnesses, capturing violence using the same tools that, in different moments, might allow them to share sexy selfies with a lover or scenes of themselves dancing with friends.

The virtual world was colliding with the physical one in horrifying ways. A national debate on the use of deadly force raged. Police and their supporters maintained that, in most cases, the responses were justified, and the courts often supported this view. Yet the images unsettled people. A cell phone video showed Cleveland twelve-year-old Tamir Rice's body prone in the distance, near the pellet gun police had mistaken for a lethal weapon, as his sister screamed, "They killed my baby brother!" One showing Baltimore man Freddie Gray being put into a police van raised questions about what happened during the van ride, after which he died from head and neck injuries. Instantly distributed, these videos often took the place of conventional news reports in forming public opinion, and fed the wave of activism that was itself organized through social media. By summer 2016, when Diamond Reynolds live-streamed the aftermath of the fatal shooting of her boyfriend, Philando Castile, during a traffic stop, Black Lives Matter had become the most significant grassroots movement confronting racial inequality in America since the 1960s.[2]

As the Black Lives Matter movement grew, mainstream musicians like Beyoncé, who had mostly steered clear of forthright political statements in the past, began to reckon with it. The pop world of carefully generated sounds and images, already opened up by social media, now had to deal with raw material that preoccupied the public precisely because it was not prettied up. Black activists' insistence that others see systematic violence as the day-to-day experience they endure, despite the gains in civil rights that reached a high point when Barack Obama became the first African American president in 2008, is now backed up by evidence they themselves can generate. Just as the photographs of lynchings had shocked people in the 1930s, when Billie Holiday sang, in "Strange Fruit," of bodies "hanging from the poplar trees," now these videos reinforce the truth of racism: that it is not abstract, not merely an idea or a flaw in the system, but a visceral reality.[3]

With *Lemonade,* Beyoncé negotiated a turn that few would have expected even a few years before, when consciousness about these issues was rising but the pop world was still distracted by Miley Cyrus's twerking and other titillations. Cyrus was only an "It" girl for a season. Blunders like the interview in which she spoke of some media outlets' editing of her racy "We Can't Stop" video in the same breath as Martin's killing made her a less-than-viable spokesperson either for a new attitude among youth or for increased interracial understanding within pop. Few who were engaged in the push for change furthered by Black Lives Matter saw anything progressive in Cyrus's gyrations.[4]

The hip-wagging dancers of 2013 did not still themselves, and sometimes they spoke up, too. The rapper Nicki Minaj has emerged as a major star in this era, a skilled verbalist who is also an expert dancer; her song "Anaconda" extolls the power of the good booty while openly criticizing white America's simultaneous denigration and appropriation of the black female form. Beyoncé herself, who has been championing good booty since Destiny's Child had a hit with "Bootylicious" in 2001, continues to perform her own versions of the shimmy-shake even as she calls for greater respect for herself and her spiritual sisters. But a new sobriety, even censoriousness, now dominates the cultural mood, and this includes a certain discomfort about sexual self-expression. People are talking openly again about the problems of cultural appropriation, and about how black women often represent sexuality in music without being granted the right to their own self-possession. In league with these concerns, women musicians and fans of all races are speaking out in greater numbers about feeling exploited or suffering abuse within the good-time environments of their rock and hip-hop scenes.

The music writer Jessica Hopper started a firestorm in August 2015 when she called for "gals/other marginalized folks" within the popular music world to post personal experiences of sexism on her Twitter feed. Hundreds of responses poured in. Hopper's outreach inspired others. More women began speaking out about being harassed or raped by male musicians or music-industry executives. This mostly happened on an individual or grassroots level, in private online groups or through personal social media pages. But the secrets of the pop machine also threatened to leak when the pop singer and songwriter Kesha Rose Sebert sued her long-time producer, Lukasz Gottwald, in 2014. Seeking to terminate the contract that tied her to his company, Sebert accused Gottwald of drugging and raping her, and being "tyrannical and abusive since our relationship began." She lost in court, but other artists voiced their support for her, feeding an ongoing critique of music's pleasure culture that demands a reassessment of the fine lines between artists' self-expression and exploitation by others, and between

erotic encounters that enrich people's lives and the kinds of en-
croachments that can destroy them.[5]

These events within the music world reflect and intertwine
with larger developments within American culture. Within the expanded realities of online life, people may feel more free, but new
perils also present themselves, along with a great awareness of the
ones that have always been present within the often unequal power
exchanges that structure even our most tender interactions. The
shocking yet all too commonplace revelations of Black Lives Matter show how black people's bodies remain under siege; other forms
of activism do the same for women's bodies. A new generation of
college students is fighting back against sexual assault on campus,
reviving the "take back the night" activism of earlier feminist generations, now across cyberspace. Online sexual harassment and
"slut shaming" have also become the focus of activists standing
up to male "trolls" empowered by the anonymity and mobility the
Internet affords. Women online are waging real, terrifying battles with harassers, whose behavior goes beyond lewd comments
to include practices like "doxxing"—the procurement and online
sharing of personal material including home addresses, intimate
photographs, and credit information. Women have always known
they need to protect themselves as they move through spaces dominated by men. Now the identities they shape in virtual space are
proving just as vulnerable. Yet it's also much easier to expose and
organize against violators, thanks to the ability to share information instantly and widely. A new generation of activists believes
that there is reason to rage, and reason to hope.[6]

How music's erotic expressions fit into these challenging but
absolutely crucial conversations isn't always clear. Protest makes
sense: great new works like the rapper Kendrick Lamar's 2015 album *To Pimp a Butterfly* have given activism a fresh soundtrack by
expressing community pride and voicing the urgency of the public
moment. It's more difficult to figure out how to express intimacies,

or make room for pleasure, at times when thinking about the body demands facing the many ways it can be diminished, even extinguished, instead of serving as a vessel of joy. Yet to contemplate this disjuncture, and to use music to live with it, is to return to the very birth of it as an American art form. There we are again, among the dancers in the streets of new cities as they try to reach out to each other and—every one of them, women, men, and transgender, white and of color, all really undefinable—demand to own themselves.

"Freedom!" Beyoncé cries in her best church voice on the song by that name on *Lemonade*. And, in the same breath: "I can't move." This anthem calls down the spirit of resistance that American music has conjured for as long as these sounds, African at heart, have existed. Not only Martin Luther King Jr., but his favorite singer Mahalia Jackson, and her inspiration Bessie Smith, and the Creole women whose names no one remembers, and the market women in Congo Square—all buoy and sustain her singing. So does that cry of "I can't breathe!" from Eric Garner, which isn't a shout for liberation, but evidence of the way those in struggle keep getting knocked down. The key samples in "Freedom" reinforce this tension: one is a sermonette from a Memphis Church in 1959, with a female congregation's hymnody giving life to a male preacher's words; the other is a work song recorded in Mississippi's notorious Parchman Farm penitentiary, where men sent coded messages of hope and defiance within the chants they shared under guards' watch. Blending these elements as history has done, Beyoncé and her cowriters created a freedom song that lives within the loop of uplift and oppression always present in American popular music, which can seem confoundingly accelerated today.

"Freedom, cut me loose!" Beyoncé begs. She's just an entertainer; this is just music. But as people struggle, she knows, they reach for this: a way of remembering how to be somebody. When we think we can't move, the music is always there to say we can.

ACKNOWLEDGMENTS

When you finally finish the book you've wanted to write for most of your life, it's difficult to know how to begin thanking people. A music writer's career is one of constant dialogue: with the songs and sounds that make what you do possible, the people who play that music and help bring it to audiences, and the fellow writers who tease out its meanings, share its stories, obsess about its details. If you've crossed my path within this glorious, noisy, body-rocking art world, you've probably left a mark on this manuscript.

Specifically, however . . .

Any set of acknowledgments has to begin with Eric Weisbard. I would not be the writer I am today without him. He is my partner in all things, a brilliant mind, and a wonderfully supportive human being. Endless gratitude, Eric, for seeing me through six years of turning a vague dream into a viable manuscript; for serving as my in-house editor; and for being an award-winning dad and husband. I can't wait to read your next book. Deep thanks also to my daughter, Bebe Weisbard, for her patience during all the late nights, research trips, and other book-related interruptions in our family life. Your hugs sustained me many times when I was at the end of my rope. Over the past six years, you've become an amazing young woman, not to mention a punk rock star. I can't wait to hear what you play next.

There's one other person without whom *Good Booty* would not exist, and that's my agent, Sarah Lazin. Sarah had the patience of Job as I spent a decade mulling over how to even approach this book's subject, and she unwaveringly fought for my vision through its arduous and sometimes unclear path to publication. I couldn't have had a better advocate. Thanks, too, to Sarah's colleagues, Manuela Jessel, Amelia Bienstock, and Julia Conrad, for their contributions to the health of the manuscript.

Denise Oswald is an unfailingly calm, insightful editor who believed in this project from the first time she heard about it, and I'm so happy she's shepherding it into existence. I'm also honored to have the support of publisher Lynn Grady and the rest of the Dey Street Books team. Encouragement was provided along the way by Dominick V. Anfuso, Jonathan Karp, Nan Graham, Brant Rumble, and Kathy Belden. I'm thankful for Patty Romanowski Bashe for her copyediting skills, Amanda Wicks for help in securing permissions, and Corinne Cummings for fact checking above and beyond the call of duty. Jessi Zazu created the cover of my dreams, as well as illustrations that truly capture the spirit of the good booty. She is a remarkable person and a consistent inspiration.

I have the best day job in the world, and my colleagues at NPR have been more patient and understanding than I could have hoped. Deep gratitude to Anya Grundmann, Jessica Goldstein, and the whole NPR Music team, to my former colleagues Frannie Kelley and Saidah Blount, and especially to editor supreme Jacob Ganz. Thanks also to my dear friends in the many cities I've called home, especially Nick Popovich, Nora Carria, Greg Powers, Victoria Burwell and Carl Zytowski, Josh Goldfein and Yvonne Brown, Jill Sternheimer, Rebecca and Josh Rothman, Margaret Peacock and D. Jay Cervino, Jamie and Stefanie Livers, Loretta and Christopher Lynn, Shelly and Marianne Rosenzweig, Olivia Scibelli, Tim

Higgins, and Aaron Head. Jenny Toomey gave me a place to stay on a crucial archival visit to New York. Love always to the Weisbard and Powers families, especially to Nate and Wendy Weisbard for constant support.

The idea of this book had been percolating for a while when I grabbed lunch one day with Josh Kun in downtown Los Angeles, but he was the first to enthusiastically encourage me to pursue it. Not long after that, Lauren Onkey invited me to give the first Jane Scott Memorial Lecture at the Rock and Roll Hall of Fame, and the project was off and running. Josh and Lauren are part of my beloved community of music writers, scholars, and nerds, too many to list in total here. Some whose insights have helped me the most, in conversation and through their work, are Jody Rosen, Gayle Wald, Carl Wilson, Sonnet Retman, Alex Ross, Holly George-Warren, Elijah Wald, Daphne Carr, Jason King, Jewly Hight, Oliver Wang, Lucy O'Brien, Joan Morgan, Jayna Brown, Tavia Nyong'o, Nelson George, Greg Tate, Richard Goldstein, and Vince Aletti. I want to give a particularly strong shout-out to a few writers who have broken the ground I travel in this book: Evelyn McDonnell, Daphne Brooks, Alice Echols, Simon Reynolds, and Joy Press, and the late Ellen Willis. I am indebted to many experts who helped me traverse a wide range of material. Anthony Heilbut was exceedingly generous in sharing his extensive knowledge of gospel music. Dwight Cammeron was exceedingly generous in sharing the working material for his outstanding documentary on Dorothy Love Coates. Steve Propes offered valued information on the early years of doo-wop. Andy Zax located a pristine copy of the Mom's Apple Pie album cover. Jim Farber helped me see the connections between glam rock and gay coming of age. Rey Roldan pointed me toward some key Britney Spears material. I thank Curtis Bonney and Michael Udesky for helping me to see the humor in Jim Morrison.

I hope everyone reads this book, an inspiration: *The Spirituals and the Blues,* by James T. Cone.

Archives are essential in preserving the history of American music, and I've been lucky enough to dig into some of the best. Thanks to Bruce Raeburn at Tulane University's Hogan Jazz Archive; Andy Leach, Jennie Thomas, and Anastasia Karel at the Rock and Roll Hall of Fame Library and Archives; Paul Friedman at the New York Public Library; the entire staff of the Music Division at Lincoln Center; Sharon M. Howard and the staff of the Schomburg Center for Research in Black Culture; Jessica Lacher-Feldman and the staff at the W. S. Hoole Division of Special Collections at Gorgas Library, the University of Alabama; Steven Weiss at the Southern Folklife Collection at the University of North Carolina at Chapel Hill; Lucinda Cockrell and the staff of the Center for Popular Music at Middle Tennessee State University; and Aisha M. Johnson, who guided me through the remarkable special collections at Fisk University. I also found material online through the Louisiana Digital Library, Rock's Backpages, and the New York Public Library's AIDS/HIV Collections.

Writing an archivally based book like this one can be a very lonely project. I'm very thankful that occasionally people brought me into the world to present some of the work as it took form. Those people include Terry Stewart at the Rock and Roll Hall of Fame; Kathryn Metz and the Popular Music Section of the Society for Ethnomusicology; Greil Marcus at the New School for Social Research; the graduate students of UNC Chapel Hill, who brought me to speak at the Carolina Symposia in Music and Culture; Daniel Goldmark at Case Western Reserve University; Lisa Cockrell at the Festival of Faith and Music in Grand Rapids; Daphne Brooks at Yale; and the many members of the program committee at the annual Pop Conference. That conference is my home away from home, intellectually and spiritually, and I have presented much material from the book there. Thanks also to Jasen Emmons for being the Pop Con's champion in Seattle, and to the staff of EMP (now the Museum of Popular Culture) for herding music-critic cats every year.

To my dear friends Robert Christgau and Carola Dibbell—I hope I did you proud. Thanks for decades of love and dining-room-table talk. I dedicate this project to you. And to the memory of Prince: I'm blessed to have shared time and space with an artist whose music could teach me everything. May U live 2 see the dawn.

NOTES

INTRODUCTION

1. Eileen Southern, *Readings in Black American Music,* second edition (New York: W. W. Norton & Co., 1983), p. 63.
2. Martin Luther King Jr., "Address at Public Meeting of the Southern Christian Ministers Conference of Mississippi," Jackson, MS, September 23, 1959.
3. Joseph Roach, *Cities of the Dead: Circum-Atlantic Performance* (New York: Columbia University Press, 1996), p. 28.

CHAPTER 1: THE TABOO BABY

1. Dancers: Ann Ostendorf, *Sounds American: National Identity and the Music Cultures of the Lower Mississippi River Valley, 1800–1860* (Athens, GA: University of Georgia Press, 2011), p. 202; bandleaders: Samuel A. Floyd Jr. and Marsha J. Reisser, "Social Dance Music of Black Composers in the Nineteenth Century and the Emergence of Classic Ragtime," in *The Black Perspective in Music,* vol. 8, no. 2 (Autumn 1980).
2. Lyle Saxon, *Old Louisiana* (Gretna, LA: Pelican Publishing Company, paperback edition, 1989), pp. 108–109.
3. Thomas Ashe, *Travels in America* (London: Richard Phillips, 1808), pp. 266–67.
4. Ronald Walters, "The Erotic South: Civilization and Sexuality in American Abolitionism," *American Quarterly* 25, no. 2 (May 1973), p. 187.
5. Tavia Amolo Ochieng Nyong'o, *The Amalgamation Waltz: Race, Perfor-*

mance, and the Ruses of Memory (Minneapolis: University of Minnesota Press, 2009).

6. Eric Lott, *Love and Theft: Blackface Minstrelsy and the American Working Class* (London and New York: Oxford University Press, 1993). For other viewpoints, see Daphne Brooks, *Bodies in Dissent: Spectacular Performances of Race and Freedom, 1850–1910* (Durham, NC: Duke University Press, 2006); Dale Cockrell, *Demons of Disorder: Early Blackface Minstrels and Their World* (London: Cambridge University Press, 1997); and W. T. Lhamon, *Raising Cain: Blackface Performance from Jim Crow to Hip Hop* (Cambridge: Harvard University Press, 2000).

7. New Orleans *Daily Picayune*, January 22, 1850.

8. Walters, "The Erotic South," p. 183.

9. The classic history of early New Orleans music is Henry A. Kmen, *Music in New Orleans: The Formative Years, 1791–1841* (Baton Rouge: Louisiana State University Press, 1966). An important recent history is Ned Sublette, *The World That Made New Orleans: From Spanish Silver to Congo Square* (Chicago: Lawrence Hill Books/Chicago Review Press, 2008).

10. Ostendorf, *Sounds American*, p. 73.

11. Benjamin Henry Latrobe, *Impressions Respecting New Orleans: Diary and Sketches, 1818–1820* (New York: Columbia University Press, 1951), p. 34.

12. Marshall and Jean Stearns, *Jazz Dance: The Story of American Vernacular Dance* (New York: Macmillan, 1968), p. 17.

13. Joseph Roach, *Cities of the Dead: Circum-Atlantic Performance* (New York: Columbia University Press, 1966), p. 27.

14. Rixford J. Lincoln, *Historical New Orleans 'in Verse'* (1911), p. 10.

15. Kenneth Aslakson, "The 'Quadroon-Plaçage' Myth of Antebellum New Orleans: Anglo-American (Mis)interpretations of a French-Caribbean Phenomenon," *Journal of Social History* (2011), pp. 1–26. See also Alecia P. Long, *The Great Southern Babylon: Sex, Race, and Respectability in New Orleans, 1865–1920* (Baton Rouge: Louisiana State University Press, 2005); and Emily Clark, *The Strange History of the American Quadroon: Free Women of Color in the Revolutionary Atlantic World* (Chapel Hill: University of North Carolina Press, 2013).

16. Juretta Jordan Heckscher, "Our National Poetry: The Afro-Chesapeake Inventions of American Dance," in Julie Malnig, ed., *Ballroom, Boogie, Shimmy Sham, Shake: A Social and Popular Dance Reader* (Champaign: University of Illinois Press, 2009), p. 26.

17. Robert Tallant, *The Romantic New Orleanians* (New York: Dutton, 1950), p. 109.

18. George Washington Cable, introduction to Michael Kreyling, *The Grandissimes* (New York: Penguin, 1988), p. 3.

19. Kmen, *Music in New Orleans,* p. 44.

20. "La Belle Zoraïde," in *The Complete Works of Kate Chopin* (Baton Rouge: Louisiana State University Press, 2006), p. 303.

21. James Burton Pond, *Eccentricities of Genius: Memories of Famous Men and Women of the Platform and Stage* (New York: G. W. Dillingham Company, 1900), p. 231.

22. Mary Wyman Bryan, "Hitherto Unpublished Songs of New Orleans," *New Orleans Item-Tribune,* Magazine section, March 8, 1925, p. 5.

23. Sybil Kein, "The Use of Louisiana Creole in Southern Literature," in Sybil Kein, ed., *Creole: The History and Legacy of Louisiana's Free People of Color* (Baton Rouge: Louisiana State University Press, 2000), p. 260.

24. Doris Garraway, *The Libertine Colony: Creolization in the Early French Caribbean* (Durham, NC: Duke University Press, 2005).

25. Deborah Jenson, *Beyond Slave Narrative: Politics, Sex, and Manuscripts in the Haitian Revolution* (Liverpool: Liverpool University Press, 2012), p. 261.

26. Kein, "The Use of Louisiana Creole in Southern Literature," p. 123.

27. Mina Monroe and Kurt Schindler, *Bayou Ballads* (New York: G. Schirmer, 1921).

28. Henry Edward Krehbiel, *Afro-American Folksongs: A Study in Racial and National Music* (New York: G. Schirmer, 1914), p. 151.

29. Samuel A. Floyd Jr., *The Power of Black Music: Interpreting Its History from Africa to the United States* (New York: Oxford University Press, 1995), p. 156.

30. Solomon Northrop, *Twelve Years a Slave* (New York: Miller, Orton & Mulligan, 1855).

31. Jenson, *Beyond Slave Narrative,* p. 257.

32. Edwin C. Hill, *Black Soundscapes White Stages: The Meaning of Francophone Sound in the Black Atlantic* (Baltimore: Johns Hopkins University Press, 2013), p. 19. For another view of the *doudou,* see Lachelle Rénee Hannickel, "From Cultural Transgressions to Literary Transformations: Recasting Feminine Archetypes in French Caribbean Women's Autobiography," dissertation, University of California, Santa Barbara, 2007.

33. Derek Scott, *From the Erotic to the Demonic: On Critical Musicology* (New York: Oxford University Press, 2003), p. 195.

34. Vivian Perlis and Libby Van Cleve, *Composers' Voices from Ives to El-*

lington: An Oral History of American Music (New Haven: Yale University Press, 2005), p. 384.

35. George Washington Cable, "The Dance in Place Congo," *Century Magazine*, February 1886, pp. 517–31.

36. E. W. Kemble, *A Coon Alphabet* (New York: R. H. Russell, 1898).

37. Ted Widmer, "The Invention of a Memory: Congo Square and African Music in Nineteenth-Century New Orleans," *Revue Française D'études Américaines*, vol. 98 (December 2003), pp. 69–78.

38. Freddi Williams Evans, *Congo Square: African Roots in New Orleans* (Lafayette: University of Louisiana at Lafayette Press, 2011).

39. Latrobe, *Impressions Respecting New Orleans*, p. 49.

40. Grace King, *New Orleans: The Place and the People* (New York: Macmillan and Sons, 1895).

41. "The Dance in Place Congo," *New York Times*, March 24, 1918, section 1, p. 19.

42. Herbert Asbury, *The French Quarter: An Informal History of the New Orleans Underworld* (New York: Basic Books, 2003), p. 244.

43. Bryan Wagner, *Disturbing the Peace: Black Culture and the Police Power After Slavery* (Boston: Harvard University Press, 2010), pp. 58–116.

CHAPTER 2:
THAT DA DA STRAIN: SHIMMYING, SHAKING, SEXOLOGY

1. Walter H. Ford, *The Tryst: An Original Dramatic Sketch in One Act* (Washington, DC: Rare Book and Special Collections Division, Library of Congress, 1895).

2. "Last Week's Bills," *New York Dramatic Mirror*, December 19, 1896.

3. Steven Seidman, *Romantic Longings: Love in America, 1830–1980* (New York: Routledge, 1991), p. 19.

4. Kurt F. Stone, *The Jews of Capitol Hill: A Compendium of Jewish Congressional Members* (Lanham, MD: Scarecrow Press, 2010), p. 138.

5. Rachel Shteir, *Striptease: The Untold History of the Girlie Show* (New York: Oxford University Press, 2004), p. 43.

6. For the history of Little Egypt and the advent of the hootchie-kootch, see Donna Carlton, *Looking for Little Egypt* (Bloomington, IN: International Dance Discovery, 1994); Fahreda Mazar obituary, April 6, 1937, source unknown; Little Egypt clip file, Billy Rose Theater Collection, New York Public Library for the Performing Arts.

7. Ray Argyle, *Scott Joplin and the Age of Ragtime* (Jefferson, NC: McFarland, 2009), p. 107.

8. Terry Waldo, *This Is Ragtime* (New York: Da Capo, 1991), p. 4.

9. Edward A. Berlin, *Ragtime: A Musical and Cultural History* (Berkeley: University of California Press, 1980), p. 69.

10. Seidman, *Romantic Longings*, p. 2; Niagara Falls honeymoons: Angus McLaren, *Twentieth Century Sexuality: A History* (New York: Wiley, 1999), p. 50.

11. Havelock Ellis, "The Philosophy of Dancing," *Atlantic Monthly*, February 1914, pp. 197–206.

12. Isaac Goldberg, *Tin Pan Alley: A Chronicle of the American Popular Music Racket* (New York: John Day Co., 1930).

13. Recorded interview, "The Perry Bradford Story—Pioneer of the Blues," Folkways Records. Originally released by the Crispus Attucks Record Company, 1957.

14. Ethel Waters, *His Eye Is on the Sparrow* (New York: Jove/HBJ, 1978), p. 72.

15. Susan Glenn, *Female Spectacle: The Theatrical Roots of Modern Feminism* (Cambridge: Harvard University Press, 2000), pp. 100–14. For more on the Salome craze, see Daphne Brooks, *Bodies in Dissent.*

16. Rebecca A. Bryant, "Shaking Things Up: Popularizing the Shimmy in America," *American Music*, vol. 20, no. 2 (Summer 2002), pp. 168–87.

17. For a lively account of dance music in the jazz age, see Elijah Wald, *How The Beatles Destroyed Rock 'n' Roll: An Alternative History of Popular Music* (New York: Oxford University Press, 2009).

18. Bee Palmer interview, *New York Telegram*, October 4, 1919.

19. *American Dancer*, March–April 1928.

20. Lewis Erenberg, *Steppin' Out: New York Nightlife and the Transformation of American Culture* (Chicago: University of Chicago Press, 1984), p. 167.

21. Gilda Gray, "The Story of Me," *Dance Magazine*, August 1928. In Gilda Gray clip file, Jerome Robbins Dance Collection, New York Public Library for the Performing Arts.

22. Alice Eis scrapbook, Jerome Robbins Dance Division, New York Public Library for the Performing Arts.

23. Marybeth Hamilton, *When I'm Bad, I'm Better: Mae West, Sex, and American Entertainment* (Berkeley: University of California Press, 1997), p. 26.

24. Danielle Robinson, "Performing American: Ragtime Dancing as Participatory Minstrelsy," *Dance Chronicle*, vol. 32, issue 1, 2009.

25. Waters, *His Eye Is on the Sparrow*, p. 156.

26. Donald Bogle, *Heat Wave: The Life and Career of Ethel Waters* (New York: HarperCollins, 2011), p. 54.

27. Shimmy clip file, Jerome Robbins Dance Division, New York Public Library for the Performing Arts.

28. Marshall and Jean Stearns, *Jazz Dance: The Story of American Vernacular Dance* (New York: Macmillan, 1968), p. 236.

29. Mura Dehn with James Berry, "Harlem Jazz Dance," *Jazz Hot*, no. 355.

30. Louise Brooks, "Charlie Chaplin Remembered," *Film Culture*, Spring 1966, p. 5.

31. Charles J. Maland, *Chaplin and American Culture: The Evolution of a Star Image* (Princeton: Princeton University Press, 1991), p. 117.

32. Maurice Mouvet, *Maurice's Art of Dancing: An Autobiographical Sketch* (New York: G. Schirmer, 1915), pp. 26–34.

33. "The Dance Bizarre," unidentified newspaper clipping, 1912, Billy Rose Theatre Division, New York Public Library for the Performing Arts.

34. Erenberg, *Steppin' Out*, p. 147.

35. David A. Jasen and Gene Jones, *Spreadin' Rhythm Around: Black Popular Songwriters, 1880–1930* (New York: Schirmer Books, 1998), p. 258.

36. Stearns, *Jazz Dance*.

37. Erenberg, *Steppin' Out*, p. 1.

38. Film excerpt, Jerome Robbins Dance Division, New York Public Library for the Performing Arts.

39. Jayna Brown, *Babylon Girls: Black Women Performers and the Shaping of the Modern* (Durham, NC: Duke University Press, 2009), p. 171.

40. Elizabeth Drake-Boyt, *Latin Dance* (Santa Barbara, CA: ABC-CLIO, 2011), p. 67.

41. Niven Busch Jr., "Fire Sign," *New Yorker*, April 20, 1929.

42. Barbara Grossman, *Funny Woman: The Life and Times of Fanny Brice* (Bloomington: Indiana University Press, 1992), p. 132.

43. Fanny Brice clip file, Billy Rose Theater Collection, Lincoln Center Public Library.

44. Ibid.

45. Robert Kimball, liner notes, *Shuffle Along* Cast Recording rerelease, New World Records, 2002.

46. The only book-length Mills biography published to date is Bill Egan, *Florence Mills: Harlem Jazz Queen* (Lanham, MD: Scarecrow Press, 2004). For excellent critical assessments, see Jayna Brown, *Babylon Girls*; and James F. Wilson, *Bulldaggers, Pansies, and Chocolate Babies: Performance, Race, and Sexuality in the Harlem Renaissance* (Ann Arbor: University of Michigan Press, 2010).

47. Egan, *Florence Mills, passim*; Florence Mills Papers, Helen Armstead-Johnson Theatre Collection, Manuscripts, Archives and Rare Books Division, Schomburg Center for Research in Black Culture, New York Public Library.

48. Herbert Hughes, "Leaves from an American Diary," *London Daily Telegraph*, March 18, 1922.

49. James Weldon Johnson, *Black Manhattan* (New York: Da Capo Press, 1991), p. 199.

50. Gilbert Seldes, *The 7 Lively Arts* (Mineola, NY: Courier Dover Publications, 1957), p. 154.

51. Florence Mills Papers, Box 1, letter dated January 23, 1925.

52. Florence Mills Papers, Box 1, Theophilus Lewis, article from the *Pittsburgh Courier*, 1927.

53. Will Friedwald, *Jazz Singing: America's Great Voices from Bessie Smith to Bebop and Beyond* (New York: Da Capo, 1996), p. 6.

54. Egan, *Florence Mills*, p. 126.

55. Obituary, *New York Times*, November 2, 1927.

56. For more on the idea of public intimacy in the Harlem Renaissance, see Shane Vogel, *The Scene of Harlem Cabaret: Race, Sexuality, Performance* (Chicago: University of Chicago Press, 2009).

57. Katherine Boutry, "Black and Blue: The Female Body of Blues Writing in Jean Toomer, Toni Morrison, and Gayl Jones," in Saadi A. Simawe, ed., *Black Orpheus: Music in American Fiction from the Harlem Renaissance to Toni Morrison* (New York and London: Garland Publishing, 2000).

58. Waters, *His Eye Is on the Sparrow*, p. 129.

59. Arnold Shaw, *The Jazz Age: Popular Music in the 1920s* (New York: Oxford University Press, 1989), p. 77.

CHAPTER 3: LET IT BREATHE ON ME: SPIRITUAL EROTICS

1. Audre Lorde, "Uses of the Erotic: The Erotic as Power," *Sister Outsider* (Berkeley, CA: Crossing Press, 1984).

2. Thomas Fulbright, "Ma Rainey & I," *Jazz Journal*, March 1956.

3. Michelle R. Scott, *Blues Empress in Black Chattanooga: Bessie Smith and the Emerging Urban South* (Champaign: University of Illinois Press, 2008), p. 121.

4. Most biographical detail about Dorsey in this chapter comes from the definitive biography by Michael A. Harris, *The Rise of Gospel Blues: The*

Music of Thomas Andrew Dorsey in the Urban Church (New York: Oxford, 1994).

5. Jim O'Neal and Amy Van Singel, eds., *The Voice of the Blues: Classic Interviews from Living Blues Magazine* (New York: Routledge, 2013), p. 31.

6. Harris, *Rise of Gospel Blues,* p. 68.

7. O'Neal and Van Singel, *Voice of the Blues,* p. 31.

8. Harris, *Rise of Gospel Blues,* p. 148.

9. Ibid., p. 69.

10. Horace Clarence Boyer and Lloyd Yearwood, *How Sweet the Sound: The Golden Age of Gospel* (Washington, DC: Elliott and Clark, 1995), p. 43.

11. For accounts of this period, see Robert Darden, *People Get Ready!: A New History of Black Gospel Music* (New York: Continuum, 2004); and Eileen Southern, *The Music of Black Americans: A History* (New York: W. W. Norton & Company, 1997).

12. Postcard, Thomas Andrew Dorsey Collection, Fisk University Special Collections and Archives, Nashville, Tennessee.

13. Harris, *Rise of Gospel Blues,* p. 128.

14. James H. Cone, *The Spirituals and the Blues: An Interpretation* (Maryknoll, NY: Orbis Books, 1972), p. 82.

15. Correspondence, clippings file, Thomas Andrew Dorsey Collection.

16. William Thomas Dargan and Kathy White Bullock, "Willie Mae Ford Smith of St. Louis: A Shaping Influence upon Black Gospel Singing Style," in Judith Weisenfeld and Richard Newman, eds., *This Far by Faith: Readings in African American Women's Religious Biography* (New York: Routledge, 1996), p. 37.

17. Glenn Hinson, *Fire in My Bones: Transcendence and The Holy Spirit in African American Gospel* (Philadelphia: University of Pennsylvania Press, 2004), pp. 142, 130.

18. Craig Hansen Werner, *A Change Is Gonna Come: Music, Race & the Soul of America* (Ann Arbor: University of Michigan Press, 2006), p. 28.

19. The groundbreaking history of gospel music that best captures this period is Anthony Heilbut, *The Gospel Sound: Good News and Bad Times* (New York: Hal Leonard Corporation, 1975).

20. Laurraine Goreau, *Just Mahalia, Baby: The Mahalia Jackson Story* (Gretna, LA: Pelican Publishing, 1975), p. 91.

21. Boyer and Yearwood, *How Sweet the Sound,* p. 192.

22. Anthony Heilbut, "The Children and Their Secret Closet," *The Fan Who Knew Too Much* (New York: Random House, 2012), p. 3.

23. Horace Clarence Boyer interview transcripts, by Dwight Cammeron, "Still Holding On: The Music of Dorothy Love Coates and the Gospel Harmonettes," 1999, courtesy of the filmmaker.

24. Pamphlet, Hoole Special Collections Library, University of Alabama.

25. Daniel Wolff quoted in Darden, *People Get Ready!*, p. 190.

26. Douglas Seroff and Lynn Abbot, *To Do This, You Must Know How: Music Pedagogy in the Black Gospel Quartet Tradition* (Jackson: University Press of Mississippi, 2012), pp. 145–61.

27. Ibid., p. 154.

28. Ibid., p. 129.

29. Isabel Wilkerson, *The Warmth of Other Suns: The Epic Story of America's Great Migration* (New York: Random House, 2010), p. 11.

30. For an excellent overview of Memphis gospel quartets, see Kip Lornell, *"Happy in the Service of the Lord": African-American Sacred Vocal Harmony Quartets in Memphis* (Knoxville: University of Tennessee Press, 1995).

31. Unpublished interview with Robert Reed, Douglas Seroff Collection of Tennessee Black Gospel Quartet Materials, Center for Popular Music, Middle Tennessee State University.

32. Seroff and Abbot, *To Do This You Must Know How,* p. 155.

33. Sister Flute: Jerry Zolten, *Great God A'Mighty! The Dixie Hummingbirds: Celebrating the Rise of Soul Gospel Music* (New York: Oxford University Press, 2002), p. 64; Ira Tucker: Darden, *People Get Ready!*, p. 189; Five Blind Boys: Evelyn Starks Hardy and Nathan Hale Turner, *The Sweetest Harmony: Evelyn Starks Hardy and the Original Gospel Harmonettes, An Autobiography and Short History of the Pioneer American Musical Ensemble* (Jonesboro, AR: Grant House Publishers, 2009).

34. Hinson, *Fire in My Bones,* p. 206.

35. Unpublished interview with Mary L. Thomas and Doris Jean Gary, February 3, 1983, Seroff Collection, Center for Popular Music MTSU.

36. Christine Beebe, producer, and Rhys Ernst, director, *Little Axe* (Nonetheless Productions/Focus Features, 2016).

37. Michael K. Honey, *Southern Labor and Black Civil Rights: Organizing Memphis Workers* (Champaign: University of Illinois Press, 1993), p. 111. Center for Popular Music, MTSU.

38. "Walk on the Water": William Barlow, *Voice Over: The Making of Black Radio* (Philadelphia: Temple University Press, 1999), p. 119; babynaming, photo and caption: *The Memphis World,* undated; Cadillac: *The Memphis World,* September 2, 1949, Center for Popular Music, MTSU.

39. WDIA event program, Center for Popular Culture, MTSU.

40. Clipping, *The Memphis World*, October 28, 1947, Center for Popular Culture, MTSU.

41. Interview with Nathaniel Peck of the Brewsteraires, January 31, 1981, Seroff Collection, Center for Popular Culture, MTSU.

42. Louis Cantor, *Dewey and Elvis: The Life and Times of a Rock 'n' Roll Deejay* (Champaign: University of Illinois Press, 2005), pp. 82–85.

43. Ibid. p. 84.

44. Nathaniel Peck interview.

45. Peter Guralnick, *Last Train to Memphis: The Rise of Elvis Presley* (Boston: Little Brown & Company, 1994), p. 77.

46. Jimmy McDonough, *Tammy Wynette: Tragic Country Queen* (New York: Penguin Viking Press, 2010).

47. *Billboard* Gospel Charts, April 19, 1952.

48. Kree Jake Racine, *Above All: The Story of the Famous Blackwood Brothers* (Memphis: Jarodoce Publications, 1967).

49. Blackwood Brothers Family Album, Blackwood Brothers folder, the Center for Popular Culture, MTSU.

50. Racine, *Above All*, p. 125.

51. James M. Curtis, *Rock Eras: Interpretations of Music and Society, 1954–1984* (Bowling Green, OH: Popular Press, 1987), p. 30.

52. Guralnick, *Last Train to Memphis*, p. 417.

53. Charles K. Wolfe, "Presley and the Gospel Tradition," in Jac. L. Tharpe, ed., *Elvis: Images and Fancies* (Jackson: University of Mississippi Press, 1975), p. 142.

54. Douglas Harrison, *Then Sings My Soul: The Culture of Southern Gospel Music* (Champaign, IL: University of Illinois Press, 2012), p. 161.

CHAPTER 4: TEEN DREAMS AND GROWN-UP URGES

1. Isabel Morse Jones, "Croo-Hoo-Hooning: Just an Old Music Custom," *Los Angeles Times*, September 25, 1932, p. B-15.

2. Brian Ward, *Just My Soul Responding: Rhythm and Blues, Black Consciousness and Race Relations* (Berkeley: University of California Berkeley Press, 1998), pp. 71–80.

3. Joli Jensen, "Honky-Tonking: Mass Mediated Culture Made Personal," George Lewis, ed. *All That Glitters: Country Music in America*, (Bowling Green, OH: Popular Press, 1993), pp. 118–30.

4. Steve Leggett, review of *The First Rock and Roll Record*, allmusic.com.
5. "R&B Ramblings," *The Cashbox*, May 29, 1954.
6. Dick Huggs interview transcript, personal correspondence, January 29, 2014, transcript of courtesy Steve Propes.
7. Adam Phillips, "Talking Nonsense, and Knowing When to Stop," in Leslie Caldwell, ed., *Sex and Sexuality: Winnicottian Perspectives* (London: Karnac Books, 2005), pp. 154–55.
8. Johnny Keyes, *DuWop* (Chicago: Vesti Press, 1991).
9. Jeffrey Melnick, "Story Untold: The Black Men and White Sounds of Doo Wop," in Mike Hill, ed., *Whiteness: A Critical Reader* (New York: New York University Press, 1997), p. 134–50.
10. Record Reviews column, *Billboard*, May 27, 1957.
11. "Frankie Lymon Says He's Too Young for Love," *Daily Defender (Daily Edition) (1956–1960)*, November 1, 1956, p. 30.
12. Anthony J. Gribin and Matthew M. Schiff, *Doo Wop: The Forgotten Third of Rock 'n Roll* (Iola, WI: Krause Publications, 1992).
13. Beth L. Bailey, *From Front Porch to Back Seat: Courtship in Twentieth-Century America* (Baltimore: Johns Hopkins University Press, 1989), p. 48.
14. Ward, *Just My Soul Responding*, p. 60.
15. Gertrude Samuels, "Why They Rock 'n' Roll—And Should They?," *New York Times Magazine*, January 12, 1958.
16. Edward Comentale, *Sweet Air: Modernism, Regionalism, and American Popular Song*, Music in American Life series (Urbana and Chicago: Illinois University Press, 2013), p. 171.
17. Ken Burke, "Billy Lee Riley," in Jake Austen, ed., *Flying Saucers Rock 'n' Roll: Conversations with Unjustly Obscure Rock 'n' Soul Eccentrics* (Durham, NC: Duke University Press, 2011), p. 140.
18. Craig Morrison, *Go Cat Go! Rockabilly Music and Its Makers* (Urbana and Chicago: University of Illinois Press, 1996), p. 43.
19. Robert Palmer, "Sam Phillips: The Sun King," *Memphis*, December 1978, p. 32.
20. Elvis pictorial, *Teenage Rock and Roll Review*, vol. 1, no. 1, October 1956.
21. Charles White, *The Life and Times of Little Richard: The Quasar of Rock* (New York: Harmony Books, 1985), pp. 23–25.
22. W. T. Lhamon, *Deliberate Speed: The Origins of a Cultural Style in the American 1950s* (Washington, DC: Smithsonian Institution Press, 1990), p. 88.
23. Lester A. Kirkendall, "Understanding Sex," in William C. Menninger

et al., *How to Be a Successful Teen-Ager* (New York: Sterling Publishing Company, 1954), p. 184.

24. John Goldrosen and John Beecher, *Remembering Buddy: The Definitive Biography of Buddy Holly* (New York: Da Capo Press, 1996), p. 46.

25. Goldrosen and Beecher, *Remembering Buddy*, p. 86.

26. The literature on Holly's singing style includes Dave Ling, *Buddy Holly* (New York: Macmillan, 1971); Jonathan Cott, "Buddy Holly," in *The Rolling Stone Illustrated History of Rock & Roll* (New York: Random House, 1976); Barbara Bradley and Brian Torode, "Pity Peggy Sue," in *Popular Music*, vol. 4, January 1984, and Comentale, *Sweet Air*.

27. H. H. Remmers and C. G. Hackett, *Let's Listen to Youth: A Better Living Booklet for Parents and Teenagers* (Chicago: Science Research Associates, 1950), p. 5.

28. Teen magazine collection, Rock and Roll Hall of Fame Library and Archive, Cleveland, Ohio.

29. Grace Palladino, *Teenagers: An American History* (New York: Westview Press, 1996), p. 157.

30. Barbara Ehrenreich et al., "Beatlemania: A Sexually Defiant Consumer Subculture?," in Ken Gelder and Sarah Thornton, eds., *The Subcultures Reader* (London and New York: Routledge, 1997), p. 524.

31. Ralph E. Koger, "'Rock and Roll' . . . Is It Good or Bad?: Rock and Roll Moves Them the . . . ," *Pittsburgh Courier*, July 28, 1956.

32. Phyllis Batelle, "Rock 'N Roll Fad Reflects Unsettled Spirit of World," *Washington Post and Times Herald*, January 26, 1956.

33. Jon Savage, *Teenage: The Prehistory of Youth Culture, 1875–1945* (New York: Viking Books, 2007), p. 442.

34. Eddie Cochran Collection, Rock and Roll Hall of Fame Library and Archives, Cleveland, Ohio.

35. Genie Wicker, "The Kiss Letter," Southern Folklife Collection Archive, University of North Carolina at Chapel Hill, North Carolina.

36. Chuck Berry, *Chuck Berry: The Autobiography* (New York: Harmony Books, 1987), p. 32.

37. Berry, *Chuck Berry*, p. 211.

38. Alan Light, "Ballad of the 13-Year-Old Bride," *Cuepoint*, October 27, 2014.

39. Nick Tosches, *Hellfire: The Jerry Lee Lewis Story* (New York: Delta Publishing, 1982).

40. Pricilla Beaulieu Presley with Sandra Harmon, *Elvis and Me* (New York: Putnam, 1985).

41. Robert Chalmers, "Legend: Little Richard," in Men of the Year, *GQ*, November 2010.

42. Paul H. Landis, *Understanding Teenagers* (New York: Appleton-Century Crofts, 1955), p. 81.

43. Remmers and Hackett, *Let's Listen to Youth*, pp. 32–34.

44. Undated clipping, "What Do You Know About Necking . . . and Your Reputation?" Teen Magazine Collection, Rock and Roll Hall of Fame Library and Archive, Cleveland, Ohio.

45. Katharine Whiteside Taylor, *Do Adolescents Need Parents?* (East Norwalk, CT: Appleton-Century-Crofts, 1938).

CHAPTER 5:
THE SEXUAL REVOLUTION AND ITS DISCONTENTS

1. Theodore Roszak, *The Making of a Counter Culture: Reflections on the Technocratic Society and Its Youthful Opposition* (New York: Anchor Books, 1969), p. 101.

2. Ken Emerson, *Always Magic in the Air: The Bomp and Brilliance of the Brill Building Era* (New York: Viking, 2005), pp. 87–100; Carole King, *A Natural Woman* (New York: Grand Central Publishing, 2012).

3. Jacqueline Warwick, *Girl Groups, Girl Culture* (New York: Routledge, 2007), p. 36.

4. "Are American Dating Customs Dangerous?," *Ebony*, June 1960, pp. 140–44.

5. Alex Poinsett, "A Despised Minority: Unwed Mothers Are Targets of Abuse from a Harsh Society," *Ebony*, August 1966, p. 48.

6. Gerald Early, *One Nation Under a Groove: Motown & American Culture* (Hopewell, NJ: Ecco Press, 1995), pp. 95, 109.

7. Richard Buskin, *Inside Tracks: A First-hand History of Popular Music from the World's Greatest Record Producers and Engineers* (London: Spike Books, 1999), p. 123.

8. Ed Ifkovic, *Diana's Dogs: Diana Ross and the Definition of a Diva* (Lincoln, NE: iUniverse, 2007).

9. Jim Henke, ed., *I Want to Take You Higher: The Psychedelic Era, 1965–1969* (San Francisco: Chronicle Books, 1997), p. 25.

10. Tom Robbins, "To Dance," in Jesse Kornbluth, ed., *Notes from the New Underground* (New York: Ace Books/Viking, 1968).

11. Michael J. Kramer, "The Civics of Rock: Sixties Countercultural Music and the Transformation of the Public Sphere," dissertation, University of North Carolina at Chapel Hill, 2006, p. 101.

12. Alice Echols, *Shaky Ground: The Sixties and Its Aftershocks* (New York: Columbia University Press, 2002), p. 35; festivals: Gina Arnold, "'As Real as Real Can Get': Race, Representation and Rhetoric at Wattstax, 1972," in George McKay, ed., *The Pop Festival: History, Music, Media, Culture* (New York: Bloomsbury, 2015), p. 61.

13. Jerilyn Lee Brandelius, ed., *The Grateful Dead Family Album* (New York: Warner Books, 1990).

14. Dennis McNally, *A Long Strange Trip: The Inside History of the Grateful Dead* (New York: Broadway Books, 2002), p. 10.

15. Richard Alpert, "Drugs and Sexual Behavior," *Journal of Sex Research*, vol. 5, no. 1 (February 1969), p. 51.

16. David Bromberg, "Interview: Jerry Garcia of the Grateful Dead," *Jazz & Pop*, February 1971.

17. Josh Sides, *Erotic City: Sexual Revolutions and the Making of Modern San Francisco* (New York: Oxford University Press, 2009), p. 124.

18. Mikal Gilmore, *Stories Done: Writings on the 1960s and Its Discontents* (New York: Simon & Schuster, 2008), p. 261.

19. Jerry Hopkins and Danny Sugerman, *No One Here Gets Out Alive: The Biography of Jim Morrison*, updated paperback edition (New York: Grand Central Publishing, 2006), p. 195.

20. Tuli Kupferberg, "The Hip and the Square: The Hippie Generation"; Communication Company, "Haight/Hate?," in Kornbluth, *Notes*, pp. 224, 266.

21. These and other press quotes from Doors clipping file, Rock and Roll Hall of Fame Library and Archive, Cleveland, Ohio; "implicational" comment from Paul Williams, *Outlaw Blues: A Book of Rock Music* (New York: E. P. Dutton and Co., 1969), p. 94.

22. Albert Goldman, "SuperSpade Raises Atlantis," *New York*, vol. 1, no. 23, September 9, 1968.

23. Steven Roby and Brad Schreiber, *Becoming Jimi Hendrix: From Southern Crossroads to Psychedelic London, the Untold Story of a Musical Genius* (New York: Da Capo Press, 2010), pp. 42–44.

24. Charles Shaar Murray, *Crosstown Traffic: Jimi Hendrix and the Rock 'n' Roll Revolution* (New York: St. Martin's Press, 1989).

25. Alfred G. Aronowitz, "Brash Buccaneer with a Wa-Wa," *Life*, vol. 11, March 15, 1968.

26. Charles R. Cross, *Room Full of Mirrors: A Biography of Jimi Hendrix* (New York: Hyperion, 2006), p. 142.

27. David Hajdu, *Positively Fourth Street: The Lives and Times of Joan Baez, Bob

Dylan, Mimi Baez Fariña, and Richard Fariña (New York: Farrar, Straus & Giroux, 2001), p. 74.

28. Cross, *Room Full of Mirrors*, p. 164.
29. John Perry, *Electric Ladyland*, 33 1/3 series (*New York: Continuum*, 2004), p. 40.
30. Cross, *Room Full of Mirrors*, p. 178.
31. Herbert Marcuse, *Eros and Civilization: A Philosophical Inquiry into Freud* (Boston: Beacon Press, 1966), p. xvii.
32. Chester Anderson, "Notes for the New Geology," in Kornbluth, *Notes*, pp. 77–80.
33. Jimi Hendrix interview with Steven Barker, in Steven Roby, ed., *Hendrix on Hendrix: Interviews and Encounters with Jimi Hendrix* (Chicago: Chicago Review Press, 2012), p. 264.
34. Murray, *Crosstown Traffic*, p. 69.
35. Ralph Ellison, *Invisible Man* (New York: Random House, 1952), p. 5.
36. Cross, *Room Full of Mirrors*, p. 189.
37. Jimi Hendrix interview with Jane de Mendelssohn, http://jimihendrix .forumactif.org/t664-interview-avec-jane-de-mendelssohn-11-mars -1969.
38. Ralph J. Gleason, "The Power of Non-Politics or the Death of the Square Left," in Kornbluth, *Notes*, p. 234; Tom Wolfe, *Radical Chic & Mau-Mauing the Flak Catchers* (New York: Macmillan, 2010), p. 85; "dissolving": unidentified press clip, Hendrix press file, Rock and Roll Hall of Fame Library and Archive.
39. Steve Waksman, *Instruments of Desire: The Electric Guitar and the Shaping of Musical Experience* (Cambridge: Harvard University Press, 2001), p. 167.
40. "Singers: Passionate and Sloppy," *Time*, August 9, 1968.
41. Laura Joplin, *Love, Janis* (New York: Villard, 1992), p. 220.
42. Karl Dallas, "Janis Joplin: Lock Up Your Sons," *Melody Maker*, August 17, 1968.
43. Nona Willis Aronowitz, ed., *Out of the Vinyl Deeps: Ellen Willis on Rock Music* (Minneapolis: University of Minnesota Press, 2011), p. 125.
44. Michael Lydon: *Eyewitness Accounts of the Rock Revolution* (New York: Psychology Press, 2003), *Flashbacks*, pp. 80–81.
45. Myra Friedman, *Buried Alive: The Biography of Janis Joplin* (New York: Bantam, 1974), p. 75.
46. Deborah Landau, *Janis Joplin: Her Life and Times* (New York: Coronet Paperback Library, 1971), p. 40.

47. Landau, *Janis Joplin,* p. 46.

48. Joplin, *Love, Janis,* p. 307.

49. Richard Goldstein, "Next Year in San Francisco," *Village Voice,* January 1, 1968.

50. Joe Whitaker, in Alice Echols, ed., *Scars of Sweet Paradise: The Life and Times of Janis Joplin* (New York: Macmillan, 2000), p. 78.

51. "Do I Ball?": Echols, *Scars of Sweet Paradise,* p. 180; Miss America, http://www.redstockings.org/index.php/themissamericaprotest.

52. Joplin, *Love, Janis,* p. 247.

53. Draft for *Hullabaloo* quiz, Doors press clippings file, Rock and Roll Hall of Fame Archive and Library.

54. "A real vengeance": Murray, *Crosstown Traffic,* p. 91; "I wrote the part": Joplin, *Love, Janis,* p. 289.

55. "Lament": recording released on the Doors, *An American Prayer,* 1995 remastered edition, Rhino Records, track 15.

56. Richard Goldstein, *Another Little Piece of My Heart: My Life of Rock and Revolution in the '60s* (New York: Bloomsbury Publishing, 2015), p. 88.

57. *Jazz & Pop,* vols. 7–8, 1968, p. 40.

58. *Mad* magazine: Stephen Davis, *Jim Morrison: Life, Death, Legend* (New York: Penguin, 2005), p. 12; "seriousness of intent": Greil Marcus, *The Doors: A Lifetime of Listening to Five Mean Years* (New York: Public Affairs Press, 2011), p. 62; "like a bird's wing": Hopkins, *No One,* p. 70.

59. "Plumage and punch": Howard Smith, "Scenes," *Village Voice,* February 22, 1968; Nadya Zimmerman, *Countercultural Kaleidoscope: Musical and Cultural Perspectives on Late Sixties San Francisco* (Ann Arbor: University of Michigan Press, 2008), p. 140.

60. David Allyn, *Make Love Not War: The Sexual Revolution: An Unfettered History* (New York: Little, Brown and Company, 2000), p. 159.

61. Goldstein, *Piece of My Heart,* p. 127.

62. Echols, *Scars,* p. 307.

63. "The Doors Open Up," *Freakout,* no. 2, February 1967.

64. Pamela Des Barres, *I'm with the Band: Confessions of a Groupie* (New York: William Morrow/Jove, 1988), p. 57.

65. Bernard Wolfe, "The Real-Life Death of Jim Morrison," *Esquire,* June 1972, pp. 106–10.

66. Various articles, Doors press clips file, Rock and Roll Hall of Fame Library and Archive.

67. Jerry Hopkins, "The Rolling Stone Interview: Jim Morrison," *Rolling*

Stone, July 26, 1969; "little revolution": reporter's notes, Doors press clips file, Rock and Roll Hall of Fame Library and Archive.

68. Bob Chorush, *Los Angeles Free Press* interview manuscript, 1971; Doors press clips file, Rock and Roll Hall of Fame Library and Archive.

CHAPTER 6: HARD AND SOFT REALITIES

1. Legs McNeil and Gillian McCain, *Please Kill Me: The Uncensored Oral History of Punk* (New York: Grove Press, 1996), p. 95.

2. Angela Bowie with Patrick Carr, *Backstage Passes: Life on the Wild Side with David Bowie* (New York: G. P. Putnam's Sons, 1993), p. 152.

3. Dave Thompson, *Your Pretty Face Is Going to Hell: The Dangerous Glitter of David Bowie, Iggy Pop, and Lou Reed* (Milwaukee: Backbeat Books, 2009), p. 113.

4. Robert Hilburn, "David Bowie Arrives with a Burst of Stardust," *Los Angeles Times,* November 5, 1972.

5. "Consciousness-raising": Jessica Grogan, *Encountering America: Humanistic Psychology, Sixties Culture & the Shaping of the Modern Self* (New York: Harper Perennial, 2013), p. 262; "Vietnam vets": Andreas Killen, *1973 Nervous Breakdown: Watergate, Warhol, and the Birth of Post-Sixties America* (New York: Bloomsbury, 2006), p. 84.

6. "Gay Woodstock": "Parade," *The New Yorker,* July 11, 1970, p. 19.

7. Laurence O'Toole, *Pornocopia: Porn, Sex, Technology and Desire,* expanded edition (London: Serpent's Tail, 1999), p. 73.

8. Lisa Robinson, "Looking for a Kiss in Parking Lot Babylon," *Creem,* December 1973, p. 42.

9. Lori Mattix as told to Michael Kaplan, "I Lost My Virginity to David Bowie," *Thrillist,* November 3, 2015; Paul Trynka, *David Bowie: Starman* (New York: Little Brown, 2011), p. 209.

10. "High at the Hyatt," *Time,* September 3, 1973, p. 66.

11. "The Rock and Roll Sexindex," *Circus,* June 1974, p. 40.

12. Lisa Rhodes, *Electric Ladyland: Women and Rock Culture* (Philadelphia: University of Pennsylvania Press, 2005), p. 247.

13. "Bands are power": Michael Walker, *What You Want Is in the Limo: On the Road with Led Zeppelin, Alice Cooper, and the Who in 1973, the Year the Sixties Died and the Modern Rock Star Was Born* (New York: Spiegel & Grau, 2013), p. 143; David Johansen: Ben Edmonds, "The New York Dolls Greatest Hits Vol. 1," *Creem,* October 1973, p. 41.

14. Rick Perlstein, *The Invisible Bridge: The Fall of Nixon and the Rise of Reagan* (New York: Simon & Schuster, 2014), p. 103; Robinson, "Looking for a Kiss," p. 44.

15. Linda Williams, *Hard Core: Power, Pleasure and the "Frenzy of the Visible"* (Berkeley: University of California Press, 1989), p. 120.

16. Porn as musical: Williams, *Hard Core*, pp. 120–26; Lovelace: Carolyn See, *Blue Money* (New York: Pocket Books, 1976), p. 135.

17. For more on Led Zeppelin's Apollonian/Dionysian split, see Erik Davis, *Led Zeppelin's Led Zeppelin IV* (New York: Continuum, 2005); "below-the-belt": Charles Shaar Murray, "Led Zeppelin: Robert Plant—and That Below-the-Belt Surge," *New Musical Express*, June 1973.

18. Donna Gaines, "The Ascension of Led Zeppelin," *Rolling Stone: The '70s* (New York: Little Brown, 1998), p. 14; Pamela Des Barres, *Let's Spend the Night Together: Backstage Secrets of Rock Muses and Groupies* (Chicago: Chicago Review Press, 2007), p. 142; Brad Tolinski, in Barney Hoskyns, ed., *Trampled Under Foot: The Power and Excess of Led Zeppelin* (New York: Faber & Faber, 2012); Susan Fast, *In the Houses of the Holy: Led Zeppelin and the Power of Rock Music* (New York: Oxford University Press, 2007), p. 177.

19. This author traced the commonalities between Robert Plant and Janis Joplin in a presentation as part of the Rock and Roll Hall of Fame American Masters Program *Kozmic Blues: The Life and Music of Janis Joplin* at Case Western Reserve University, November 24, 2009. Independently, Tracy McMullen wrote of the connection in "Bring It On Home: Robert Plant, Janis Joplin and the Myth of Origin," *Journal of Popular Music Studies*, vol. 26, no. 2–3, June–September 2014, pp. 368–96.

20. Robert Plant interview with Terry Gross, *Fresh Air*, WHYY, January 22, 2004.

21. John Mendelsohn, "Led Zeppelin," *Rolling Stone*, March 15, 1969.

22. Des Barres, *I'm with the Band*, p. 262.

23. Kid Congo Powers, "How I Came Out of the Closet and into the Streets," *Huffington Post*, May 3, 2014.

24. Evelyn McDonnell, *Queens of Noise: The Real Story of the Runaways* (New York: Da Capo Press, 2013), p. 135.

25. Various issues, *Creem* and *Circus*, 1970–1976.

26. Lester Bangs, "Deep Throat," *Creem*, March 1973, p. 48.

27. Chaste groupie: Walker, p. 92; Uriah Heep: undated photo caption, *Circus*.

28. Oneida Bell, "How to Meet Rock Stars," *Circus*, December 1973, p. 45.

29. Robin Maltz, "The Perfect Groupie," *Anderbo*; Alice Cooper: Walker, *In the Limo*, p. 145; Des Barres: Barney Hoskyns, *Waiting for the Sun: A Rock 'n' Roll History of Los Angeles* (Milwaukee, WI: Backbeat Books, 2009), p. 270.

30. Carol Pickel, "Sunset Strip Groupies," *Star*, June 1973.

31. Cooper was never part of a gay drag scene, but always used the band name, which derived from a character on the television show *Mayberry R.F.D.*, as his own.

32. Dennis Dunaway and Chris Hodenfield, *SNAKES! GUILLOTINES! ELECTRIC CHAIRS!: My Adventures in the Alice Cooper Group* (New York: Thomas Dunne Books, 2015); Alice Cooper, *Alice Cooper, Golf Monster* (New York: Crown Publishers, 2007), p. 57.

33. Joshua Gamson, *The Fabulous Sylvester: The Legend, the Music, the Seventies in San Francisco* (New York: MacMillan, 2005), pp. 53–54; Rex Reed, "The Cockettes: Better a Tinsel Queen Than a Golden Toad," *Chicago Tribune*, September 19, 1971.

34. Ibid., p. 92.

35. "Androgyny: A Short Introduction" and "Androgyny Hall of Fame," *Creem*, August 1973.

36. "Ungay gay": Simon Frith, "What's the Ugliest Part of YOUR Body?," *Creem*, May 1974; "Alice Is a Liar": Ben Edmonds, "Alice Cooper Blows His Wad," *Creem*, June 1973.

37. "Terminal confusion": Steve Waksman, *This Ain't the Summer of Love: Conflict and Crossover in Heavy Metal and Punk* (Berkeley: University of California Press, 2009), p. 84.

38. Tom Wolfe, "The 'Me' Decade and the Third Great Awakening," *New York*, August 23, 1976.

39. Mike Jahn, "Watch the Freak: Iggy Pop," *New York Times*, April 3, 1970; "Punched him": Lester Bangs and Esther Korinsky-Woodward, "'Honey, Come & Be My Enemy, I Can Love You Too': Iggy and the Stooges Take America by the Spleen," *Creem*, April 1974.

40. Robinson, "Looking for a Kiss"; Ronson: Peter Doggett, *The Man Who Sold the World: David Bowie and the 1970s* (New York: HarperCollins, 2012), p. 156.

41. Jim Farber, "The Androgynous Mirror," *Rolling Stone: The '70s*, p. 142; Vince Aletti, "Tighten Up," *Creem*, May 1972.

42. Edmonds, "The New York Dolls Greatest Hits Volume 1."

43. Stuard Werrin, "Jobriath Breaks All the Rules," *Rolling Stone*, December 6, 1973; Bob Weiner, "Jobriath," *Interview*, October 1973; Ben

Windham, "Album of the Late Glam-Rock Great Reissued," *Tuscaloosa News,* February 25, 2005.

44. Tuscaloosa: Leigh W. Rutledge, *The Gay Decades: From Stonewall to the Present, the People and Events That Shaped Gay Lives* (New York: Plume, 1992), p. 64; Freddie Mercury: Farber, *Androgynous Mirror,* p. 145.

45. Miss America: Alice Echols, *Daring to Be Bad: Radical Feminism in America, 1967–1975* (Minneapolis: University of Minnesota Press, 1989), p. 92; Dance-ins: Benjamin Shepard, *Queer Political Performance and Protest* (New York: Routledge, 2009), p. 46; Aquarius Day: Gamson, *Fabulous Sylvester,* p. 58.

46. Ann Powers, "Labelle Was Always More Than a 'Lady,'" *Los Angeles Times,* October 12, 2008.

47. Jean Williams, "Trio Labelle: Patti, Sarah and Nona Favor Revolutionary Songs, Attitude," *Billboard,* March 29, 1975.

48. John Rockwell, "Labelle at the Met: Sequins, Regions and Acoustics," *New York Times,* October 11, 1974; Vince Aletti, "Labelle: Flowing over the Met," *Village Voice,* October 17, 1974; John Crittendon, "Black Trio's Historic Night at the Met," undated clip from file, Rock and Roll Hall of Fame Museum and Archive.

49. Jane DeLynn, "I Flunked Masturbation Class," in Peter Knobler and Greg Mitchell, eds., *Very Seventies: A Cultural History of the 1970s, from the Pages of* Crawdaddy (New York: Fireside, 1995), p. 282.

50. Jared Johnson, "Hard Rock vs. Soft Rock," *Atlanta Constitution,* May 23, 1970.

51. Jared Johnson, "'Soft Rock' Back Again," *Atlanta Constitution,* August 21, 1971.

52. *Redbook* article quoted in Bruce Schulman, *The Seventies: The Great Shift in American Culture, Society, and Politics* (New York: Da Capo, 2002), p. 178.

53. Alex Comfort, *The Joy of Sex: A Gourmet Guide to Lovemaking* (New York: Fireside, 1972); Ariel Levy, "Doing It," *The New Yorker,* January 5, 2009; Douglas Martin, "Alex Comfort Dies; a Multifaceted Man Best Known for Writing 'The Joy of Sex,'" *New York Times,* March 29, 2000; Cordelia Hebblethwaite, "How *The Joy of Sex* Was Illustrated," *BBC News,* October 26, 2011.

54. Rutledge, *Gay Decades,* p. 69.

55. Abraham I. Friedman, *How Sex Can Keep You Slim* (Englewood Cliffs, NJ: Prentice-Hall, 1972).

56. Tom Shales, "Trying to Like 'Love!'," *Washington Post,* February 9, 1972.

57. Near: Gillian G. Gaar, *She's a Rebel: The History of Women in Rock & Roll* (New York: Seal Press, 1992), p. 139.

58. Gary Deeb, "For Sheer Sensuality, It's Country Music," *Chicago Tribune,* September 17, 1973.

59. Nelson George, "Fools, Suckas, and Baadasssss Brothers," *Rolling Stone: The '70s,* p. 59.

60. Les Bridges, "What Sort of Man Runs Down *Playboy*?: A Former Marketing Director for *Playboy*," *Chicago Tribune,* May 21, 1972; James Auer, "The Nabokov of Epoxy Resin," *Milwaukee Journal,* September 27, 1981.

61. Bowie, *Backstage Passes,* pp. 131–34.

62. Tim Lawrence, *Love Saves the Day: A History of American Dance Music Culture, 1970–1979* (Durham, NC: Duke University Press, 2004), p. 25.

63. Gay Talese, *Thy Neighbor's Wife* (New York: Harper Perennial updated edition, 2009), p. 272; Barbara Williamson and Nancy Bacon, *An Extraordinary Life* (San Francisco: Balboa Press, 2014), p. 83.

64. Patrick Pacheco, "Before Out Was In," *Rolling Stone: The '70s,* p. 221.

65. Alice Echols, *Hot Stuff: Disco and the Remaking of American Culture* (New York: Norton, 2010), pp. 101–10; Summer quote: "There's Sex in Them Lyrics, But the Point Is Not to Beat Us over the Head with It," *Atlanta Journal Constitution,* January 22, 1977.

66. Elana Levine, *Wallowing in Sex: The New Sexual Culture of 1970s American Television* (Durham, NC: Duke University Press, 2007), p. 156.

67. Davitt Sigerson, "Sylvester," *Sounds,* August 26, 1978.

68. Apollo: Trynka, *Starman,* p. 257; Bobby Bland: David Bowie Fan Club bulletin, April 4, 1975.

69. Peter Doggett, *The Man Who Sold the World: David Bowie and the 1970s* (New York: HarperCollins, 2012), p. 260.

CHAPTER 7:
OH NO, IT HURTS: AIDS, REAGAN, AND THE BACKLASH

1. "A question mark": Lynn Norment, "The Outrageous Grace Jones," *Ebony,* July 1979; "alienation": Simon Reynolds and Joy Press, *The Sex Revolts: Gender, Rebellion, and Rock 'n' Roll* (Cambridge: Harvard University Press, 1996), p. 294.

2. Grace Jones and Paul Morley, *I'll Never Write My Memoirs* (New York: Simon & Schuster, 2015); "Grace Jones Has Baby Shower in Gay Disco," *Jet,* October 18, 1979.

3. Howell Raines, "Reagan Vows US Will Press Effort to Build Defenses," *New York Times,* May 28, 1981.

4. Dudley Clendinen and Adam Nagourney, *Out for Good: The Struggle to Build a Gay Rights Movement in America* (New York: Simon & Schuster, 2013), p. 468.

5. John Mintz, "Growing Number of Area Cases," *Washington Post,* June 28, 1983.

6. Hemphill: Martin Duberman, *Hold Tight Gently: Michael Callen, Essex Hemphill, and the Battlefield of AIDS* (New York: The New Press, 2014), p. 123.

7. Jones and Morley, *I'll Never Write.*

8. Jeremy Gerard, "Creative Arts Being Reshaped by the Epidemic: Entertainers Confront AIDS Crisis," *New York Times,* June 9, 1987.

9. Lindsy Van Gelder, "Death in the Family," *Rolling Stone,* February 9, 1983, p. 18.

10. Paul Attinello, "Closeness and Distance: Songs About AIDS," in Sheila Whitely and Jennifer Rycenga, eds., *Queering the Popular Pitch* (New York: Routledge, 2006); Etheridge: Judy Wieder, "Melissa Etheridge: Rock's Great Dyke Hope," *Advocate,* July 26, 1994.

11. Gay Men's Chorus: Meredith May, "Gay Men's Chorus Carries On," *SF Gate,* June 4, 2006; Tim Page, "The Ordeal of Kevin Oldham," *Tim Page on Music: Views and Reviews* (Portland, OR: Amadeus Press, 2002).

12. "No point of reference": David W. Dunlap, "As Disco Faces Razing, Gay Alumni Share Memories," *New York Times,* August 21, 1995; "amoeba-like": Tim Lawrence, "The Forging of a White Gay Aesthetic at the Saint, 1980–84," *Dancecult,* July 2, 2013.

13. Walter Hughes, "In the Empire of the Beat: Discipline and Disco," in Andrew Ross and Tricia Rose, eds., *Microphone Fiends: Youth Music & Youth Culture* (New York: Routledge, 1994), p. 147.

14. William Hayes, "Out with the Boys," *Mother Jones,* July/August 1990, p. 49.

15. Legs McNeil and Gillian McCain, *Please Kill Me* (New York: Grove Press, 1996), p. 240.

16. "Pathetic hippie crap": McNeil and McCain, *Please Kill Me,* p. 16.

17. "Fat arse": Jon Savage, "Tainted Love: The Influence of Male Homosexuality and Sexual Divergence on Pop Music and Culture Since the War," in Alan Tomlinson, ed., *Consumption, Identity, and Style: Marketing, Meanings, and the Packaging of Pleasure* (New York: Routledge, 1990), p. 111; Johnny Rotten: Jon Savage, *England's Dreaming: Anarchy, Sex Pistols, Punk Rock, and Beyond* (New York: St. Martin's Press, 1992), p. 187;

Wolcott: *Lucking Out: My Life Getting Down and Semi-Dirty in Seventies New York* (New York: Doubleday, 2011), p. 152; John Robb, *Punk Rock: An Oral History* (Oakland, CA: PM Press, 2012), p. 388.

18. Cheetah Chrome: Mark Huddle, "Interview: Cheetah Chrome of Rocket From the Tombs and Dead Boys," *Verbicide Magazine*, July 27, 2010. http://www.verbicidemagazine.com/2010/07/27/interview-cheetah-chrome/; Marky Ramone: Monte A. Melnick and Frank Meyer, *On the Road with the Ramones* (London: Music Sales Group, 2007); Manitoba "spit trick": Amy Wallace and Dick Manitoba, *The Official Punk Rock Book of Lists* (Minneapolis: Hal Leonard Corporation, 2007), p. 69.

19. Greil Marcus, *Lipstick Traces: A Secret History of the Twentieth Century* (Cambridge: Harvard University Press, 1989), p. 74.

20. Carola Dibbell, "Inside Was Us: Women in Punk," in Barbara O'Dair, ed., *Trouble Girls: The Rolling Stone Book of Women in Rock* (New York: Random House, 1997), p. 277.

21. Alex Cox, director, *Repo Man* (Universal Pictures, 1984).

22. Carol Giacomo, "Senate Unit Told 'Latchkey Kids' Growing Problem for US," *Hartford Courant*, June 10, 1983; John Kass, "Milk Cartons to Carry Missing Kids' Pictures," *Chicago Tribune*, January 1, 1985.

23. Alice Bag, *Violence Girl: East L.A. Rage to Hollywood Stage, A Chicana Punk History* (Port Townsend, WA: Feral House, 2011), p. 603.

24. Bret Easton Ellis, *Less Than Zero* (New York: Simon & Schuster, 1985), p. 11.

25. Steve Abbott, "Colder Than Her Eyes," in Dennis Cooper, ed., *Discontents: New Queer Writers* (New York: Amethyst Press, 1992).

26. Bill Zehme, "Madonna: The Rolling Stone Interview," *Rolling Stone*, March 23, 1989.

27. Lucy O'Brien, *Madonna: Like an Icon* (New York: HarperCollins, 2007), p. 24.

28. Harry Dean Stanton, "Madonna," *Interview*, December 1985, p. 63.

29. Debbie Miller, *Like a Virgin* album review, *Rolling Stone*, January 17, 1985.

30. Erica Jong, "Women and the Fear of AIDS," *Washington Post*, June 10, 1986.

31. Robert Hilburn, "Pop Review: Madonna Makes a Hot Topic," *Los Angeles Times*, April 22, 1985; "football players": Jonathan Takiff, "Madonna 'Boy Toy' Image," *Philadelphia Daily News*, February 28, 1985, p. 35.

32. For a full analysis of the "Lucky Star" video, see Sally Banes, "TV-Dancing Women: Music Videos, Camera-Choreography, and Feminist Theory," in *Before, Between, and Beyond: Three Decades of Dance Writing* (Madison: University of Wisconsin Press, 2007), p. 345.

33. Madonna with Steven Meisel and Glenn O'Brien, *Sex* (New York: Warner Books, 1992).

34. Andrew Goodwin, *Dancing in the Distraction Factory* (Minneapolis: University of Minnesota Press, 1992), p. 70.

35. Tom Roston, "Mr. Zappa Goes to Washington," *Spin*, May 2010, p. 42.

36. Robert Palmer, "Is Prince Leading Music to a True Biracism?," *New York Times*, December 2, 1981.

37. Touré examines Prince's use of porn scenarios in detail in *I Would Die 4 U: Why Prince Became an Icon* (New York: Atria Books, 2013).

38. Wendy and Lisa: Barry Walters, "The Revolution Will Be Harmonized," *Out*, April 16, 2006; Dez Dickerson: Touré, *I Would Die 4 U*, p. 77.

39. Marie Moore, "Prince Rules Supreme in Sex-citement," *Amsterdam News*, December 12, 1981.

40. Pauline Kael, "The Current Cinema," *The New Yorker*, August 20, 1984.

41. Raoul Abdul, "Concern About Prince's Influence on America's Youth," *Amsterdam News*, August 25, 1984.

42. Adam Sherwin, "Madonna Has Now Become 'Toxic' Figure for Millennials, Academics Say," *The Independent*, March 25, 2016.

43. Kim Gordon, "Meaty, Beaty, Big and Bouncy," *Spin*, September 1989.

44. Robin D. G. Kelley, "Kickin' Reality, Kickin' Ballistics: Gangsta Rap and Postindustrial Los Angeles," in William Eric Perkins, ed., *Droppin' Science: Critical Essays on Rap Music and Hip Hop Culture* (Philadelphia: Temple University Press, 1996), p. 117–159.

45. Nelson George, "Rappin' with Kurtis Blow," *New Amsterdam News*, July 19, 1980.

46. Gina Arnold, *Route 666: The Road to Nirvana* (New York: St. Martin's Press, 1993), p. 13.

47. Stewart Dean Ebersole, *Barred for Life: How Black Flag's Iconic Logo Became Punk Rock's Secret Handshake* (Oakland, CA: PM Press, 2013), p. 165.

48. David Seeley, "The Shaggy Club," *Texas Monthly*, May 1985, p. 130.

49. MacKaye: Stephen Blush, *American Hardcore: A Tribal History* (Port Townsend, WA: Feral House Press, 2010); Rollins: Michael Azerrad, *Our Band Could Be Your Life: Scenes from the American Indie Underground, 1981–1991* (New York: Little, Brown and Company, 2001), p. 51.

50. Joan Morgan, *When Chickenheads Come Home to Roost: A Hip-Hop Feminist Breaks It Down* (New York: Simon & Schuster, 2000), p. 102.

51. Mullen: Marc Spitz and Brendan Mullen, *We Got the Neutron Bomb: The*

Untold Story of L.A. Punk (New York: Three Rivers Press, 2001), p. 162; Hart: Azerrad, *Our Band,* p. 179.

52. Terrance Dean, *Hiding in Hip Hop: Living on the Down Low in the Entertainment Industry—from Music to Hollywood* (New York: Simon & Schuster, 2006), p. 268.

53. Nelson George, *Hip Hop America* (New York: Penguin Books, 1999), p. 49.

54. Dennis Hunt, "TLC: Condom Fashions Are a Political Statement," *Los Angeles Times,* April 26, 1992.

55. Imani Perry, *Prophets of the Hood: Politics and Poetics in Hip Hop* (Durham, NC: Duke University Press, 2004); Eithne Quinn, *Nuthin' but a "G" Thang: The Culture and Commerce of Gangsta Rap* (New York: Columbia University Press, 2013), p. 138.

56. Ann Powers, "A Surge of Sexism on the Rock Scene," *New York Times,* August 22, 1999.

57. Reynolds and Press, *The Sex Revolts,* p. 262.

58. Sean Nelson, "Let's Not Get It On," *The Stranger,* June 25, 2009.

59. Clark Humphrey, *Loser: The Real Seattle Music Story* (Seattle: MiscMedia, 1999), p. 62.

60. Lisa Darms, ed., *The Riot Grrrl Collection* (New York: The Feminist Press at CUNY, 2013), p. 39.

61. Emily White, "Revolution Girl Style Now," *L.A. Weekly,* July 10–16, 1992.

62. "Demonic": Eric L. Wee and Todd Shields, "Lilith Name 'Dangerous,' Falwell Newspaper Says: Editor Cites Tour Title's Demonic Links," *Washington Post,* June 20, 1999; "Breast-fest": Roger Catlin, "Loving Lilith," *Hartford Courant,* July 24, 1998.

63. Grunge and AIDS: Hal Sparks on *The Bob & Tom Show,* May 7, 2010.

CHAPTER 8: HUNGRY CYBORGS:
BRITNEY, BEYONCÉ, AND THE VIRTUAL FRONTIER

1. Ann Gerhart, "Nipped in the Bud: More and More Young Women Choose Surgical 'Perfection,'" *Washington Post,* June 23, 1999; Vanessa Grigoriadis, "The Tragedy of Britney Spears," *Rolling Stone,* February 21, 2008; "U.S. Teenagers Queue for Breast Implants," *Sunday Times* (London), August 1, 1999.

2. Donna Haraway, *A Cyborg Manifesto: Science, Technology and Socialist Feminism in the Late 20th Century* (Houten Springer Netherland, 2006), p. 11.

3. Sadie Plant, "Coming Across the Future," in David Bell and Barbara M. Kennedy, eds., *The Cybercultures Reader* (New York: Routledge, 2000), p. 466.

4. Alex Tresniowski, "Britney's Wild Ride," *People*, February 14, 2000.

5. Neil Strauss, "A Woodstock Concert Where Teeny Is Everything," *New York Times*, July 5, 1999.

6. Larry Flick, "After Quiet Build, Jive's Teen Star Spears Breaks Out," *Billboard*, December 12, 1998.

7. Jeff Chu and Hugh Porter, "Top of the Pops," *Time Europe*, March 19, 2001, p. 66.

8. "Hot Career Track: The Little Trooper," *Rolling Stone*, August 19, 1999; Steve Daly, "Britney Spears: Inside the Heart and Mind (and Bedroom) of America's New Teen Queen," *Rolling Stone*, April 15, 1999; Gina Arnold, "Outrageous Fortune," *The Scotsman*, March 18, 2000; Ron Moore, "Click Me, Baby, One More Time: Thousands of Sites to Behold and They're All About One Girl," *Daily Record* (Glasgow), January 20, 2000.

9. Arnold, "Outrageous Fortune"; "computer-literate children": Moore, "Click Me, Baby, One More Time."

10. "No feelings": Daly, "Heart and Mind"; "all those feelings": Jim Farber, "How Hard She Works: Teen Queen's Heavy Crown," *New York Daily News*, May 14, 2000.

11. Kelefa Sanneh, "Aaliyah, a Pioneer, Briefly, of a New Sound," *New York Times*, September 2, 2001.

12. Andy Clark, *Natural Born Cyborgs: Minds, Technologies, and the Future of Human Intelligence* (New York: Oxford University Press, 2003), p. 138.

13. Chris Mundy, "The Girl Can't Help It," *Rolling Stone*, May 25, 2000; Chuck Klosterman, "The Year in Ideas," *New York Times Magazine*, December 9, 2001.

14. Chuck Klosterman, "Bending Spoons with Britney Spears," *Esquire*, November 2003.

15. Serge F. Kovaleski and Joe Coscarelli, "Is Britney Spears Ready to Stand on Her Own?," *New York Times*, May 4, 2016.

16. Sadie Plant, "On the Matrix," in R. Shields, ed., *Cultures of the Internet: Virtual Spaces, Real Histories, Living Bodies* (London: Sage, 1996).

17. Shane Mercado on *The Bonnie Hunt Show*, https://www.youtube.com /watch?v=C4Udzyn0Ds0&list=PL37A3C961B0056BE5&index=4; Harmony Bench, "'Single Ladies' Is Gay: Queer Performances and Mediated Masculinities on YouTube," in Melanie Bales and Karen El-

iot, eds., *Dance on Its Own Terms: Histories and Methodologies* (New York: Oxford University Press, 2013).

18. Dance parodies: http://www.urlesque.com/2009/10/19/single-ladies -dance-parodies/.

19. Sherry Turkle, *Alone Together: Why We Expect More from Technology and Less from Each Other* (New York: Basic Books, 2011), p. 227.

20. John G. Palfrey and Urs Gasser, *Born Digital: Understanding the First Generation of Digital Natives* (New York: Basic Books, 2008); Turkle, *Alone Together*, p. 169.

21. Ibid., p. 31.

22. Touré, "Beyoncé: A Woman Possessed," *Rolling Stone*, March 4, 2004.

23. Zack O'Malley-Greenburg, "The Top-Earning Women in Music 2014," *Forbes*, November 4, 2014; "Beyoncé Pregnancy News at the MTV VMAS," TechCrunch, August 29, 2011.

24. Anne Helen Petersen, "Decoding the Beyoncé Tumblr," *Gawker*, April 9, 2012.

25. Keith Caulfield, "It's Official: Beyoncé Makes History with Fifth No. 1 Album," *Billboard*, December 17, 2013; Jenna Wortham, "Bingeing on Beyoncé: The Ripple Effect," *New York Times*, December 20, 2013.

26. Neil McCormick, *Beyoncé*, album review, *The Telegraph*, December 13, 2013.

27. bell hooks et al., "Are You Still a Slave?: Liberating the Black Female Body," panel discussion, The New School, May 6, 2014.

28. Ben Todd, "Children 'at Risk from Pop Charts Porn,'" *Daily Mail*, August 11, 2010.

29. Jon Caramanica, "Business and Pleasure," *New York Times*, September 5, 2012.

30. Chris Richards, "T-Pain: In Auto-Tune with His Audience," *Washington Post*, November 26, 2008; Sasha Frere-Jones, "The Gerbil's Revenge," *The New Yorker*, June 6, 2008.

31. Alison Fensterstock, "Stripper Chic: A Review Essay," in Danielle Egan, Katherine Frank, and Merri Lisa Johnson, eds., *Flesh for Fantasy: Producing and Consuming Exotic Dance* (Seattle: Seal Press, 2005), p. 194.

32. Ariel Levy, *Female Chauvinist Pigs: Women and the Rise of Raunch Culture* (New York: Simon & Schuster, 2005).

33. Elizabeth Bernstein, *Temporarily Yours: Intimacy, Authenticity, and the Commerce of Sex* (Chicago: University of Chicago Press, 2010).

34. Palfrey and Gasser, *Born Digital*, p. 36.

35. John Schwartz, "File-Swapping Is New Route for Internet Pornogra-

phy," *New York Times,* July 28, 2001; Saul Hansell, "Aiming at Pornography to Hit Music Piracy," *New York Times,* September 7, 2003.

36. Samuel Craig Watkins, *The Young and the Digital: What the Migration to Social-Network Sites, Games, and Anytime, Anywhere Media Means for Our Future* (Boston: Beacon Press, 2009), p. 43.

37. James Rettig, "Will Someone Please Right-Swipe Adam Duritz on Tinder?," *Stereogum,* August 7, 2014; Hanna Rosin, "Why Kids Sext," *The Atlantic,* November 2014.

38. Eric Ducker, "Q&A: Veteran Music Video Director Diane Martel on Her Controversial Videos for Robin Thicke and Miley Cyrus," *Grantland,* June 26, 2013; Jocelyn Vena, "Robin Thicke's 'Blurred Lines' Director Filmed Clothed Version as a 'Favor,'" *MTV News,* July 16, 2013.

39. "Robin Thicke's Naked 'Blurred Lines' Video Gets YouTube Ban," Associated Press, March 1, 2013; Lisa Huynh, "Robin Thicke's Rape Song," Feminist in L.A. blog, April 2, 2013; Sezin Koehler, "From the Mouths of Rapists: The Lyrics of Robin Thicke's 'Blurred Lines,'" Sociological Images blog, September 17, 2013; Maura Johnston, "The Way You Grab Me," *Maura Magazine,* July 23, 2013.

EPILOGUE

1. Beyoncé, *Lemonade* CD/DVD, Sony Music, 2016.

2. Kimberly Kindy et al., "A Year of Reckoning: Police Fatally Shoot Nearly 1000," *Washington Post,* December 26, 2015.

3. Kanye West sampled Nina Simone's 1965 version of "Strange Fruit" in his song "Blood on the Leaves," but the political message in the rapper's reference was unclear; his lyrics were about a romantic relationship, not racial violence.

4. Cyrus interview: Fay Strang, "'They took out literally everything': Cyrus Reveals Raunchy Video for 'We Can't Stop' Was MORE Explicit as She Opens Up About Shedding Her Squeaky Clean Past," *Daily Mail,* July 20, 2013.

5. Hopper: Annie Zaleski, "Music Writer's Twitter Feed Exposes Industry's Harsh Sexism, Marginalization," *A.V. Club,* August 26, 2015; Kesha: Danielle Bacher, "The Saga of Kesha, Dr. Luke and a Mother's Fight: 'He Almost Destroyed Us,'" *Billboard,* March 10, 2016.

6. Vanessa Grigoriadis, "Meet the Women Who Are Starting a Revolution Against Campus Sexual Assault," *New York,* September 21, 2014.

LIST OF ILLUSTRATIONS

Introduction and epilogue illustrations by Jessi Zazu.

Page 1: E. W. Kemble, "The Bamboula," 1886

Page 39: Gilda Gray photographed by Madam D'Ora, circa 1920

Page 75: The Spirit of Memphis Quartet, promotional photograph, circa 1951, from the collection of Kip Lornell

Page 111: Little Richard and fans from *Sepia* magazine, courtesy of the African American Museum, Dallas, Texas

Page 155: Dancers at the Human Be-In, San Francisco, 1967, by Jim Marshall, courtesy of the estate of Jim Marshall

Page 199: Mom's Apple Pie album cover, 1972, from the collection of Andy Zax

Page 245: Gay Men's Health Crisis Showers invitation poster, 1982, courtesy of the New York Public Library

Page 299: Beyoncé wearing her cyberglove, used with permission of Getty Images.

INDEX

NOTE: Page references in *italics* refer to illustrations and photos.

Coates, Dorothy, 90–93, 106

Cobain, Kurt, 294–295, 297–298

Cochran, Eddie, 139–141

Cockettes (performance troupe), 191, 218, 226–227

cocottes (Creole archetype), 21–27

Code Noir, 31

code-switching, by Hendrix, 174

Cole, Richard, 215

Coleman, Lisa, 276

Columbia Records, 74, 132

Combs, Sean "Puffy," 283

Comentale, Edward P., 126

Comfort, Alex, 232–233

"Coming Across the Future" (Plant), 301

Congo Square
Creole musical expression and, 27–32
illustration of, *1*
legends and written accounts of, 32–37
modern-day comparison, xxi–xxii
Shimmy influence by, 54

Continentals, 173

Control (Jackson), 307

Cooke, Sam, 84, 90–91, 94–96, 99, 142

Coon Alphabet, A (Kemble), 29

Cooper, Alice, 212, 217–218, 220, 222

Corigliano, John, 254

cosmetic surgery, popularity of, 300

Costello, Elvis, 263

Cotton Club (New York), 55

country music
early popularity of, 112–113
soft rock and, 231, 235
Southern gospel and, 104

County, Jayne (Wayne), 199–200, 288–289

"coupling," xxiv–xxv

Cowley, Patrick, 242–243, 252, 254

Cox, Alex, 262

Crawdaddy (magazine), 230

"Crazy Blues" (Bradford), 58, 71

Crazy House (short film), 54

Creem (magazine), 213, 219–220, 223, 227

Creole Heritage Center, 17

"Creole Love Call" (Ellington), 26–27, 122

Creoles
cocotte and candio archetypes, 21–27
Congo Square and musical expression of, 27–32 (*see also* Congo Square)
Creole song tradition, 15–21
defined, 4–5
terminology controversy, 18

Creolettes, 117

Crewe, Bob, 229

Crickets, 132, 135

crime and violence
cybercrime threats, 316–318, 348–349
depiction of, in apache dances, 55–59, 63
domestic violence, 261–263, 335
feminist rock (1990s) about, 296
gangs, 121, 283
rape, 143–144, 170–171, 212, 215, 288, 292, 296, 347–349
underage groupies and, 202–206, 211–216

Crosby, Bing, 96, 112

Rape, Abuse and Incest
National Network
(RAINN), 296
victims speaking out against,
347–349
rap music
gangsta rap, 292
homophobia and, 288–291
rise of, 280–285, 293
women's roles and, 288
"Rapper's Delight" (Sugarhill
Gang), 284
Ravan, Genya, 257–258
Ravizee Family Singers, 82
Ray, Johnnie, 127, 138
RCA-Victor Records, 105, 128
Reagan, Ronald, 202, 247–249,
251, 270, 278, 290
"realm of public privacy," 60
Reasonable Doubt (Jay Z), 283
Rebel Heart Tour (Madonna),
279–280
recording industry. *see also
individual names of recording
studios*
advent of recording studios, 71
early use of recording studios,
123–125
45 RPM singles, 124, 136
music file sharing, 326–327,
333–334
ribbon microphones, 112
Recording Industry of America, 333
Redding, Noel, 175
"Red House" (Hendrix), 176
Redstockings, 186
Reed, Lou, 192, 200, 218
Reed, Rex, 218

Reed, Robert, 97–98
Reems, Harry, 206
religious right
AIDS epidemic and, 247–249,
251
on Lilith Fair, 296
Quiverfull, 336
rise of, 270, 277
Rent (play), 254
Replacements, 293
Repo Man (film), 262
Reuben, David M., 233
Revolution, 276
Reynolds, Diamond, 345–346
Reynolds, Simon, 246, 294
Reznor, Trent, 298
Rhodes, Lisa, 183, 204
ribbon microphones, 112
Rice, Tamir, 345
Rice, Thomas, 7
Rich, Charlie, 235
Richards, Keith, 168, 174
Ridley, Ethel, 53
Rihanna, 310, 319, 335
Riley, Billy Lee, 124
ring shout, xvi, xx, xxi
riot grrrl, 295–296, 298
Ritchie Family, 248, 249
River Rovers, 100
Roach, Joseph, xxv, 9
Robb, John, 258
Robbins, Tom, 163
Robertson, Pat, 270
Robinson, Danielle, 52
Robinson, Lisa, 202, 205–206, 223
Robinson, Smokey, 160
roboglove, 314
Robyn, 310